A REVOLUTION IN THREE ACTS

A REVOLUTION IN THREE ACTS

THE RADICAL VAUDEVILLE OF
BERT WILLIAMS, EVA TANGUAY, AND JULIAN ELTINGE

David Hajdu and John Carey

COLUMBIA UNIVERSITY PRESS / NEW YORK

Columbia University Press
Publishers Since 1893
New York Chichester, West Sussex
cup.columbia.edu

Library of Congress Cataloging-in-Publication Data

Names: Hajdu, David, author. | Carey, John (John Whitney), 1958- illustrator.
Title: A revolution in three acts : the story of Bert Williams, Eva Tanguay, and Julian Eltinge / David Hajdu and John Carey [illustrator].
Description: New York : Columbia University Press, [2021]
Identifiers: LCCN 2021013069 (print) | LCCN 2021013070 (ebook) | ISBN 9780231191821 (hardback ; acid-free paper) | ISBN 9780231549547 (ebook)
Subjects: LCSH: Entertainers—United States—Biography—Comic books, strips, etc. | Vaudeville—United States—History—20th century—Comic books, strips, etc. | Williams, Bert, 1874-1922—Comic books, strips, etc. | Tanguay, Eva, 1878-1947—Comic books, strips, etc. | Eltinge, Julian, 1883-1941—Comic books, strips, etc. | LCGFT: Biographical comics. | Graphic novels.
Classification: LCC PN2285 .H28 2021 (print) | LCC PN2285 (ebook) | DDC 792.702/8092273—dc23
LC record available at https://lccn.loc.gov/2021013069
LC ebook record available at https://lccn.loc.gov/2021013070

Columbia University Press books are printed on permanent and durable acid-free paper.

Printed in the United States of America

Cover design and illlustrations: John Carey

For
Archie and Harry Abramson and Clark Hajdu
and
in memory of
Margaret and Glenn Carey

Foreword

Michele Wallace

It is my privilege to invite you to David Hajdu and John Carey's *A Revolution in Three Acts*, a book of graphic history that will carry you through the vaudeville era by way of the sagas of three unique performers: Julian Eltinge, Eva Tanguay, and Bert Williams. Each had a signature routine, an unprecedented combination of boldness and physical attributes that would have ordinarily been cause for rejection in the society in which they lived.

Julian Eltinge was famous for his elegant and meticulous cross-dressing imitations of conventional turn-of-the-century femininity. His preparations included pouring his portly masculine frame into a corset in a reshaping process that could take hours. Eva Tanguay played the irrepressible wild woman whose signature song was "I Don't Care," in an age when such cavorting by a white woman was both unexpected and censured. The third member of Hajdu and Carey's revolutionary triumvirate was Bert Williams, the once internationally famous Black entertainer.

We have not been accustomed to thinking of vaudeville in the context of revolutions of any kind. But Hajdu and Carey show us otherwise, presenting the performance careers of these three as foreshadowing future trends. The popularity of vaudeville arose with the rise of the cities. Vaudeville theaters were a highly urban phenomenon and gave rise to New York's theater district, the Great White Way.

Of these stars, Bert Williams is my particular favorite. From the outset of his career, Williams and his partner, George Walker, were bent upon elevating the level of depictions of Blacks on stage from the denigration of white blackface minstrel performances before the Civil War. As did other Black performers late in the nineteenth century and early in the twentieth century, they billed themselves as "real coons" to pick up on the audience already built, counting perhaps too heavily on the assumption that there was a genuine, not solely hateful, curiosity about Black life.

The thing that has most hampered our appreciation for Williams's work, and indeed the work of many early Black entertainers, is the strong, enduring prejudice against all blackface performance. It is still read purely as a marker of racism, so much so that we don't even care whether the face under the blackface is white or Black. The first famous blackface performer, Thomas Rice, dubbed himself Jim Crow, the name still given to the racist and segregation practices that have persistently dogged the economic and social advancement of African Americans since the Civil War despite the myriad legislative acts designed to ameliorate their disadvantages.

Blackface minstrels, performers sometimes referred to as Ethiopian Delineators, provided the first uniquely American stage entertainment format in the 1830s. Minstrelsy arose out of a paradoxical combination of an admiring fascination with the poorly understood folkways of African Americans and a contemptuous disregard for their humanity.

As early as the 1830s, white men donned black cork and outlandish ill-fitting costumes in imitation of how whites imagined Blacks when they were among themselves. They sang and spoke in a style that combined bizarre exaggeration with some actual observation of African American speech, dance, and song. Ironically, this period coincided with demands for the immediate end of slavery among abolitionists and the development of the Underground Railroad as a subterranean means of ferrying escaped slaves to the North and, once the Fugitive Slave Law took effect, on through to Canada. This was also the period in which communities of free Blacks and slave Black communities grew in the cities of the North and the South, together with an influx of celebrated former slaves who had written books documenting their adventures and who toured the lecture circuit telling white audiences about their lives, providing a stark contrast with the depiction of Black life on the minstrel stage. These authors complained of the ill treatment of freed Blacks in the North even as they advocated for the liberation of the slaves.

There were many Black abolitionists who made the journey from moral suasion with William Lloyd Garrison to the political abolitionism that finally helped usher in the Civil War, the most celebrated of whom was Frederick Douglass, because of his great powers as writer and orator. In the 1850s, Harriet Beecher Stowe's *Uncle Tom's Cabin* became the most internationally celebrated abolitionist work, which also unwittingly gave blackface minstrelsy yet another boost, launching entire Tom Companies that took on even greater numbers and strength after the Civil War, touring the world in both pro- and anti-Black versions, sometimes including troupes of Black dancers and singers along with white performers in blackface. Indeed, there were perhaps as many as a dozen silent film versions of *Uncle Tom's Cabin*. The first of these, made in 1903 by the Edison Company, featured a white Uncle Tom in blackface.

If Bert Williams had been white, he no doubt would have had a silent film career comparable to those of his famous white contemporaries Charlie Chaplin and Buster Keaton. Comedies on film in the early silent period were often short set pieces highlighting the performer's strengths in visual humor. Keaton had the sad visage and physical grace. Chaplin had the crazy tattered suit, the big shoes, the funny walk, and the white face makeup that all white actors wore in those days because the black-and-white nitrate film read the pinks and tans of "white" skin as dark.

We can only imagine Bert Williams's celebrated stage presence by piecing together bits of evidence remaining in his popular recordings (often made with George Walker) and his appearances in three surviving silent film projects. In the film *The Natural Born Gambler* (1916) in particular, we witness the subtle powers of his pantomime and agility of face and expression. The handsome, well-built Williams, who in real life was nothing like the comic character he created, would hunch over in ragged clothing and through the alchemy of burnt cork create a caricature of the innocent and naïve Black country bumpkin.

In the existing excerpts from the unfinished *The Lime Kiln Club Field Day*, from the silent film collection of the Museum of Modern Art, we see Williams in burnt cork among a troupe of elegant and comedic Black performers. He plays the romantic lead with charm and consummate grace. He has the *je ne sais quoi* that invariably marks the greatest stars.

A hundred years after the prime of Bert Williams, Eva Tanguay, and Julian Eltinge in vaudeville, popular culture continues to play a significant part in reminding us simultaneously of the shortcomings of our pasts and the promise of our future as a nation in which equality for all, regardless of race, gender, religion, or sex, remains a distinct possibility, if not yet a reality.

A REVOLUTION IN THREE ACTS

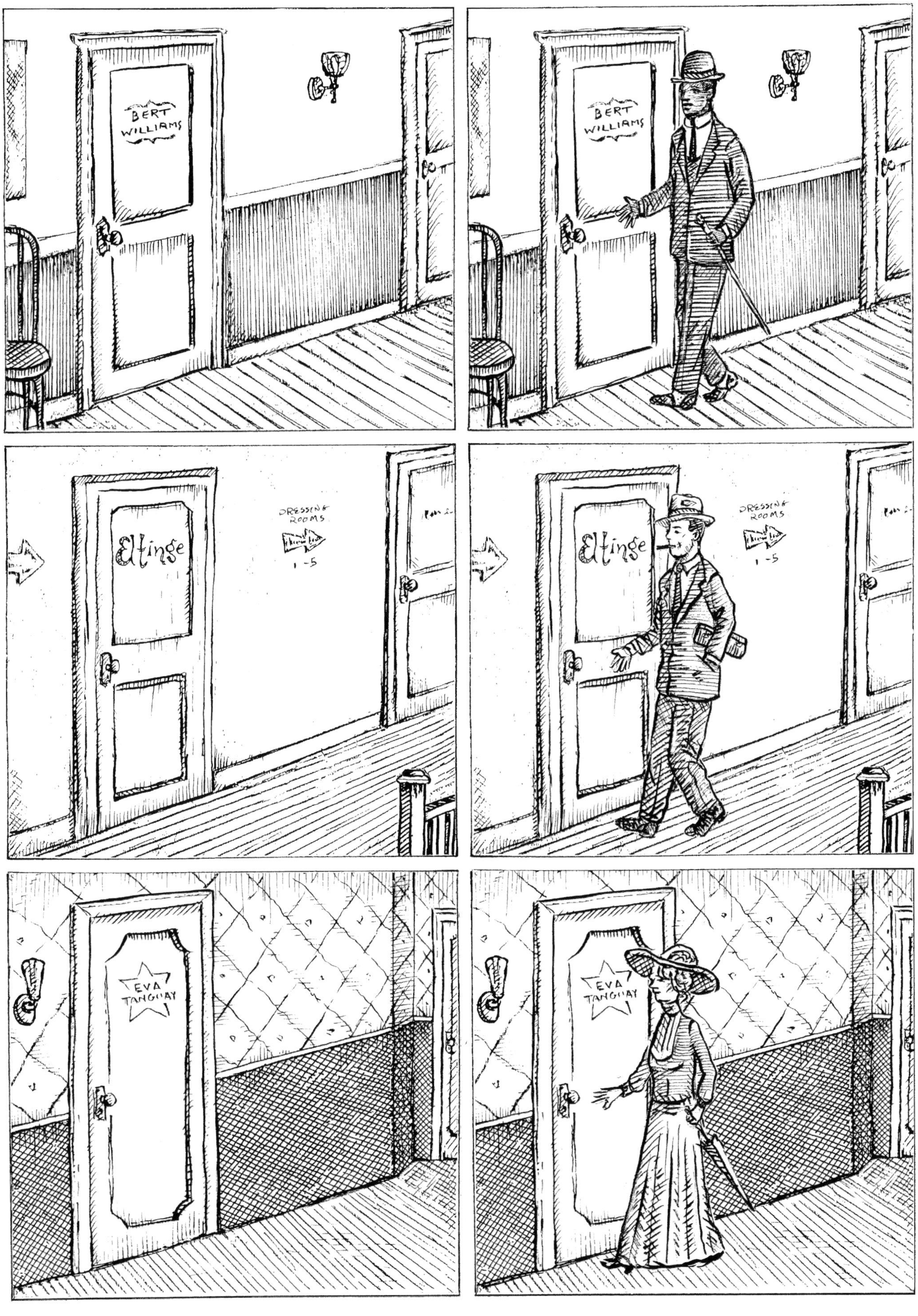
BERT WILLIAMS
BERT WILLIAMS
Eltinge
DRESSING ROOMS
1 - 5
Eltinge
DRESSING ROOMS
1 - 5
EVA TANGUAY
EVA TANGUAY

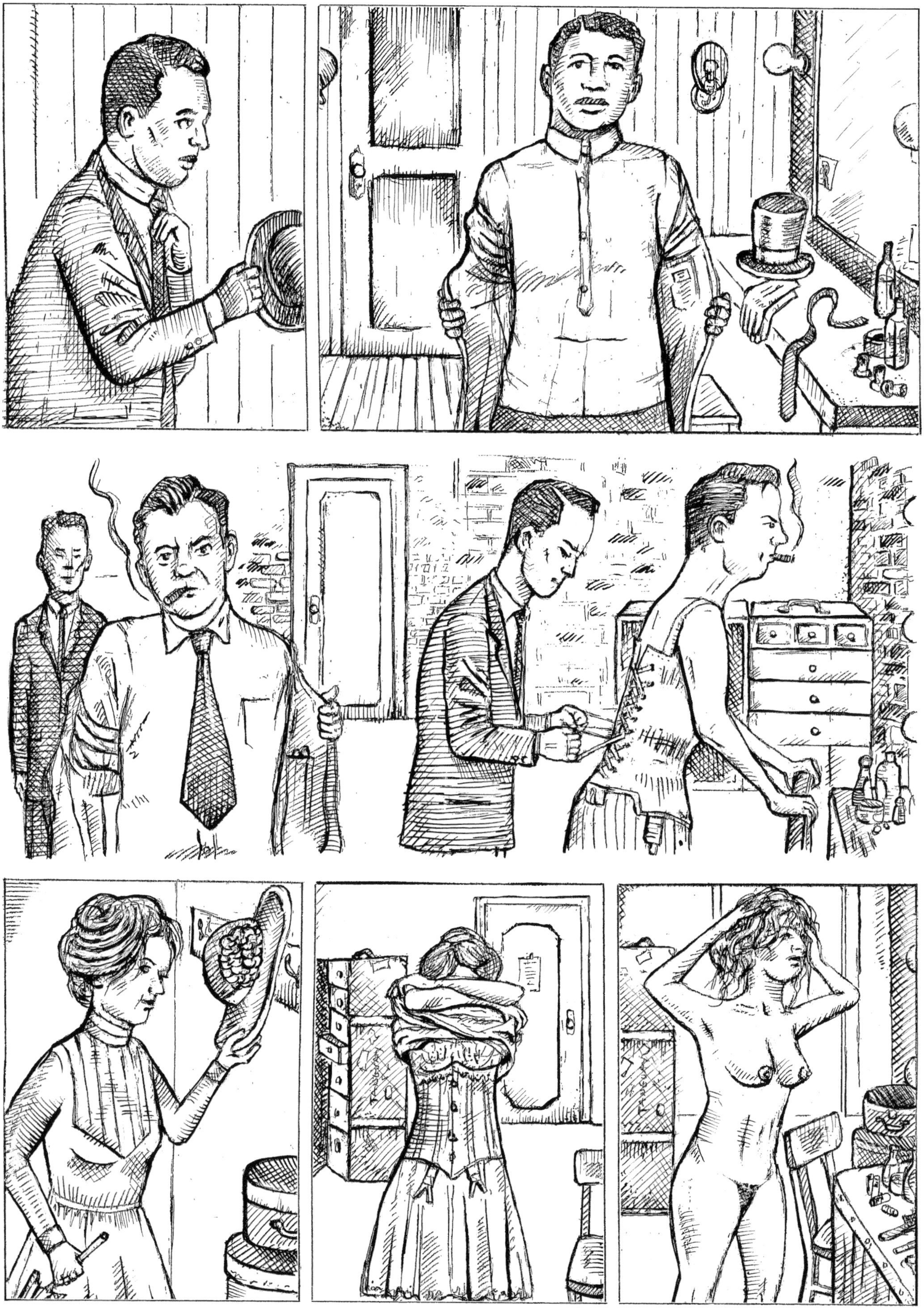

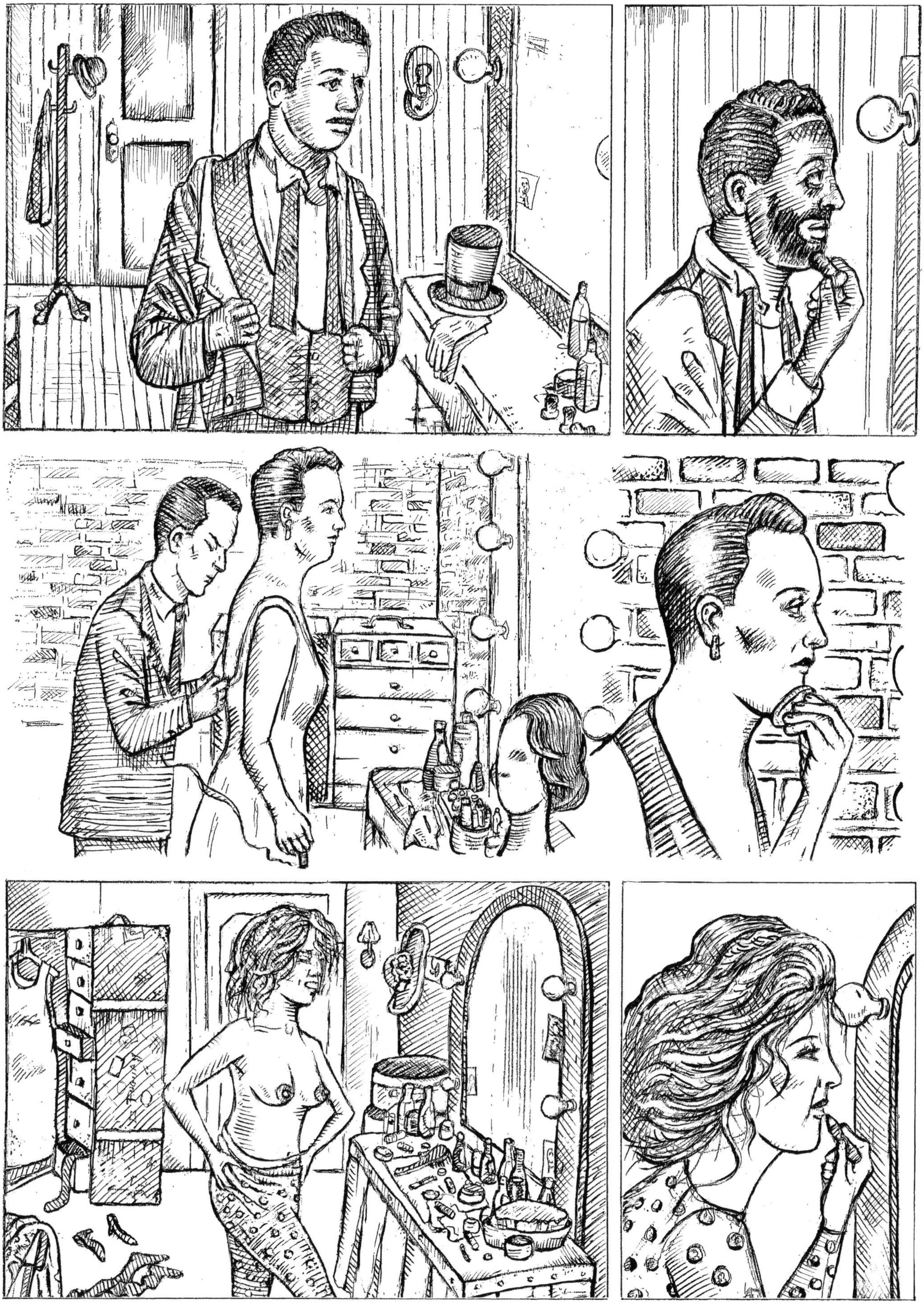

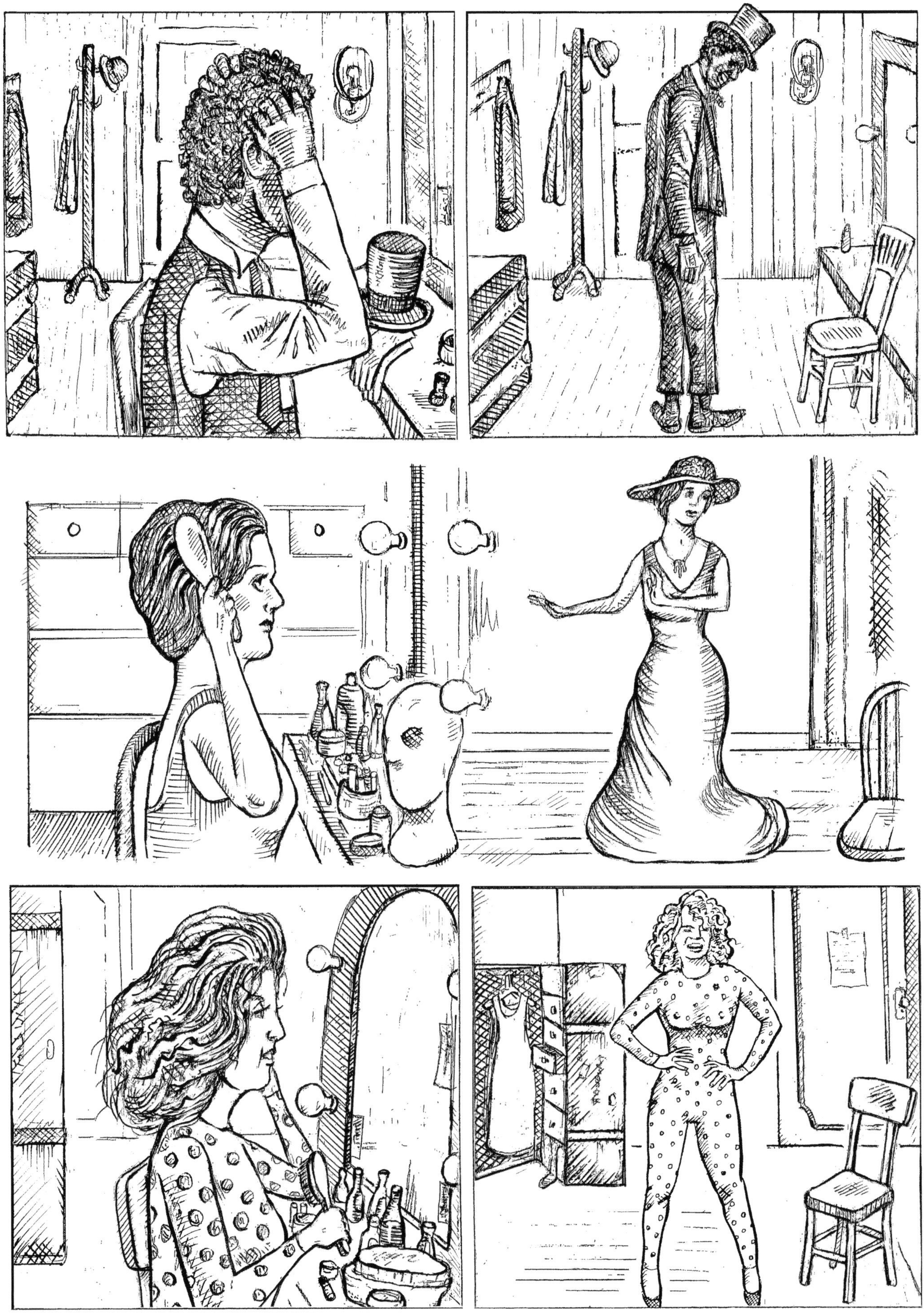

WHAT DOES IT MEAN TO BE AN AMERICAN?
A WOMAN? A BLACK MAN? OR SOMEONE WHO
DOESN'T QUITE FIT ANY CATEGORY?
IN THE TIME OF THE TURN OF THE TWENTIETH
CENTURY, AMERICAN LIFE WAS IN THE MIDST
OF UPHEAVAL, AND SO WAS ITS ENTERTAINMENT.
WITH GREASEPAINT AND COSTUMES, THREE
PERFORMING ARTISTS TRANSFORMED THEMSELVES
FOR THE VAUDEVILLE STAGE, AND THEIR AUDIENCE
WAS TRANSFORMED IN THE PROCESS.
THIS IS THE STORY OF THOSE PERFORMERS.
ONE WAS THE MOST POPULAR ACT IN VAUDEVILLE.
ONE, THE STRANGEST. AND ONE, THE FUNNIEST
AND, AT THE SAME TIME, THE SADDEST.

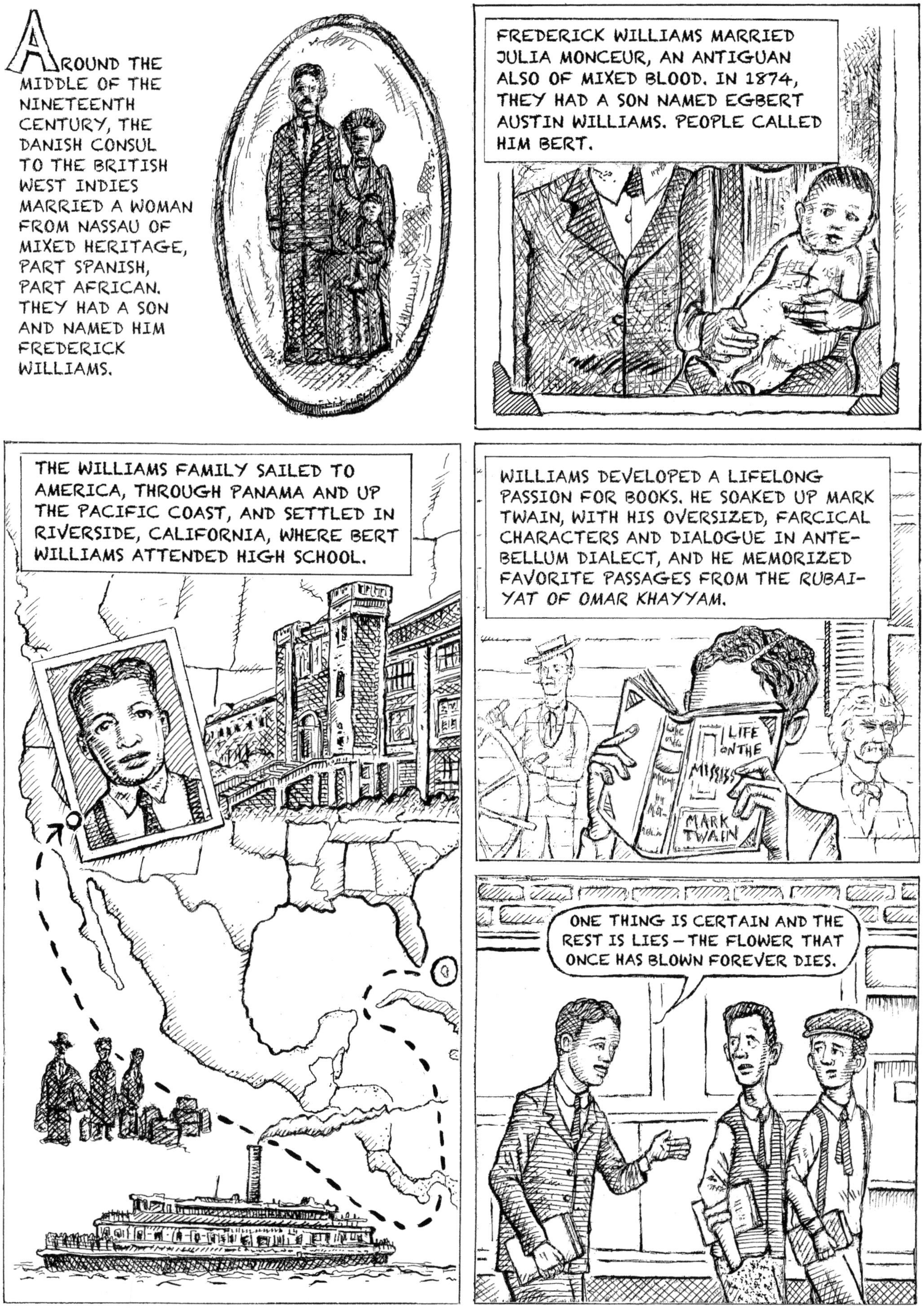
AROUND THE MIDDLE OF THE NINETEENTH CENTURY, THE DANISH CONSUL TO THE BRITISH WEST INDIES MARRIED A WOMAN FROM NASSAU OF MIXED HERITAGE, PART SPANISH, PART AFRICAN. THEY HAD A SON AND NAMED HIM FREDERICK WILLIAMS.
FREDERICK WILLIAMS MARRIED JULIA MONCEUR, AN ANTIGUAN ALSO OF MIXED BLOOD. IN 1874, THEY HAD A SON NAMED EGBERT AUSTIN WILLIAMS. PEOPLE CALLED HIM BERT.
THE WILLIAMS FAMILY SAILED TO AMERICA, THROUGH PANAMA AND UP THE PACIFIC COAST, AND SETTLED IN RIVERSIDE, CALIFORNIA, WHERE BERT WILLIAMS ATTENDED HIGH SCHOOL.
WILLIAMS DEVELOPED A LIFELONG PASSION FOR BOOKS. HE SOAKED UP MARK TWAIN, WITH HIS OVERSIZED, FARCICAL CHARACTERS AND DIALOGUE IN ANTE-BELLUM DIALECT, AND HE MEMORIZED FAVORITE PASSAGES FROM THE *RUBAIYAT OF OMAR KHAYYAM*.
LIFE ON THE
MARK TWAIN
ONE THING IS CERTAIN AND THE REST IS LIES—THE FLOWER THAT ONCE HAS BLOWN FOREVER DIES.

AFTER HE GRADUATED FROM HIGH SCHOOL, ITSELF A RARE ACHIEVEMENT FOR A YOUNG BLACK MAN IN THE 1890s, WILLIAMS ENROLLED IN STANFORD TO STUDY CIVIL ENGINEERING, OR SO HE WOULD SAY IN LATER INTERVIEWS. GOING TO COLLEGE, OR BEING RECOGNIZED AS SOMEONE WHO COULD HAVE GONE TO COLLEGE, WAS IMPORTANT TO HIM. THE FACTS ARE UNCLEAR, THOUGH THE SCHOOL ACCEPTED AT LEAST ONE BLACK STUDENT IN 1891, THE YEAR WILLIAMS WOULD HAVE STARTED AS A FRESHMAN.

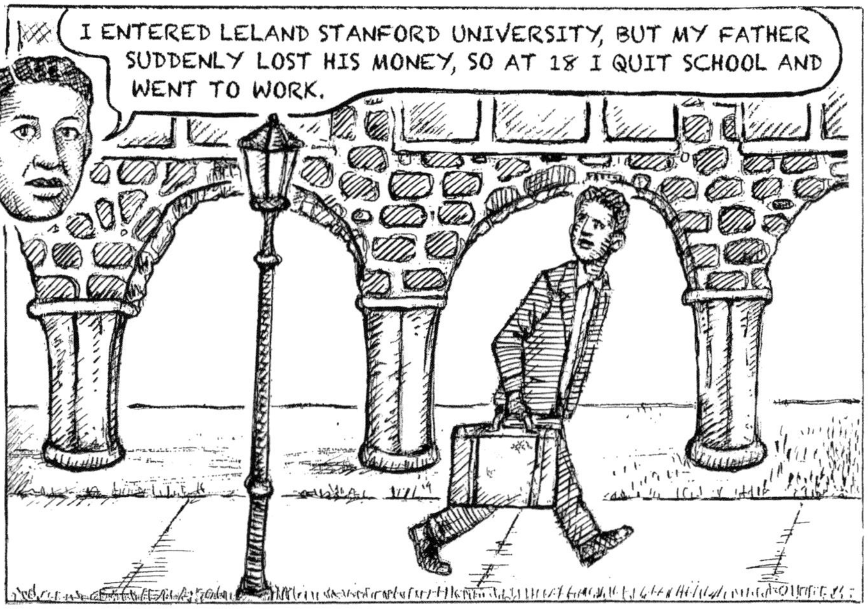
I ENTERED LELAND STANFORD UNIVERSITY, BUT MY FATHER SUDDENLY LOST HIS MONEY, SO AT 18 I QUIT SCHOOL AND WENT TO WORK.

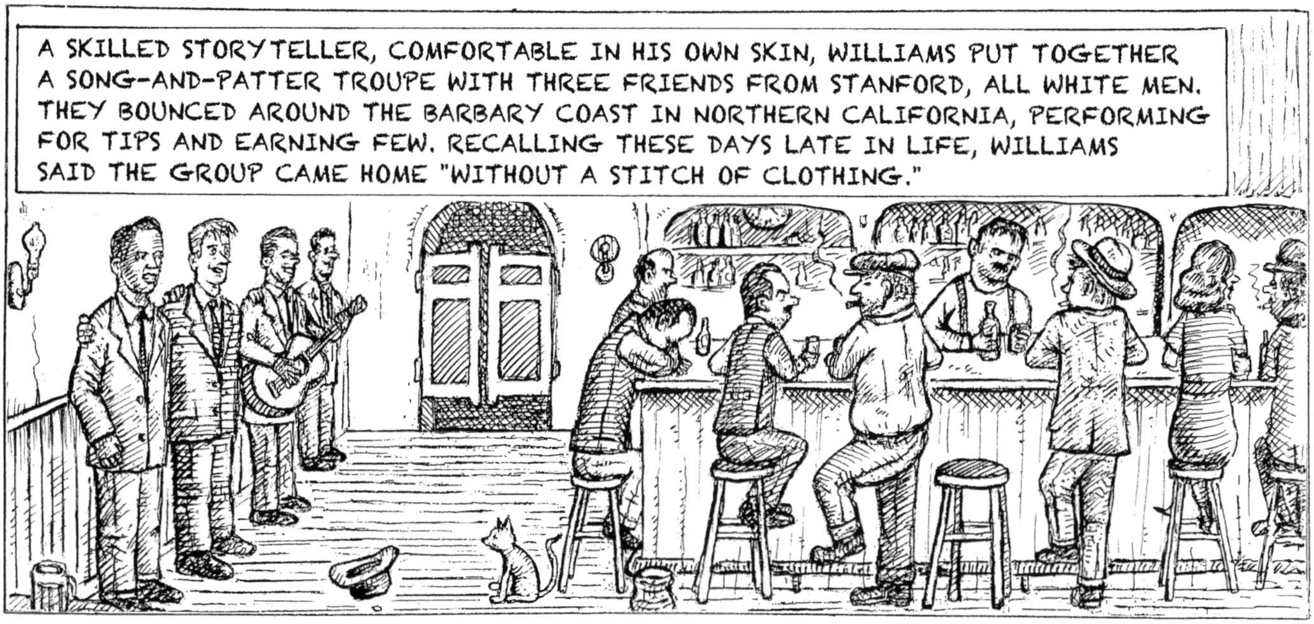
A SKILLED STORYTELLER, COMFORTABLE IN HIS OWN SKIN, WILLIAMS PUT TOGETHER A SONG-AND-PATTER TROUPE WITH THREE FRIENDS FROM STANFORD, ALL WHITE MEN. THEY BOUNCED AROUND THE BARBARY COAST IN NORTHERN CALIFORNIA, PERFORMING FOR TIPS AND EARNING FEW. RECALLING THESE DAYS LATE IN LIFE, WILLIAMS SAID THE GROUP CAME HOME "WITHOUT A STITCH OF CLOTHING."

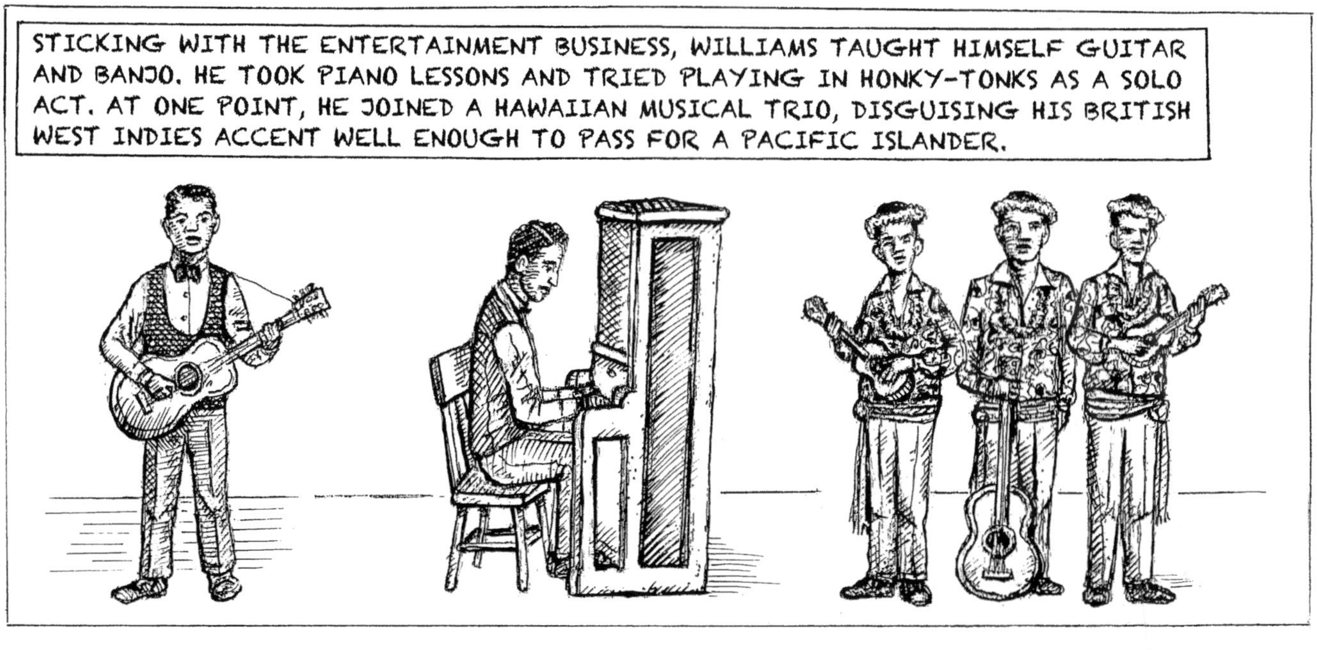
STICKING WITH THE ENTERTAINMENT BUSINESS, WILLIAMS TAUGHT HIMSELF GUITAR AND BANJO. HE TOOK PIANO LESSONS AND TRIED PLAYING IN HONKY-TONKS AS A SOLO ACT. AT ONE POINT, HE JOINED A HAWAIIAN MUSICAL TRIO, DISGUISING HIS BRITISH WEST INDIES ACCENT WELL ENOUGH TO PASS FOR A PACIFIC ISLANDER.

IN THE LAST DECADE OF THE NINETEENTH CENTURY, WHEN SLAVERY WAS A LIVING MEMORY FOR AMERICANS, THE CAREER OPTIONS FOR BLACK MEN AND WOMEN WERE CRIMINALLY LIMITED, EVEN IN THE PERFORMING ARTS, WHERE AFRICAN AMERICANS WERE GRANTED THE DUBIOUS PRIVILEGE OF SERVING WHITES BY PROVIDING THEM WITH AMUSEMENT.

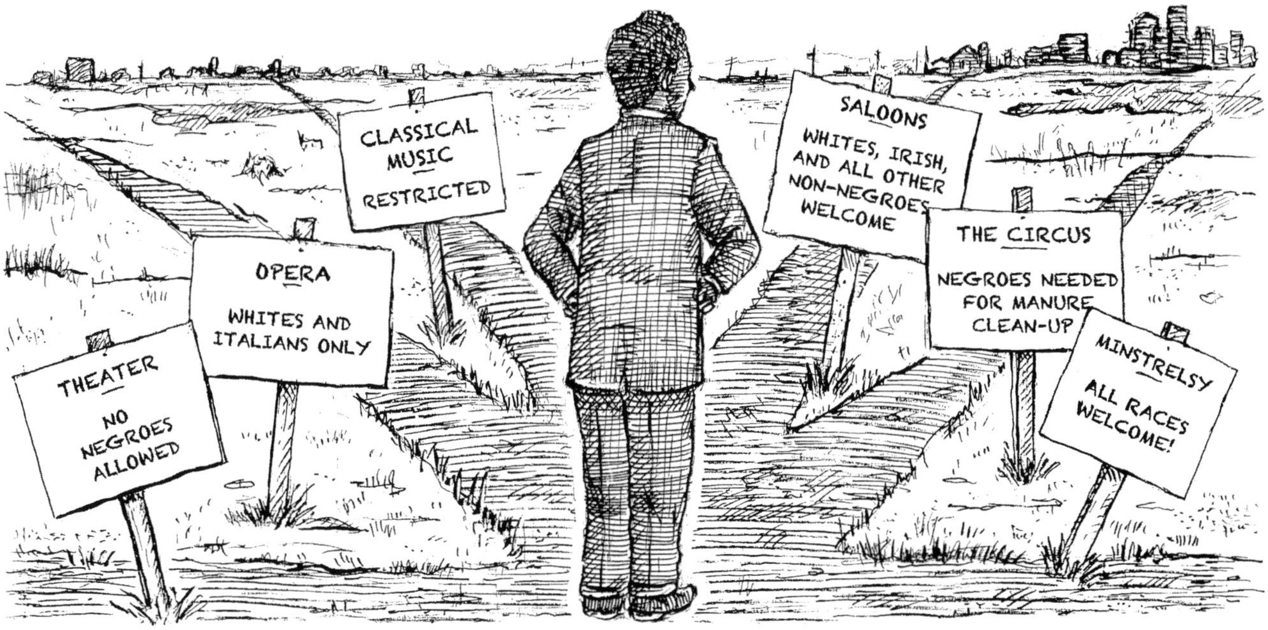
CLASSICAL MUSIC RESTRICTED
OPERA WHITES AND ITALIANS ONLY
THEATER NO NEGROES ALLOWED
SALOONS WHITES, IRISH, AND ALL OTHER NON-NEGROES WELCOME
THE CIRCUS NEGROES NEEDED FOR MANURE CLEAN-UP
MINSTRELSY ALL RACES WELCOME!

IN 1893, BERT WILLIAMS AUDITIONED FOR WILLIAM N. SELIG, A WHITE IMPRESARIO IN SAN FRANCISCO WHO RAN A TOURING COMPANY CALLED THE MASTODON MINSTRELS. IT WAS A TEN-MAN TROUPE OF FIVE WHITES, ONE LATINO, AND THREE AFRICAN AMERICANS, PLUS WILLIAMS. THE ACT WAS BILLED AS A PRESENTATION OF "ETHIOPIAN DELINEATION": A DEGRADING, RACIST CONCEPTION OF BLACKNESS PERFORMED BY PEOPLE OF VARIOUS RACES. WILLIAMS WAS PAID $7 PER WEEK, "PLUS CAKES."

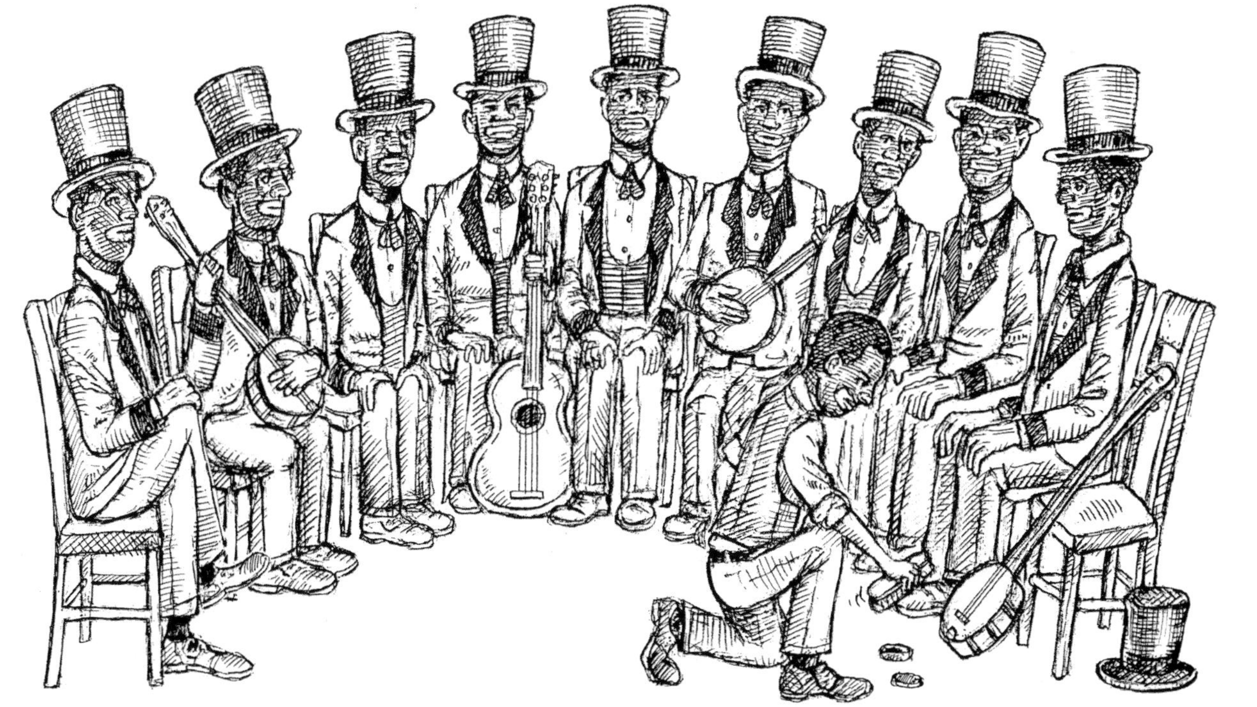

AS THE JUNIOR MEMBER OF THE ORGANIZATION, HIS JOB WAS TO SHINE ALL THE PERFORMERS' SHOES AND SET UP THE STAGE BEFORE JOINING THE COMPANY TO SING AND PLAY THE BANJO FOR A SONG CALLED "SEE YER COLORED MAN."

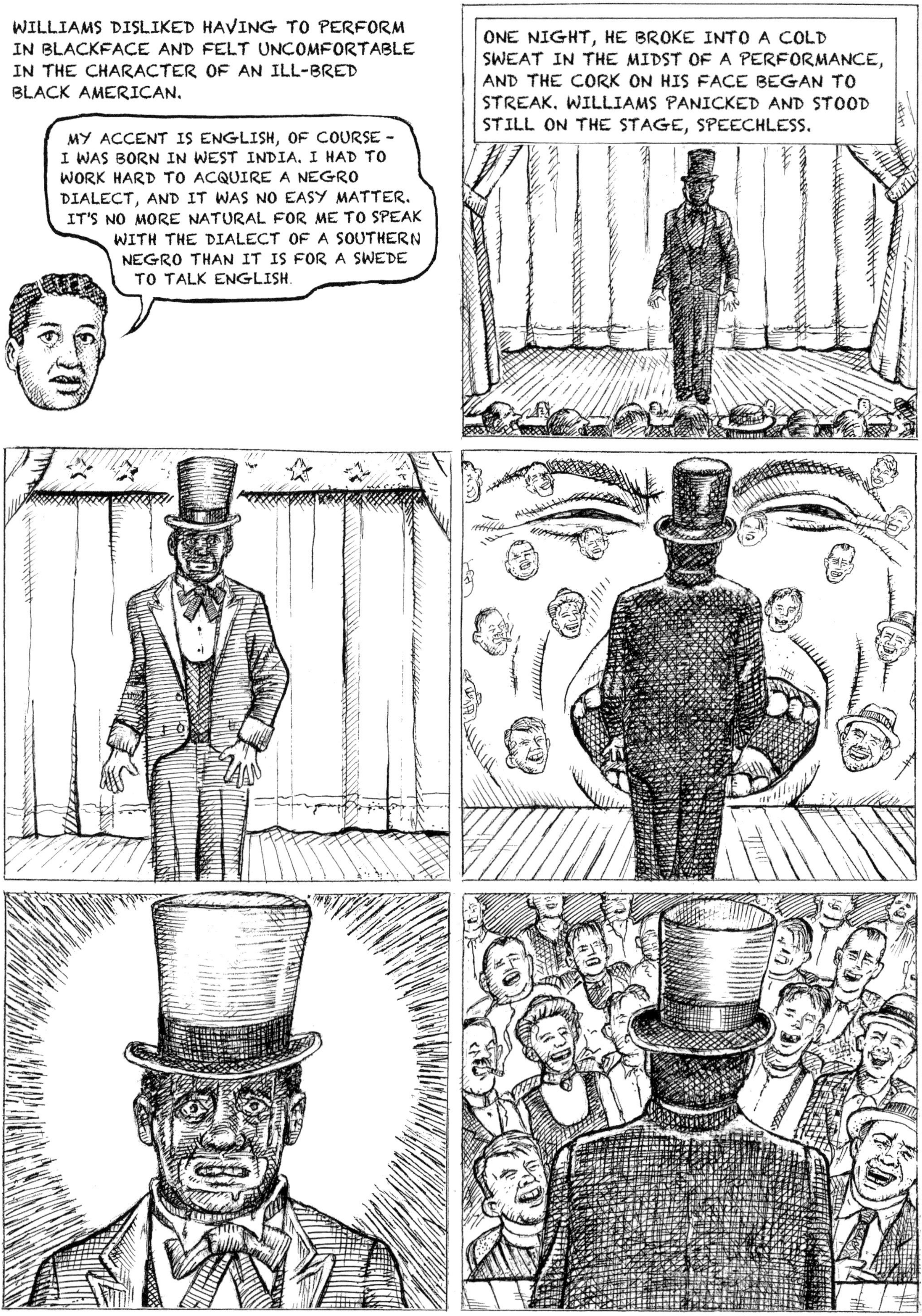
WILLIAMS DISLIKED HAVING TO PERFORM IN BLACKFACE AND FELT UNCOMFORTABLE IN THE CHARACTER OF AN ILL-BRED BLACK AMERICAN.
MY ACCENT IS ENGLISH, OF COURSE - I WAS BORN IN WEST INDIA. I HAD TO WORK HARD TO ACQUIRE A NEGRO DIALECT, AND IT WAS NO EASY MATTER. IT'S NO MORE NATURAL FOR ME TO SPEAK WITH THE DIALECT OF A SOUTHERN NEGRO THAN IT IS FOR A SWEDE TO TALK ENGLISH.
ONE NIGHT, HE BROKE INTO A COLD SWEAT IN THE MIDST OF A PERFORMANCE, AND THE CORK ON HIS FACE BEGAN TO STREAK. WILLIAMS PANICKED AND STOOD STILL ON THE STAGE, SPEECHLESS.

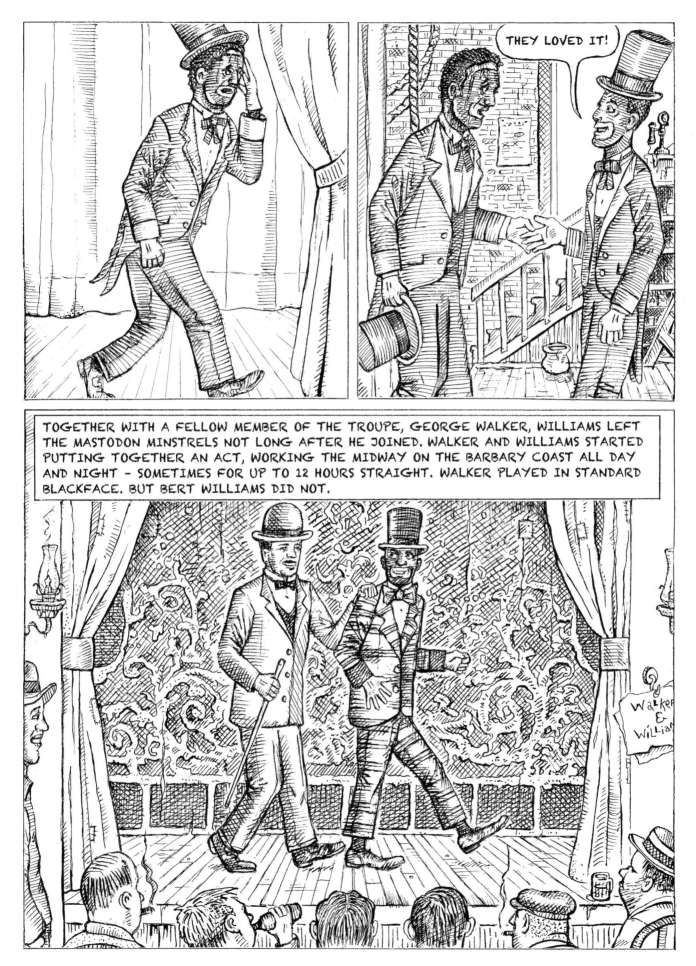

TOGETHER WITH A FELLOW MEMBER OF THE TROUPE, GEORGE WALKER, WILLIAMS LEFT THE MASTODON MINSTRELS NOT LONG AFTER HE JOINED. WALKER AND WILLIAMS STARTED PUTTING TOGETHER AN ACT, WORKING THE MIDWAY ON THE BARBARY COAST ALL DAY AND NIGHT – SOMETIMES FOR UP TO 12 HOURS STRAIGHT. WALKER PLAYED IN STANDARD BLACKFACE. BUT BERT WILLIAMS DID NOT.

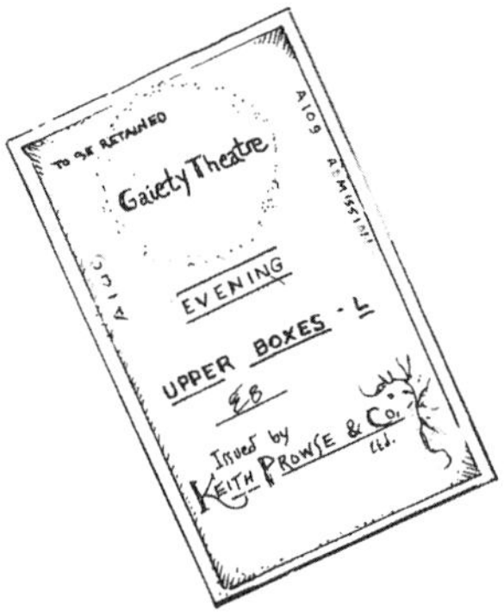

Gaiety Theatre
A109
EVENING
UPPER BOXES
Issued by
KEITH PROWSE & Co.
Ltd.

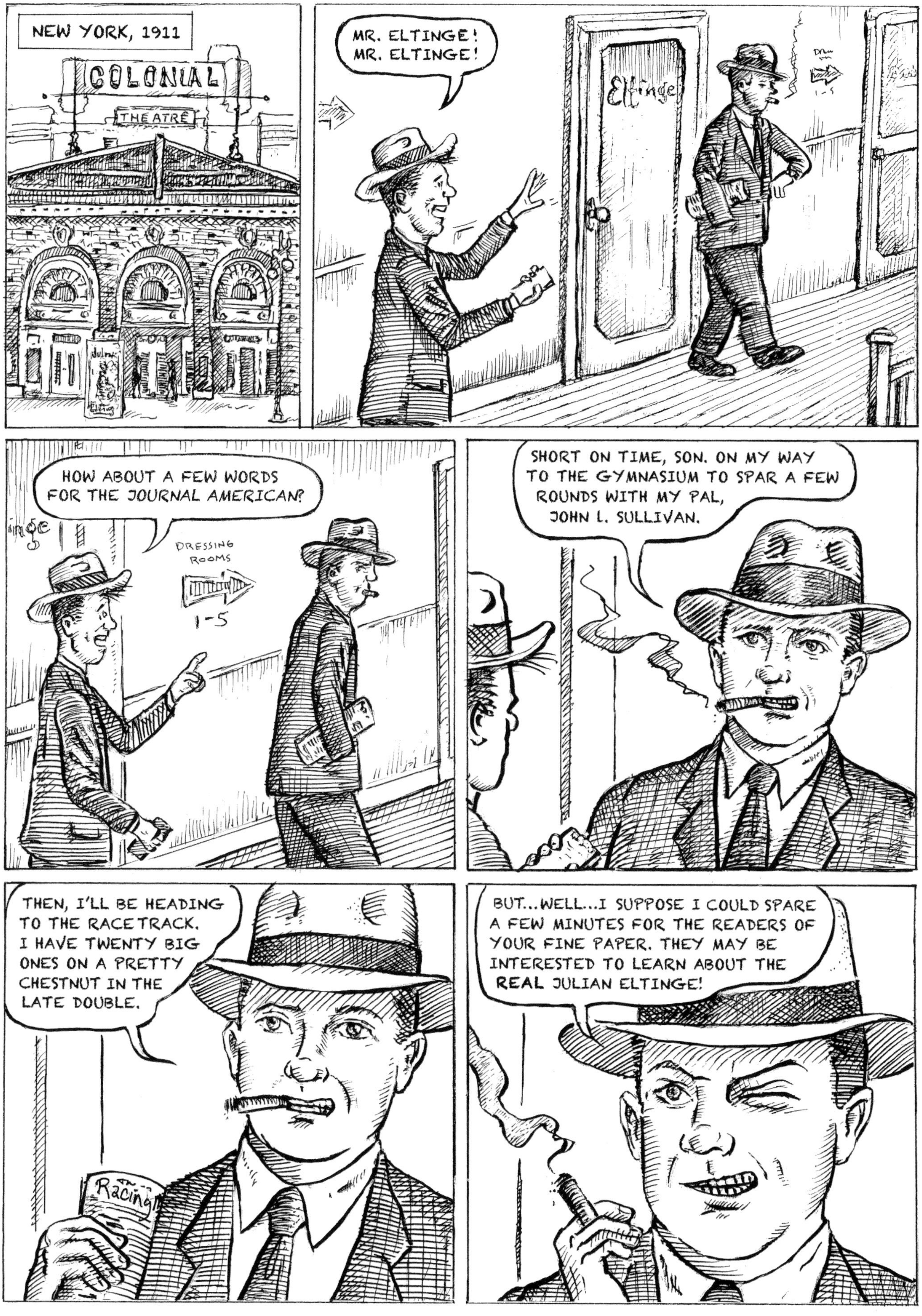
NEW YORK, 1911
COLONIAL
THEATRE
MR. ELTINGE!
MR. ELTINGE!
Eltinge
HOW ABOUT A FEW WORDS FOR THE JOURNAL AMERICAN?
DRESSING ROOMS
1-5
SHORT ON TIME, SON. ON MY WAY TO THE GYMNASIUM TO SPAR A FEW ROUNDS WITH MY PAL, JOHN L. SULLIVAN.
THEN, I'LL BE HEADING TO THE RACETRACK. I HAVE TWENTY BIG ONES ON A PRETTY CHESTNUT IN THE LATE DOUBLE.
Racing
BUT...WELL...I SUPPOSE I COULD SPARE A FEW MINUTES FOR THE READERS OF YOUR FINE PAPER. THEY MAY BE INTERESTED TO LEARN ABOUT THE **REAL** JULIAN ELTINGE!

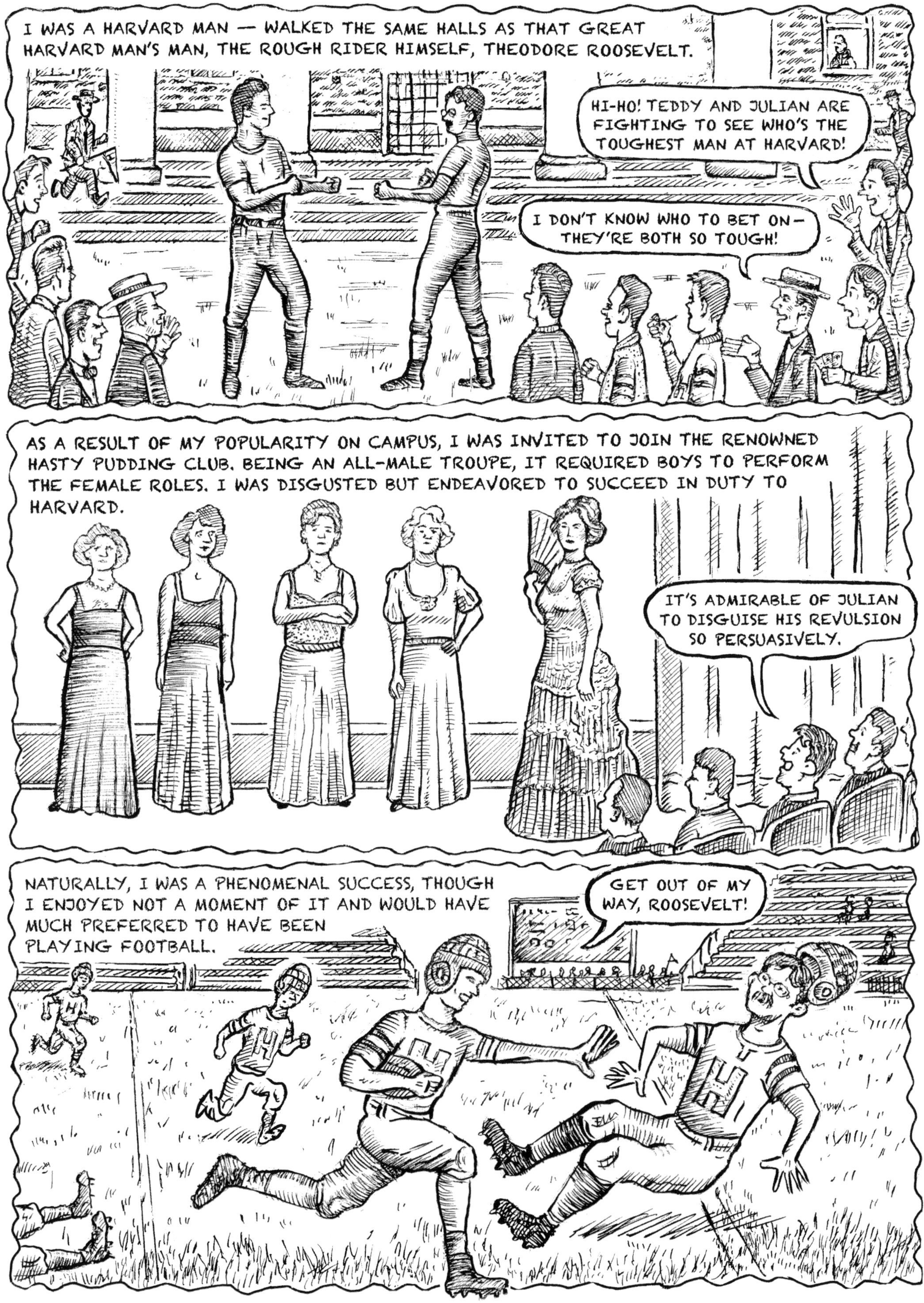
I WAS A HARVARD MAN — WALKED THE SAME HALLS AS THAT GREAT HARVARD MAN'S MAN, THE ROUGH RIDER HIMSELF, THEODORE ROOSEVELT.
HI-HO! TEDDY AND JULIAN ARE FIGHTING TO SEE WHO'S THE TOUGHEST MAN AT HARVARD!
I DON'T KNOW WHO TO BET ON— THEY'RE BOTH SO TOUGH!
AS A RESULT OF MY POPULARITY ON CAMPUS, I WAS INVITED TO JOIN THE RENOWNED HASTY PUDDING CLUB. BEING AN ALL-MALE TROUPE, IT REQUIRED BOYS TO PERFORM THE FEMALE ROLES. I WAS DISGUSTED BUT ENDEAVORED TO SUCCEED IN DUTY TO HARVARD.
IT'S ADMIRABLE OF JULIAN TO DISGUISE HIS REVULSION SO PERSUASIVELY.
NATURALLY, I WAS A PHENOMENAL SUCCESS, THOUGH I ENJOYED NOT A MOMENT OF IT AND WOULD HAVE MUCH PREFERRED TO HAVE BEEN PLAYING FOOTBALL.
GET OUT OF MY WAY, ROOSEVELT!

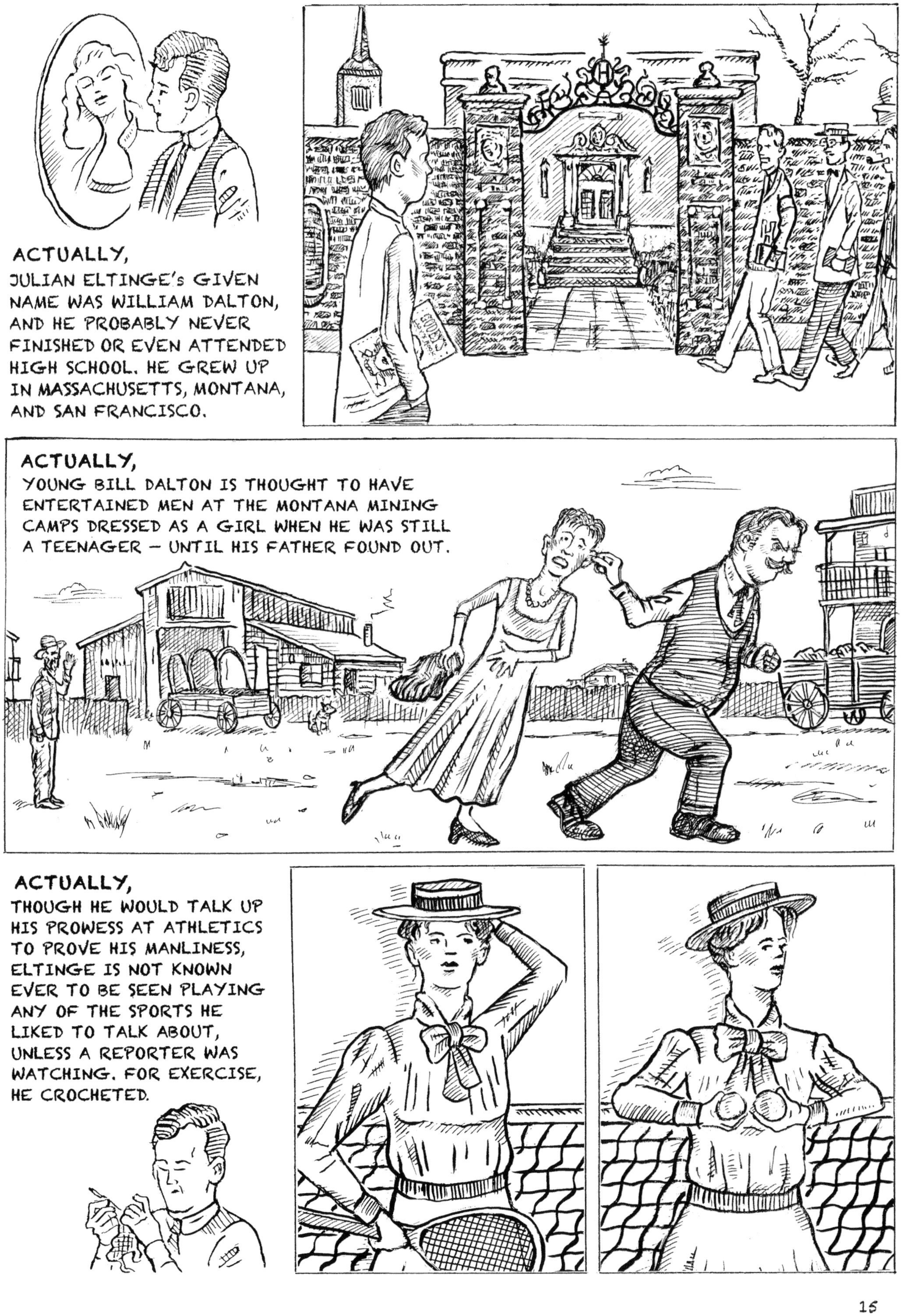
ACTUALLY,
JULIAN ELTINGE's GIVEN NAME WAS WILLIAM DALTON, AND HE PROBABLY NEVER FINISHED OR EVEN ATTENDED HIGH SCHOOL. HE GREW UP IN MASSACHUSETTS, MONTANA, AND SAN FRANCISCO.
ACTUALLY,
YOUNG BILL DALTON IS THOUGHT TO HAVE ENTERTAINED MEN AT THE MONTANA MINING CAMPS DRESSED AS A GIRL WHEN HE WAS STILL A TEENAGER – UNTIL HIS FATHER FOUND OUT.
ACTUALLY,
THOUGH HE WOULD TALK UP HIS PROWESS AT ATHLETICS TO PROVE HIS MANLINESS, ELTINGE IS NOT KNOWN EVER TO BE SEEN PLAYING ANY OF THE SPORTS HE LIKED TO TALK ABOUT, UNLESS A REPORTER WAS WATCHING. FOR EXERCISE, HE CROCHETED.

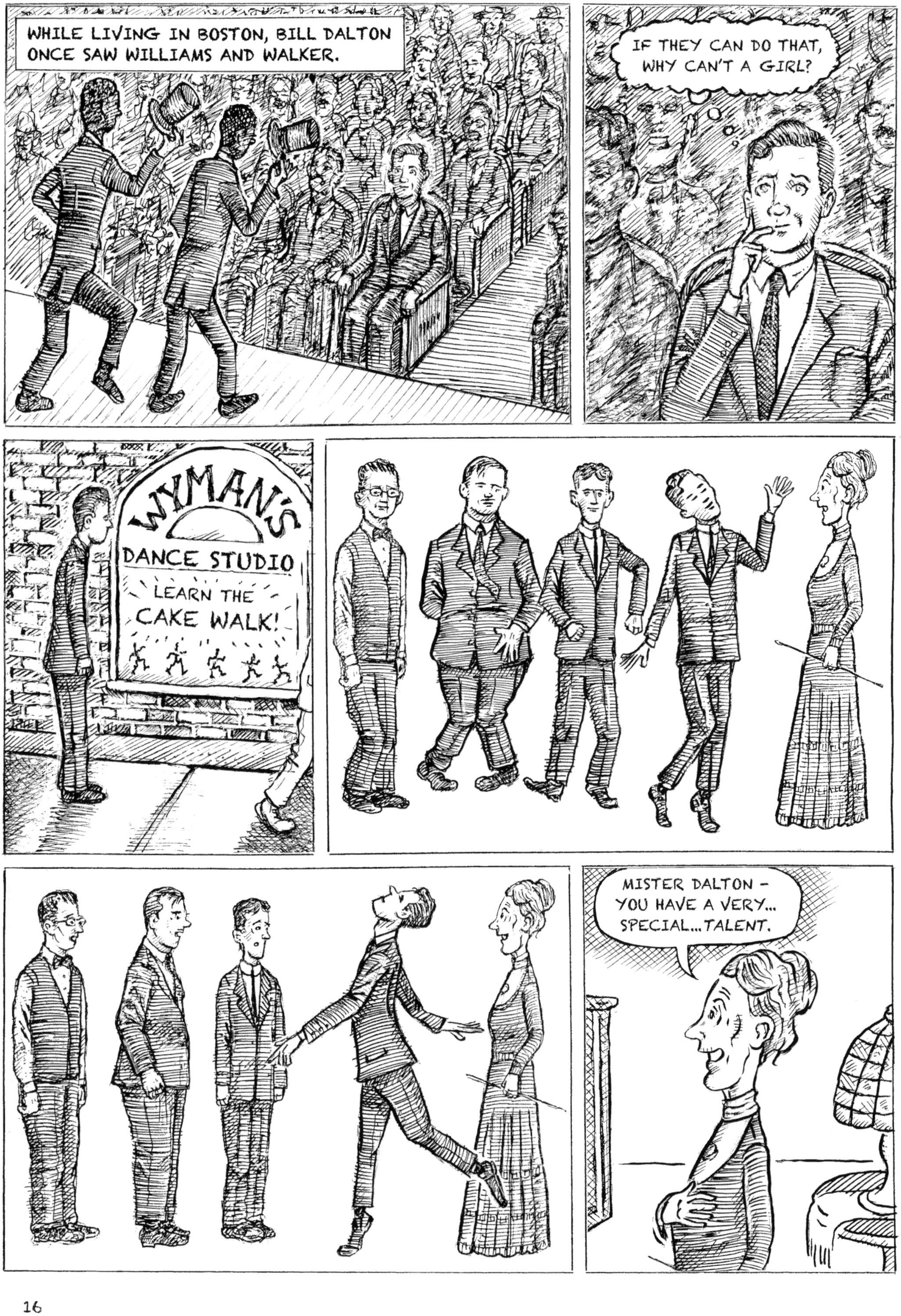
WHILE LIVING IN BOSTON, BILL DALTON ONCE SAW WILLIAMS AND WALKER.
IF THEY CAN DO THAT, WHY CAN'T A GIRL?
WYMAN'S DANCE STUDIO
LEARN THE CAKE WALK!
MISTER DALTON - YOU HAVE A VERY... SPECIAL... TALENT.

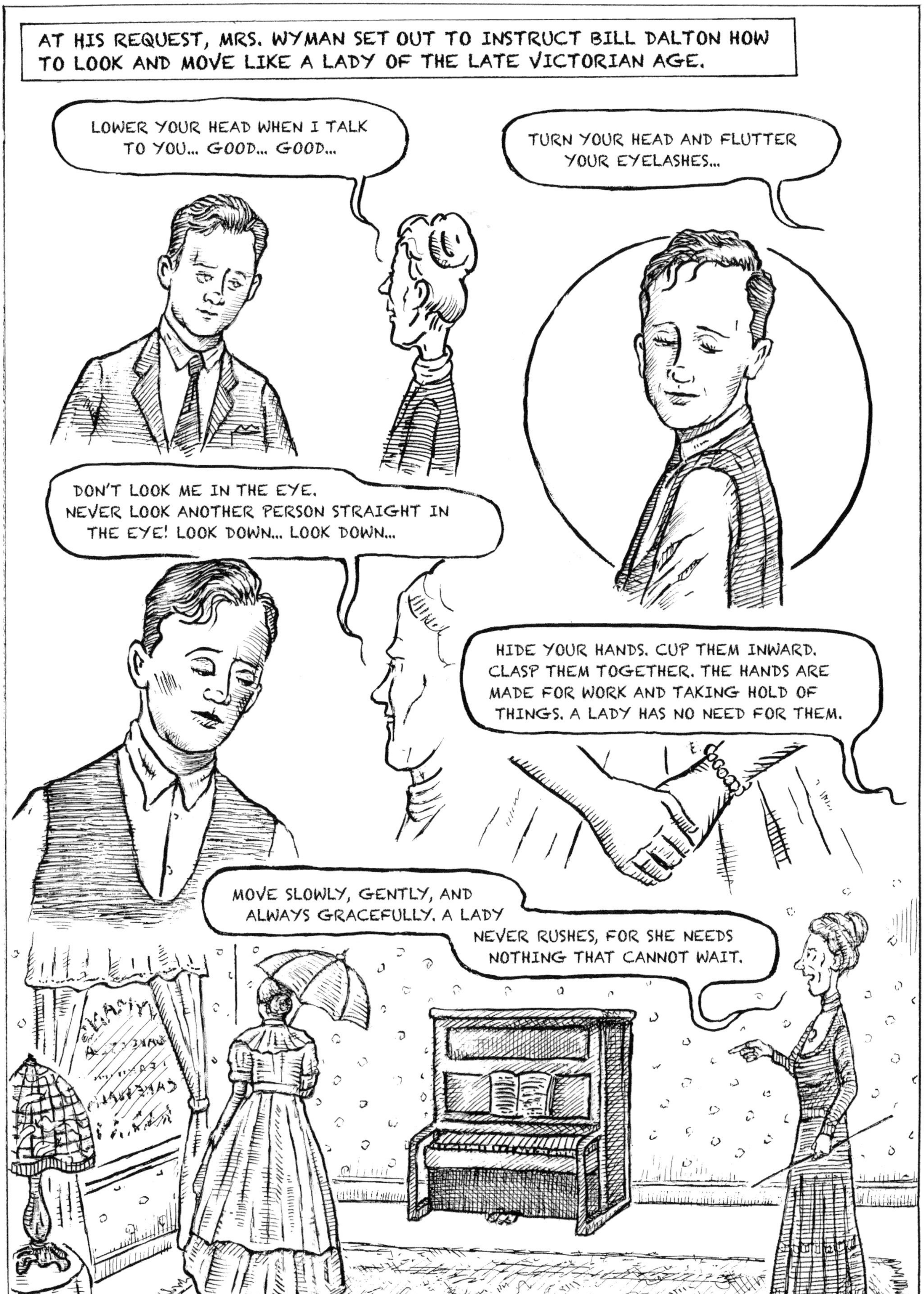
AT HIS REQUEST, MRS. WYMAN SET OUT TO INSTRUCT BILL DALTON HOW TO LOOK AND MOVE LIKE A LADY OF THE LATE VICTORIAN AGE.
LOWER YOUR HEAD WHEN I TALK TO YOU... GOOD... GOOD...
TURN YOUR HEAD AND FLUTTER YOUR EYELASHES...
DON'T LOOK ME IN THE EYE. NEVER LOOK ANOTHER PERSON STRAIGHT IN THE EYE! LOOK DOWN... LOOK DOWN...
HIDE YOUR HANDS. CUP THEM INWARD. CLASP THEM TOGETHER. THE HANDS ARE MADE FOR WORK AND TAKING HOLD OF THINGS. A LADY HAS NO NEED FOR THEM.
MOVE SLOWLY, GENTLY, AND ALWAYS GRACEFULLY. A LADY NEVER RUSHES, FOR SHE NEEDS NOTHING THAT CANNOT WAIT.

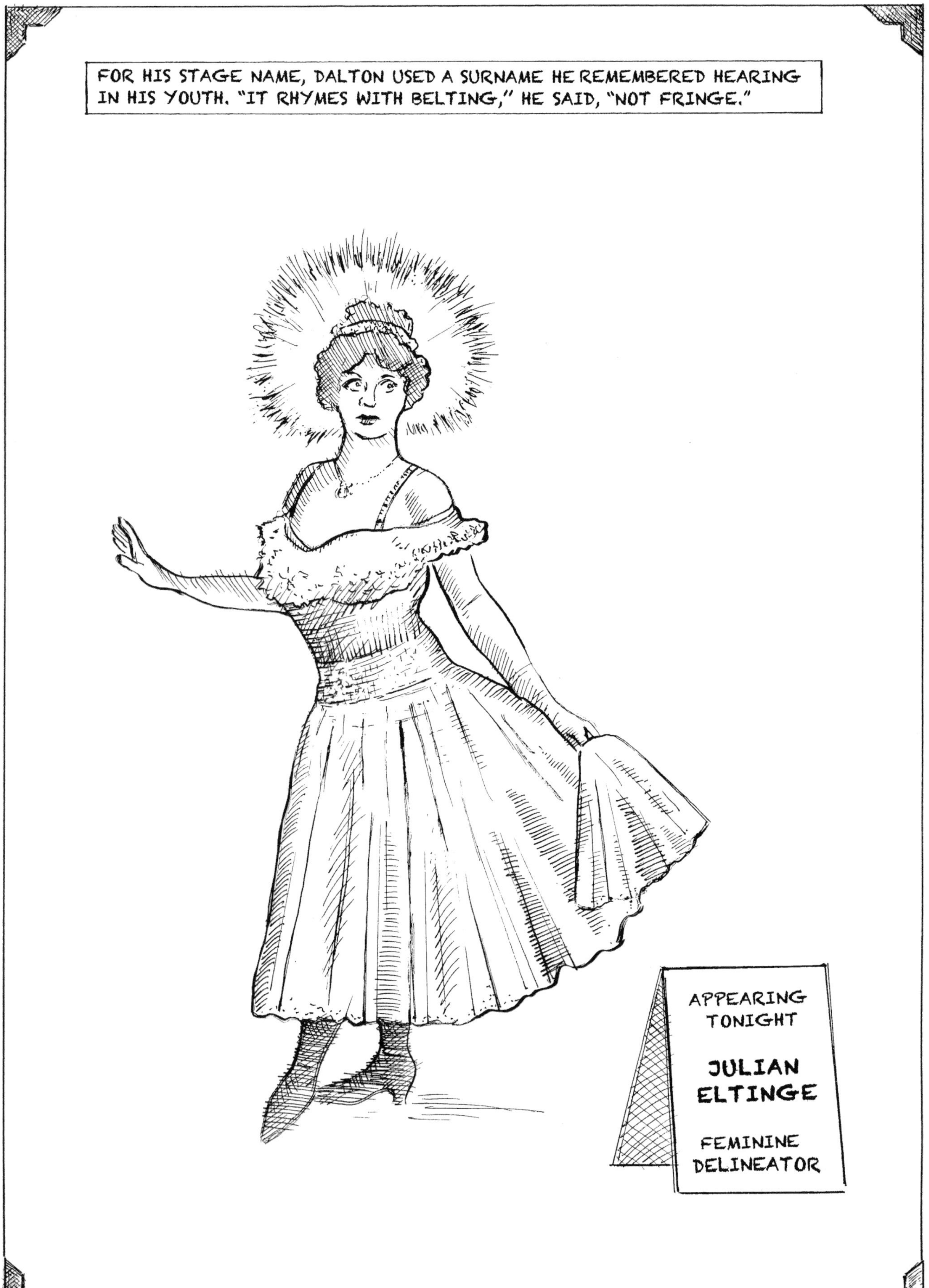
FOR HIS STAGE NAME, DALTON USED A SURNAME HE REMEMBERED HEARING IN HIS YOUTH. "IT RHYMES WITH BELTING," HE SAID, "NOT FRINGE."
APPEARING TONIGHT
JULIAN ELTINGE
FEMININE DELINEATOR

WITH THE HELP OF MRS. WYMAN, JULIAN ELTINGE JOINED THE BOSTON CADETS, A TROUPE IN THE VEIN OF THE HASTY PUDDING CLUB (BUT NOT THE HASTY PUDDING CLUB). HE EXCELLED IN FEMALE ROLES, PLAYING THE INGENUE IN A COMIC TAKE ON DUMAS CALLED *MILADI AND THE MUSKETEERS.*

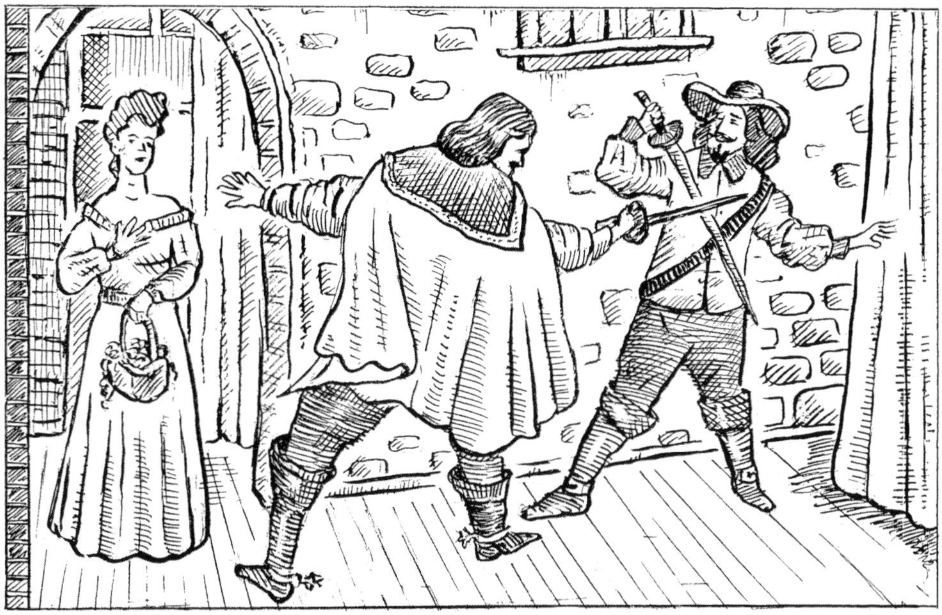

WITHIN A YEAR, *MILADI AND THE MUSKETEERS* WOULD BE STAGED ON BROADWAY WITH A NEW TITLE, *MY LADY,* AND WOMEN IN WOMEN'S ROLES. ONE OF THE CHORUS GIRLS WAS A 23-YEAR-OLD NAMED EVA TANGUAY. HER JOB WAS TO POSE AND SWAY IN THE BACKGROUND WHILE THE LEADS SHOWED OFF THEIR STUFF.

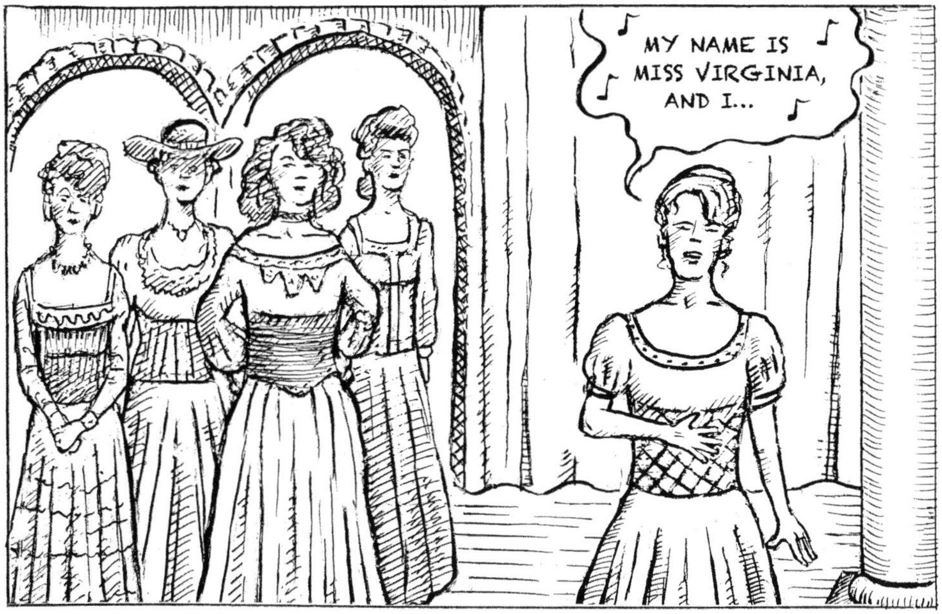
MY NAME IS MISS VIRGINIA, AND I...

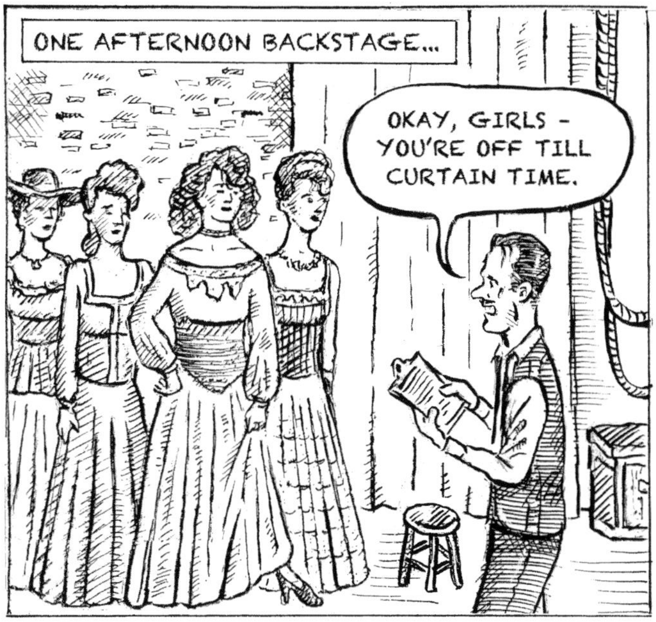
ONE AFTERNOON BACKSTAGE...
OKAY, GIRLS - YOU'RE OFF TILL CURTAIN TIME.

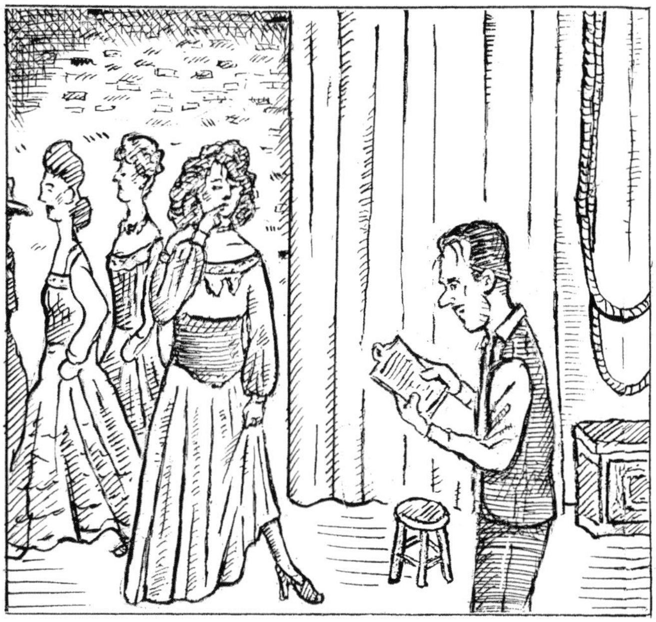

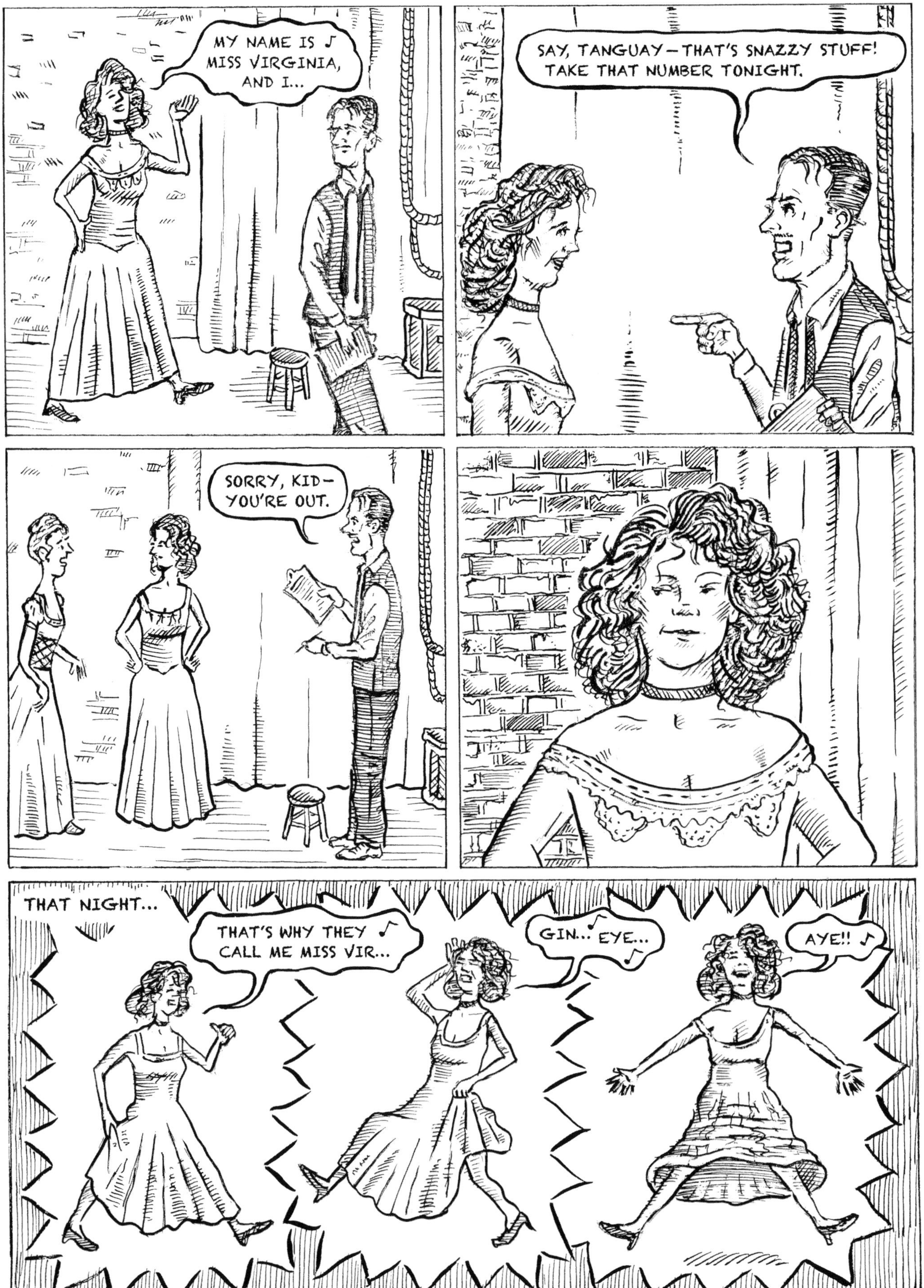
MY NAME IS ♪ MISS VIRGINIA, AND I...
SAY, TANGUAY—THAT'S SNAZZY STUFF! TAKE THAT NUMBER TONIGHT.
SORRY, KID—YOU'RE OUT.
THAT NIGHT...
THAT'S WHY THEY ♪ CALL ME MISS VIR...
GIN... ♪ EYE... ♪
AYE!! ♪

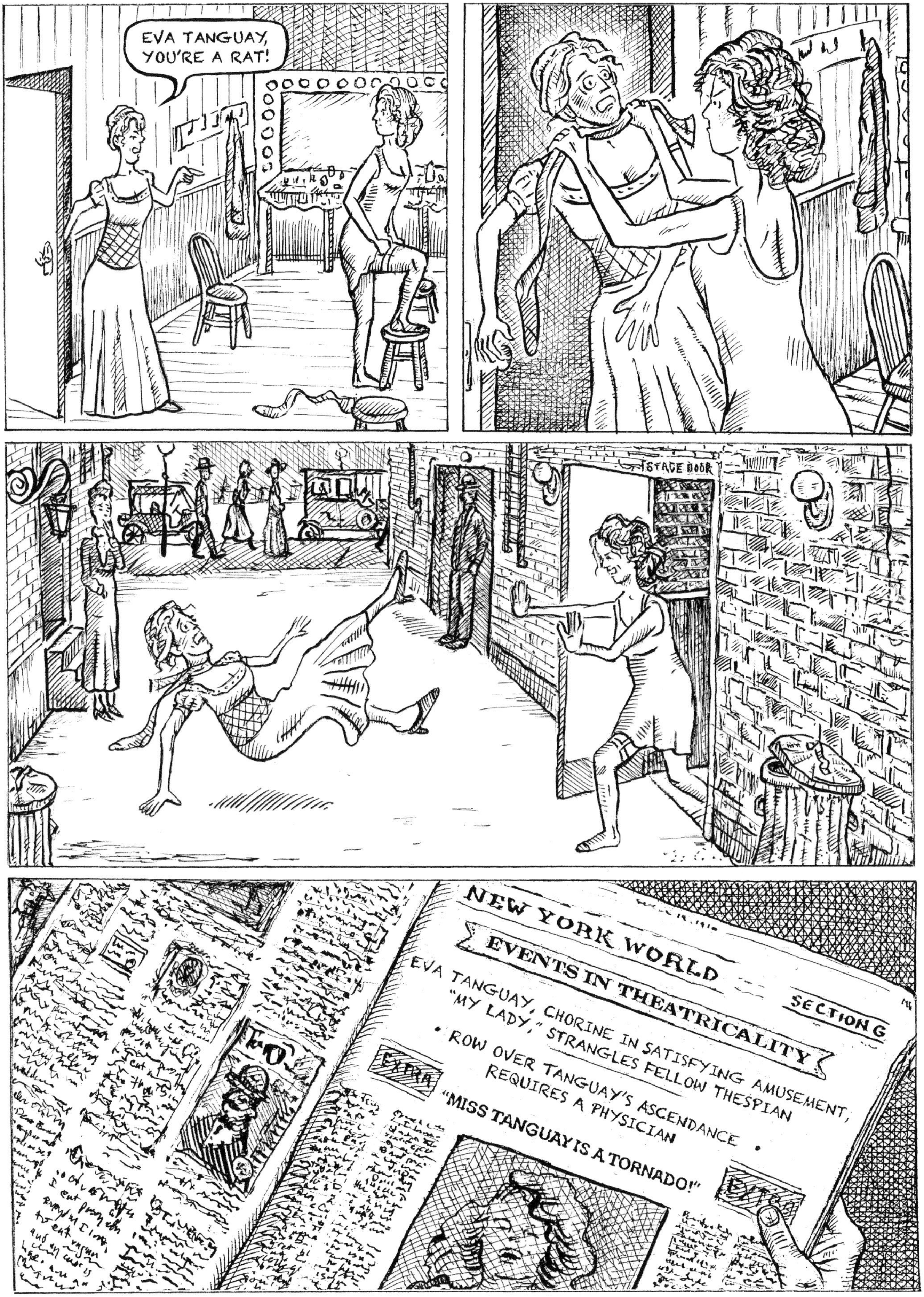
EVA TANGUAY, YOU'RE A RAT!
STAGE DOOR
NEW YORK WORLD
EVENTS IN THEATRICALITY
SECTION G
EVA TANGUAY, CHORINE IN SATISFYING AMUSEMENT, "MY LADY," STRANGLES FELLOW THESPIAN
• ROW OVER TANGUAY'S ASCENDANCE REQUIRES A PHYSICIAN •
EXTRA
"MISS TANGUAY IS A TORNADO!"
EXTRA

HOW A HIT WAS MADE
IN THE SHEET-MUSIC ERA

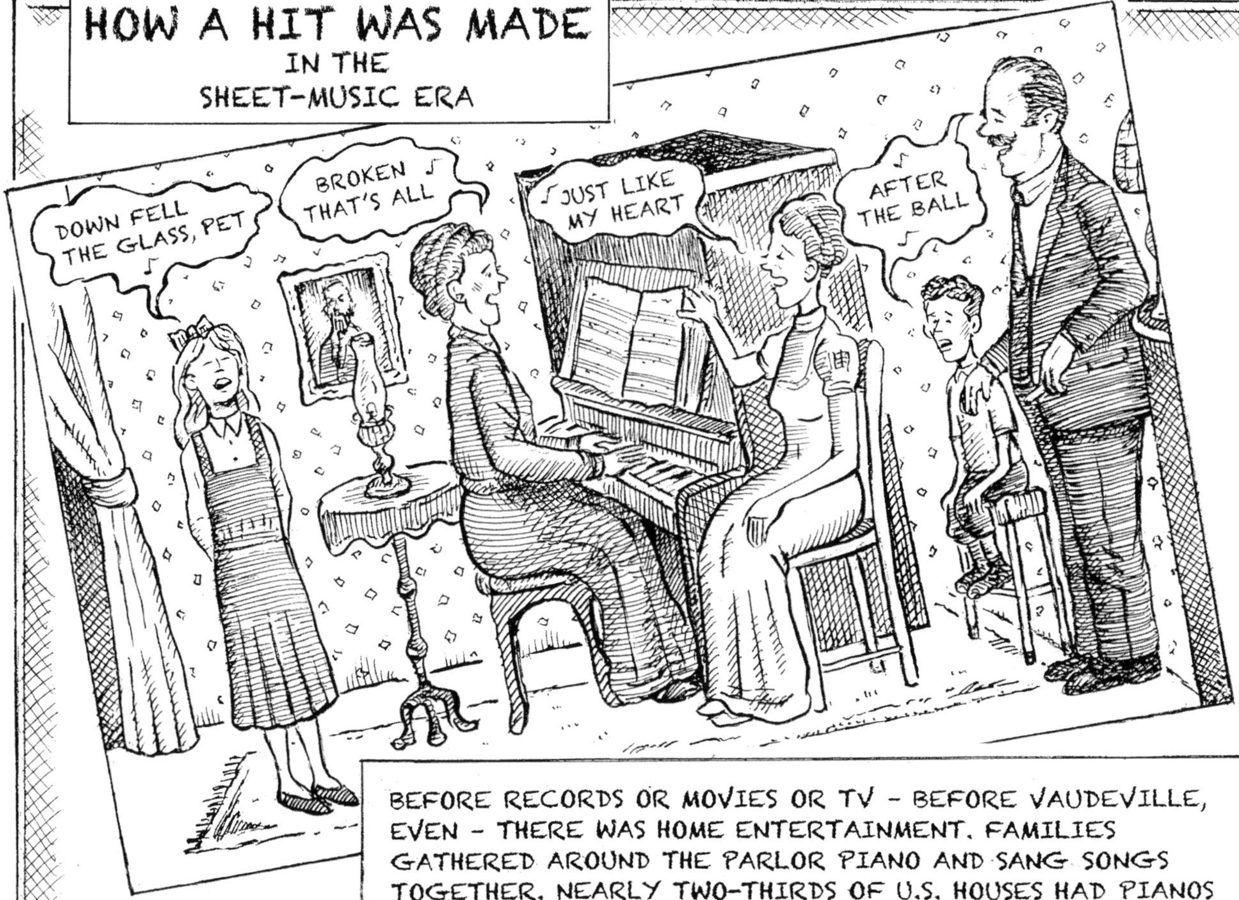
DOWN FELL THE GLASS, PET
BROKEN THAT'S ALL
JUST LIKE MY HEART
AFTER THE BALL

BEFORE RECORDS OR MOVIES OR TV - BEFORE VAUDEVILLE, EVEN - THERE WAS HOME ENTERTAINMENT. FAMILIES GATHERED AROUND THE PARLOR PIANO AND SANG SONGS TOGETHER. NEARLY TWO-THIRDS OF U.S. HOUSES HAD PIANOS AT THE TURN OF THE TWENTIETH CENTURY.

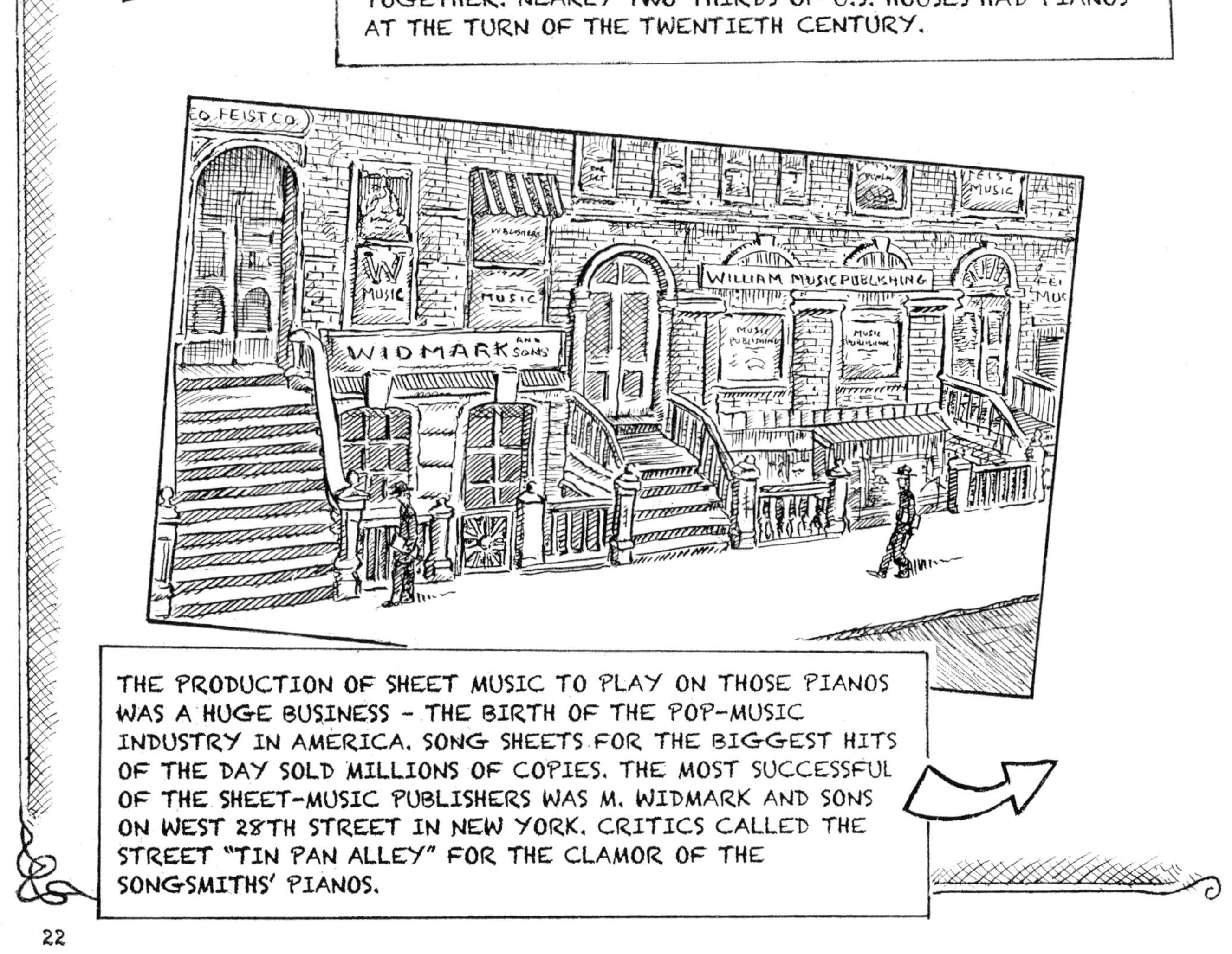
FEIST CO.
W MUSIC
MUSIC
WIDMARK AND SONS
WILLIAM MUSIC PUBLISHING
FEIST MUSIC

THE PRODUCTION OF SHEET MUSIC TO PLAY ON THOSE PIANOS WAS A HUGE BUSINESS - THE BIRTH OF THE POP-MUSIC INDUSTRY IN AMERICA. SONG SHEETS FOR THE BIGGEST HITS OF THE DAY SOLD MILLIONS OF COPIES. THE MOST SUCCESSFUL OF THE SHEET-MUSIC PUBLISHERS WAS M. WIDMARK AND SONS ON WEST 28TH STREET IN NEW YORK. CRITICS CALLED THE STREET "TIN PAN ALLEY" FOR THE CLAMOR OF THE SONGSMITHS' PIANOS.

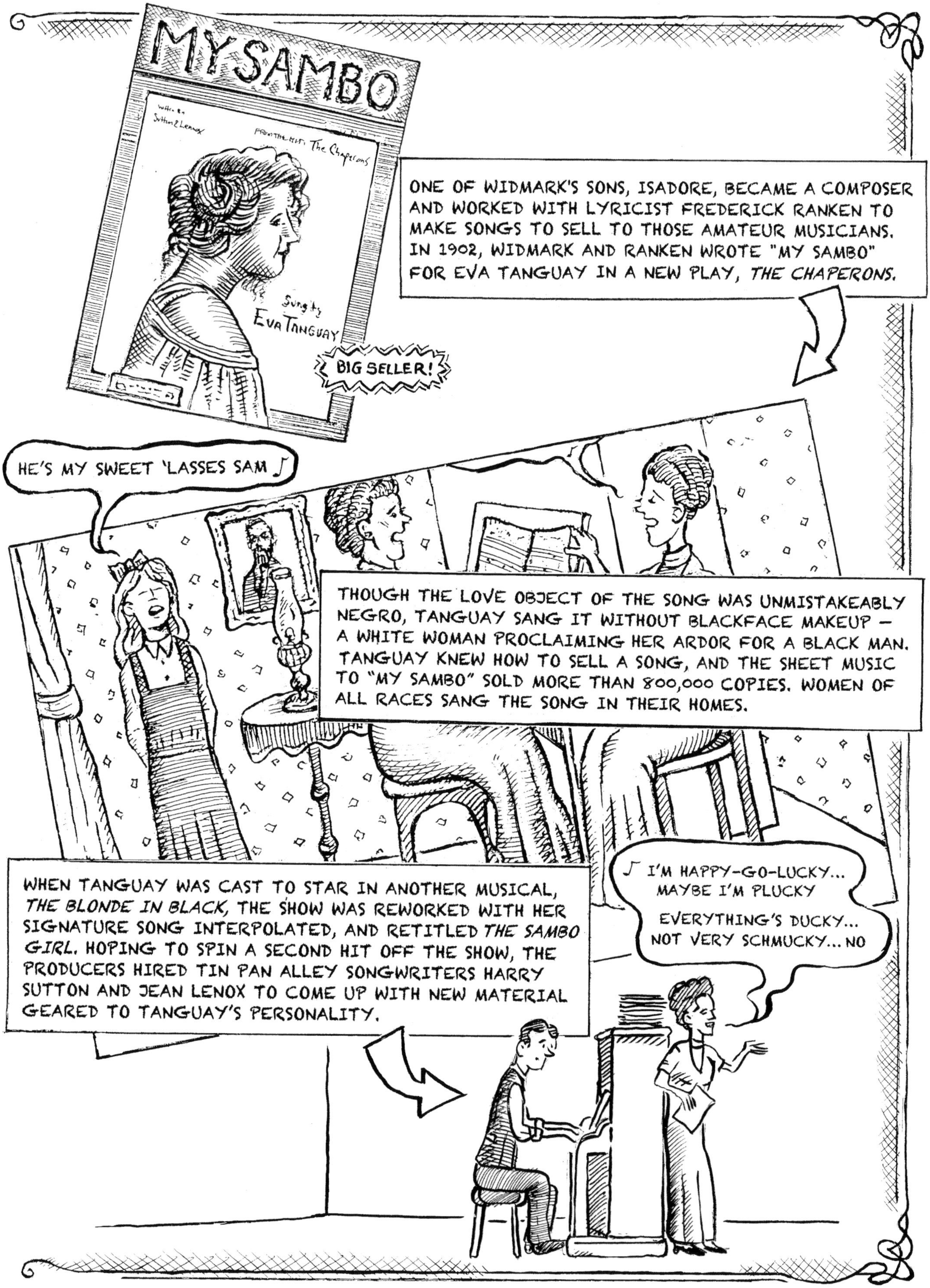
MY SAMBO
Sung by Eva Tanguay
BIG SELLER!
ONE OF WIDMARK'S SONS, ISADORE, BECAME A COMPOSER AND WORKED WITH LYRICIST FREDERICK RANKEN TO MAKE SONGS TO SELL TO THOSE AMATEUR MUSICIANS. IN 1902, WIDMARK AND RANKEN WROTE "MY SAMBO" FOR EVA TANGUAY IN A NEW PLAY, *THE CHAPERONS.*
HE'S MY SWEET 'LASSES SAM ♪
THOUGH THE LOVE OBJECT OF THE SONG WAS UNMISTAKEABLY NEGRO, TANGUAY SANG IT WITHOUT BLACKFACE MAKEUP — A WHITE WOMAN PROCLAIMING HER ARDOR FOR A BLACK MAN. TANGUAY KNEW HOW TO SELL A SONG, AND THE SHEET MUSIC TO "MY SAMBO" SOLD MORE THAN 800,000 COPIES. WOMEN OF ALL RACES SANG THE SONG IN THEIR HOMES.
WHEN TANGUAY WAS CAST TO STAR IN ANOTHER MUSICAL, *THE BLONDE IN BLACK,* THE SHOW WAS REWORKED WITH HER SIGNATURE SONG INTERPOLATED, AND RETITLED *THE SAMBO GIRL.* HOPING TO SPIN A SECOND HIT OFF THE SHOW, THE PRODUCERS HIRED TIN PAN ALLEY SONGWRITERS HARRY SUTTON AND JEAN LENOX TO COME UP WITH NEW MATERIAL GEARED TO TANGUAY'S PERSONALITY.
♪ I'M HAPPY-GO-LUCKY... MAYBE I'M PLUCKY
EVERYTHING'S DUCKY... NOT VERY SCHMUCKY... NO

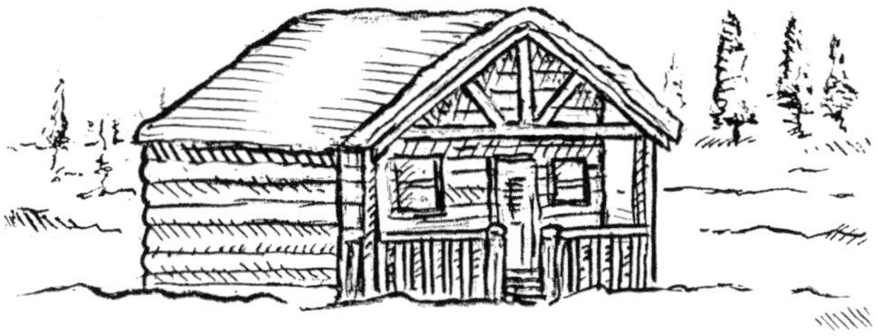

BY THE TIME OF *MY LADY,* TANGUAY HAD BEEN PERFORMING FOR 15 YEARS. BORN IN RURAL QUEBEC, SHE WAS THE DAUGHTER OF A DOCTOR AND A MOTHER WITH AN INTEREST IN THE THEATER. ACCORDING TO TANGUAY, SHE WEIGHED LESS THAN A POUND AND WAS ONLY SEVEN INCHES AT BIRTH. HER PARENTS PUT HER IN A WOODEN BOX AND KEPT HER UNDER THE WOOD STOVE — A HOMEMADE INCUBATOR.

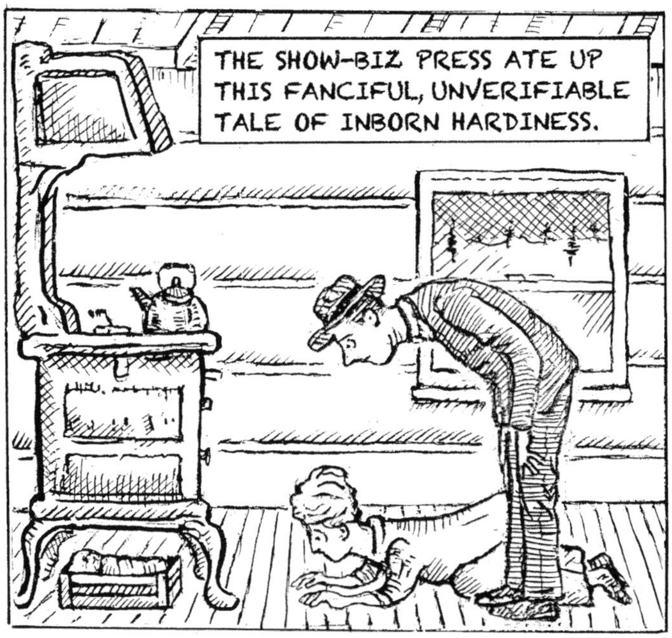
THE SHOW-BIZ PRESS ATE UP THIS FANCIFUL, UNVERIFIABLE TALE OF INBORN HARDINESS.

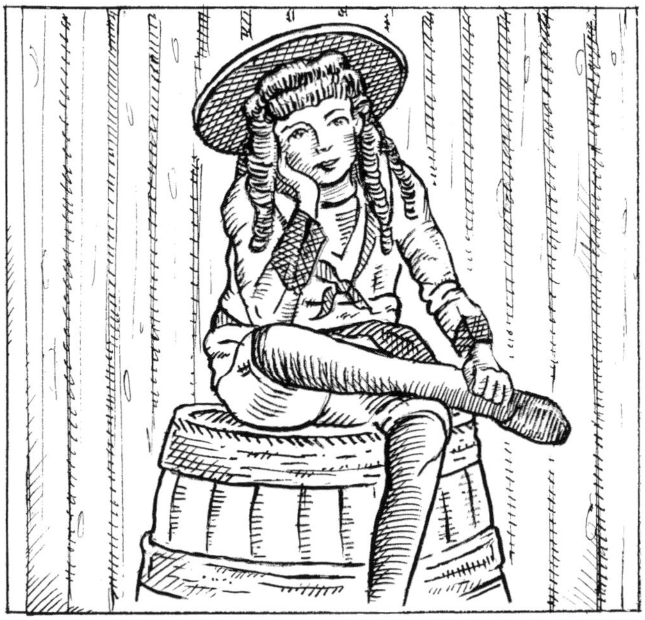

WHEN TANGUAY WAS A YOUNG GIRL, HER FAMILY MOVED TO THE U.S., SETTLING IN A FRENCH-CANADIAN COMMUNITY IN HOLYOKE, MASSACHUSETTS. HER FATHER DIED WHEN SHE WAS EIGHT. NOT LONG AFTER HIS DEATH, SHE GAVE UP SCHOOL AND JOINED THE REDDING-STANTON REPERTOIRE COMPANY, A TOURING TROUPE. SHE PLAYED LITTLE LORD FAUNTLEROY AND "SOUBRETTE" ROLES - TOMBOY GIRLS WHO SERVED AS DRAMATIC CONTRAST TO THE WOEFUL INGENUE. SHE TAUGHT HERSELF TO SING AND DANCE, IN A MANNER, ENTERED SINGING CONTESTS AND PERHAPS WON SOME, AND FOUND HER WAY TO NEW YORK, EARNING $15 A WEEK AS A CHORUS GIRL.

AFTER *MY LADY,* TANGUAY BROKE THROUGH IN A BIGGER WAY WITH *THE CHAPERONS,* A TIMELY SPOOF OF THE "CHAPERONING MOVEMENT" THAT PROTECTED THE "BACHELOR GIRLS" WHO WERE BEGINNING TO SOCIALIZE OUTSIDE THE HOME WITHOUT THEIR PARENTS. TANGUAY'S "MY SAMBO" WAS THE SHOWSTOPPER.

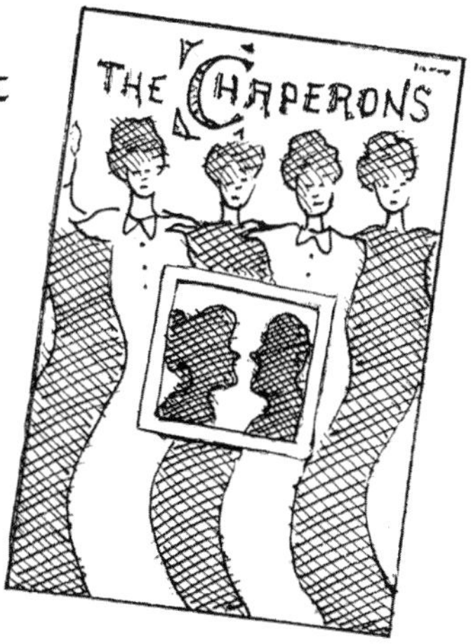
THE CHAPERONS

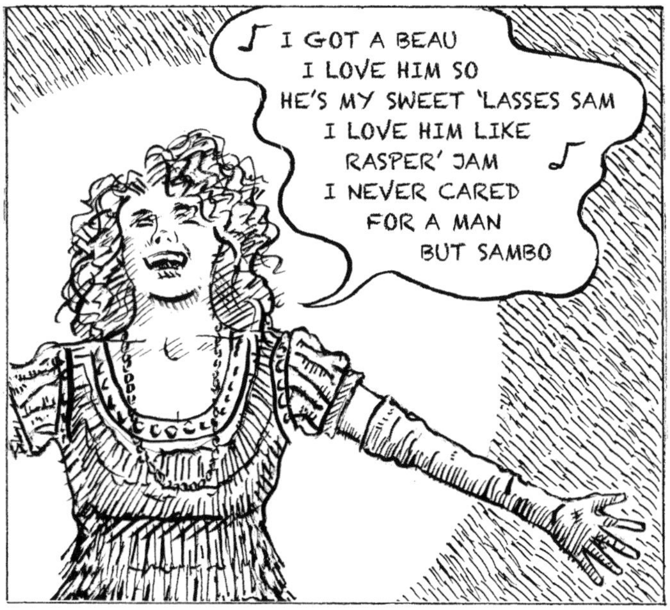
I GOT A BEAU
I LOVE HIM SO
HE'S MY SWEET 'LASSES SAM
I LOVE HIM LIKE
RASPER' JAM
I NEVER CARED
FOR A MAN
BUT SAMBO

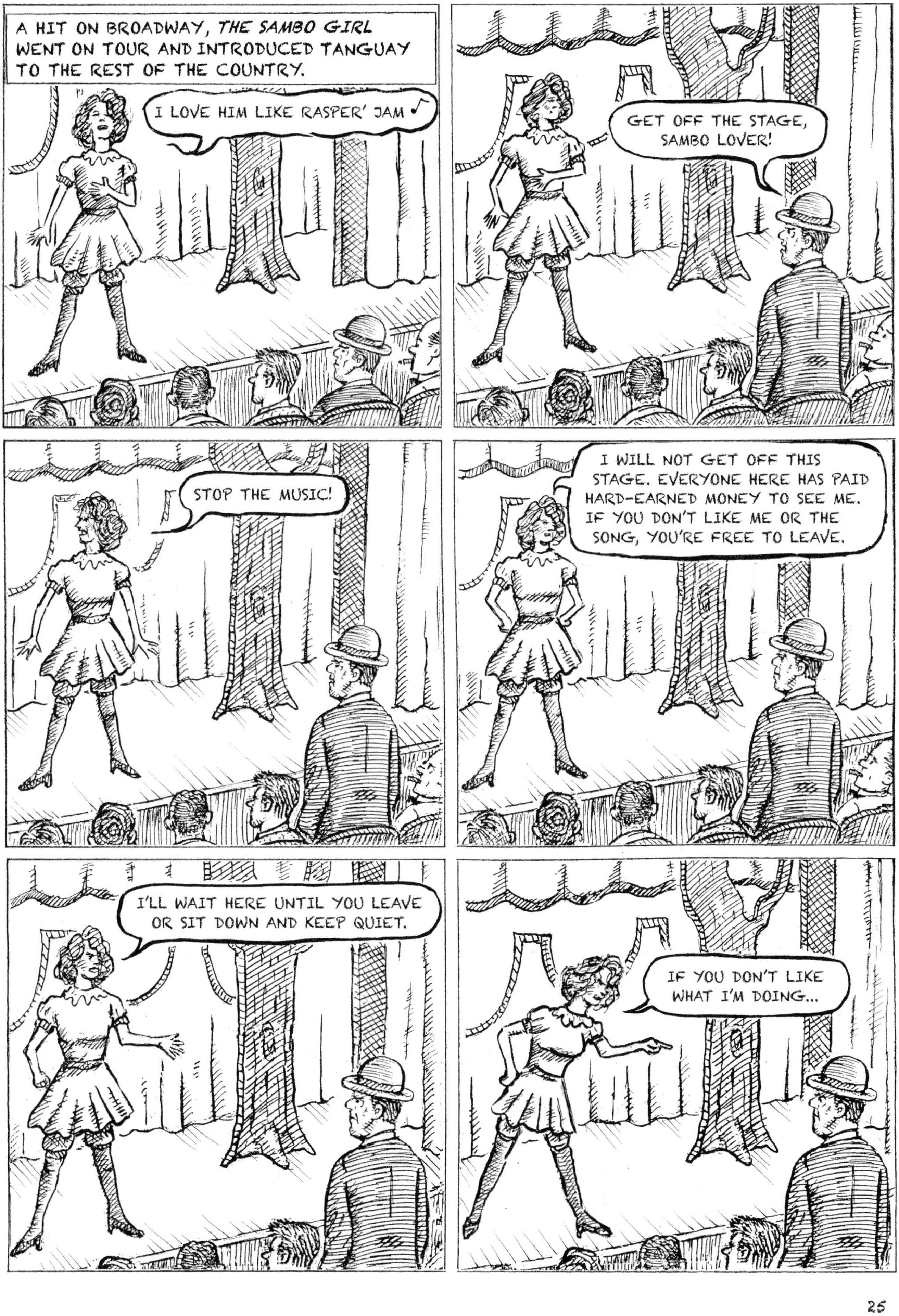
A HIT ON BROADWAY, *THE SAMBO GIRL* WENT ON TOUR AND INTRODUCED TANGUAY TO THE REST OF THE COUNTRY.
I LOVE HIM LIKE RASPER' JAM
GET OFF THE STAGE, SAMBO LOVER!
STOP THE MUSIC!
I WILL NOT GET OFF THIS STAGE. EVERYONE HERE HAS PAID HARD-EARNED MONEY TO SEE ME. IF YOU DON'T LIKE ME OR THE SONG, YOU'RE FREE TO LEAVE.
I'LL WAIT HERE UNTIL YOU LEAVE OR SIT DOWN AND KEEP QUIET.
IF YOU DON'T LIKE WHAT I'M DOING...

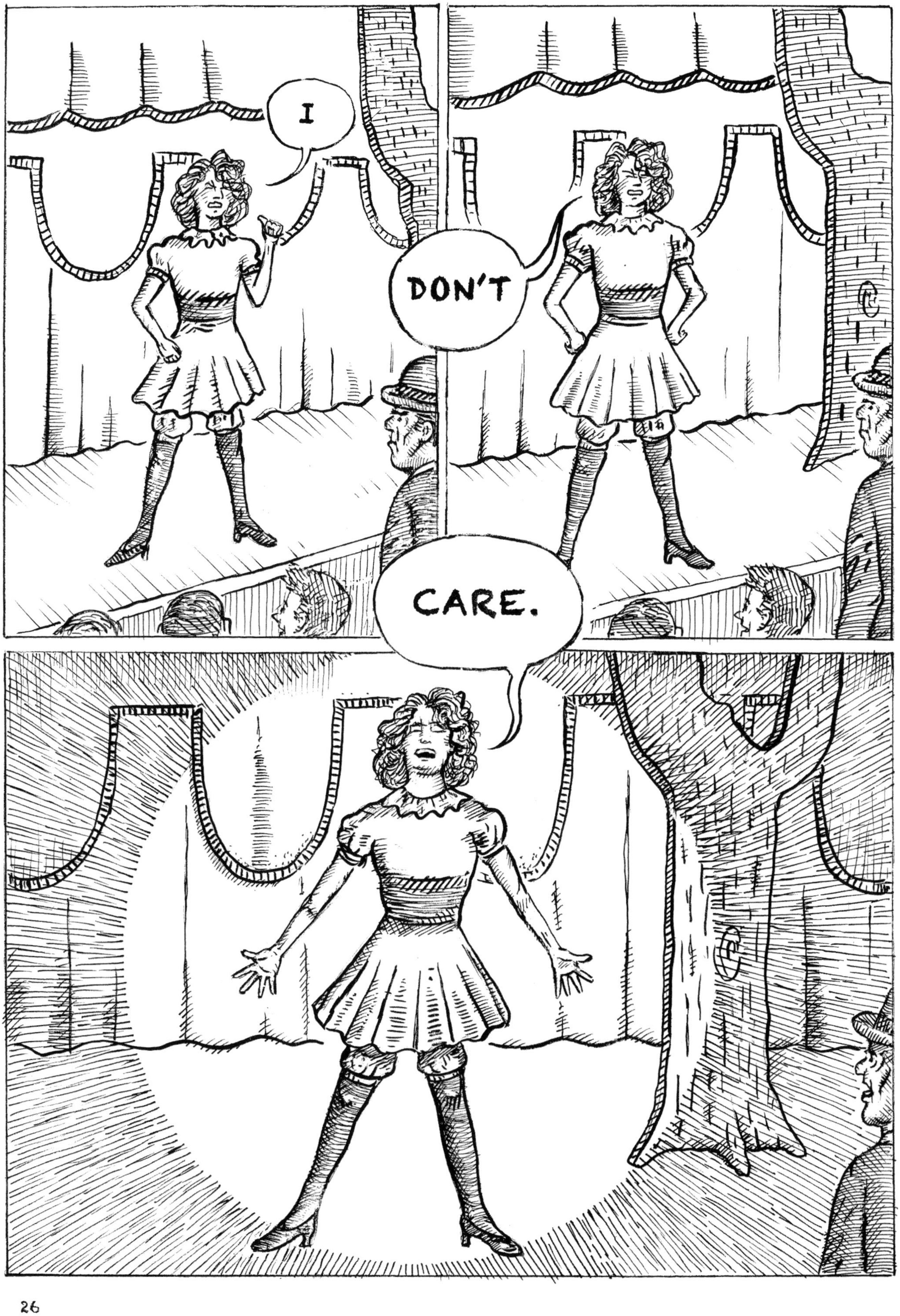
I
DON'T
CARE.

THE ARISING OF VARIETY

Whereby the Entertainment to Be Known as "Vaudeville" Captivates the Citizenry

WHILE WALKER AND WILLIAMS, JULIAN ELTINGE, AND EVA TANGUAY WERE MAKING THEIR NAMES IN MINSTRELSY AND MUSICAL THEATER, A NEW FORM OF ENTERTAINMENT WAS TAKING FORM IN AMERICAN CITIES, MOST PROMINENTLY (THOUGH NOT SOLELY) IN NEW YORK.

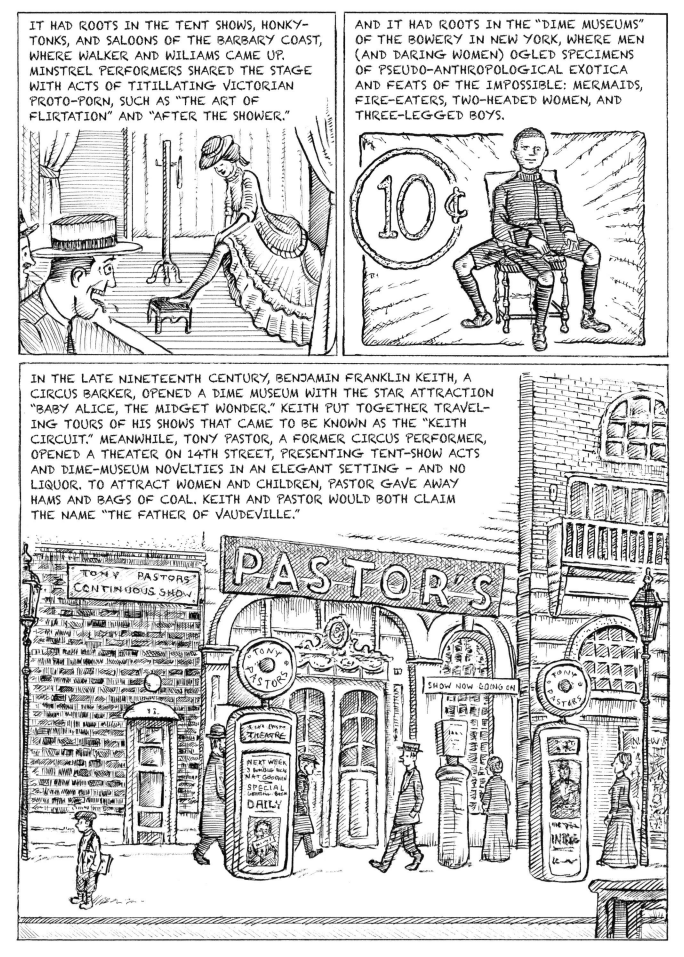

IT HAD ROOTS IN THE TENT SHOWS, HONKY-TONKS, AND SALOONS OF THE BARBARY COAST, WHERE WALKER AND WILIAMS CAME UP. MINSTREL PERFORMERS SHARED THE STAGE WITH ACTS OF TITILLATING VICTORIAN PROTO-PORN, SUCH AS "THE ART OF FLIRTATION" AND "AFTER THE SHOWER."
AND IT HAD ROOTS IN THE "DIME MUSEUMS" OF THE BOWERY IN NEW YORK, WHERE MEN (AND DARING WOMEN) OGLED SPECIMENS OF PSEUDO-ANTHROPOLOGICAL EXOTICA AND FEATS OF THE IMPOSSIBLE: MERMAIDS, FIRE-EATERS, TWO-HEADED WOMEN, AND THREE-LEGGED BOYS.
10¢
IN THE LATE NINETEENTH CENTURY, BENJAMIN FRANKLIN KEITH, A CIRCUS BARKER, OPENED A DIME MUSEUM WITH THE STAR ATTRACTION "BABY ALICE, THE MIDGET WONDER." KEITH PUT TOGETHER TRAVELING TOURS OF HIS SHOWS THAT CAME TO BE KNOWN AS THE "KEITH CIRCUIT." MEANWHILE, TONY PASTOR, A FORMER CIRCUS PERFORMER, OPENED A THEATER ON 14TH STREET, PRESENTING TENT-SHOW ACTS AND DIME-MUSEUM NOVELTIES IN AN ELEGANT SETTING - AND NO LIQUOR. TO ATTRACT WOMEN AND CHILDREN, PASTOR GAVE AWAY HAMS AND BAGS OF COAL. KEITH AND PASTOR WOULD BOTH CLAIM THE NAME "THE FATHER OF VAUDEVILLE."
TONY PASTORS CONTINUOUS SHOW
PASTOR'S
TONY PASTORS
SHOW NOW GOING ON
THEATRE
NEXT WEEK
NAT GOODWIN
SPECIAL
DAILY
TONY PASTORS

THEATERS LIKE PASTOR'S SPROUTED UP ALONG 14TH STREET IN NEW YORK, AND IN BOSTON, PHILADELPHIA, CLEVELAND, CHICAGO, AND EVERY OTHER MAJOR AMERICAN CITY. THEY PRESENTED PROGRAMS OF ACTS SENT OUT BY KEITH AND A STRING OF COPYCAT CIRCUITS. MOST PEOPLE CALLED THE ENTERTAINMENT "VARIETY" – OR "CONTINUOUS" USED AS A NOUN. OVER TIME, THE GALLIC-SOUNDING WORD "VAUDEVILLE" TOOK HOLD. IT CAME FROM THE FRENCH *VOIX DE VILLE*, FOR "VOICE OF THE CITY STREETS." IT SOUNDED EXOTIC BUT FANCY AND, BEING FRENCH, NAUGHTY, TOO.

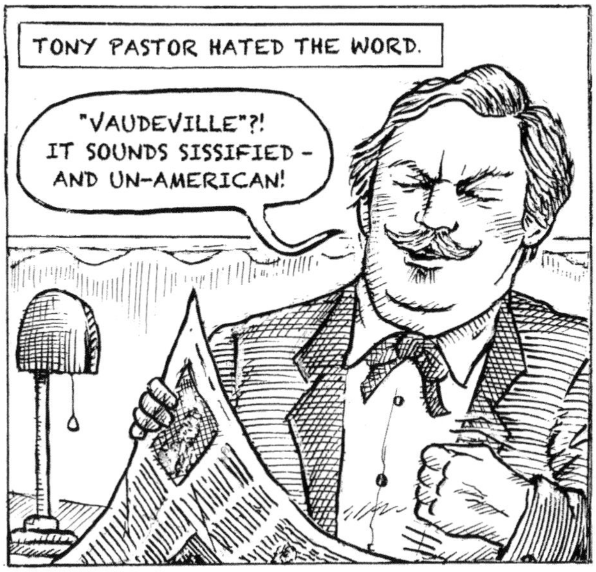
TONY PASTOR HATED THE WORD.
"VAUDEVILLE"?! IT SOUNDS SISSIFIED – AND UN-AMERICAN!

BETWEEN 1900 AND 1920, AMERICA SHIFTED FROM AN AGRARIAN TO AN INDUSTRIAL ECONOMY. THE POPULATION IN U.S. CITIES BALLOONED BY 80%, TO 54 MILLION PEOPLE. THE MAJORITY OF AMERICANS WERE NOW LIVING IN CITIES – AND WERE HUNGRY FOR ENTERTAINMENT. BY 1910, SOME 5,000 VARIETY THEATERS HAD OPENED ALL ACROSS THE COUNTRY.

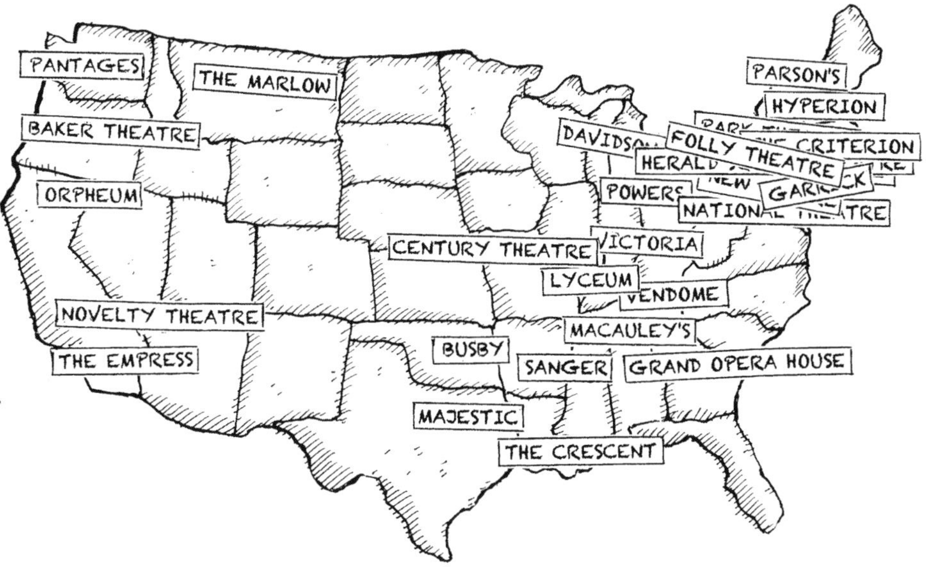
PANTAGES
THE MARLOW
BAKER THEATRE
ORPHEUM
NOVELTY THEATRE
THE EMPRESS
PARSON'S
HYPERION
CRITERION
FOLLY THEATRE
HERALD
POWERS
CENTURY THEATRE
LYCEUM
VENDOME
MACAULEY'S
BUSBY
SANGER
GRAND OPERA HOUSE
MAJESTIC
THE CRESCENT

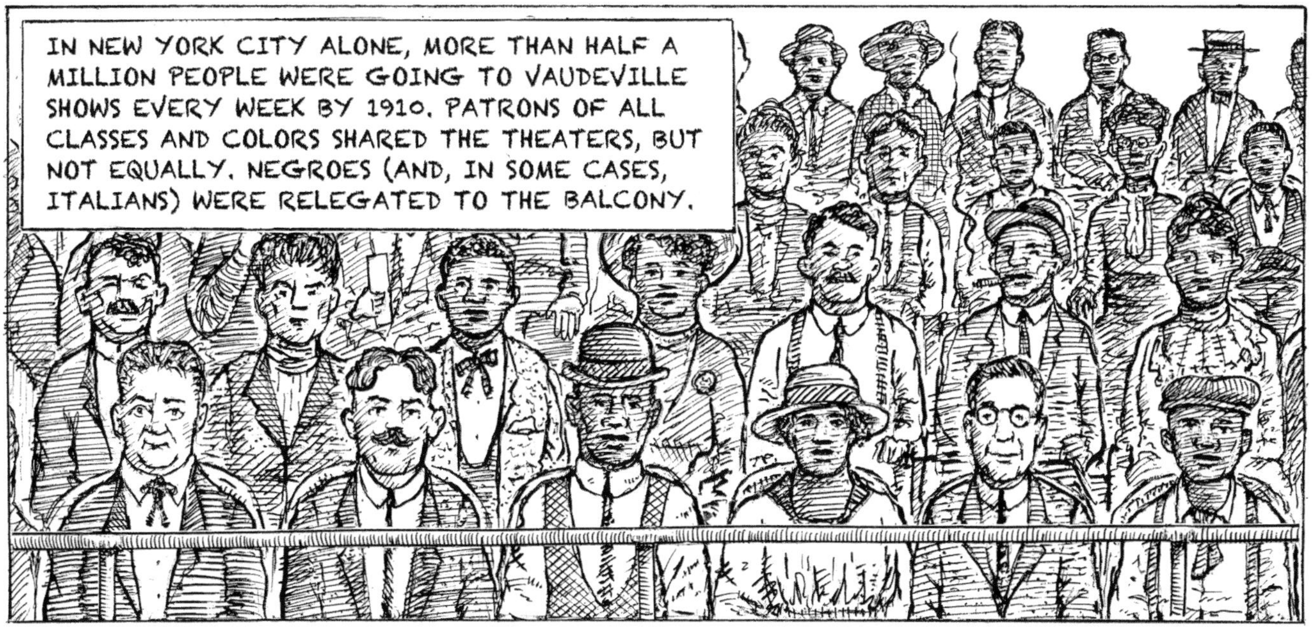
IN NEW YORK CITY ALONE, MORE THAN HALF A MILLION PEOPLE WERE GOING TO VAUDEVILLE SHOWS EVERY WEEK BY 1910. PATRONS OF ALL CLASSES AND COLORS SHARED THE THEATERS, BUT NOT EQUALLY. NEGROES (AND, IN SOME CASES, ITALIANS) WERE RELEGATED TO THE BALCONY.

BUY A TICKET FOR A VAUDEVILLE SHOW, AND YOU CAN STAY AS LONG AS YOU WANT - FROM OPENING (USUALLY AT 10 a.m.) TO CLOSING (USUALLY 11 p.m.). GOOD SEAT AT A GOOD HOUSE: 50¢. FRONT ROW: $1.00. BALCONY: 25¢. "CONTINUOUS" IT WAS. A TYPICAL BILL HAD NINE ACTS PLUS INTERMISSION AND RAN FOR THREE HOURS, THEN STARTED OVER AGAIN - FOUR TIMES EVERY DAY, EXCEPT SUNDAYS.

MOST SHOWS OPENED WITH ACROBATS, ACTS DEMANDING LITTLE FROM THE AUDIENCE, WHILE PEOPLE SETTLED INTO THEIR SEATS.

A COMIC DANCER OR DANCE TEAM WOULD PERFORM SECOND, IN FRONT OF THE CURTAIN - "IN ONE" - WHILE THE STAGE WAS SET UP FOR THE THIRD ACT.

THE THIRD ACT WAS THE BIG ACT OF THE FIRST HALF OF THE PROGRAM - A "FLASH ACT," OFTEN A REVUE OR GIRLIE SHOW, ON THE FULL STAGE.

WITH THE CURTAIN CLOSED AGAIN, A "SMART" COMEDY TEAM OR "TALKING ACT" WOULD PERFORM "IN ONE." LIKE BILLY MURRAY AND STEVE PORTER, GEORGE BURNS AND GRACIE ALLEN GOT THEIR START AS A "TALKING ACT." DONE "IN ONE."

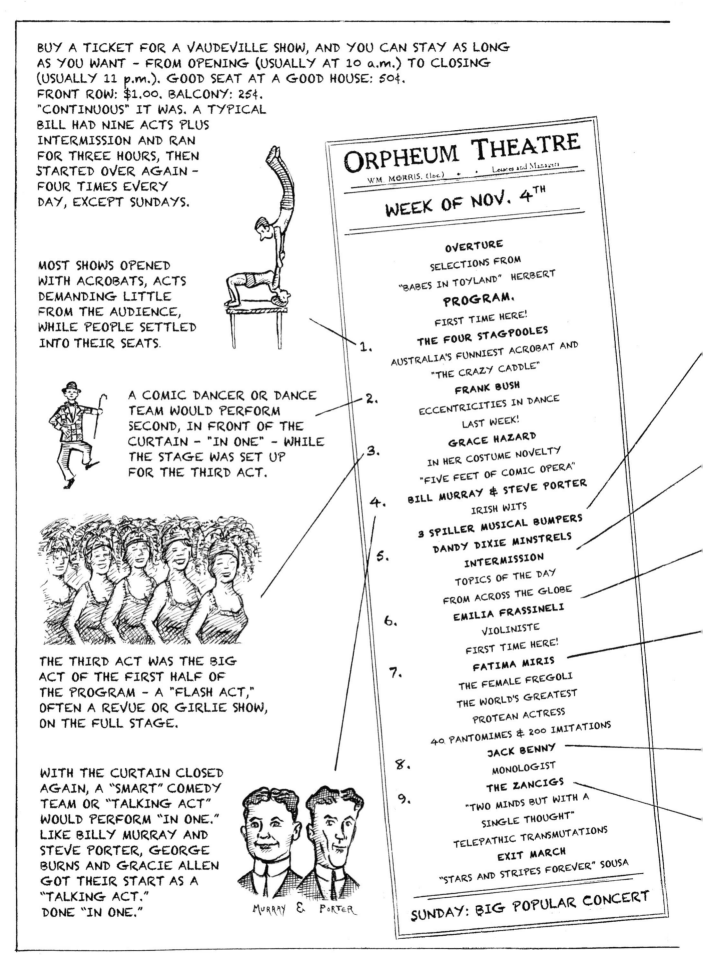

MURRAY & PORTER

ORPHEUM THEATRE
WM. MORRIS, (Inc.) · Lessees and Managers

WEEK OF NOV. 4TH

OVERTURE
SELECTIONS FROM
"BABES IN TOYLAND" HERBERT

PROGRAM.

FIRST TIME HERE!
1. THE FOUR STAGPOOLES
AUSTRALIA'S FUNNIEST ACROBAT AND
"THE CRAZY CADDLE"
2. FRANK BUSH
ECCENTRICITIES IN DANCE
LAST WEEK!
3. GRACE HAZARD
IN HER COSTUME NOVELTY
"FIVE FEET OF COMIC OPERA"
4. BILL MURRAY & STEVE PORTER
IRISH WITS
3 SPILLER MUSICAL BUMPERS
5. DANDY DIXIE MINSTRELS
INTERMISSION
TOPICS OF THE DAY
FROM ACROSS THE GLOBE
6. EMILIA FRASSINELI
VIOLINISTE
FIRST TIME HERE!
7. FATIMA MIRIS
THE FEMALE FREGOLI
THE WORLD'S GREATEST
PROTEAN ACTRESS
40 PANTOMIMES & 200 IMITATIONS
8. JACK BENNY
MONOLOGIST
9. THE ZANCIGS
"TWO MINDS BUT WITH A
SINGLE THOUGHT"
TELEPATHIC TRANSMUTATIONS
EXIT MARCH
"STARS AND STRIPES FOREVER" SOUSA

SUNDAY: BIG POPULAR CONCERT

30

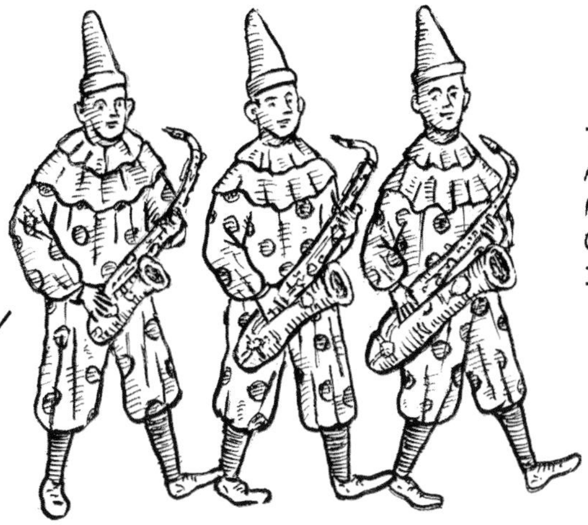

THE FIRST HALF WOULD CLOSE WITH A ROUSING MUSICAL ACT, OFTEN A MINSTREL GROUP OR A NOVELTY COMBO USING THAT COMICAL NEW INSTRUMENT, THE "SAXOPHONE."

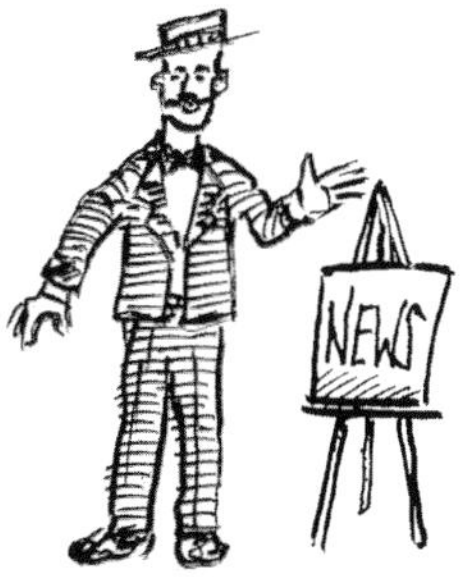
NEWS

15-MINUTE INTERMISSION, DURING WHICH A MASTER OF CEREMONIES WOULD ANNOUNCE HIGHLIGHTS OF THE NEWS OF THE DAY.

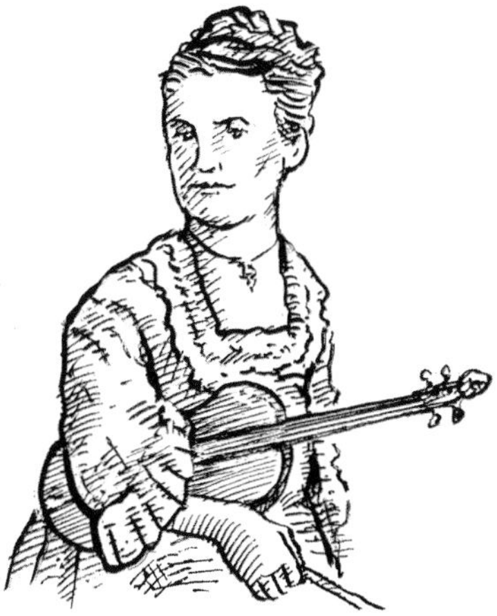

THE SECOND HALF WOULD OPEN WITH A SERIOUS MUSICIAN PLAYING CLASSICAL MUSIC WHILE THE AUDIENCE SETTLED BACK DOWN AND "SECOND-ACTERS" JUST ARRIVING FOR THE SHOW FOUND SEATS. DONE "IN ONE."

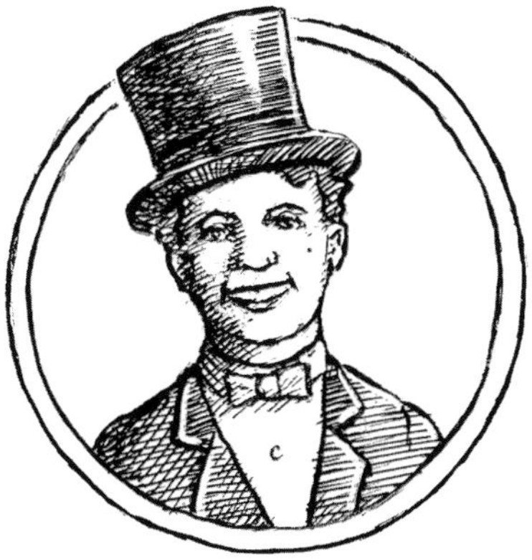

MAJOR ACT, PRESENTED WITH SETS AND COSTUMES ON THE FULL STAGE. THIS IS WHEN THE STAR ATTRACTION OF THE SHOW WOULD APPEAR. EVA TANGUAY WOULD INSIST ON APPEARING NOWHERE ELSE ON THE BILL.

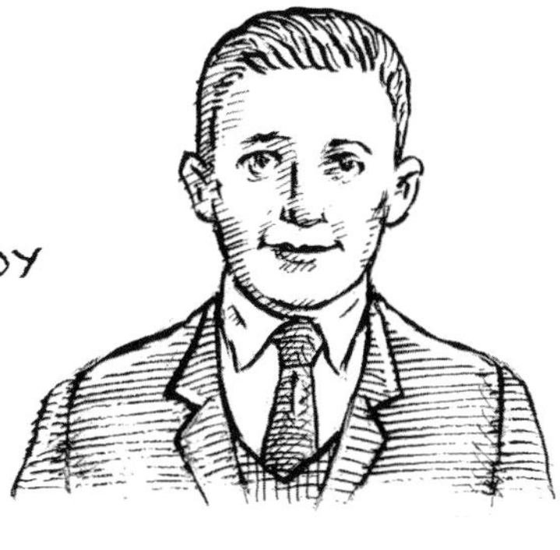

STRONG, ESTABLISHED COMEDY SINGLE OR "MONOLOGIST."

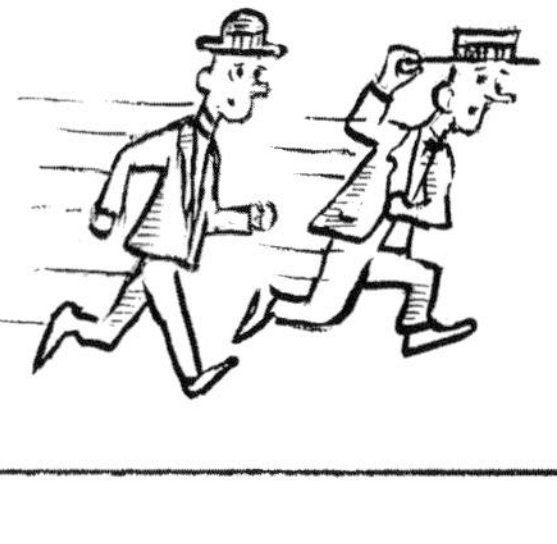

CLOSING SPOT RESERVED ESPECIALLY FOR "THE CHASER" - AN ACT SO BAD THAT IT WOULD DRIVE PEOPLE OUT OF THE HOUSE, MAKING ROOM FOR NEW PAYING CUSTOMERS.

VAUDEVILLE, A DISTINCTLY AMERICAN FORM OF ENTERTAINMENT ART, WAS CREATED MAINLY BY IMMIGRANTS AND OTHER SOCIAL OUTLIERS FOR PEOPLE LIKE THEM. A SIZABLE SHARE OF VAUDEVILLE ACTS, ESPECIALLY IN THE EARLY YEARS OF VARIETY, WERE FIXED - OR FIXATED - ON ISSUES OF IDENTITY. THROUGH ALL FORMS OF ETHNIC AND RACIAL PORTRAYAL AND PARODY, VAUDEVILLE COMEDIANS AND SINGERS EXPLORED WHAT IT MEANT TO BE AN AMERICAN MAN OR WOMAN AND ALSO IRISH OR GERMAN OR ITALIAN OR JEWISH OR ASIAN OR BLACK.

JOE WEBER AND LEW FIELDS, BOTH JEWISH AMERICANS, PERFORMED AN ACT OF "DUTCH" COMEDY, A SPOOF OF GERMAN IMMIGRANTS. BEFORE SETTLING ON THIS ACT, THEY EXPERIMENTED WITH IRISH AND ITALIAN PARODY, AND ALSO TRIED BLACKFACE.

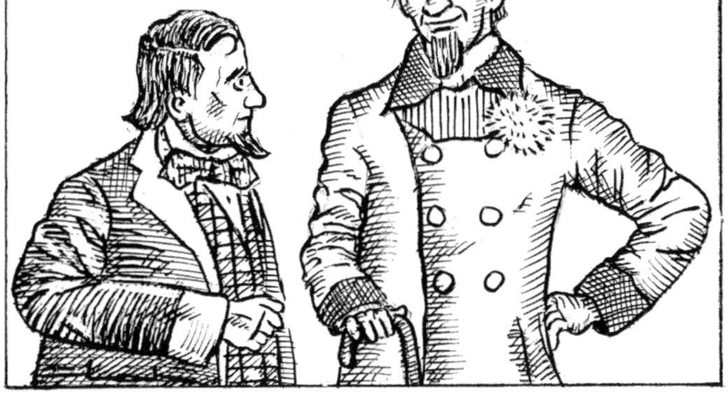

LEE TUNG FOO, CHINESE AMERICAN, PERFORMED IN COSTUME OF FESTIVE GARB FROM CHINA. HIS ACT, A MULTILAYERED PLAY ON ORIENTALIST STEREOTYPING, TOYED WITH ETHNICITY. HE SANG "MY IRISH MOLLY, O" IN BROGUE, AND CLOSED HIS SHOWS WITH A DRINKING SONG, "IM TIEFEN KELLER," SUNG IN GERMAN.

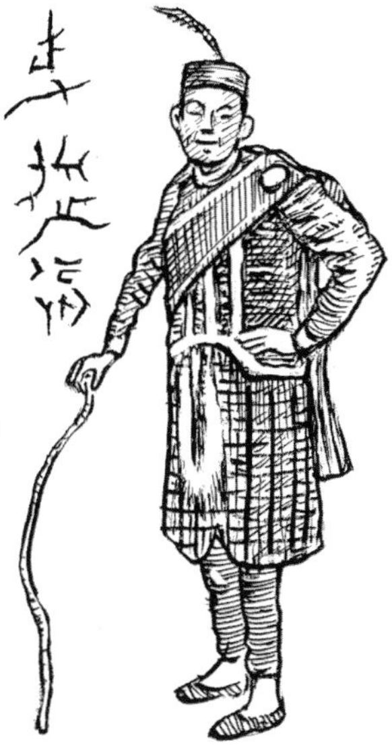

CLARK AND VERDI, PERFORMERS OF UNCERTAIN HERITAGE, DID AN ACT OF ITALIAN PARODY, THEN CALLED A "WOP ACT."

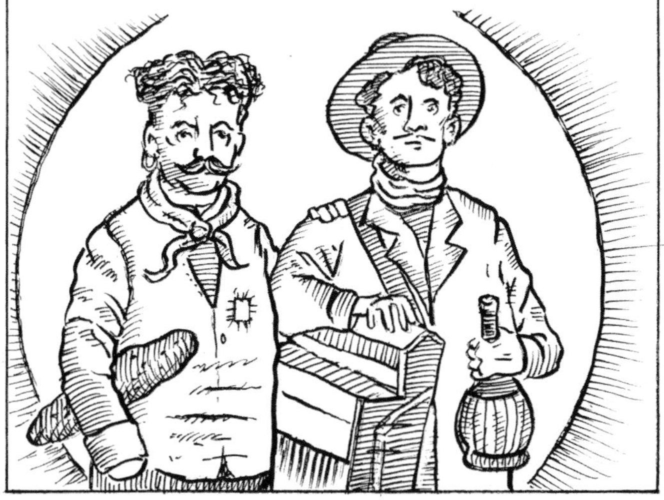

TOM BROWN, A VERSATILE AFRICAN AMERICAN SINGER AND COMEDIAN, PLAYED IN WHITEFACE - AND IN "YELLOWFACE" - TO DO IRISH, ITALIAN, GERMAN, JEWISH, AND CHINESE IMPERSONATIONS.

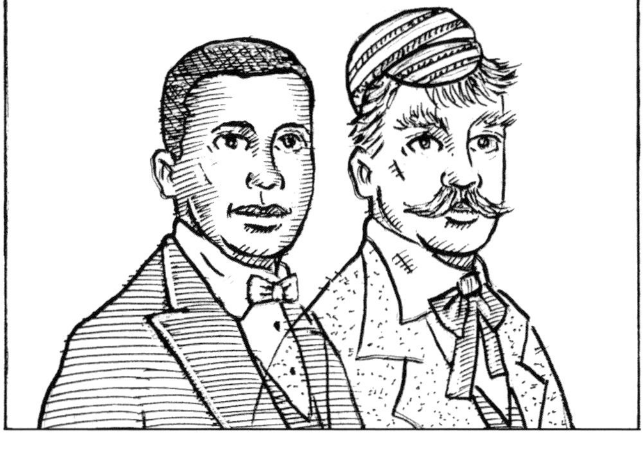

THE MARX BROTHERS, GERMAN JEWS, STARTED IN VAUDEVILLE WITH HALF THE BROTHERS DOING FORMS OF ETHNIC PARODY. GROUCHO ORIGINALLY DID "DUTCH" SATIRE, BUT DROPPED THE GERMAN ACCENT WHEN THE FIRST WORLD WAR CAME. CHICO, OF COURSE, WOULD DO AN ITALIAN IMPERSONATION THROUGHOUT HIS PROFESSIONAL LIFE. (THE BROTHERS' STAGE ACT INCLUDED THE "STRAIGHT" FOIL GUMMO, WHO LEFT TO JOIN THE SERVICE AND WAS REPLACED BY ZEPPO IN THE MOVIES.)

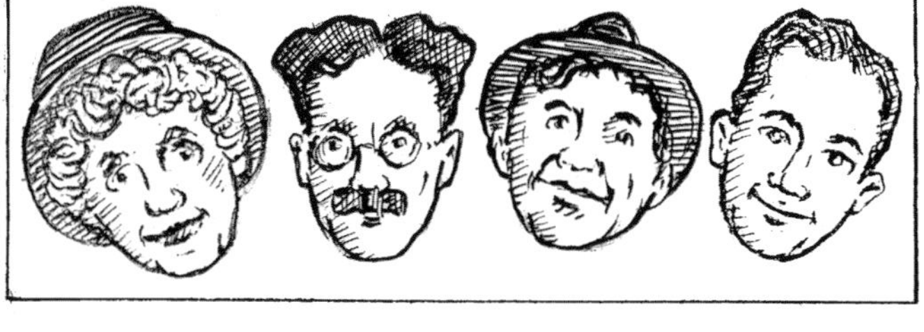

WILLIAMS AND WALKER, JULIAN ELTINGE, AND EVA TANGUAY WERE READY FOR VAUDEVILLE, AND VAUDEVILLE WAS RIPE FOR THEM.

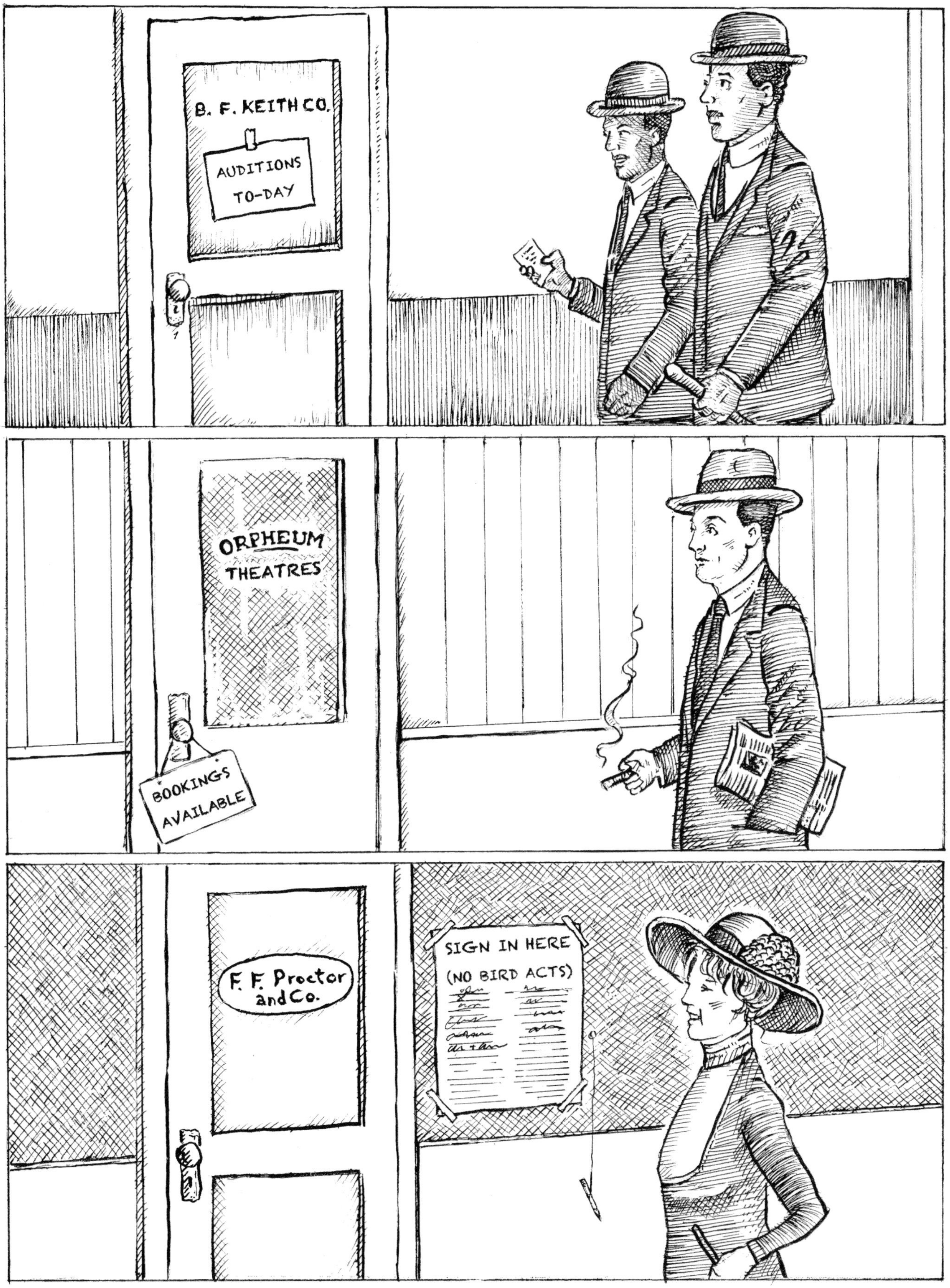
B. F. KEITH CO.
AUDITIONS TO-DAY
ORPHEUM THEATRES
BOOKINGS AVAILABLE
F. F. Proctor and Co.
SIGN IN HERE
(NO BIRD ACTS)

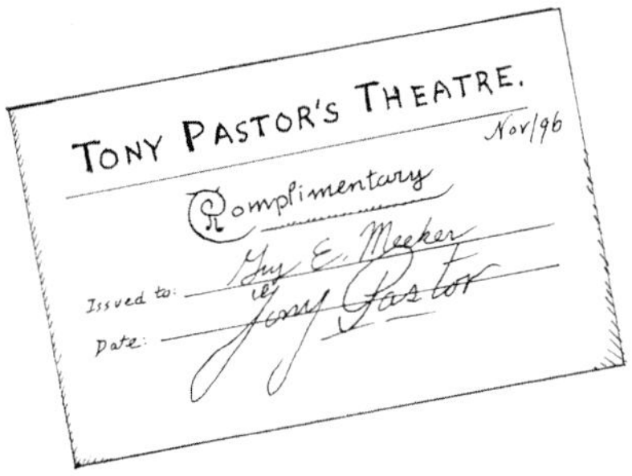
TONY PASTOR'S THEATRE.
Nov/96
Complimentary
Issued to: Guy E. Meeker
Date:
Tony Pastor

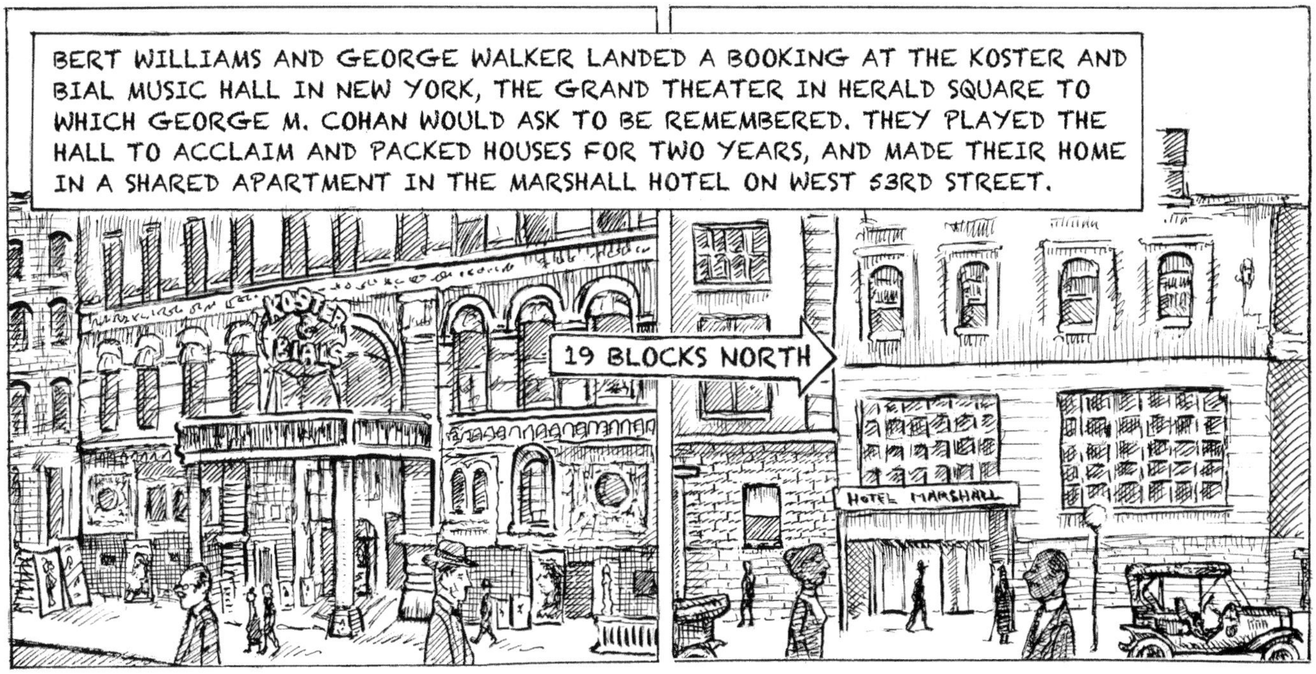
BERT WILLIAMS AND GEORGE WALKER LANDED A BOOKING AT THE KOSTER AND BIAL MUSIC HALL IN NEW YORK, THE GRAND THEATER IN HERALD SQUARE TO WHICH GEORGE M. COHAN WOULD ASK TO BE REMEMBERED. THEY PLAYED THE HALL TO ACCLAIM AND PACKED HOUSES FOR TWO YEARS, AND MADE THEIR HOME IN A SHARED APARTMENT IN THE MARSHALL HOTEL ON WEST 53RD STREET.
KOSTER & BIAL'S
19 BLOCKS NORTH
HOTEL MARSHALL

THE MARSHALL WAS A "BLACK AND TAN," WHERE PEOPLE OF ALL RACES WERE WELCOME AND SOMETIMES MIXED TENTATIVELY OVER FOOD AND DRINKS. FOR AFRICAN AMERICANS AT THE TURN OF THE CENTURY, IT WAS THE HUB OF A NEW COSMOPOLITANISM, THE SALON FOR THE EMERGING GENERATION OF ARTISTS, MUSICIANS, ACTORS, WRITERS, AND THEIR HANGERS-ON. THE HARLEM RENAISSANCE BEGAN AT THE MARSHALL BEFORE MOVING UPTOWN.

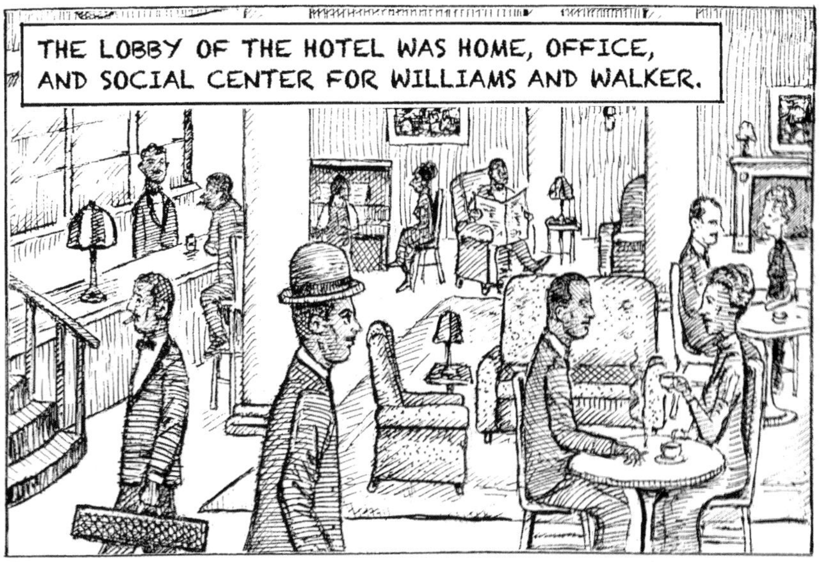
THE LOBBY OF THE HOTEL WAS HOME, OFFICE, AND SOCIAL CENTER FOR WILLIAMS AND WALKER.

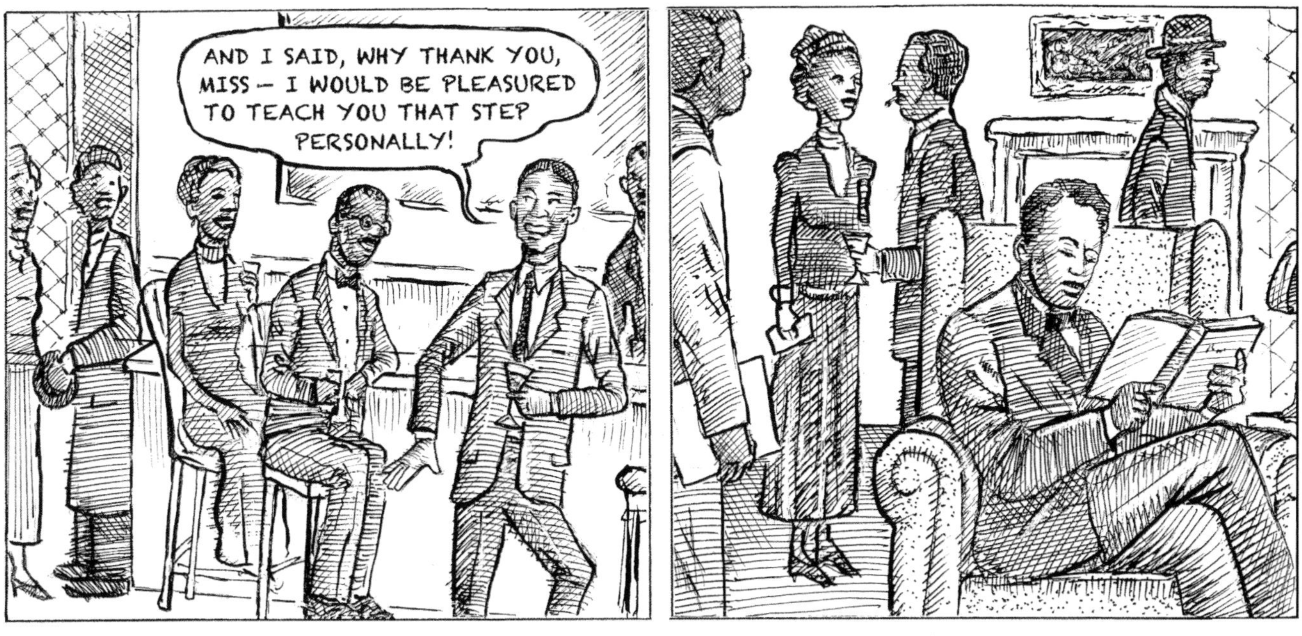
AND I SAID, WHY THANK YOU, MISS – I WOULD BE PLEASURED TO TEACH YOU THAT STEP PERSONALLY!

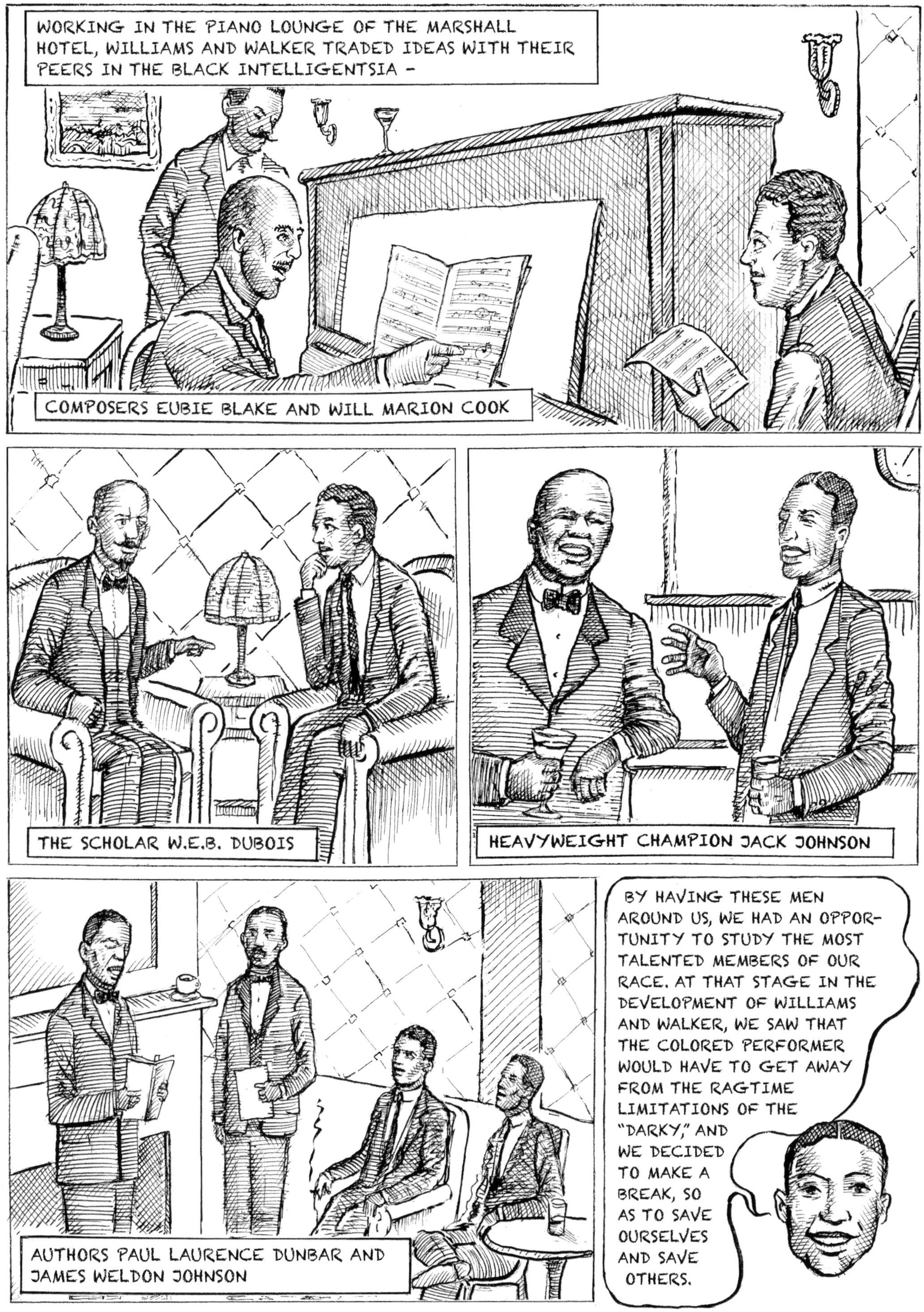
WORKING IN THE PIANO LOUNGE OF THE MARSHALL HOTEL, WILLIAMS AND WALKER TRADED IDEAS WITH THEIR PEERS IN THE BLACK INTELLIGENTSIA –
COMPOSERS EUBIE BLAKE AND WILL MARION COOK
THE SCHOLAR W.E.B. DUBOIS
HEAVYWEIGHT CHAMPION JACK JOHNSON
AUTHORS PAUL LAURENCE DUNBAR AND JAMES WELDON JOHNSON
BY HAVING THESE MEN AROUND US, WE HAD AN OPPORTUNITY TO STUDY THE MOST TALENTED MEMBERS OF OUR RACE. AT THAT STAGE IN THE DEVELOPMENT OF WILLIAMS AND WALKER, WE SAW THAT THE COLORED PERFORMER WOULD HAVE TO GET AWAY FROM THE RAGTIME LIMITATIONS OF THE "DARKY," AND WE DECIDED TO MAKE A BREAK, SO AS TO SAVE OURSELVES AND SAVE OTHERS.

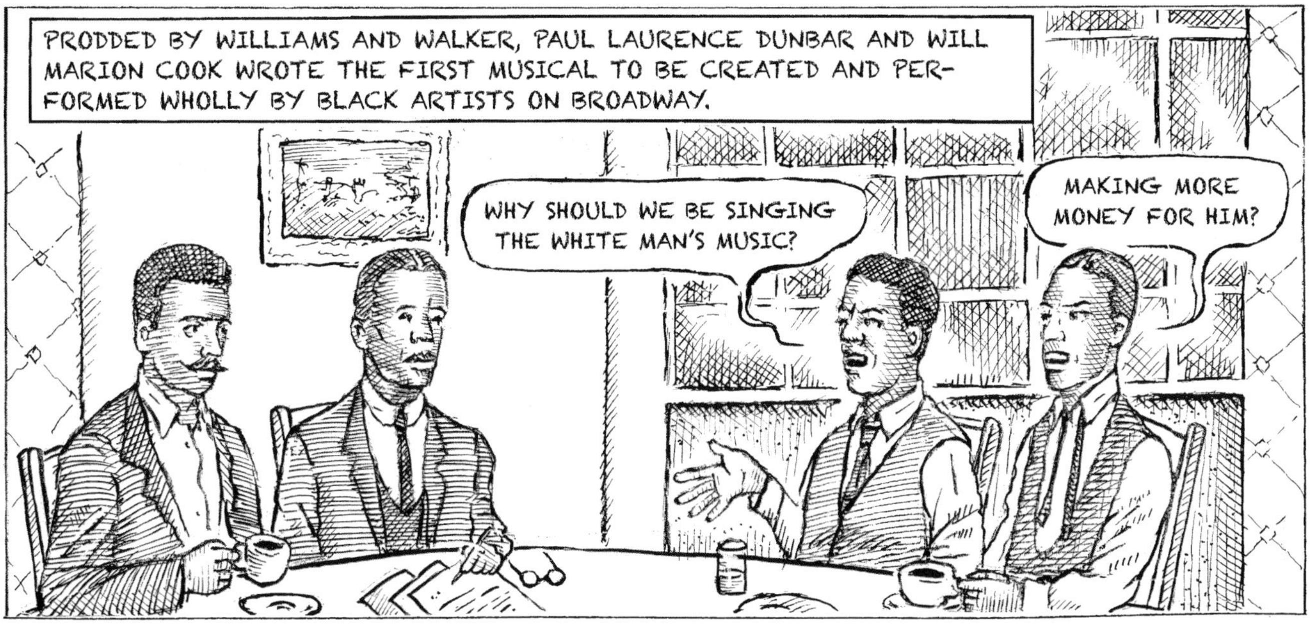
PRODDED BY WILLIAMS AND WALKER, PAUL LAURENCE DUNBAR AND WILL MARION COOK WROTE THE FIRST MUSICAL TO BE CREATED AND PERFORMED WHOLLY BY BLACK ARTISTS ON BROADWAY.
WHY SHOULD WE BE SINGING THE WHITE MAN'S MUSIC?
MAKING MORE MONEY FOR HIM?

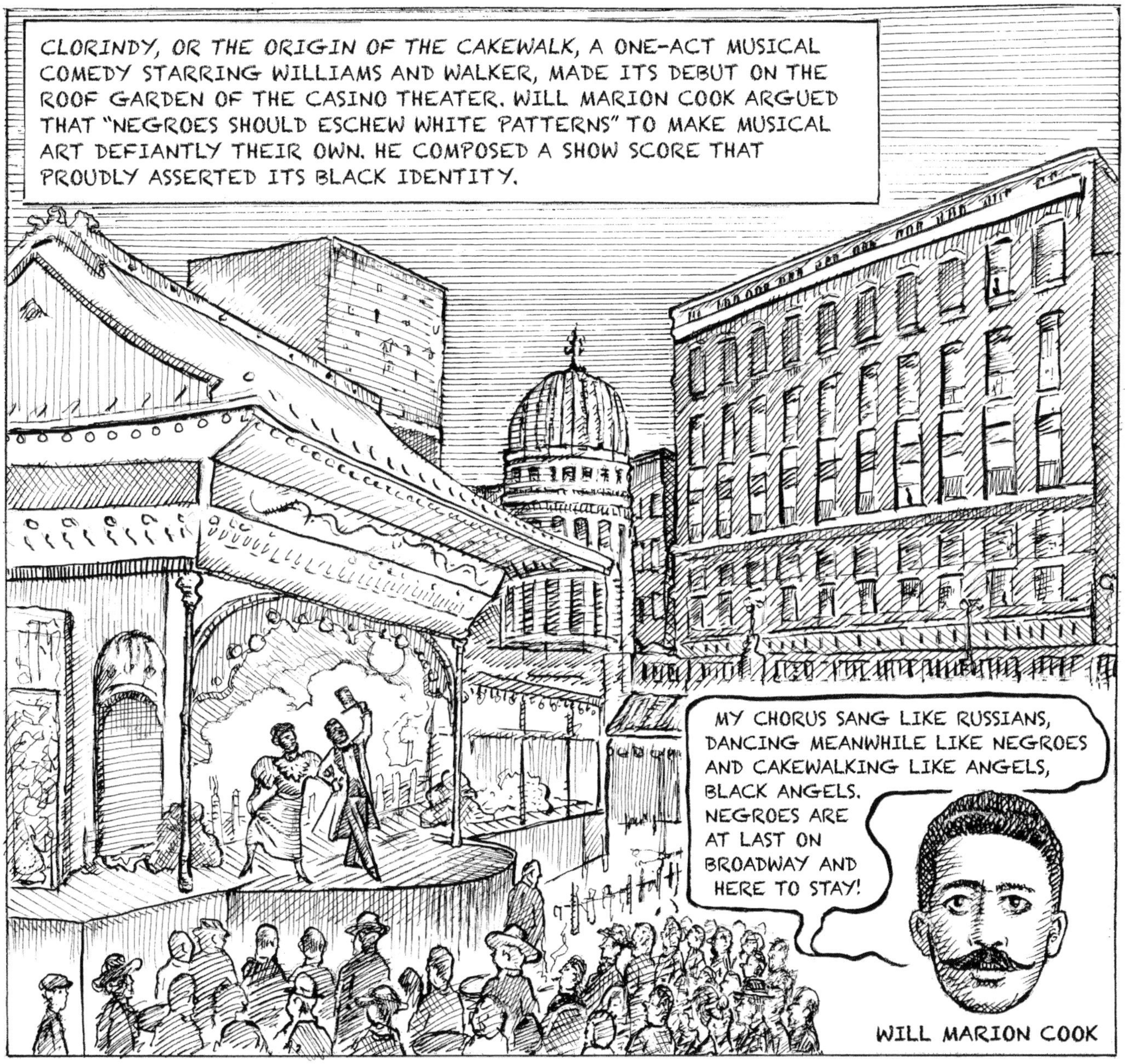
CLORINDY, OR THE ORIGIN OF THE CAKEWALK, A ONE-ACT MUSICAL COMEDY STARRING WILLIAMS AND WALKER, MADE ITS DEBUT ON THE ROOF GARDEN OF THE CASINO THEATER. WILL MARION COOK ARGUED THAT "NEGROES SHOULD ESCHEW WHITE PATTERNS" TO MAKE MUSICAL ART DEFIANTLY THEIR OWN. HE COMPOSED A SHOW SCORE THAT PROUDLY ASSERTED ITS BLACK IDENTITY.
MY CHORUS SANG LIKE RUSSIANS, DANCING MEANWHILE LIKE NEGROES AND CAKEWALKING LIKE ANGELS, BLACK ANGELS. NEGROES ARE AT LAST ON BROADWAY AND HERE TO STAY!
WILL MARION COOK

DRAWING ON THE NETWORK OF FELLOW BLACK ARTISTS THEY BUILT IN NEW YORK AND USING FUNDS THEY EARNED FROM *CLORINDY* AND OTHER SHOWS, BERT WILLIAMS AND GEORGE WALKER SET UP THEIR OWN PRODUCTION ORGANIZATION. OFFICIALLY NAMED THE WILLIAMS AND WALKER COMPANY, IT WAS SOMETIMES REFERRED TO AS THE POLICY PLAYERS, AFTER THE TITLE OF ONE OF THE MUSICAL COMEDIES THE COMPANY STAGED IN NEW YORK.

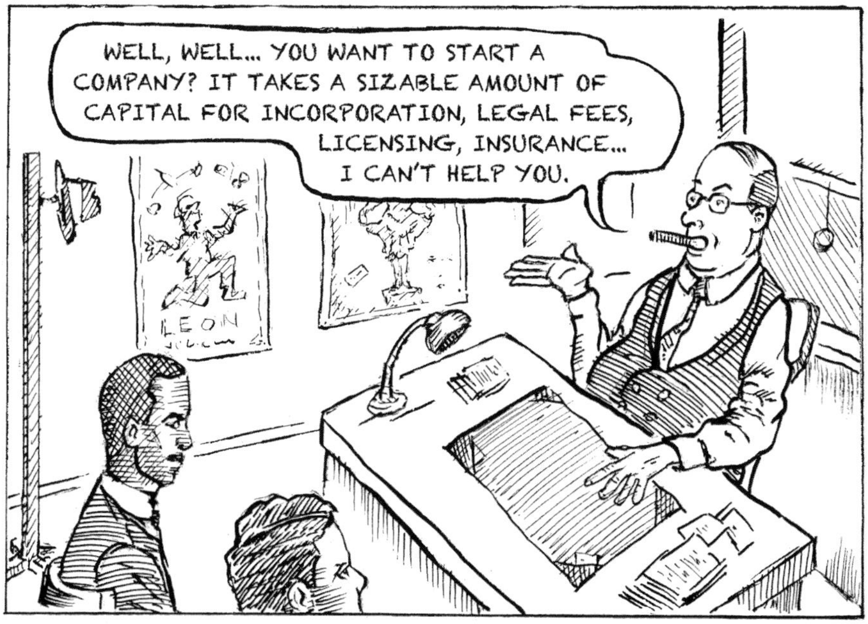
WELL, WELL... YOU WANT TO START A COMPANY? IT TAKES A SIZABLE AMOUNT OF CAPITAL FOR INCORPORATION, LEGAL FEES, LICENSING, INSURANCE... I CAN'T HELP YOU.
LEON

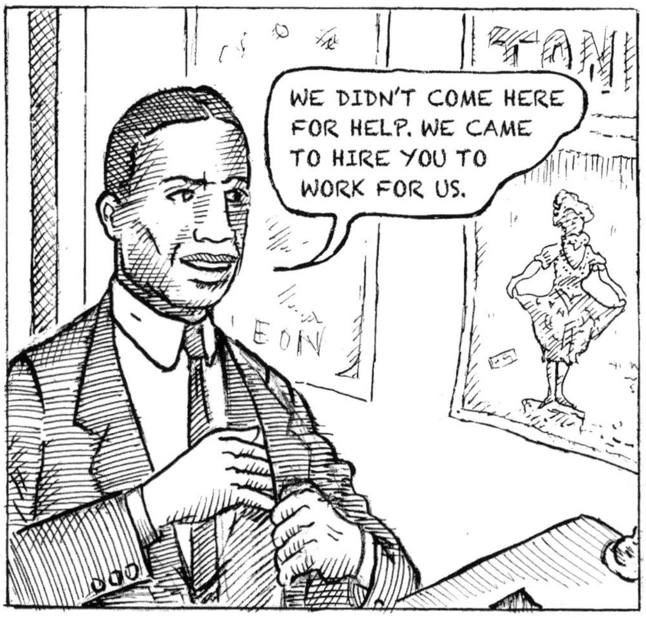
WE DIDN'T COME HERE FOR HELP. WE CAME TO HIRE YOU TO WORK FOR US.
LEON

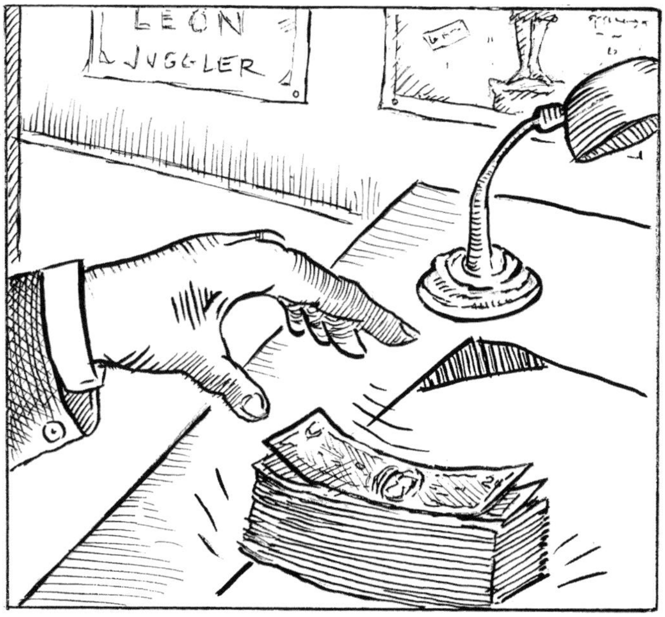
LEON
JUGGLER

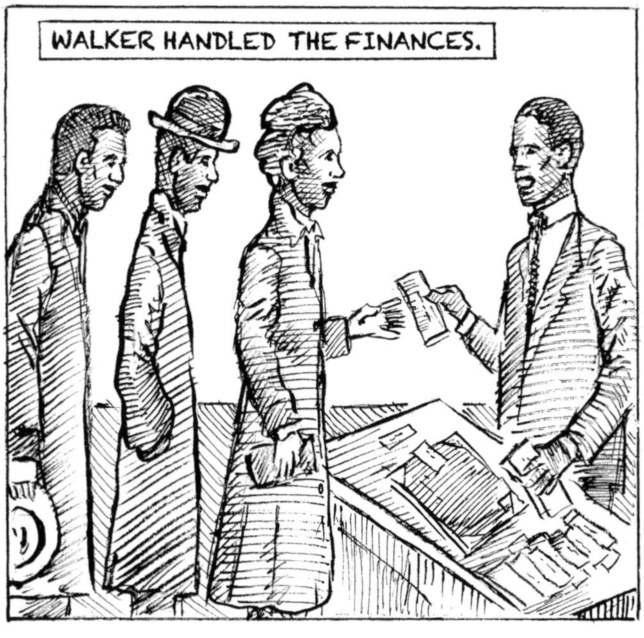
WALKER HANDLED THE FINANCES.

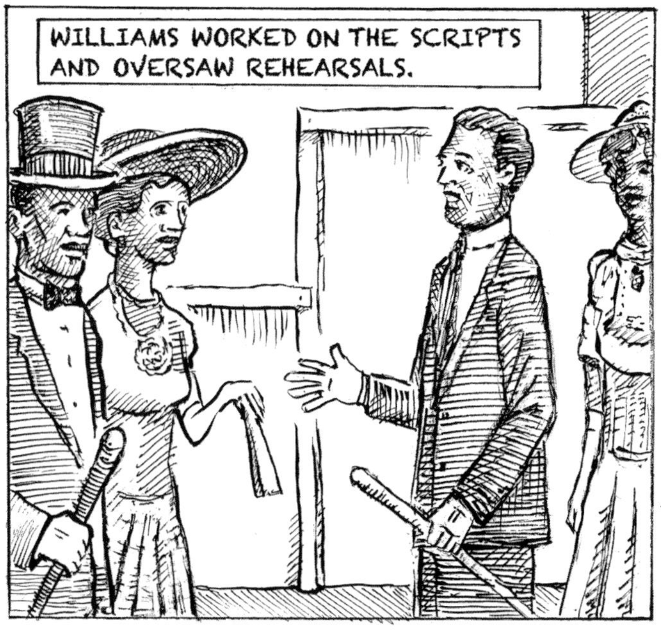
WILLIAMS WORKED ON THE SCRIPTS AND OVERSAW REHEARSALS.

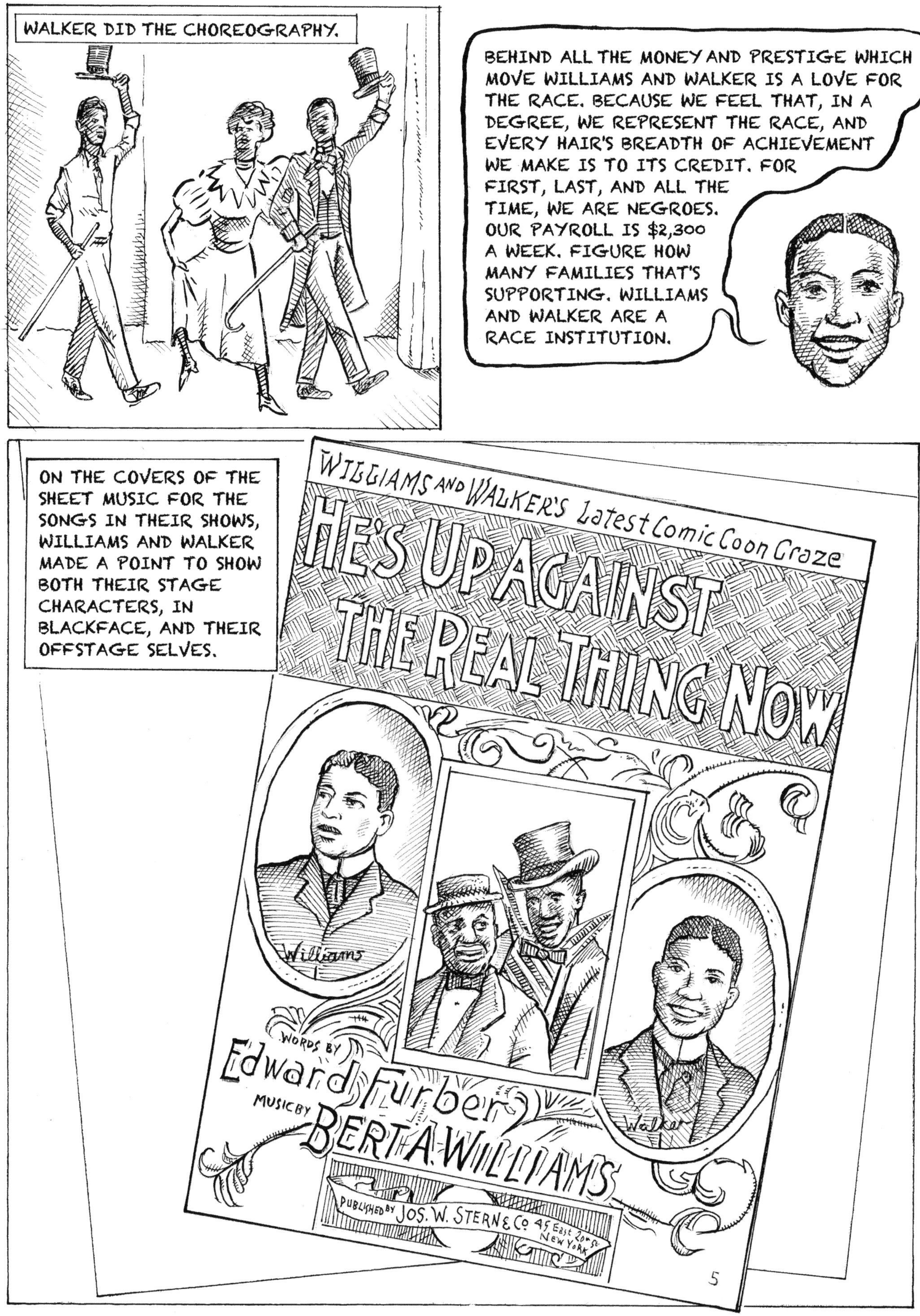
WALKER DID THE CHOREOGRAPHY.
BEHIND ALL THE MONEY AND PRESTIGE WHICH MOVE WILLIAMS AND WALKER IS A LOVE FOR THE RACE. BECAUSE WE FEEL THAT, IN A DEGREE, WE REPRESENT THE RACE, AND EVERY HAIR'S BREADTH OF ACHIEVEMENT WE MAKE IS TO ITS CREDIT. FOR FIRST, LAST, AND ALL THE TIME, WE ARE NEGROES. OUR PAYROLL IS $2,300 A WEEK. FIGURE HOW MANY FAMILIES THAT'S SUPPORTING. WILLIAMS AND WALKER ARE A RACE INSTITUTION.
ON THE COVERS OF THE SHEET MUSIC FOR THE SONGS IN THEIR SHOWS, WILLIAMS AND WALKER MADE A POINT TO SHOW BOTH THEIR STAGE CHARACTERS, IN BLACKFACE, AND THEIR OFFSTAGE SELVES.
WILLIAMS AND WALKER'S Latest Comic Coon Graze
HE'S UP AGAINST THE REAL THING NOW
Williams
Walker
WORDS BY Edward Furber
MUSIC BY BERT A. WILLIAMS
PUBLISHED BY JOS. W. STERN & Co. 45 East 20th St. NEW YORK
5

BY THE TIME OF *CLORINDY*, BERT WILLIAMS HAD RESIGNED HIMSELF TO PERFORMING IN BLACKFACE. THIS WAS A DEBASING CAPITULATION TO WHITE STEREOTYPES AND, AT THE SAME TIME, A CHALLENGE TO WHITE PERFORMERS' CLAIM TO THE RIGHT TO DEFINE BLACKNESS. WILLIAMS AND WALKER TOOK TO BILLING THEMSELVES AS "TWO REAL COONS." THE EMPHASIS, FROM THEIR POINT OF VIEW, WAS ON THE REAL.

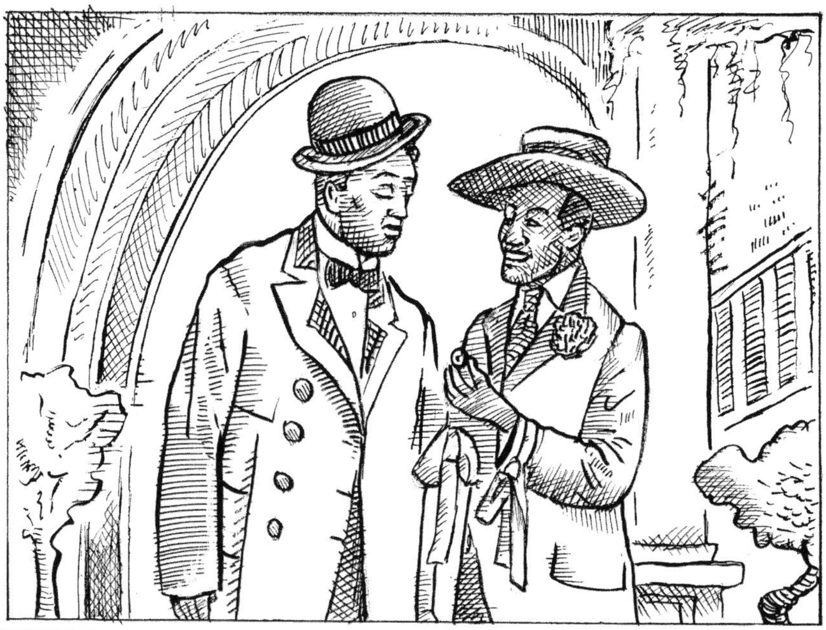

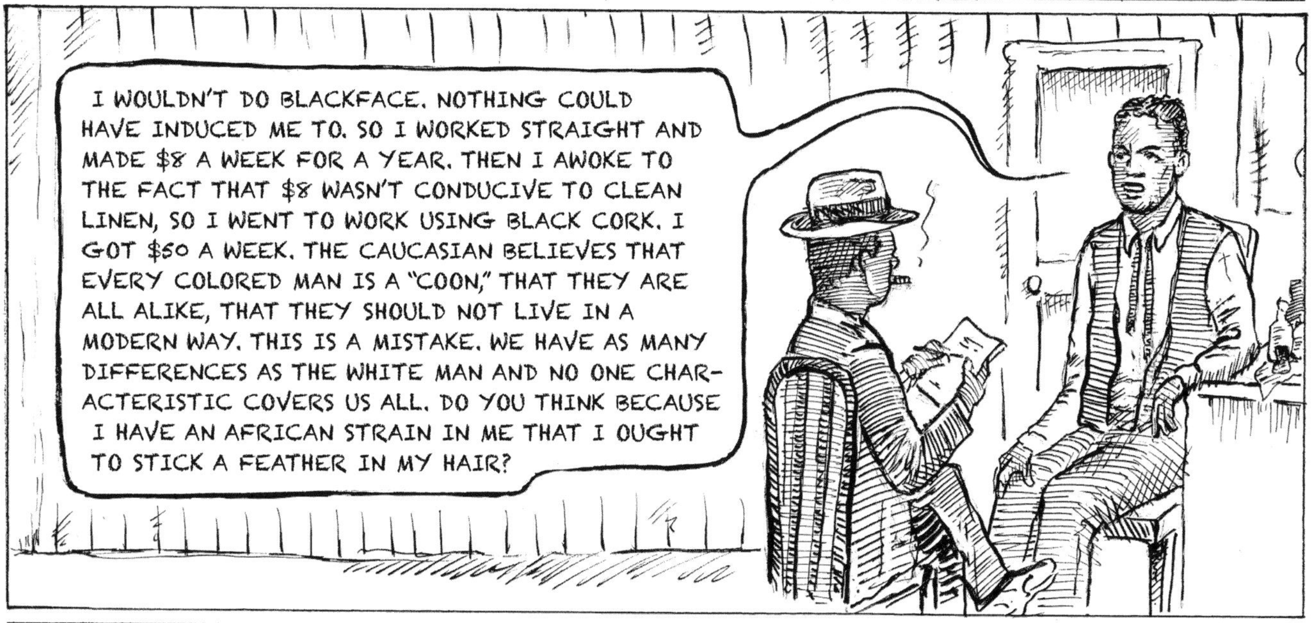
I WOULDN'T DO BLACKFACE. NOTHING COULD HAVE INDUCED ME TO. SO I WORKED STRAIGHT AND MADE $8 A WEEK FOR A YEAR. THEN I AWOKE TO THE FACT THAT $8 WASN'T CONDUCIVE TO CLEAN LINEN, SO I WENT TO WORK USING BLACK CORK. I GOT $50 A WEEK. THE CAUCASIAN BELIEVES THAT EVERY COLORED MAN IS A "COON," THAT THEY ARE ALL ALIKE, THAT THEY SHOULD NOT LIVE IN A MODERN WAY. THIS IS A MISTAKE. WE HAVE AS MANY DIFFERENCES AS THE WHITE MAN AND NO ONE CHARACTERISTIC COVERS US ALL. DO YOU THINK BECAUSE I HAVE AN AFRICAN STRAIN IN ME THAT I OUGHT TO STICK A FEATHER IN MY HAIR?

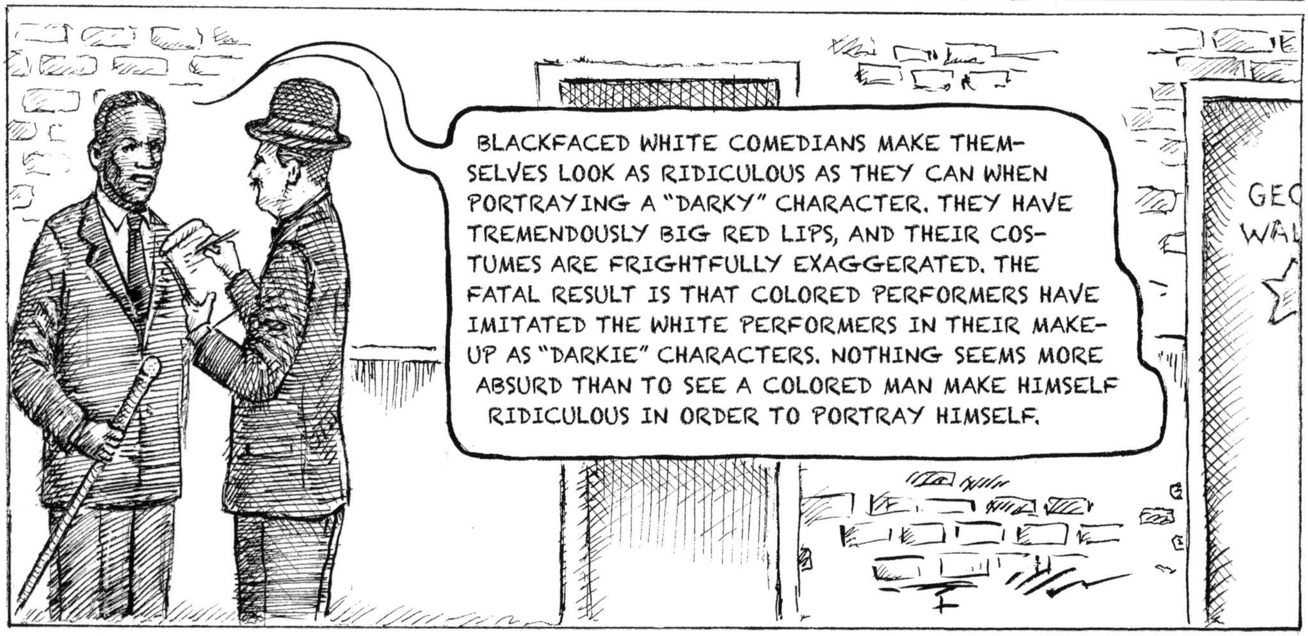
BLACKFACED WHITE COMEDIANS MAKE THEMSELVES LOOK AS RIDICULOUS AS THEY CAN WHEN PORTRAYING A "DARKY" CHARACTER. THEY HAVE TREMENDOUSLY BIG RED LIPS, AND THEIR COSTUMES ARE FRIGHTFULLY EXAGGERATED. THE FATAL RESULT IS THAT COLORED PERFORMERS HAVE IMITATED THE WHITE PERFORMERS IN THEIR MAKE-UP AS "DARKIE" CHARACTERS. NOTHING SEEMS MORE ABSURD THAN TO SEE A COLORED MAN MAKE HIMSELF RIDICULOUS IN ORDER TO PORTRAY HIMSELF.

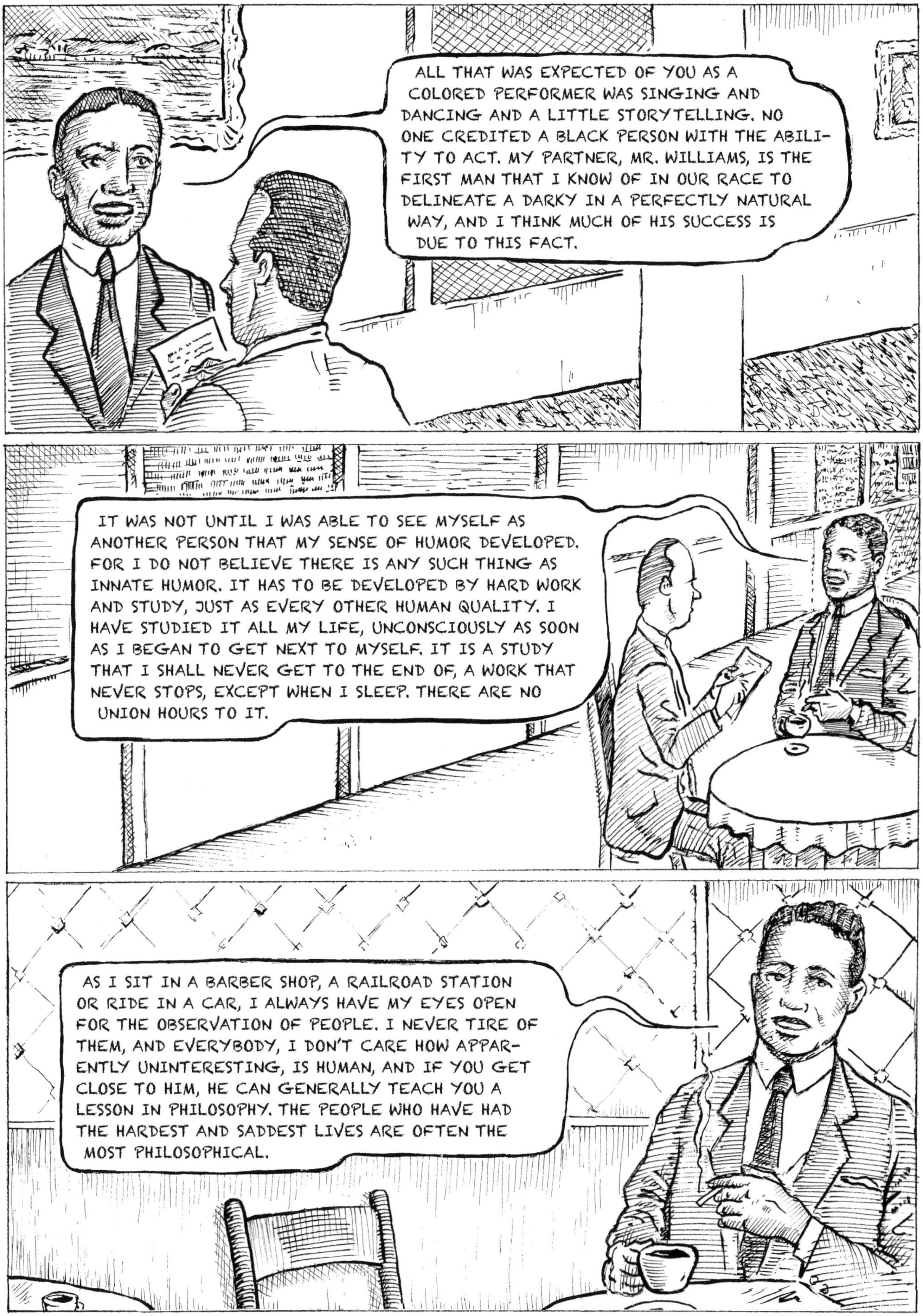
ALL THAT WAS EXPECTED OF YOU AS A COLORED PERFORMER WAS SINGING AND DANCING AND A LITTLE STORYTELLING. NO ONE CREDITED A BLACK PERSON WITH THE ABILITY TO ACT. MY PARTNER, MR. WILLIAMS, IS THE FIRST MAN THAT I KNOW OF IN OUR RACE TO DELINEATE A DARKY IN A PERFECTLY NATURAL WAY, AND I THINK MUCH OF HIS SUCCESS IS DUE TO THIS FACT.
IT WAS NOT UNTIL I WAS ABLE TO SEE MYSELF AS ANOTHER PERSON THAT MY SENSE OF HUMOR DEVELOPED. FOR I DO NOT BELIEVE THERE IS ANY SUCH THING AS INNATE HUMOR. IT HAS TO BE DEVELOPED BY HARD WORK AND STUDY, JUST AS EVERY OTHER HUMAN QUALITY. I HAVE STUDIED IT ALL MY LIFE, UNCONSCIOUSLY AS SOON AS I BEGAN TO GET NEXT TO MYSELF. IT IS A STUDY THAT I SHALL NEVER GET TO THE END OF, A WORK THAT NEVER STOPS, EXCEPT WHEN I SLEEP. THERE ARE NO UNION HOURS TO IT.
AS I SIT IN A BARBER SHOP, A RAILROAD STATION OR RIDE IN A CAR, I ALWAYS HAVE MY EYES OPEN FOR THE OBSERVATION OF PEOPLE. I NEVER TIRE OF THEM, AND EVERYBODY, I DON'T CARE HOW APPARENTLY UNINTERESTING, IS HUMAN, AND IF YOU GET CLOSE TO HIM, HE CAN GENERALLY TEACH YOU A LESSON IN PHILOSOPHY. THE PEOPLE WHO HAVE HAD THE HARDEST AND SADDEST LIVES ARE OFTEN THE MOST PHILOSOPHICAL.

WITH WILL MARION COOK AND PAUL LAURENCE DUNBAR WRITING THE WORDS AND MUSIC, WILLIAMS AND WALKER STAGED AND STARRED IN THE FIRST FULL-LENGTH MUSICAL BY AN AFRICAN AMERICAN PRODUCTION TEAM EVER PRODUCED IN A MAJOR BROADWAY THEATER. *IN DAHOMEY: A NEGRO MUSICAL COMEDY* WAS A RAUCOUS SATIRE OF THE BACK-TO-AFRICA MOVEMENT MAKING HEADLINES AND FUELING THE FERVOR OF BOTH BLACK AND WHITE SEPARATISTS.

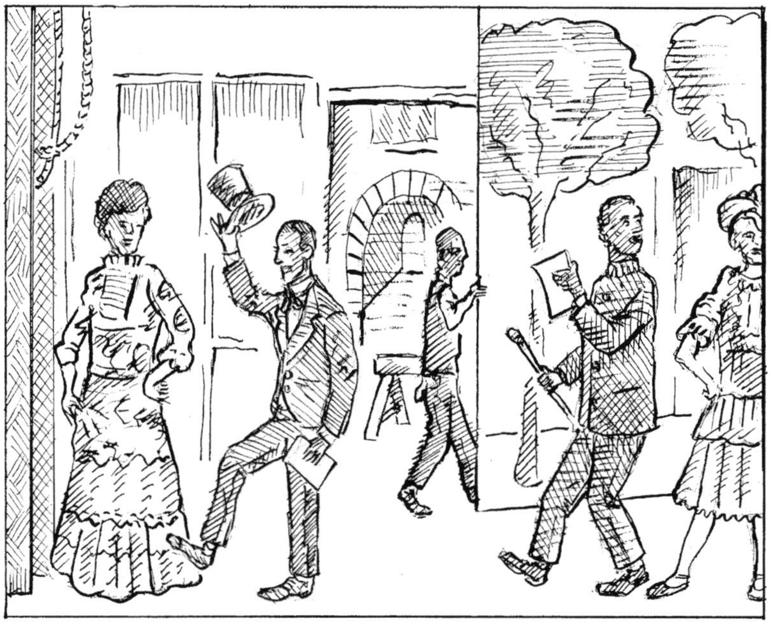

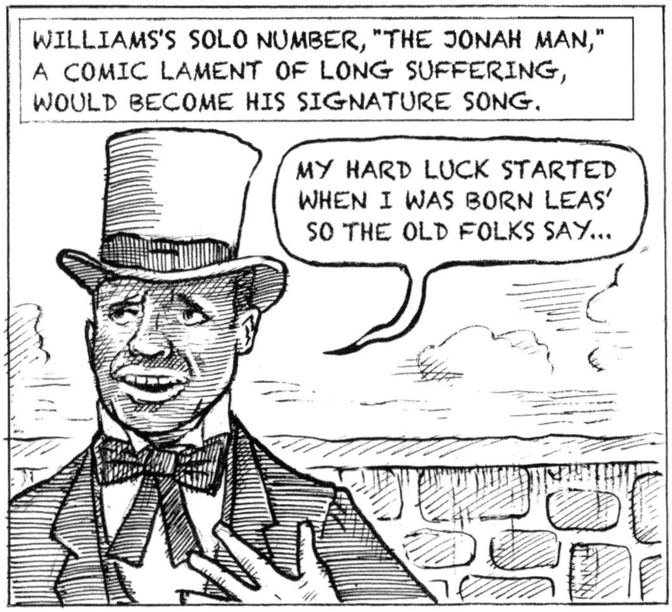
WILLIAMS'S SOLO NUMBER, "THE JONAH MAN," A COMIC LAMENT OF LONG SUFFERING, WOULD BECOME HIS SIGNATURE SONG.
MY HARD LUCK STARTED WHEN I WAS BORN LEAS' SO THE OLD FOLKS SAY...

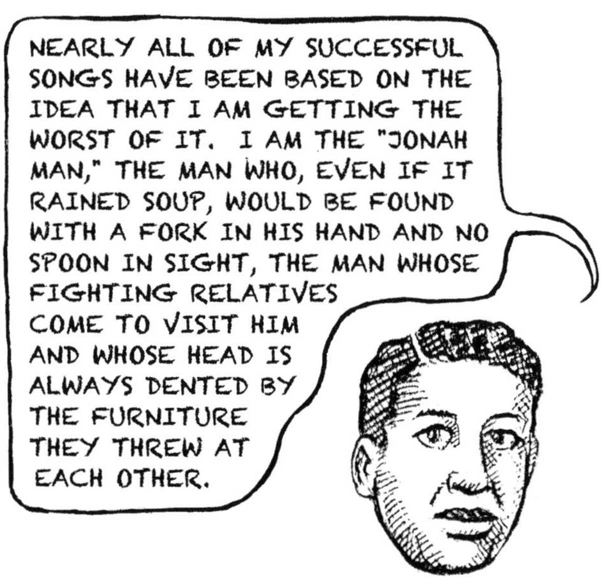
NEARLY ALL OF MY SUCCESSFUL SONGS HAVE BEEN BASED ON THE IDEA THAT I AM GETTING THE WORST OF IT. I AM THE "JONAH MAN," THE MAN WHO, EVEN IF IT RAINED SOUP, WOULD BE FOUND WITH A FORK IN HIS HAND AND NO SPOON IN SIGHT, THE MAN WHOSE FIGHTING RELATIVES COME TO VISIT HIM AND WHOSE HEAD IS ALWAYS DENTED BY THE FURNITURE THEY THREW AT EACH OTHER.

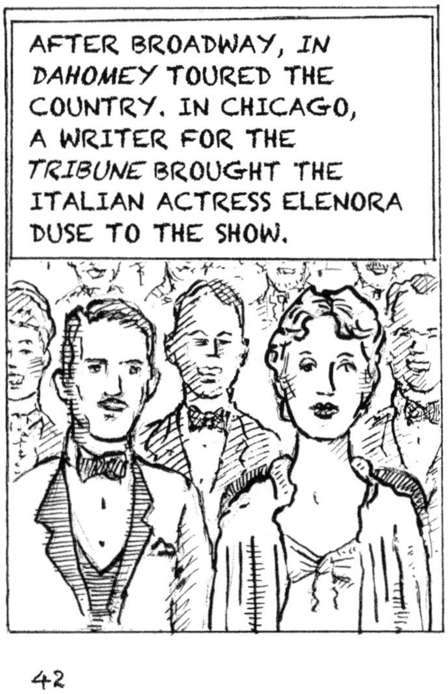
AFTER BROADWAY, *IN DAHOMEY* TOURED THE COUNTRY. IN CHICAGO, A WRITER FOR THE *TRIBUNE* BROUGHT THE ITALIAN ACTRESS ELENORA DUSE TO THE SHOW.

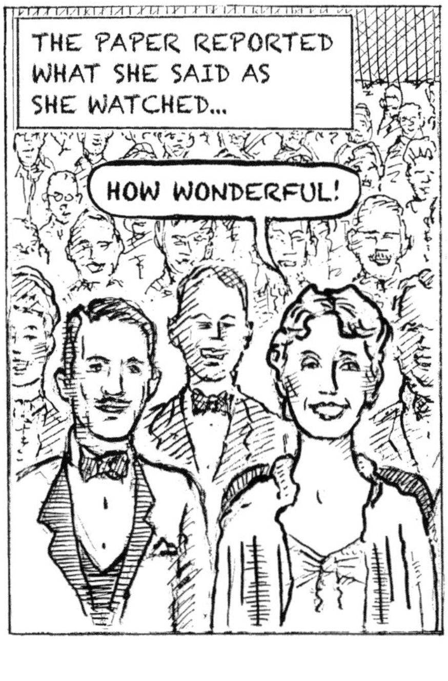
THE PAPER REPORTED WHAT SHE SAID AS SHE WATCHED...
HOW WONDERFUL!

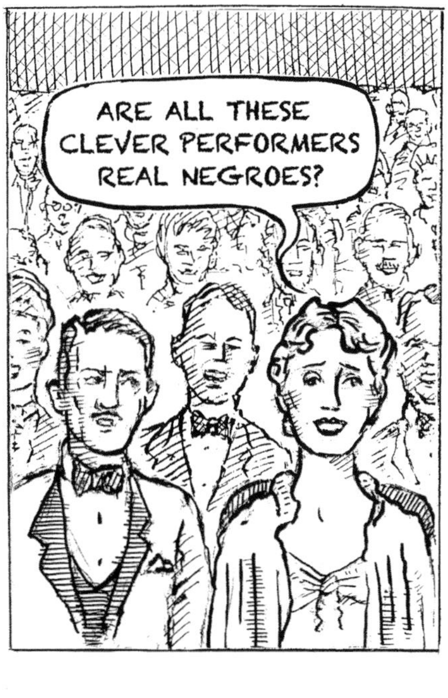
ARE ALL THESE CLEVER PERFORMERS REAL NEGROES?

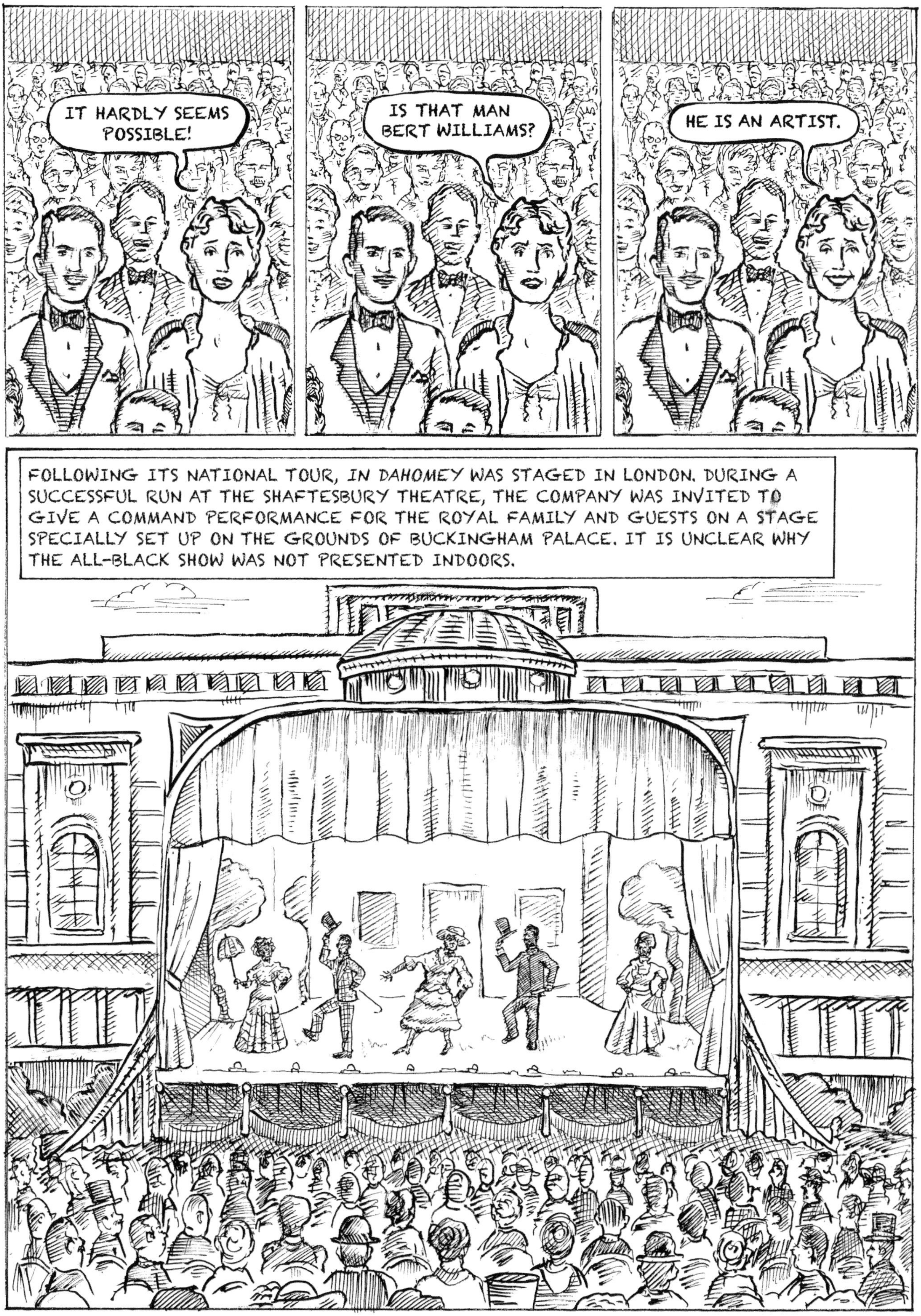
IT HARDLY SEEMS POSSIBLE!
IS THAT MAN BERT WILLIAMS?
HE IS AN ARTIST.
FOLLOWING ITS NATIONAL TOUR, *IN DAHOMEY* WAS STAGED IN LONDON. DURING A SUCCESSFUL RUN AT THE SHAFTESBURY THEATRE, THE COMPANY WAS INVITED TO GIVE A COMMAND PERFORMANCE FOR THE ROYAL FAMILY AND GUESTS ON A STAGE SPECIALLY SET UP ON THE GROUNDS OF BUCKINGHAM PALACE. IT IS UNCLEAR WHY THE ALL-BLACK SHOW WAS NOT PRESENTED INDOORS.

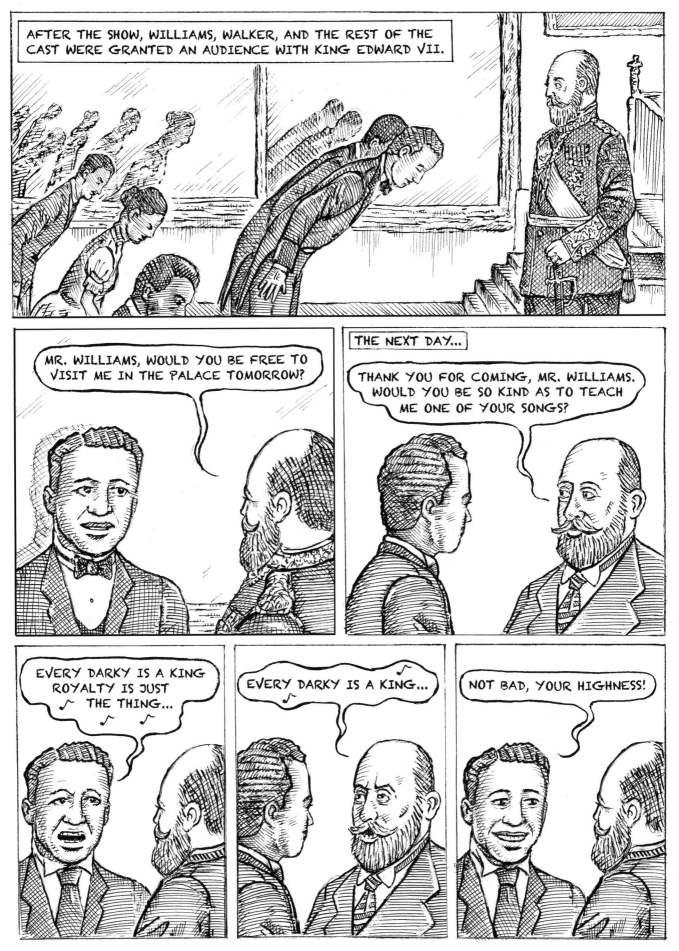

AFTER THE SHOW, WILLIAMS, WALKER, AND THE REST OF THE CAST WERE GRANTED AN AUDIENCE WITH KING EDWARD VII.

MR. WILLIAMS, WOULD YOU BE FREE TO VISIT ME IN THE PALACE TOMORROW?

THE NEXT DAY...

THANK YOU FOR COMING, MR. WILLIAMS. WOULD YOU BE SO KIND AS TO TEACH ME ONE OF YOUR SONGS?

EVERY DARKY IS A KING ROYALTY IS JUST THE THING...

EVERY DARKY IS A KING...

NOT BAD, YOUR HIGHNESS!

44

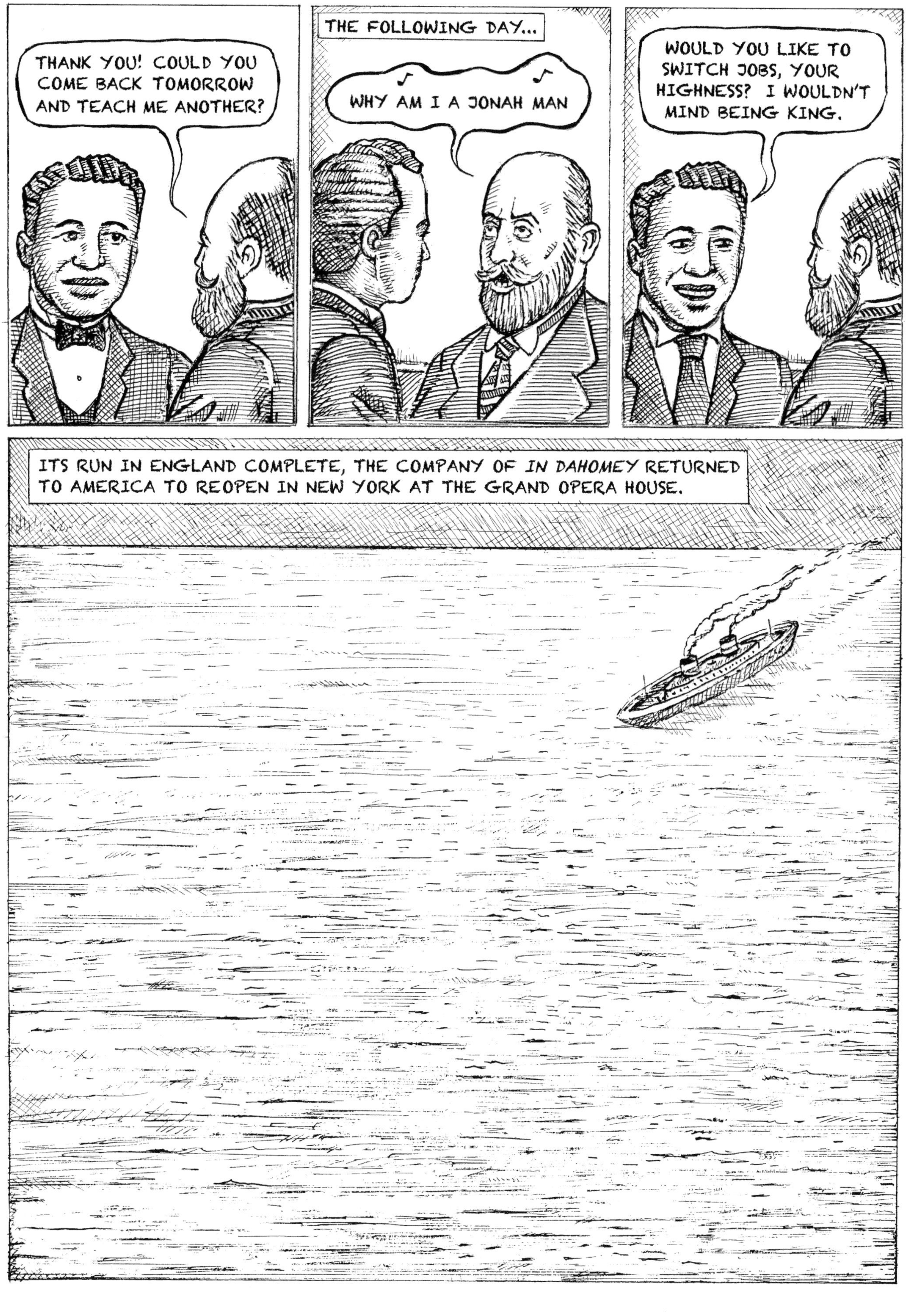
THANK YOU! COULD YOU COME BACK TOMORROW AND TEACH ME ANOTHER?
THE FOLLOWING DAY...
WHY AM I A JONAH MAN
WOULD YOU LIKE TO SWITCH JOBS, YOUR HIGHNESS? I WOULDN'T MIND BEING KING.
ITS RUN IN ENGLAND COMPLETE, THE COMPANY OF *IN DAHOMEY* RETURNED TO AMERICA TO REOPEN IN NEW YORK AT THE GRAND OPERA HOUSE.

WHILE BERT WILLIAMS AND GEORGE WALKER ESTABLISHED THEMSELVES IN NEW YORK CITY, RACIAL TENSIONS INTENSIFIED. AN ALTERCATION BETWEEN A WHITE POLICE OFFICER AND A BLACK MAN WHOM OFFICIALS LATER DESCRIBED AS A PIMP LED TO THE OFFICER'S DEATH. POLICE AROUND THE CITY, ALL OF THEM WHITE, STARTED ROUNDING UP AFRICAN AMERICANS AT RANDOM FOR PUNISHMENT. BLACK MEN WERE PULLED OFF THE SIDEWALKS AND BEATEN IN PUBLIC.

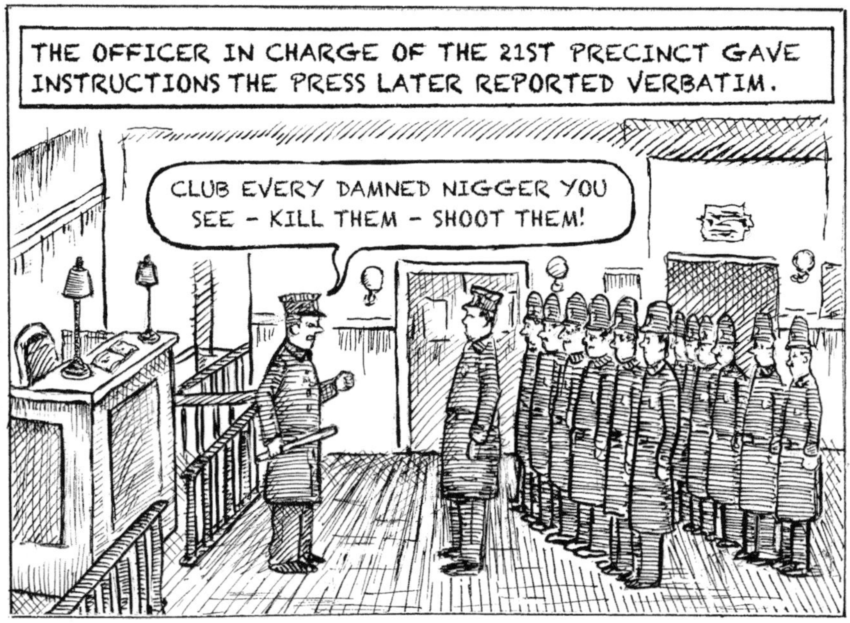
THE OFFICER IN CHARGE OF THE 21ST PRECINCT GAVE INSTRUCTIONS THE PRESS LATER REPORTED VERBATIM.
CLUB EVERY DAMNED NIGGER YOU SEE - KILL THEM - SHOOT THEM!

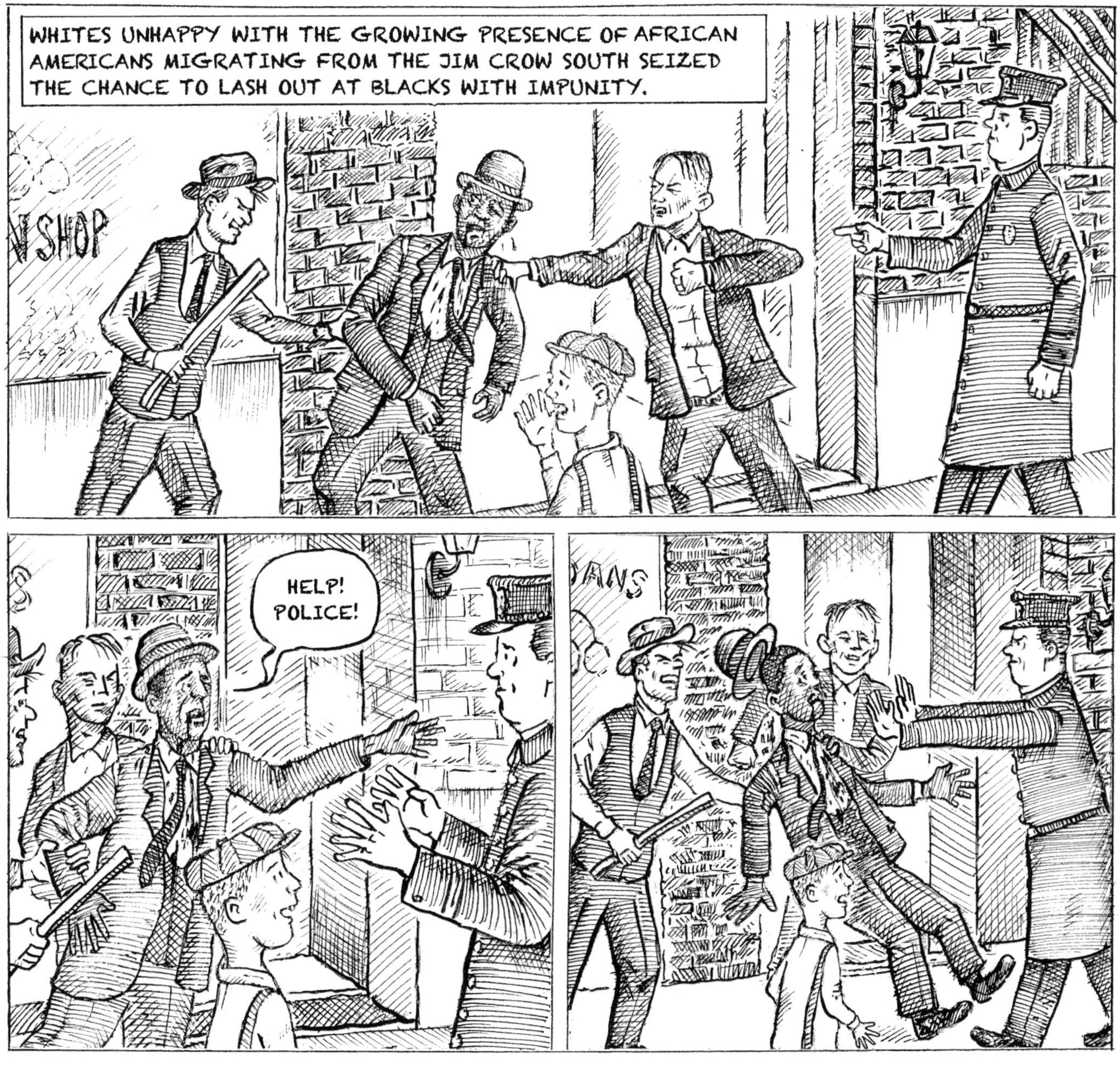
WHITES UNHAPPY WITH THE GROWING PRESENCE OF AFRICAN AMERICANS MIGRATING FROM THE JIM CROW SOUTH SEIZED THE CHANCE TO LASH OUT AT BLACKS WITH IMPUNITY.
HELP! POLICE!

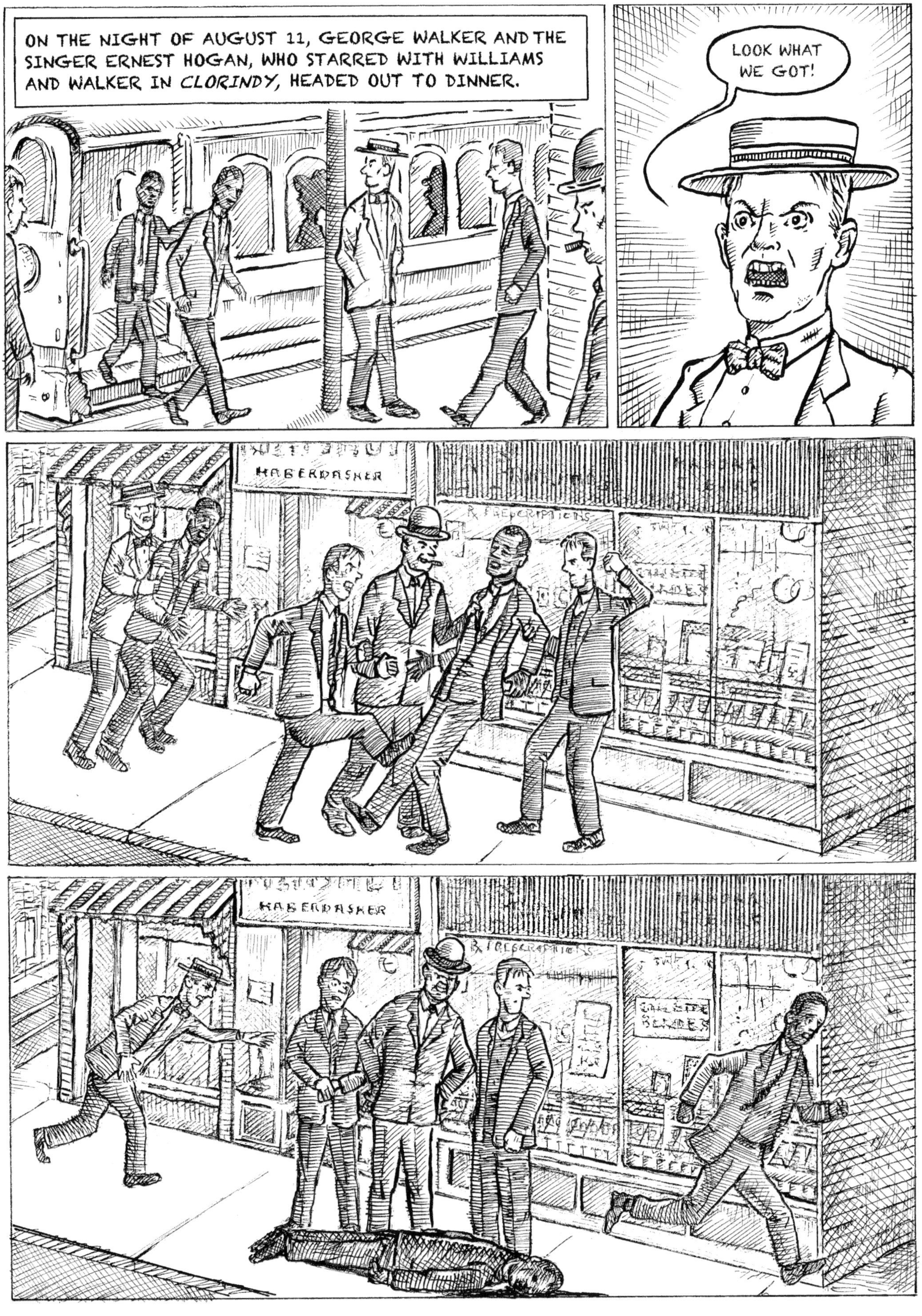
ON THE NIGHT OF AUGUST 11, GEORGE WALKER AND THE SINGER ERNEST HOGAN, WHO STARRED WITH WILLIAMS AND WALKER IN *CLORINDY*, HEADED OUT TO DINNER.
LOOK WHAT WE GOT!
HABERDASHER
HABERDASHER

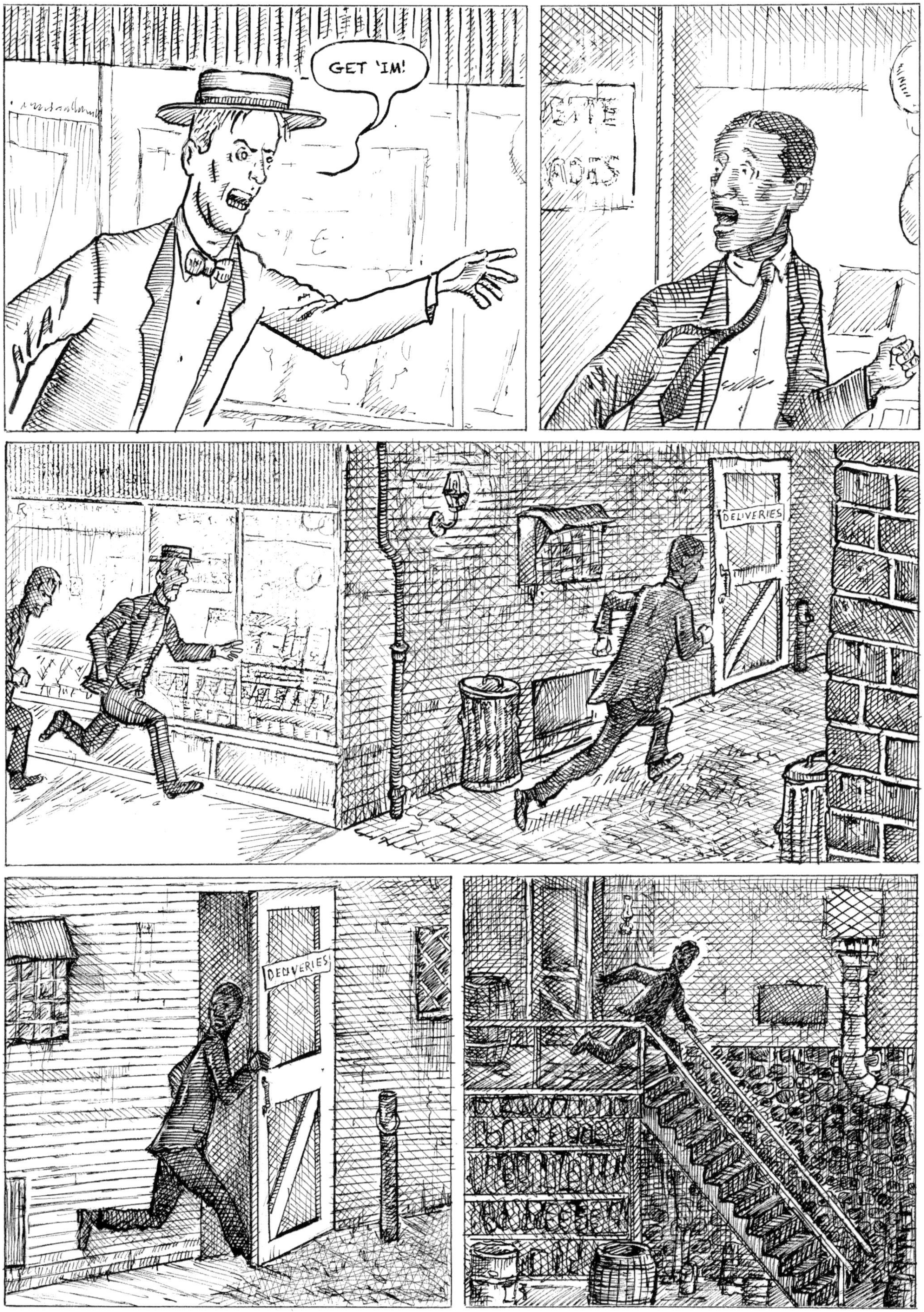
GET 'IM!
DELIVERIES
DELIVERIES

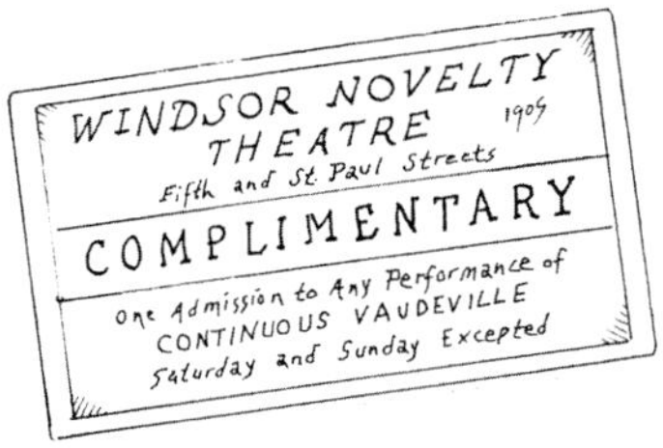
WINDSOR NOVELTY
THEATRE
1905
Fifth and St. Paul Streets
COMPLIMENTARY
One Admission to Any Performance of
CONTINUOUS VAUDEVILLE
Saturday and Sunday Excepted

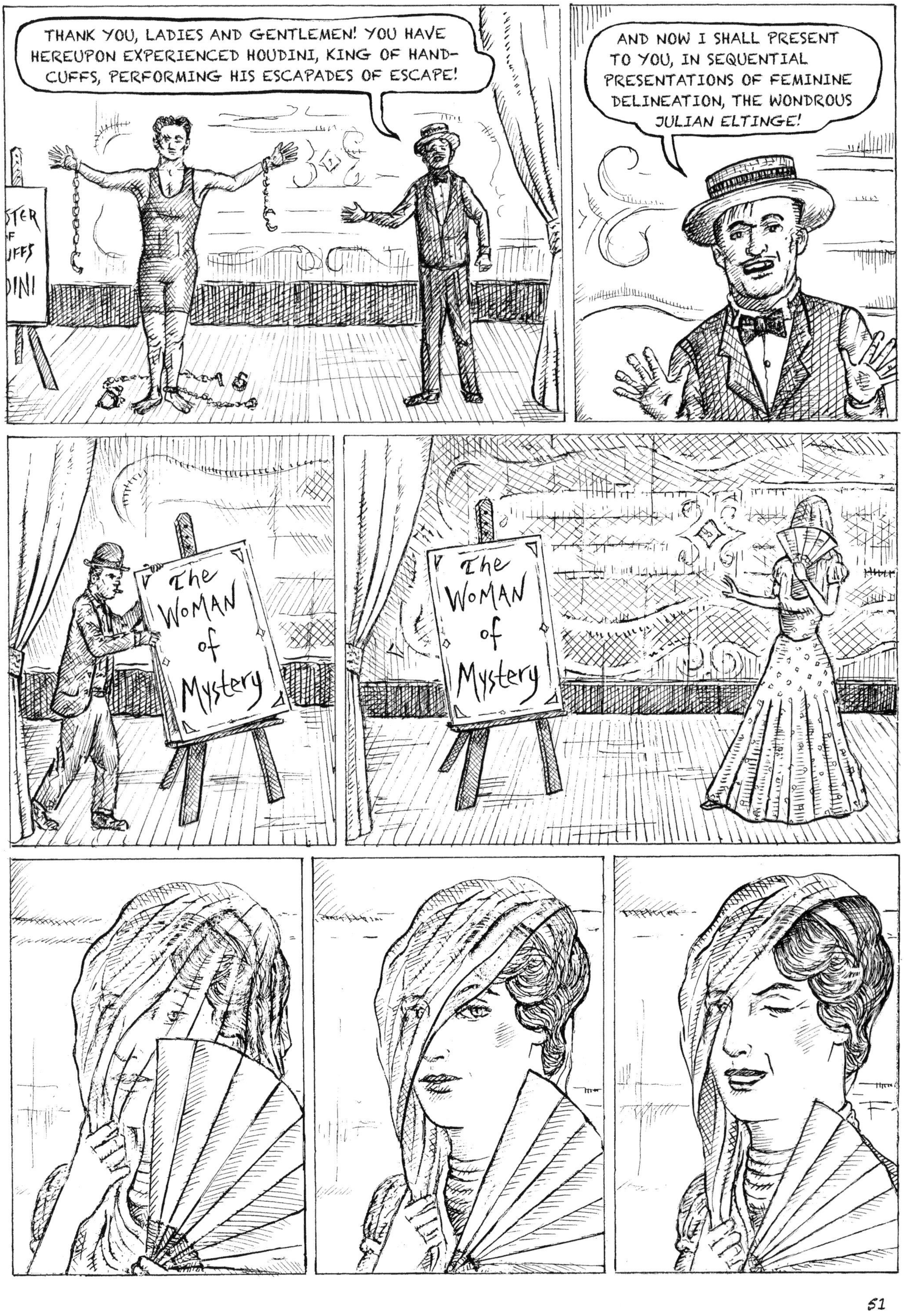
THANK YOU, LADIES AND GENTLEMEN! YOU HAVE HEREUPON EXPERIENCED HOUDINI, KING OF HAND-CUFFS, PERFORMING HIS ESCAPADES OF ESCAPE!
AND NOW I SHALL PRESENT TO YOU, IN SEQUENTIAL PRESENTATIONS OF FEMININE DELINEATION, THE WONDROUS JULIAN ELTINGE!
The WOMAN of Mystery
The WOMAN of Mystery

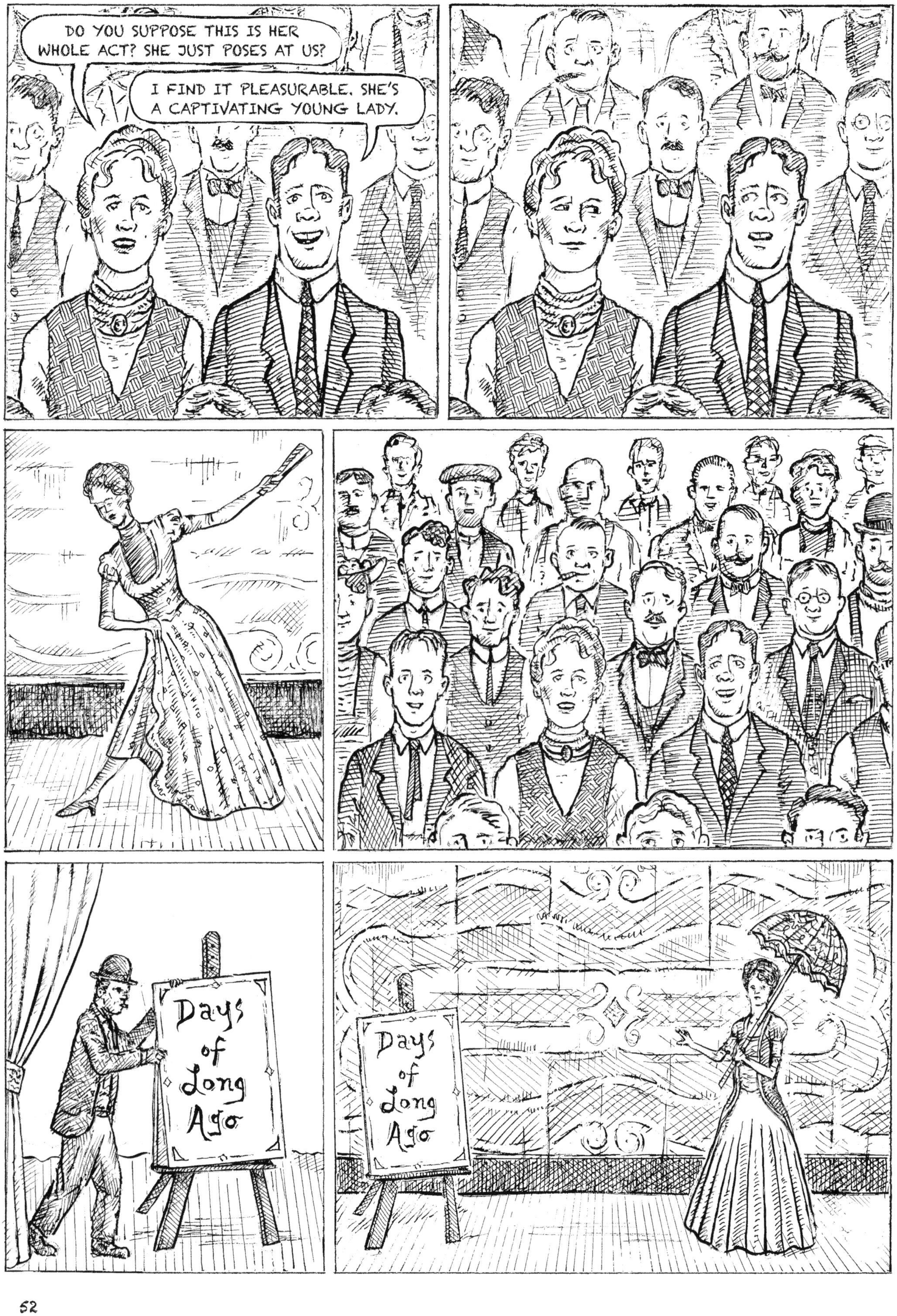
DO YOU SUPPOSE THIS IS HER WHOLE ACT? SHE JUST POSES AT US?
I FIND IT PLEASURABLE. SHE'S A CAPTIVATING YOUNG LADY.
Days of Long Ago
Days of Long Ago

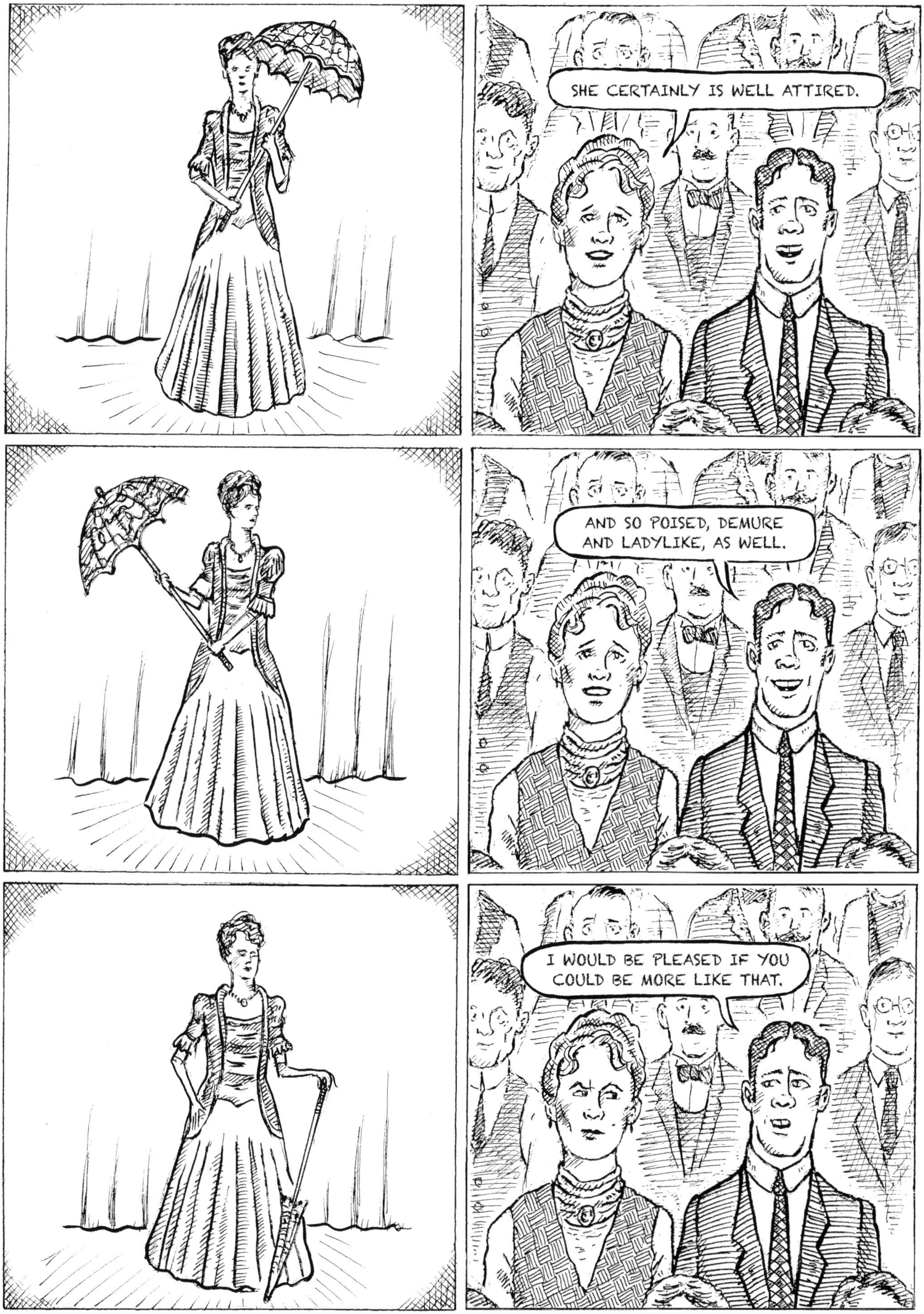
SHE CERTAINLY IS WELL ATTIRED.
AND SO POISED, DEMURE AND LADYLIKE, AS WELL.
I WOULD BE PLEASED IF YOU COULD BE MORE LIKE THAT.

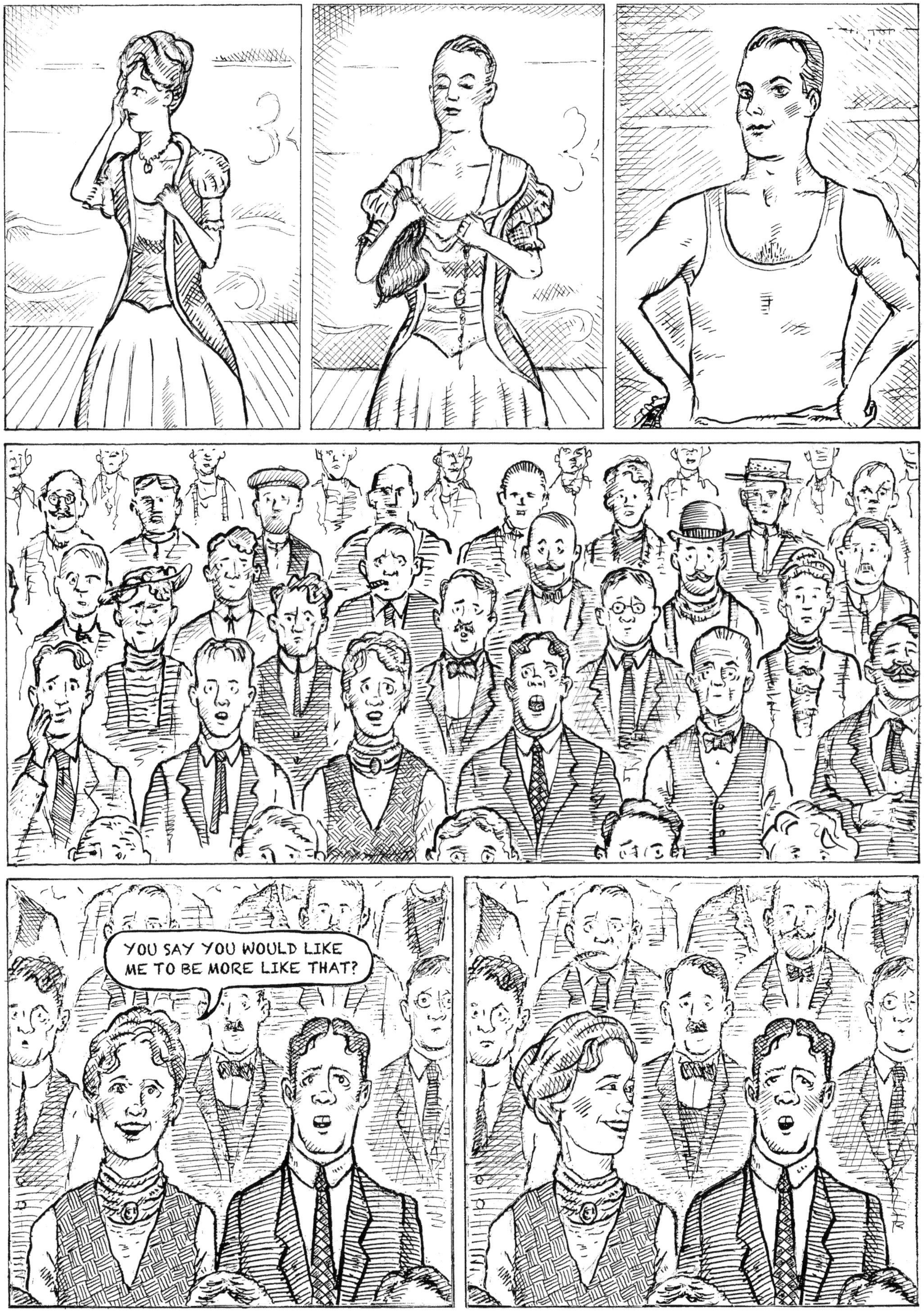
YOU SAY YOU WOULD LIKE ME TO BE MORE LIKE THAT?

THE NOVELTY IN HIS ACT WAS NOT THAT JULIAN ELTINGE PORTRAYED CHAR-
ACTERS DIFFERENT FROM HIS OFFSTAGE SELF; COUNTLESS VAUDEVILLE PER-
FORMERS DID THAT IN INNUMERABLE WAYS. THE EXTRAORDINARY THING ABOUT
JULIAN ELTINGE'S PORTRAYALS OF WOMEN WAS THE ABSENCE OF SATIRE – OR
THEATRICAL COMMENTARY OF ANY KIND, EXCEPT AFFIRMATION – IN THEM.

ELTINGE'S PRESENTATION WAS CRAFTED TO BE TAKEN AS A QUASI-SCIEN-
TIFICALLY PRECISE, UNDISTORTED REPLICATION OF THE FEMININE IDEAL.
THE FACT THAT WHAT IT REPLICATED WAS, IN FACT, AN *IDEAL* MEANT THAT IT
WAS ARTIFICIAL BY DEFINITION, HOWEVER; AND THE IDEAL IT PERPETUATED
WAS, AT THE TURN OF THE TWENTIETH CENTURY, A FADING ONE: THE VICTORI-
AN CONCEPTION OF WOMANHOOD AS A STATE OF SEXLESS VIRTUE, REGIMENTED
GRACE, AND SUBORDINATION TO THE RULES OF PROPER SOCIETY AND THE MEN
WHO RAN IT.

A FRESH IDEAL CALLED THE "NEW WOMAN," EDUCATED AND FREE-THINKING,
WAS BEGINNING TO SUPPLANT THE VICTORIAN IDEAL OF THE "TRUE WOMAN."
JULIAN ELTINGE WAS THAT "TRUE WOMAN" EMBODIED IN THE THEATRICAL
FALSE TRUTH OF A MALE STAGE ACT.

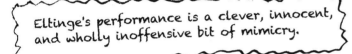

Eltinge's performance is a clever, innocent,
and wholly inoffensive bit of mimicry.

NEW YORK DRAMATIC NEWS

Julian Eltinge is an amazing mirror in which we see
ourselves, not, unfortunately, as we all are, but as we
all want to be. Women should be grateful to Mr. Eltinge,
for showing them themselves as they ought to be.

NEW YORK MIRROR

IN INTERVIEWS AND HANDOUTS TO THE PRESS, ELTINGE CAST HIS WORK AS A
PUBLIC SERVICE TO AMERICAN WOMEN.

THE WOMAN WHO PRIDES
HERSELF ON BEING AS
NATURE MADE HER IS
VERY APT TO BE
UNNECESSARILY UGLY.
THOUSANDS OF LADIES
THROUGHOUT THE
COUNTRY HAVE WRITTEN
ASKING ME WHAT FACIAL
PREPARATIONS I USE
TO TRANSFORM MYSELF
FROM MAN TO WOMAN.

THE AVERAGE WOMAN DOES NOT
KNOW HOW TO MAKE UP. SHE
SHOULD STUDY HER COMPLEXION,
THE COLOR OF HER HAIR, OF
HER EYES, THE CONSTRUCTION
OF HER EYEBROWS, SHAPE OF
HER LIPS, AND THE CHARACTER
OF HER SKIN. IF SHE HAS FINE
EYES, SHE SHOULD TRY TO
ENHANCE THEIR BEAUTY BY
TONING DOWN THE LESS PLEAS-
ING PORTIONS OF HER FACE.

Off the stage he looks more like the center rush of a football team than a
female impersonator. There is not the least bit of the effeminate about him.

BOSTON GLOBE

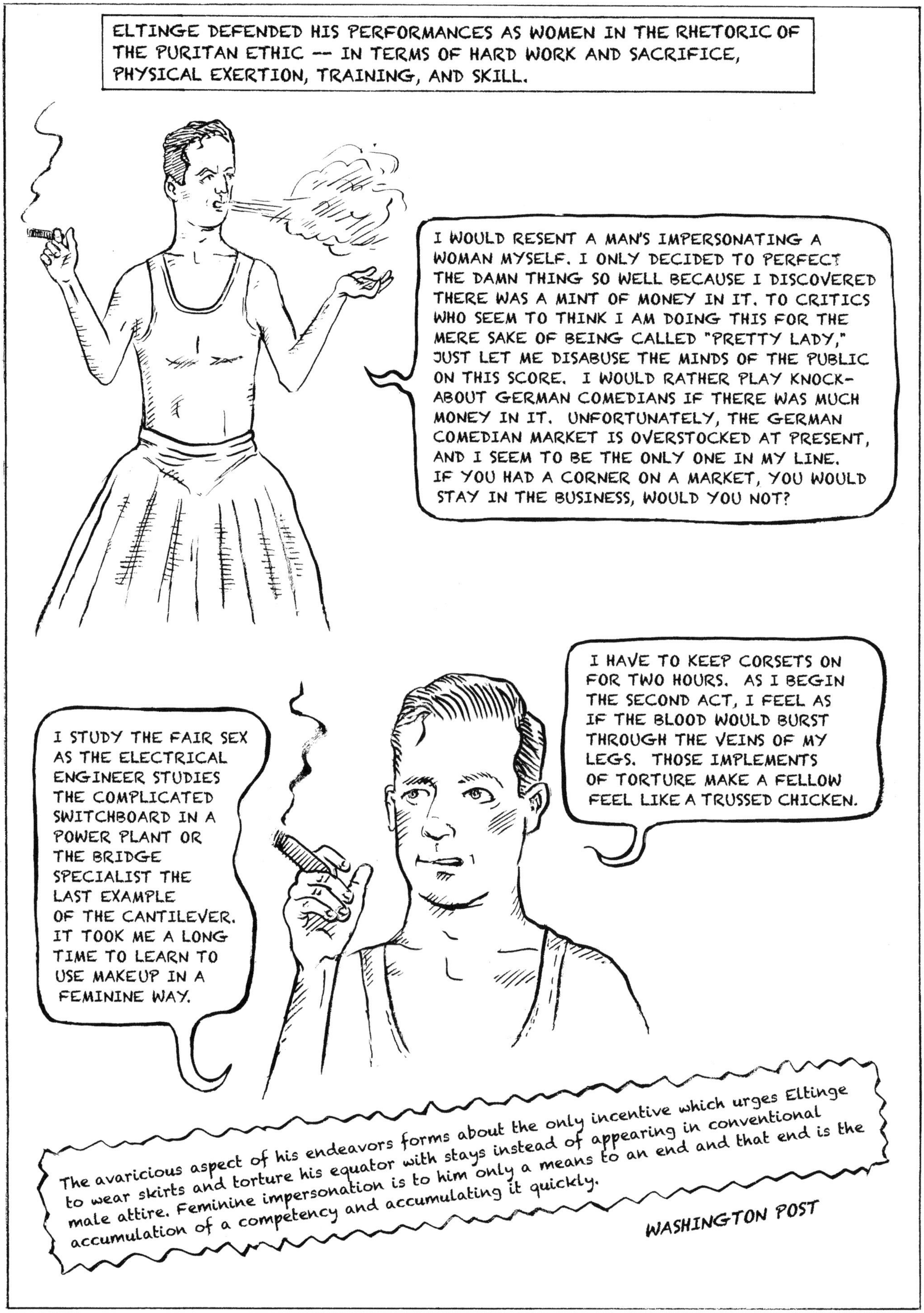
ELTINGE DEFENDED HIS PERFORMANCES AS WOMEN IN THE RHETORIC OF THE PURITAN ETHIC -- IN TERMS OF HARD WORK AND SACRIFICE, PHYSICAL EXERTION, TRAINING, AND SKILL.
I WOULD RESENT A MAN'S IMPERSONATING A WOMAN MYSELF. I ONLY DECIDED TO PERFECT THE DAMN THING SO WELL BECAUSE I DISCOVERED THERE WAS A MINT OF MONEY IN IT. TO CRITICS WHO SEEM TO THINK I AM DOING THIS FOR THE MERE SAKE OF BEING CALLED "PRETTY LADY," JUST LET ME DISABUSE THE MINDS OF THE PUBLIC ON THIS SCORE. I WOULD RATHER PLAY KNOCK-ABOUT GERMAN COMEDIANS IF THERE WAS MUCH MONEY IN IT. UNFORTUNATELY, THE GERMAN COMEDIAN MARKET IS OVERSTOCKED AT PRESENT, AND I SEEM TO BE THE ONLY ONE IN MY LINE. IF YOU HAD A CORNER ON A MARKET, YOU WOULD STAY IN THE BUSINESS, WOULD YOU NOT?
I STUDY THE FAIR SEX AS THE ELECTRICAL ENGINEER STUDIES THE COMPLICATED SWITCHBOARD IN A POWER PLANT OR THE BRIDGE SPECIALIST THE LAST EXAMPLE OF THE CANTILEVER. IT TOOK ME A LONG TIME TO LEARN TO USE MAKEUP IN A FEMININE WAY.
I HAVE TO KEEP CORSETS ON FOR TWO HOURS. AS I BEGIN THE SECOND ACT, I FEEL AS IF THE BLOOD WOULD BURST THROUGH THE VEINS OF MY LEGS. THOSE IMPLEMENTS OF TORTURE MAKE A FELLOW FEEL LIKE A TRUSSED CHICKEN.
The avaricious aspect of his endeavors forms about the only incentive which urges Eltinge to wear skirts and torture his equator with stays instead of appearing in conventional male attire. Feminine impersonation is to him only a means to an end and that end is the accumulation of a competency and accumulating it quickly.
WASHINGTON POST

BEFORE LONG, ELTINGE WAS ABLE TO BUY A THREE-STORY TOWNHOUSE ON W. 75TH STREET IN MANHATTAN. HE DID HIS OWN INTERIOR DECORATING WITH PRIDE AND FLAIR.

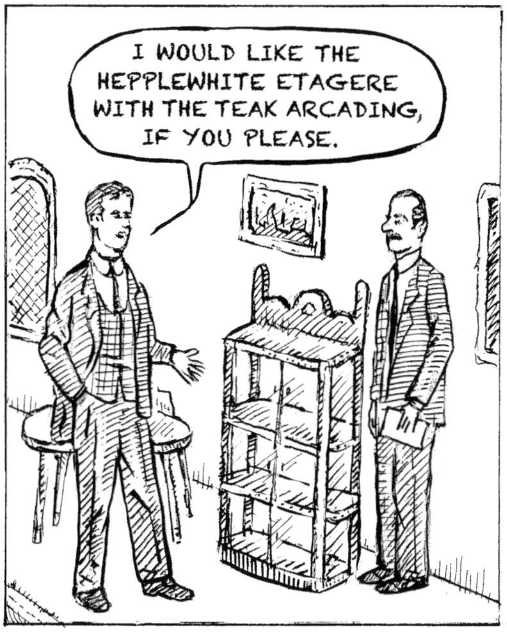
I WOULD LIKE THE HEPPLEWHITE ETAGERE WITH THE TEAK ARCADING, IF YOU PLEASE.

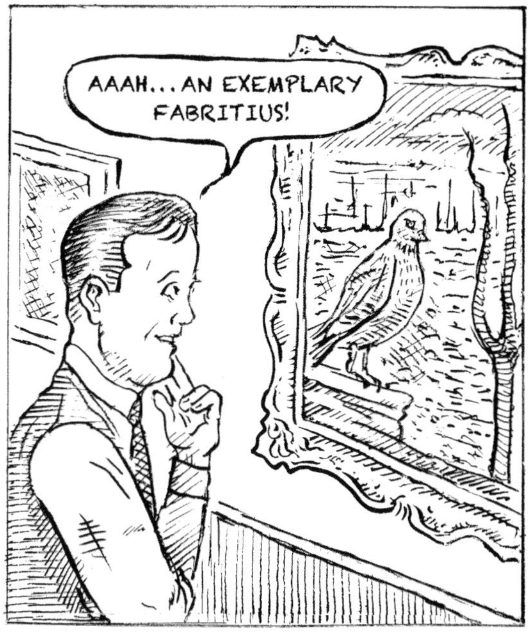
AAAH... AN EXEMPLARY FABRITIUS!

HIS PRESS AGENTS TOLD REPORTERS ELTINGE SPENT HIS OFF-DAYS ON A "WORKING FARM" IN FORT SOLANGA, LONG ISLAND.

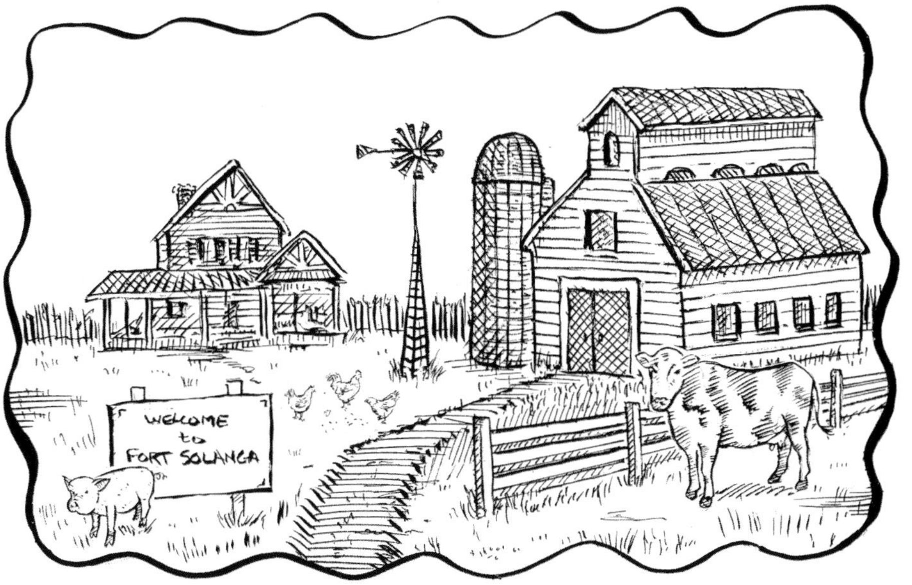
WELCOME to FORT SOLANGA

SOMETIMES, HIS PRESS AGENTS DESCRIBED HIS RETREAT AS A "100-ACRE FARM IN THE ADIRONDACKS" IN UPSTATE NEW YORK.

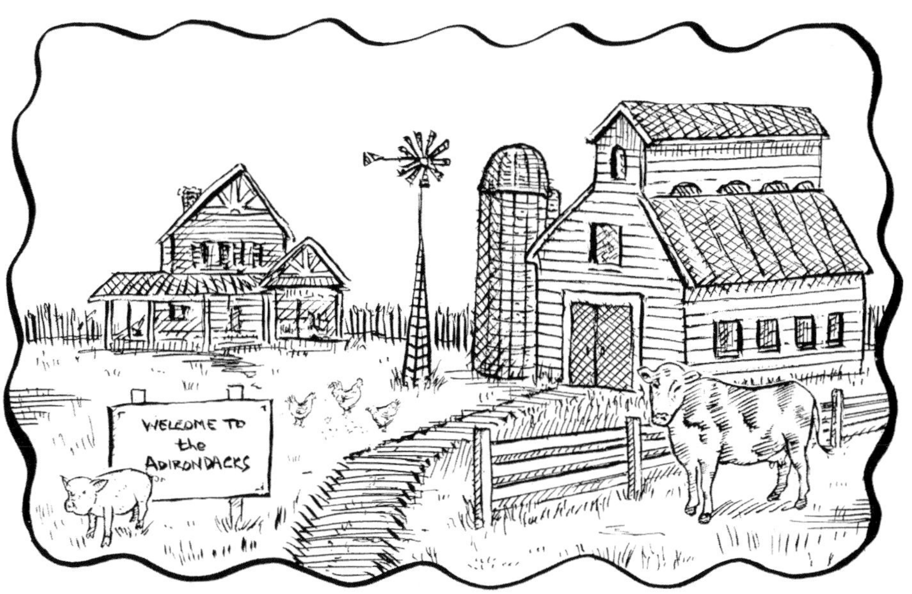
WELCOME TO the ADIRONDACKS

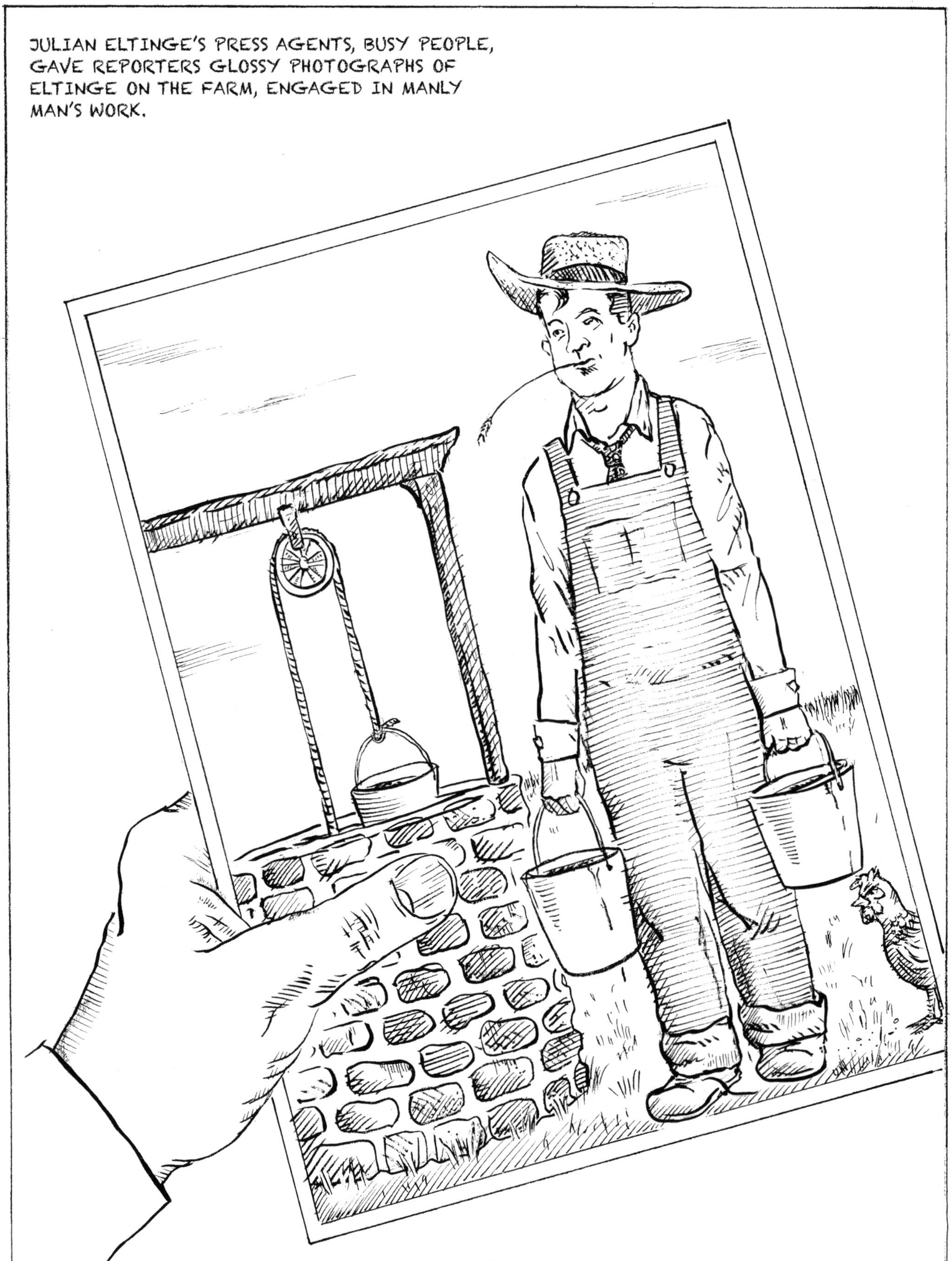
JULIAN ELTINGE'S PRESS AGENTS, BUSY PEOPLE, GAVE REPORTERS GLOSSY PHOTOGRAPHS OF ELTINGE ON THE FARM, ENGAGED IN MANLY MAN'S WORK.

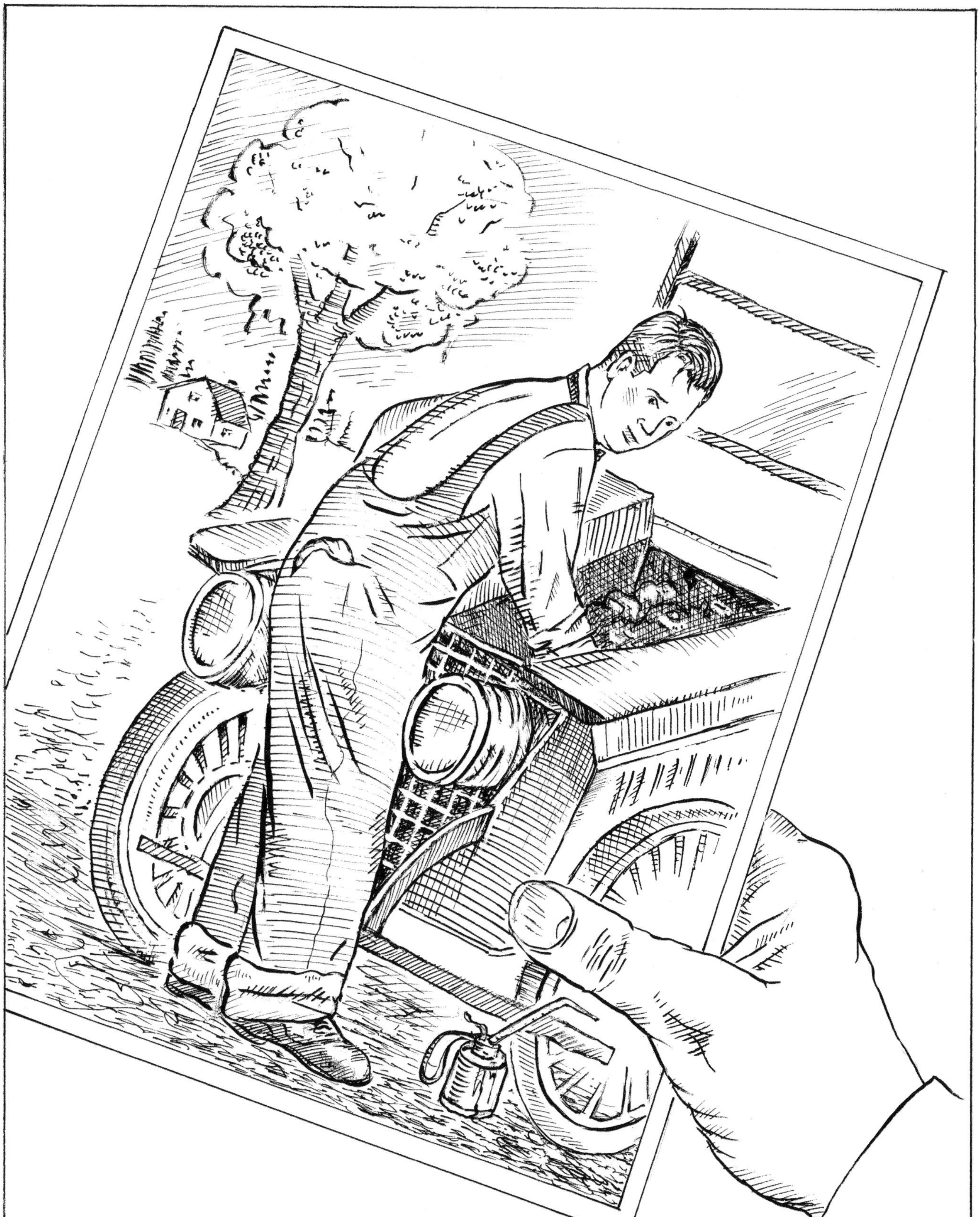
WHEN ELTINGE TOURED, NEWSPAPERS AROUND THE COUNTRY PUBLISHED THE PHOTOS, OPTING NOT TO POINT OUT THAT THEY WERE AS THEATRICAL AS HIS STAGE PERFORMANCES.

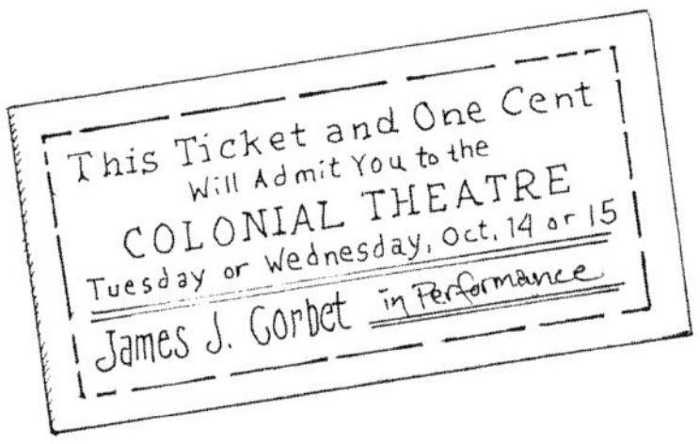
This Ticket and One Cent
Will Admit You to the
COLONIAL THEATRE
Tuesday or Wednesday, Oct. 14 or 15
James J. Corbet in Performance

IN AN ARTICLE TITLED "WOMANLINESS AS A PROFESSION," SCRIBNER'S *MAGAZINE* URGED WOMEN TO EMBRACE THE CAREGIVING ROLES OF "GOOD MOTHER, DEVOTED WIFE, GENTLE SISTER, AND QUIET GUARDIAN OF THE HEARTH FIRE." SUCH WAS THE "TRUE WOMAN" JULIAN ELTINGE TOOK UP AS *HIS* PROFESSION.

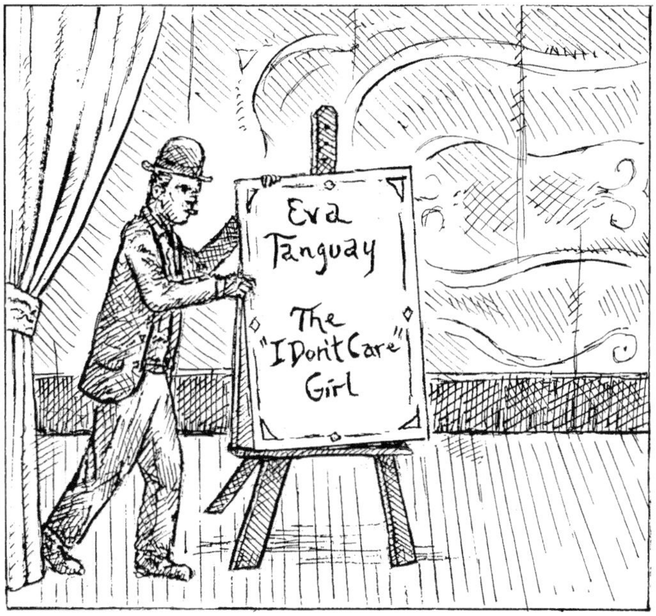
Eva Tanguay
The "I Don't Care" Girl

EVA TANGUAY ANNOUNCED THE ARRIVAL OF THE "NEW WOMAN" WITH A RADICALLY DIFFERENT VIEW OF CAREGIVING.

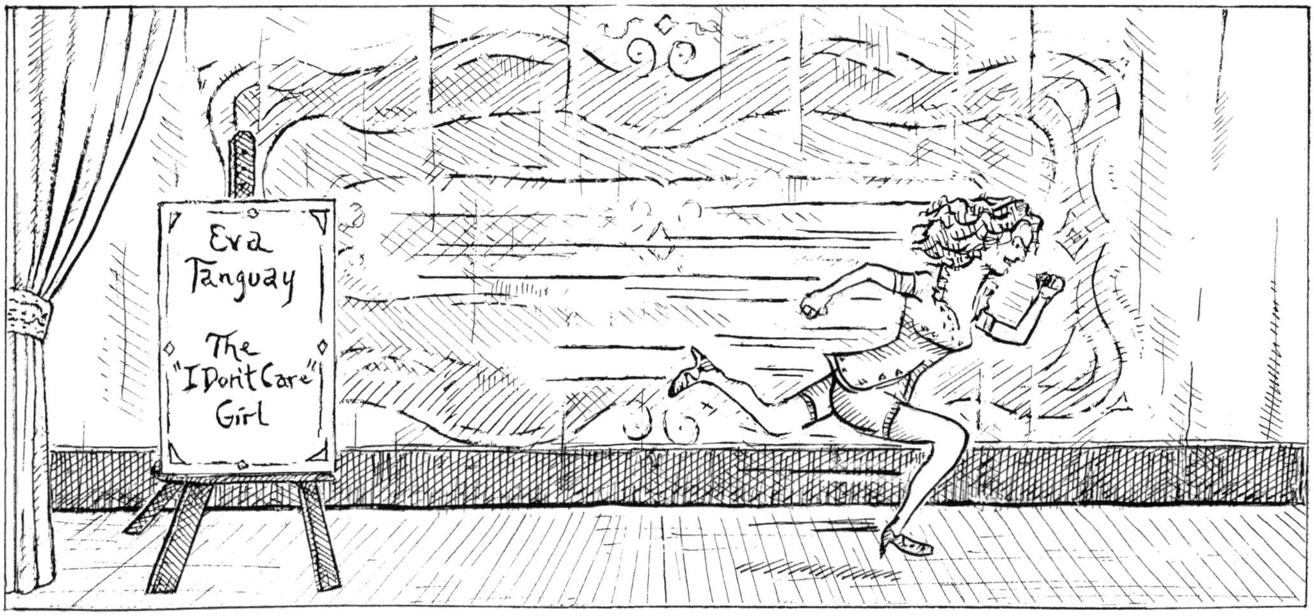
Eva Tanguay
The "I Don't Care" Girl

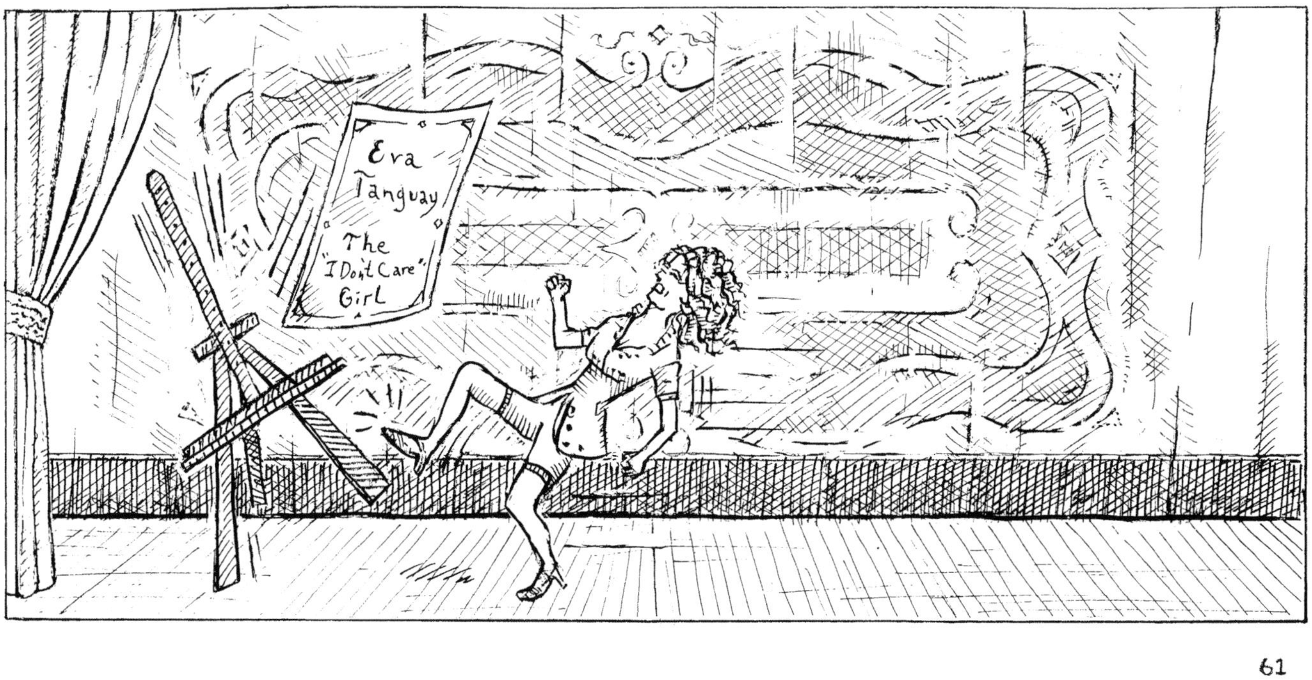
Eva Tanguay
The "I Don't Care" Girl

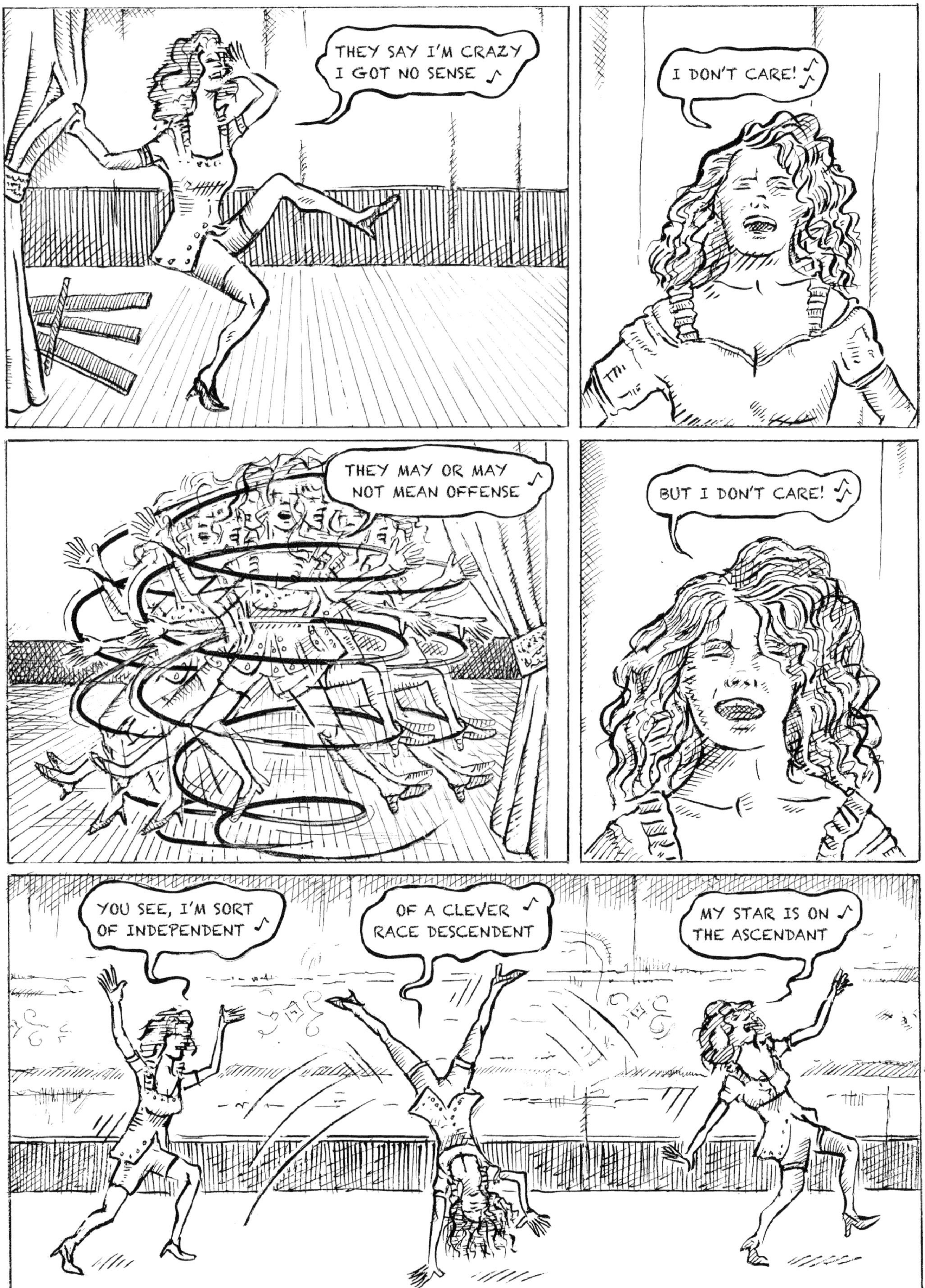
THEY SAY I'M CRAZY I GOT NO SENSE ♪
I DON'T CARE! ♪♪
THEY MAY OR MAY NOT MEAN OFFENSE ♪
BUT I DON'T CARE! ♪♪
YOU SEE, I'M SORT OF INDEPENDENT ♪
OF A CLEVER RACE DESCENDENT ♪
MY STAR IS ON THE ASCENDANT ♪

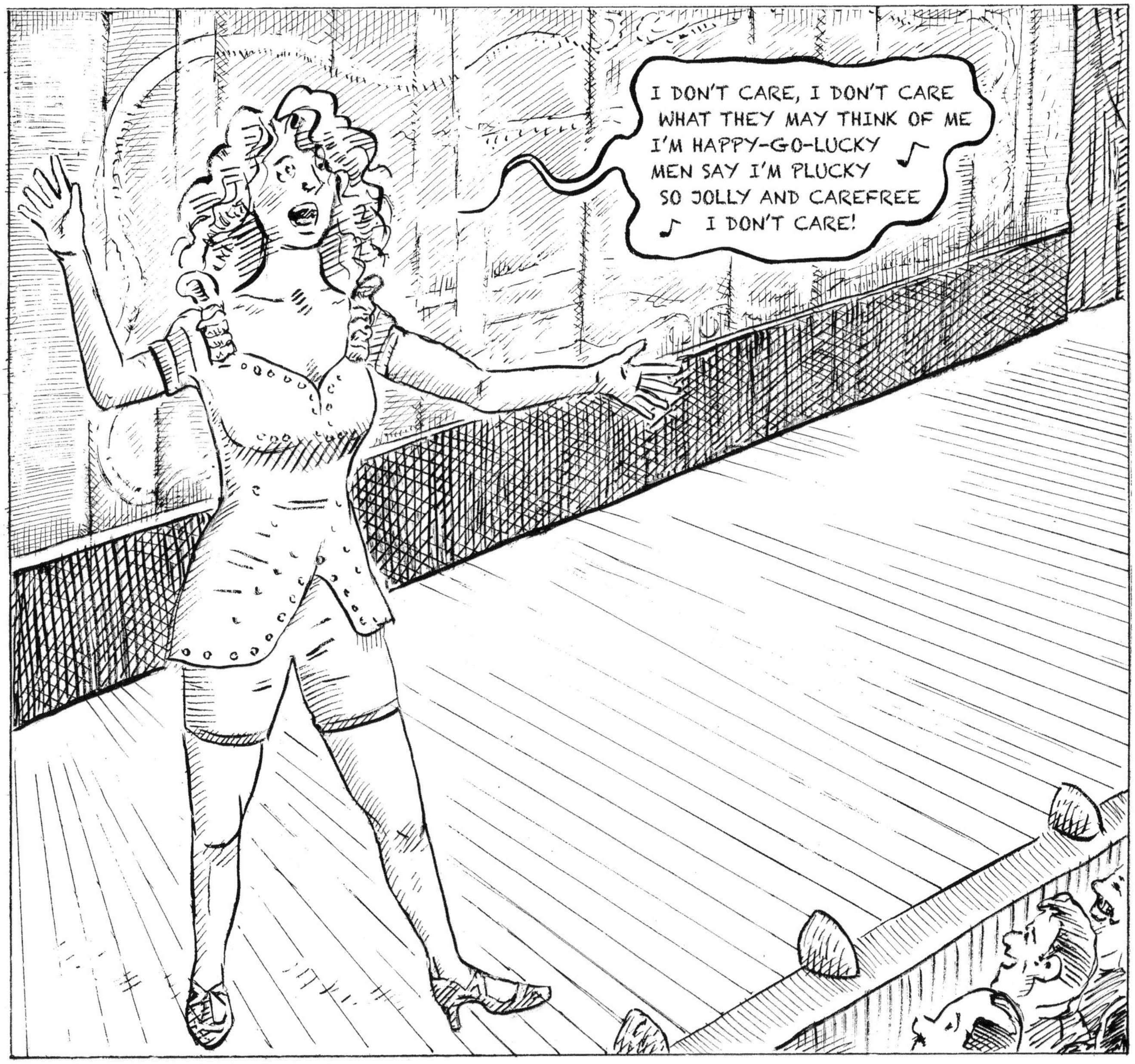
I DON'T CARE, I DON'T CARE
WHAT THEY MAY THINK OF ME
I'M HAPPY-GO-LUCKY
MEN SAY I'M PLUCKY
SO JOLLY AND CAREFREE
I DON'T CARE!

TANGUAY PROJECTED THE SAME IMAGE OFFSTAGE, MAKING CLEAR THAT THE PLUCKY, CAREFREE EVA TANGUAY WAS THE TRUE TANGUAY. IN HER FREE TIME BETWEEN SHOWS, SHE MADE HIGH DIVES INTO PUBLIC POOLS, BOXED WITH MEN IN GYMS, AND DROVE MOTORCARS AT STARTLING SPEEDS OF UP TO 60 MILES PER HOUR!

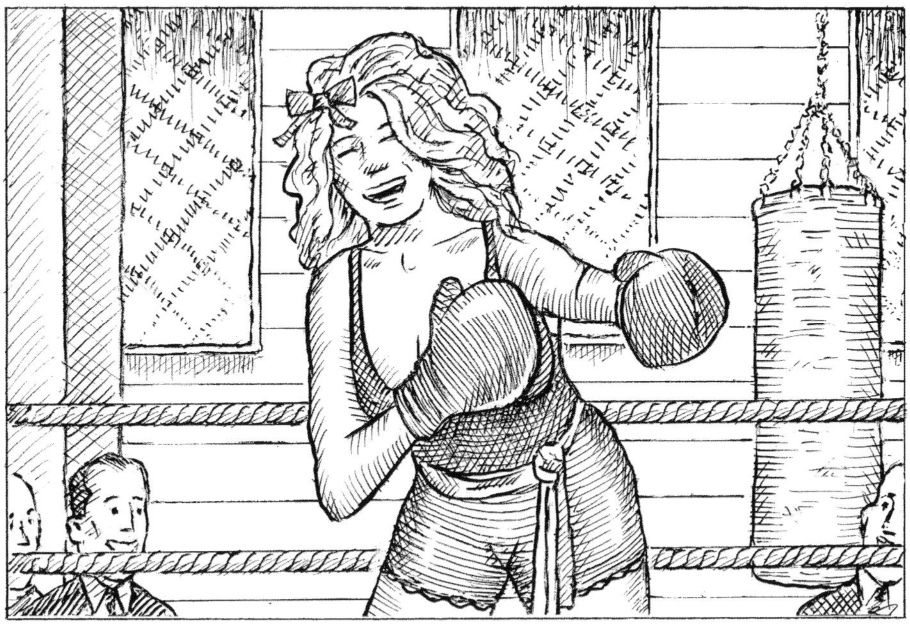

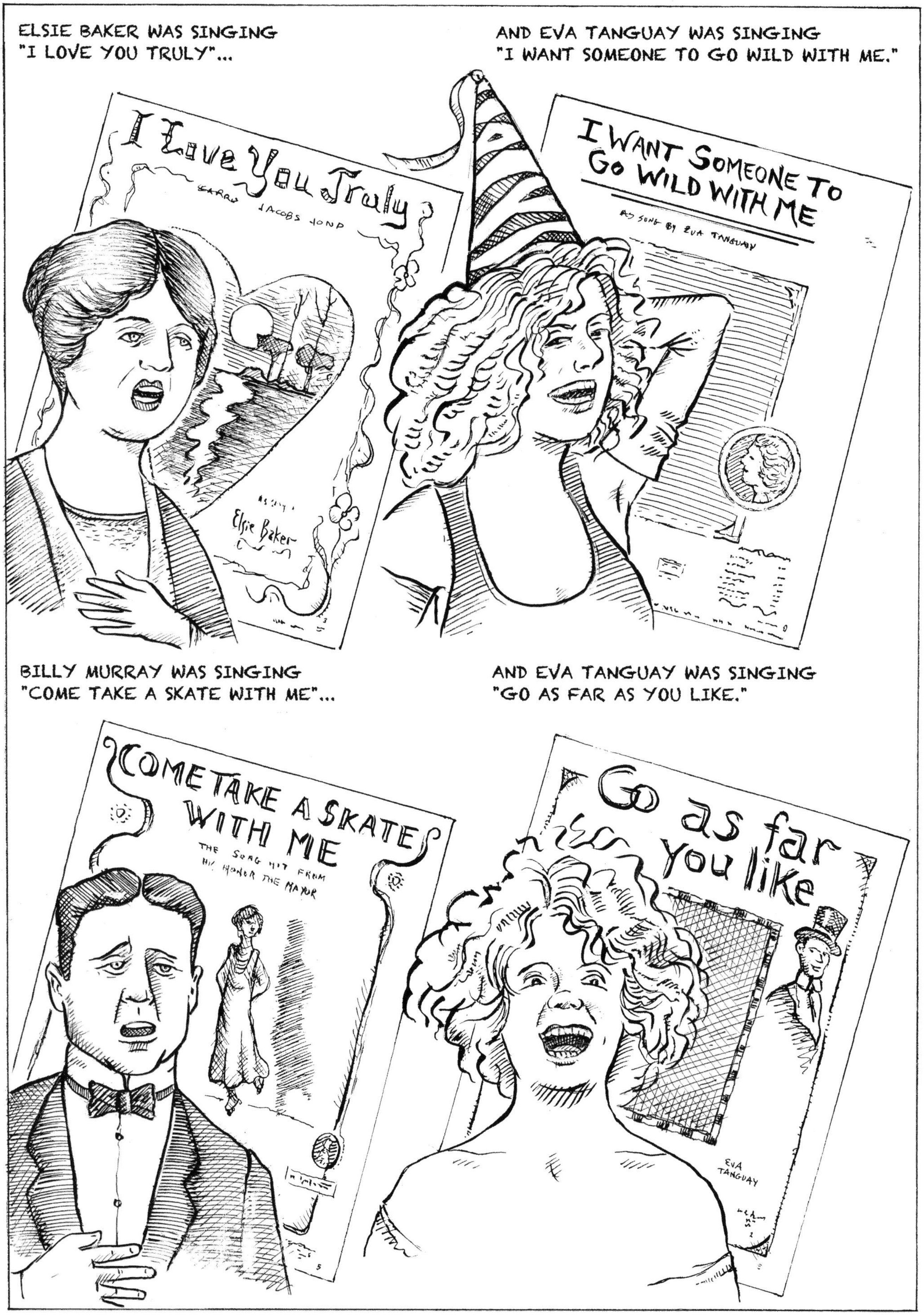
ELSIE BAKER WAS SINGING "I LOVE YOU TRULY"...
I Love You Truly
Elsie Baker
AND EVA TANGUAY WAS SINGING "I WANT SOMEONE TO GO WILD WITH ME."
I WANT SOMEONE TO GO WILD WITH ME
BILLY MURRAY WAS SINGING "COME TAKE A SKATE WITH ME"...
COME TAKE A SKATE WITH ME
AND EVA TANGUAY WAS SINGING "GO AS FAR AS YOU LIKE."
Go as far you like
EVA TANGUAY

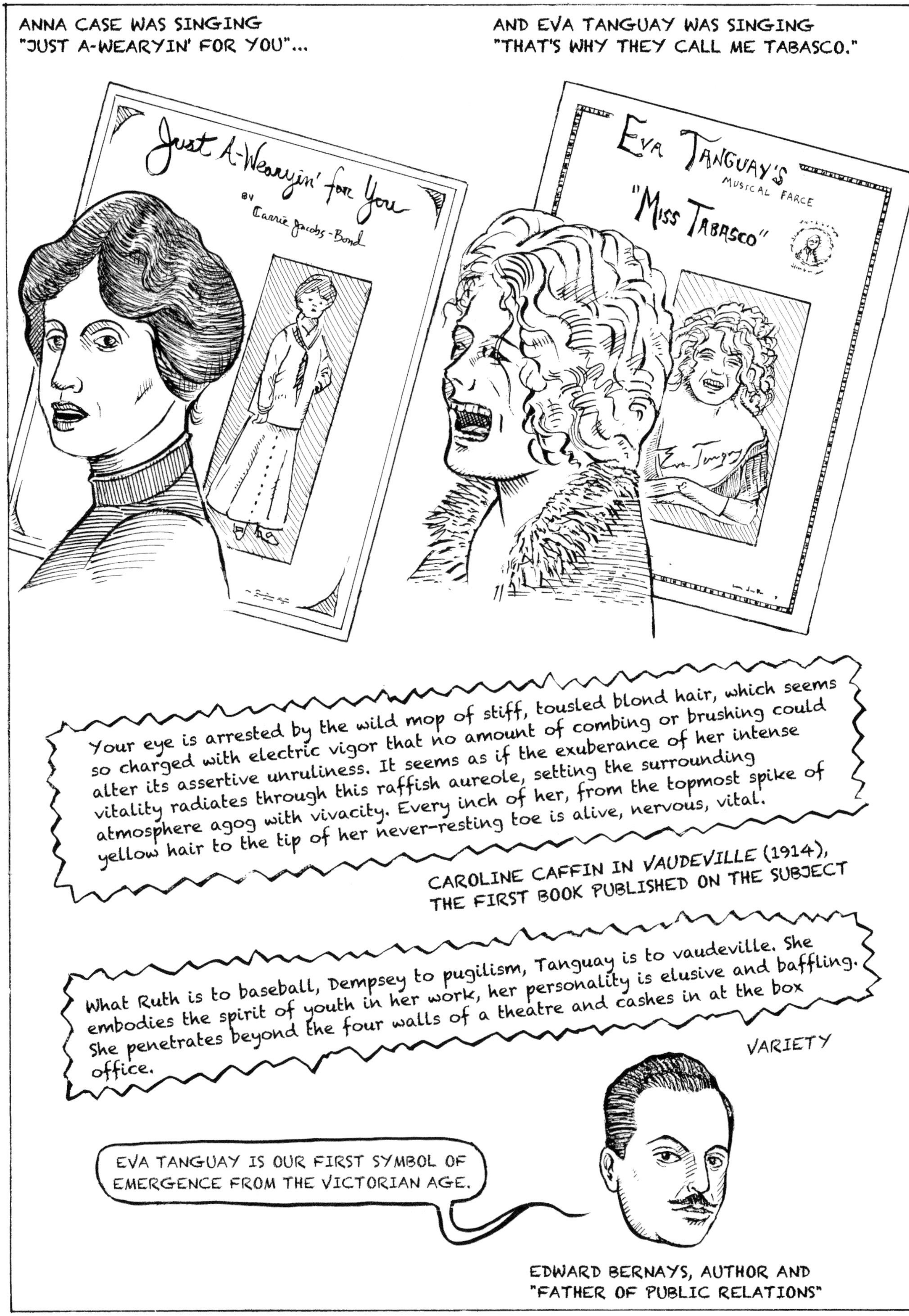
ANNA CASE WAS SINGING "JUST A-WEARYIN' FOR YOU"...
AND EVA TANGUAY WAS SINGING "THAT'S WHY THEY CALL ME TABASCO."
Just A-Wearyin' for You
BY Carrie Jacobs-Bond
EVA TANGUAY'S
MUSICAL FARCE
"MISS TABASCO"
Eva Tanguay
Your eye is arrested by the wild mop of stiff, tousled blond hair, which seems so charged with electric vigor that no amount of combing or brushing could alter its assertive unruliness. It seems as if the exuberance of her intense vitality radiates through this raffish aureole, setting the surrounding atmosphere agog with vivacity. Every inch of her, from the topmost spike of yellow hair to the tip of her never-resting toe is alive, nervous, vital.
CAROLINE CAFFIN IN VAUDEVILLE (1914), THE FIRST BOOK PUBLISHED ON THE SUBJECT
What Ruth is to baseball, Dempsey to pugilism, Tanguay is to vaudeville. She embodies the spirit of youth in her work, her personality is elusive and baffling. She penetrates beyond the four walls of a theatre and cashes in at the box office.
VARIETY
EVA TANGUAY IS OUR FIRST SYMBOL OF EMERGENCE FROM THE VICTORIAN AGE.
EDWARD BERNAYS, AUTHOR AND "FATHER OF PUBLIC RELATIONS"

TANGUAY GOT AWAY WITH PROMOTING RADICAL IDEAS BY PROJECTING A COMICAL "KOOKY" PERSONA – AS IF ONLY A MADWOMAN WOULD DARE SUCH MADNESS. HER COSTUMES WERE AS WILD AS HER THINKING.

THE AMERICAN FLAG COSTUME

THE CHANDELIER COSTUME

IN 1909, WHEN THE LINCOLN-HEAD PENNY WAS INTRODUCED, TANGUAY
HAD A COSTUME MADE OF PENNIES GLUED ONTO A BODYSUIT.

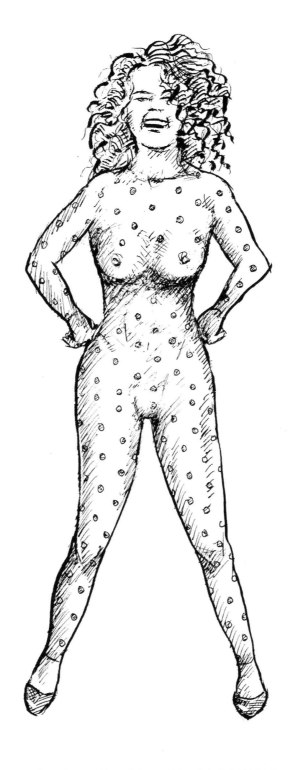

THE LINCOLN-HEAD PENNY COSTUME

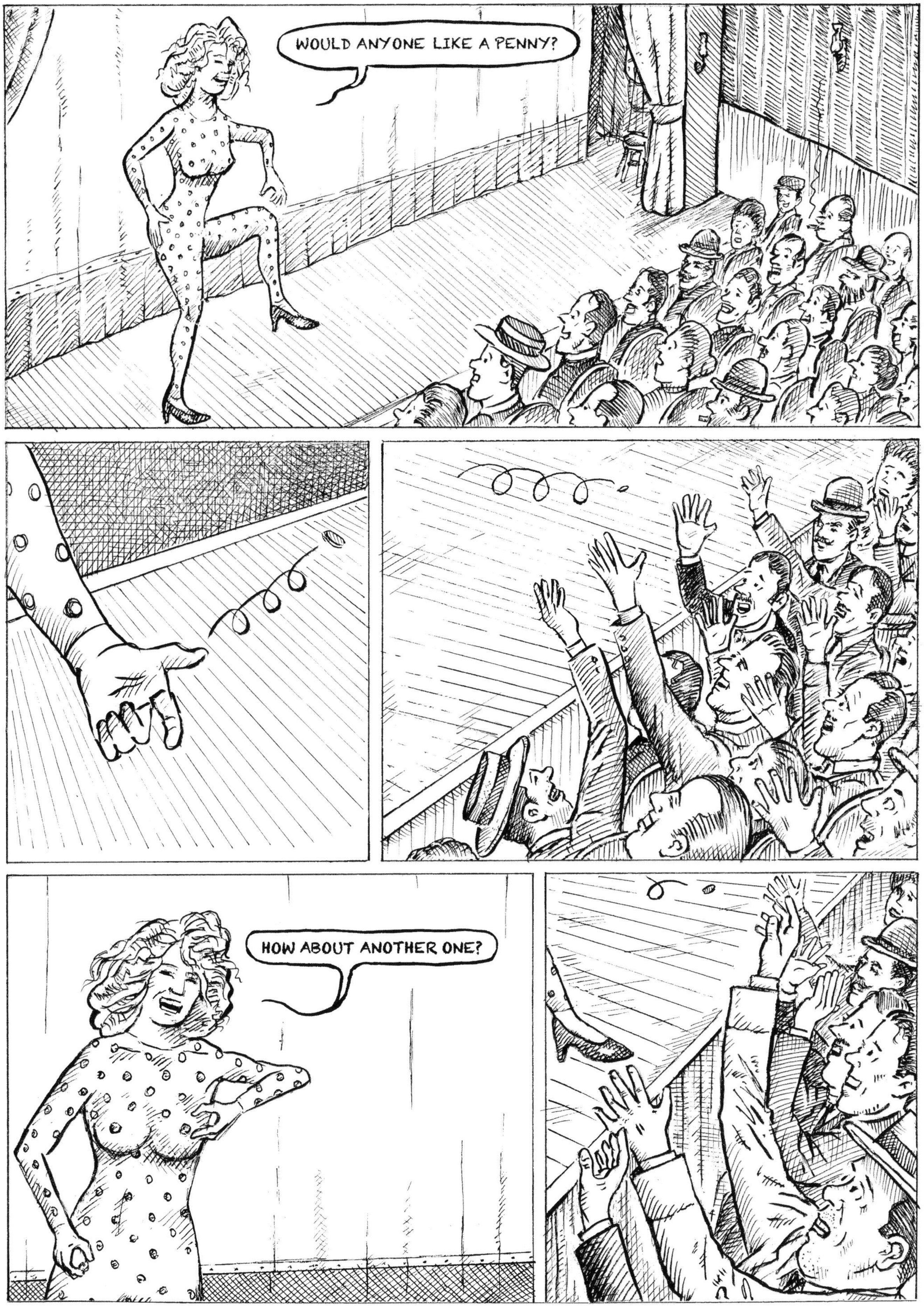
WOULD ANYONE LIKE A PENNY?
HOW ABOUT ANOTHER ONE?

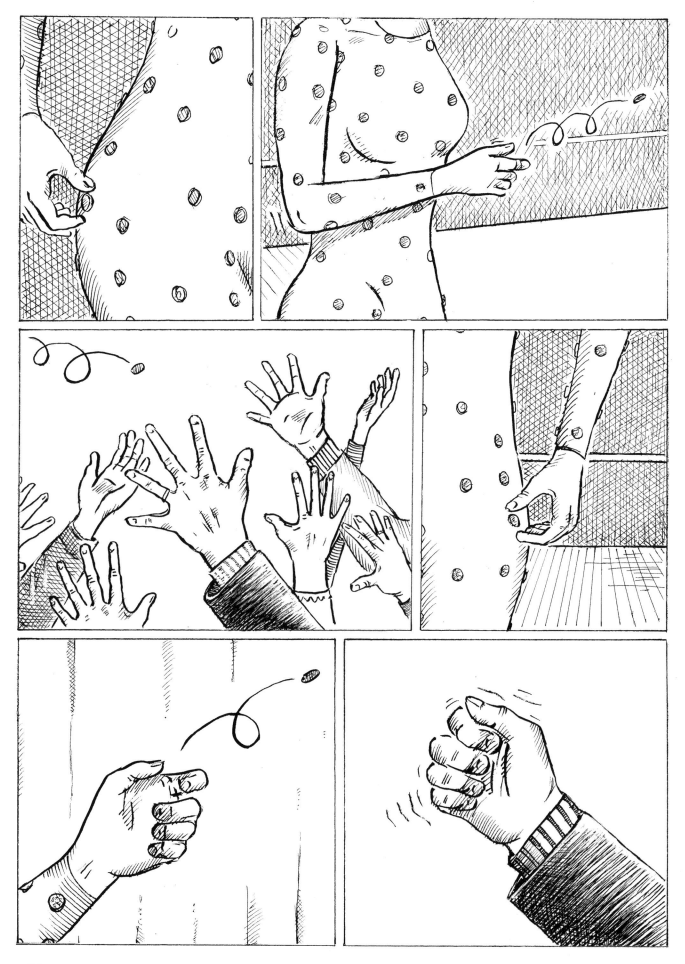

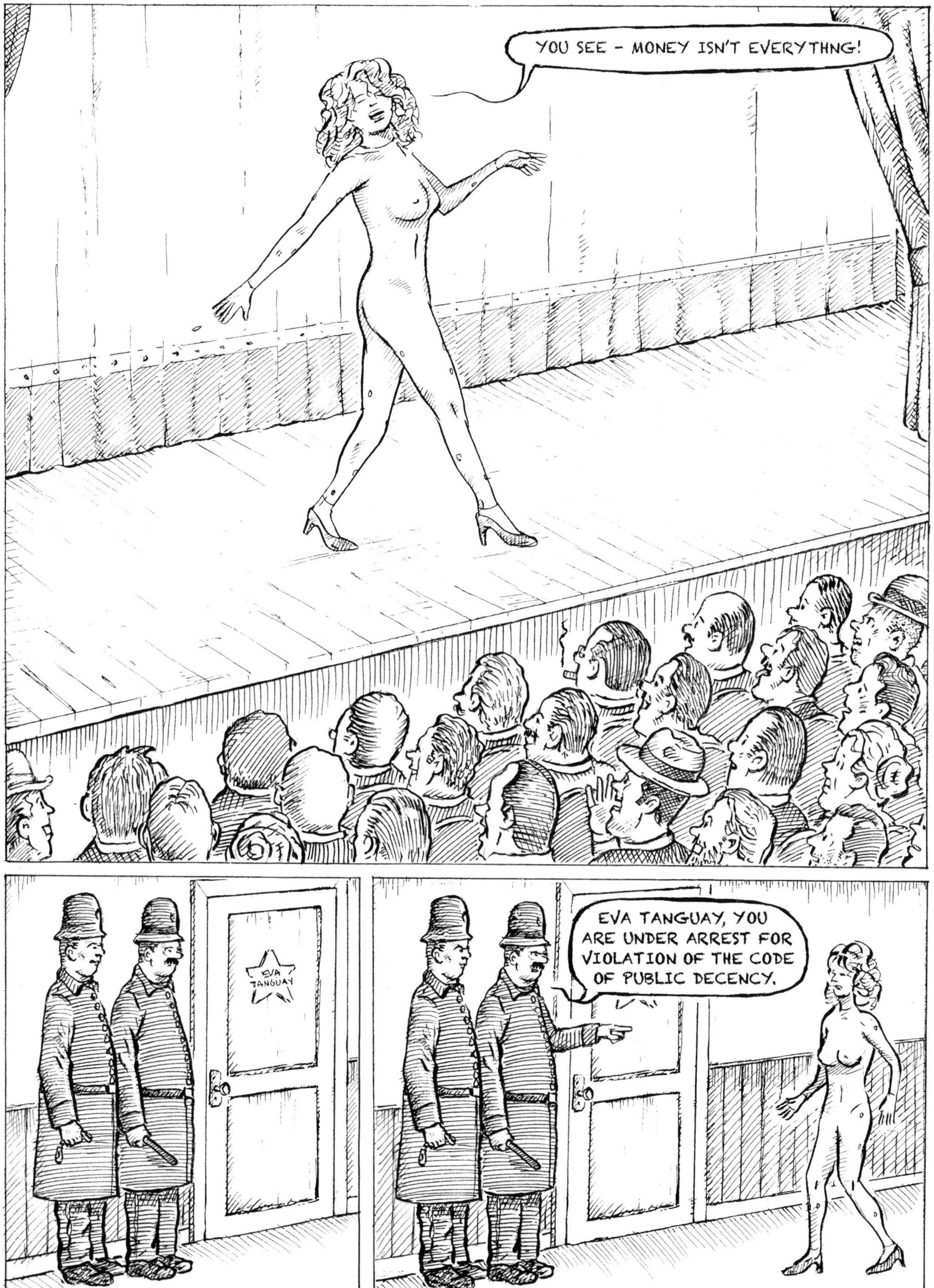
YOU SEE - MONEY ISN'T EVERYTHNG!
EVA TANGUAY
EVA TANGUAY, YOU ARE UNDER ARREST FOR VIOLATION OF THE CODE OF PUBLIC DECENCY.

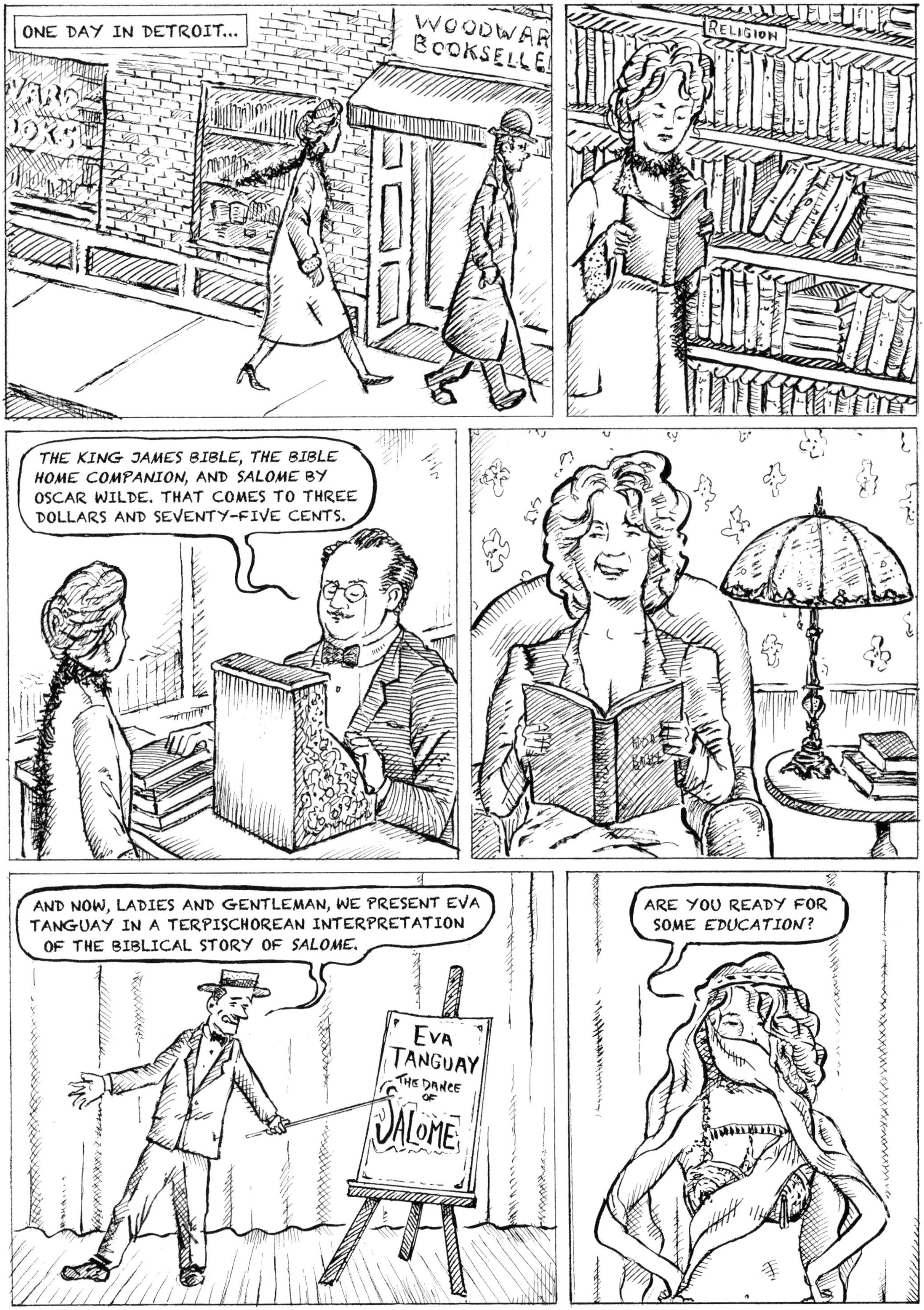

ONE DAY IN DETROIT...
WOODWAR
BOOKSELLE
RELIGION
THE KING JAMES BIBLE, THE BIBLE HOME COMPANION, AND SALOME BY OSCAR WILDE. THAT COMES TO THREE DOLLARS AND SEVENTY-FIVE CENTS.
AND NOW, LADIES AND GENTLEMAN, WE PRESENT EVA TANGUAY IN A TERPISCHOREAN INTERPRETATION OF THE BIBLICAL STORY OF SALOME.
EVA TANGUAY
THE DANCE OF
SALOME
ARE YOU READY FOR SOME EDUCATION?

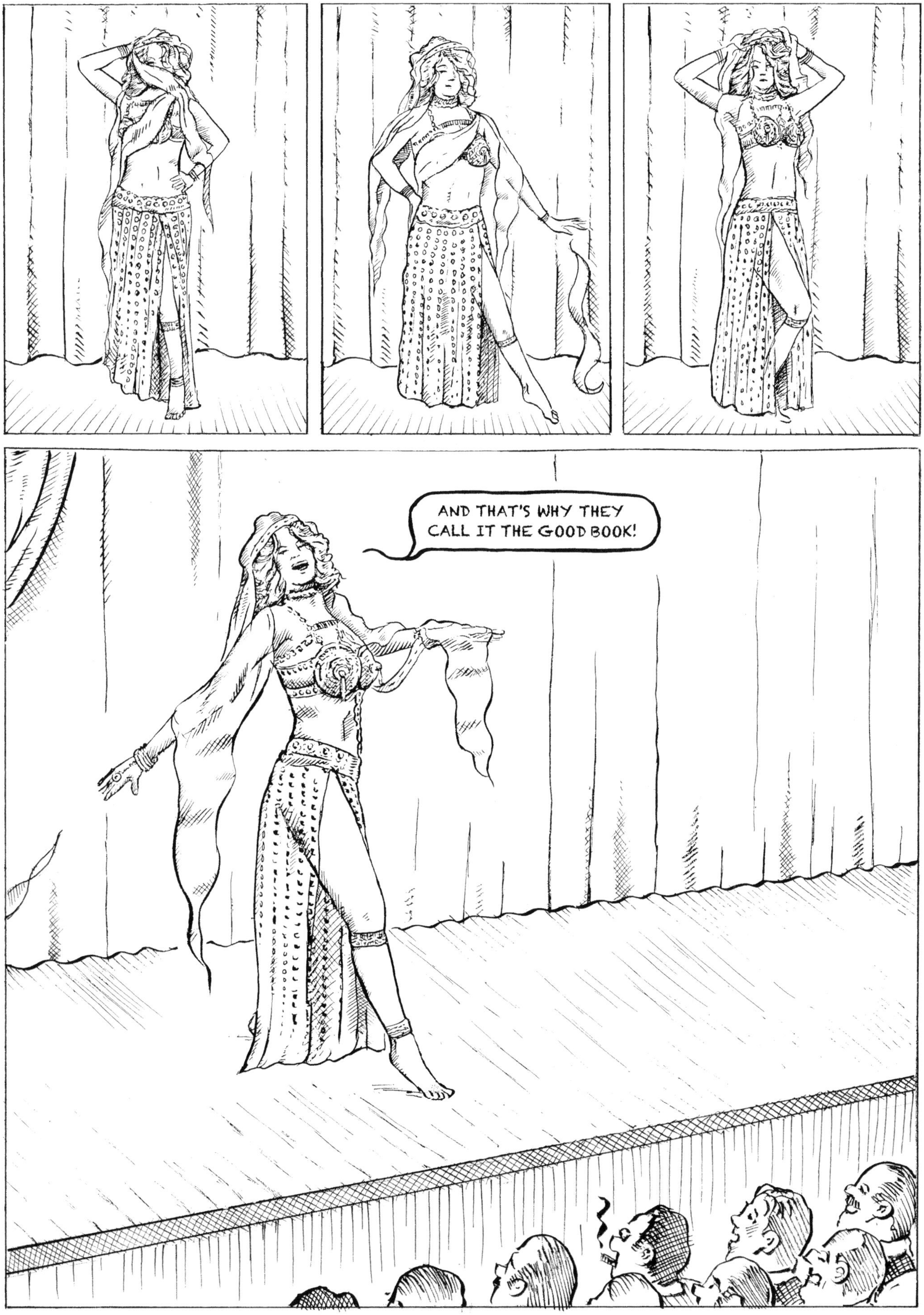
AND THAT'S WHY THEY CALL IT THE GOOD BOOK!

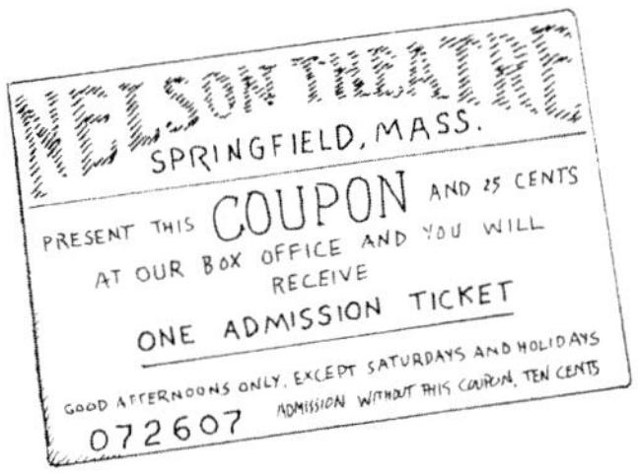
NELSON THEATRE
SPRINGFIELD, MASS.
PRESENT THIS COUPON AND 25 CENTS
AT OUR BOX OFFICE AND YOU WILL
RECEIVE
ONE ADMISSION TICKET
GOOD AFTERNOONS ONLY, EXCEPT SATURDAYS AND HOLIDAYS
ADMISSION WITHOUT THIS COUPON, TEN CENTS
072607

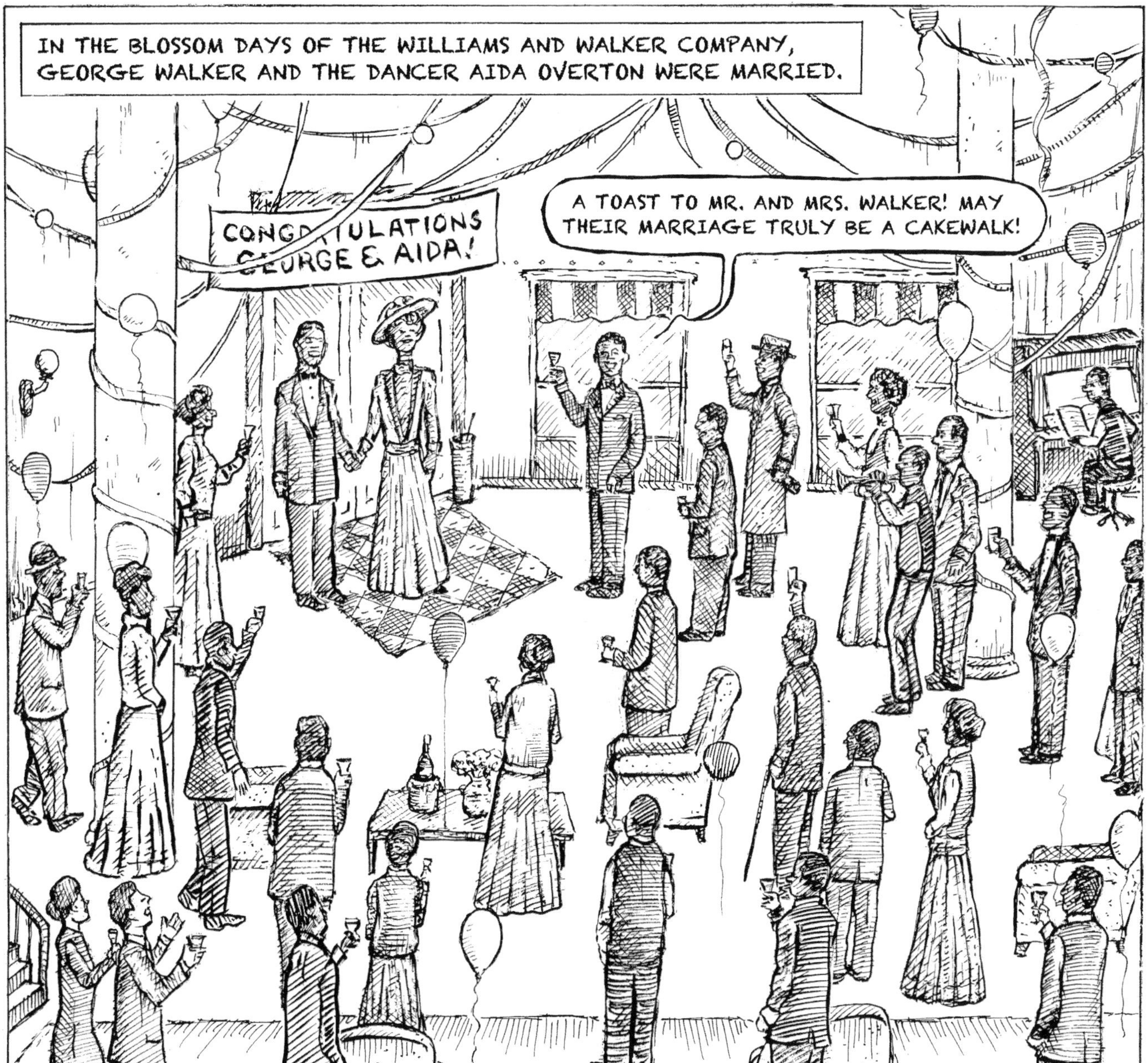
IN THE BLOSSOM DAYS OF THE WILLIAMS AND WALKER COMPANY, GEORGE WALKER AND THE DANCER AIDA OVERTON WERE MARRIED.
CONGRATULATIONS GEORGE & AIDA!
A TOAST TO MR. AND MRS. WALKER! MAY THEIR MARRIAGE TRULY BE A CAKEWALK!

A PROFESSIONAL PERFORMER FROM THE AGE OF 15, AIDA OVERTON WAS ESTABLISHED AS "THE QUEEN OF THE CAKEWALK" BEFORE JOINING WILLIAMS AND WALKER. SHE BROUGHT GRACE AND POLISH TO THE COMPANY AS A CHOREOGRAPHER AS WELL AS A FEATURED SINGER AND DANCER, NOW OFTEN BILLED AS AIDA OVERTON WALKER.

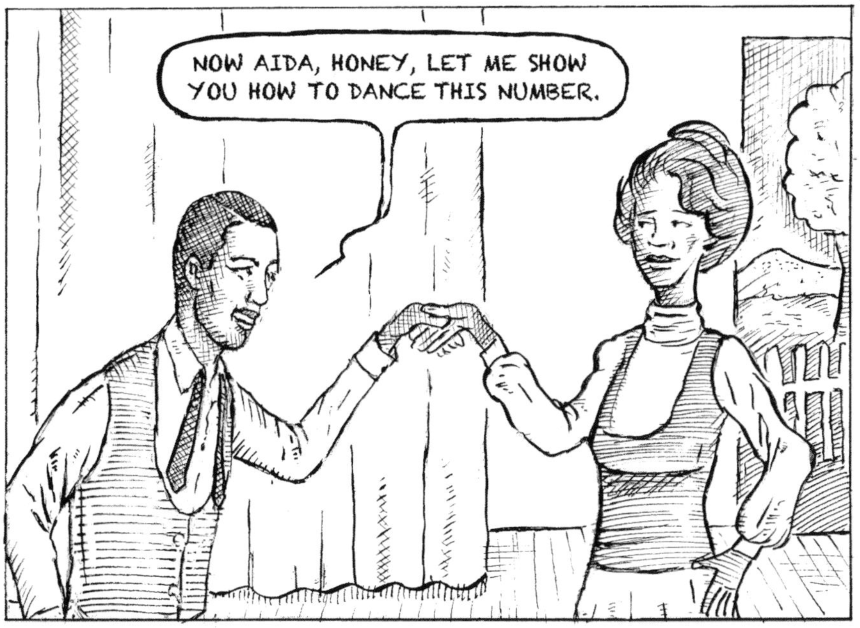
NOW AIDA, HONEY, LET ME SHOW YOU HOW TO DANCE THIS NUMBER.

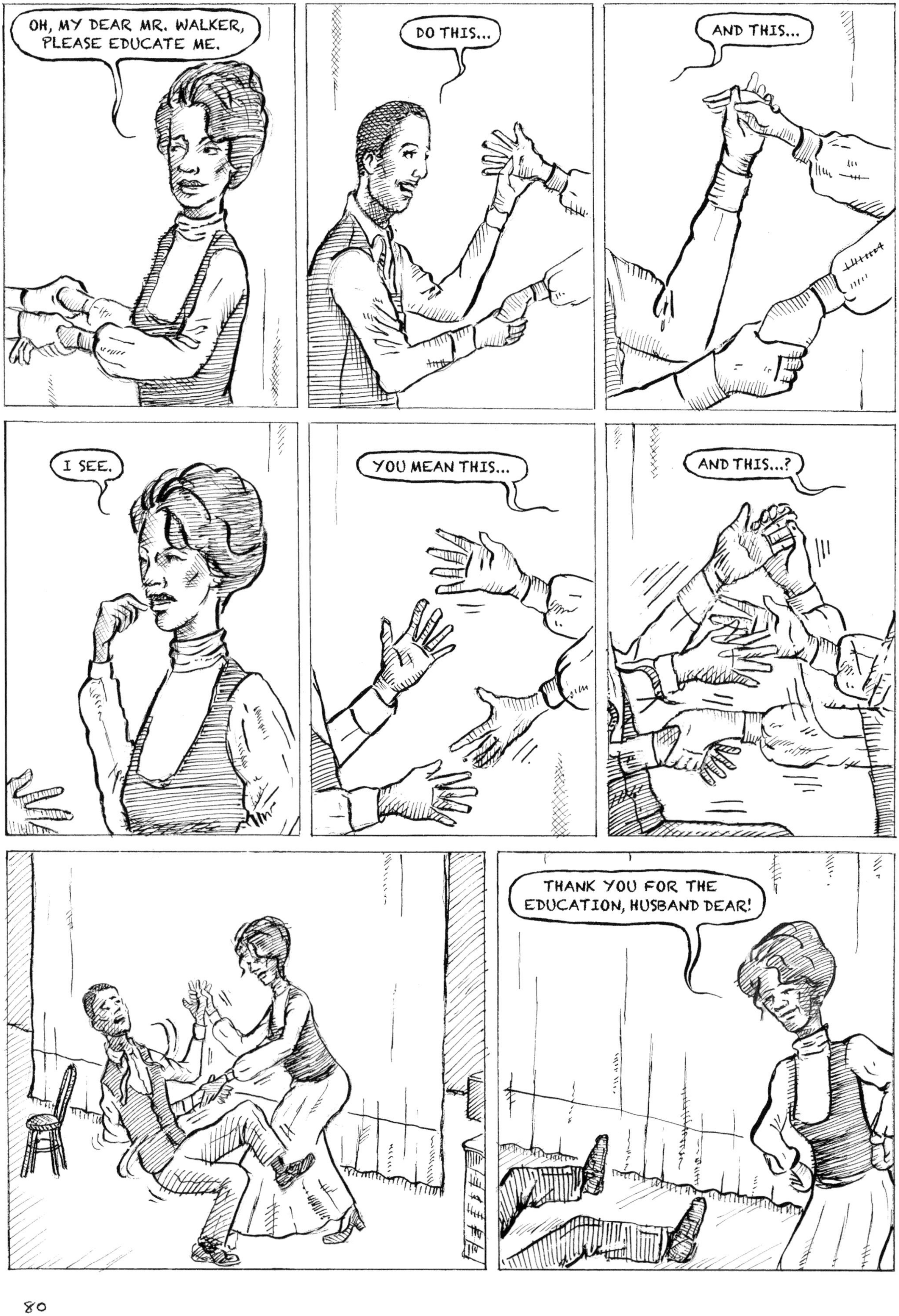
OH, MY DEAR MR. WALKER, PLEASE EDUCATE ME.
DO THIS...
AND THIS...
I SEE.
YOU MEAN THIS...
AND THIS...?
THANK YOU FOR THE EDUCATION, HUSBAND DEAR!

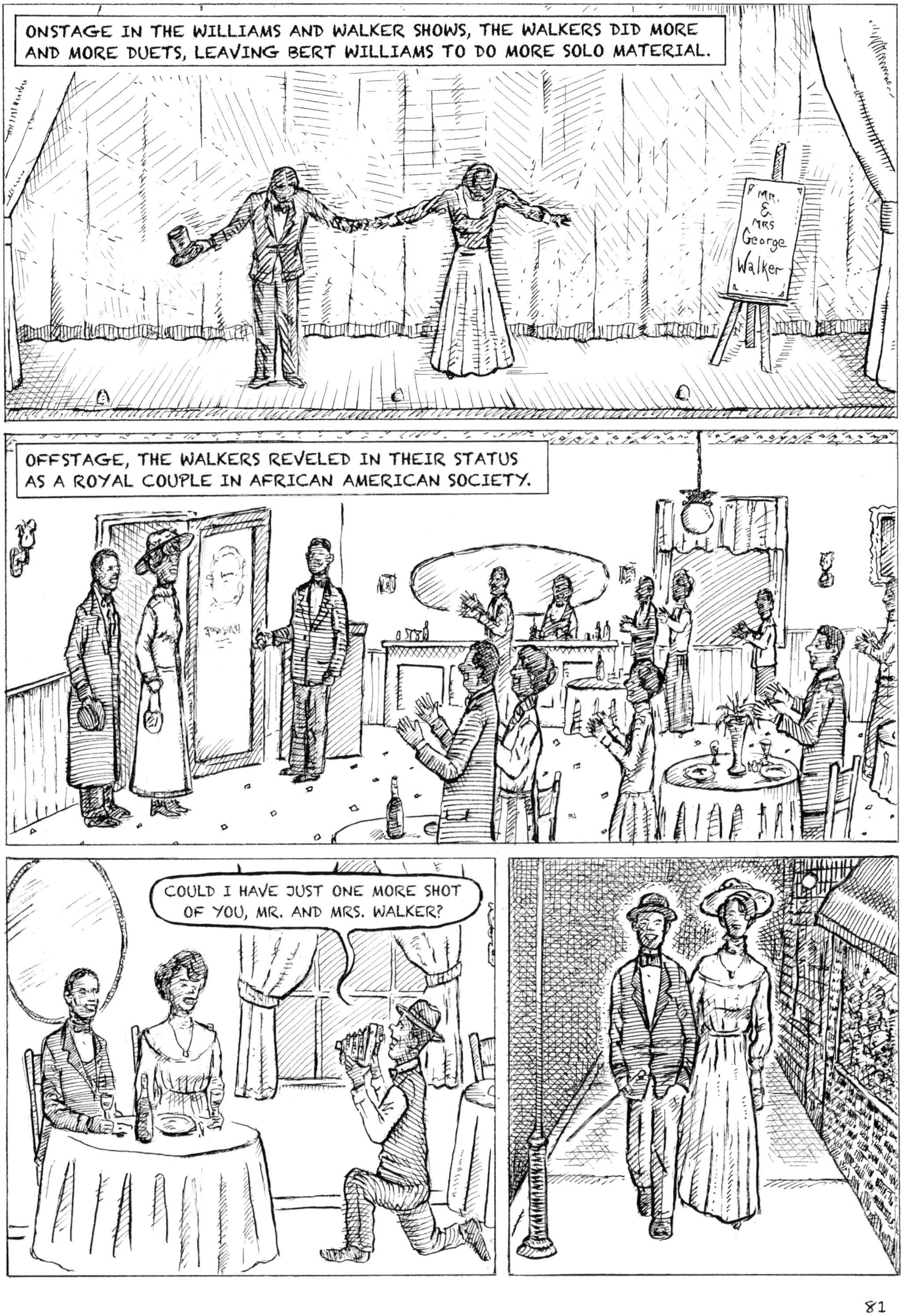
ONSTAGE IN THE WILLIAMS AND WALKER SHOWS, THE WALKERS DID MORE AND MORE DUETS, LEAVING BERT WILLIAMS TO DO MORE SOLO MATERIAL.
MR. & MRS George Walker
OFFSTAGE, THE WALKERS REVELED IN THEIR STATUS AS A ROYAL COUPLE IN AFRICAN AMERICAN SOCIETY.
COULD I HAVE JUST ONE MORE SHOT OF YOU, MR. AND MRS. WALKER?

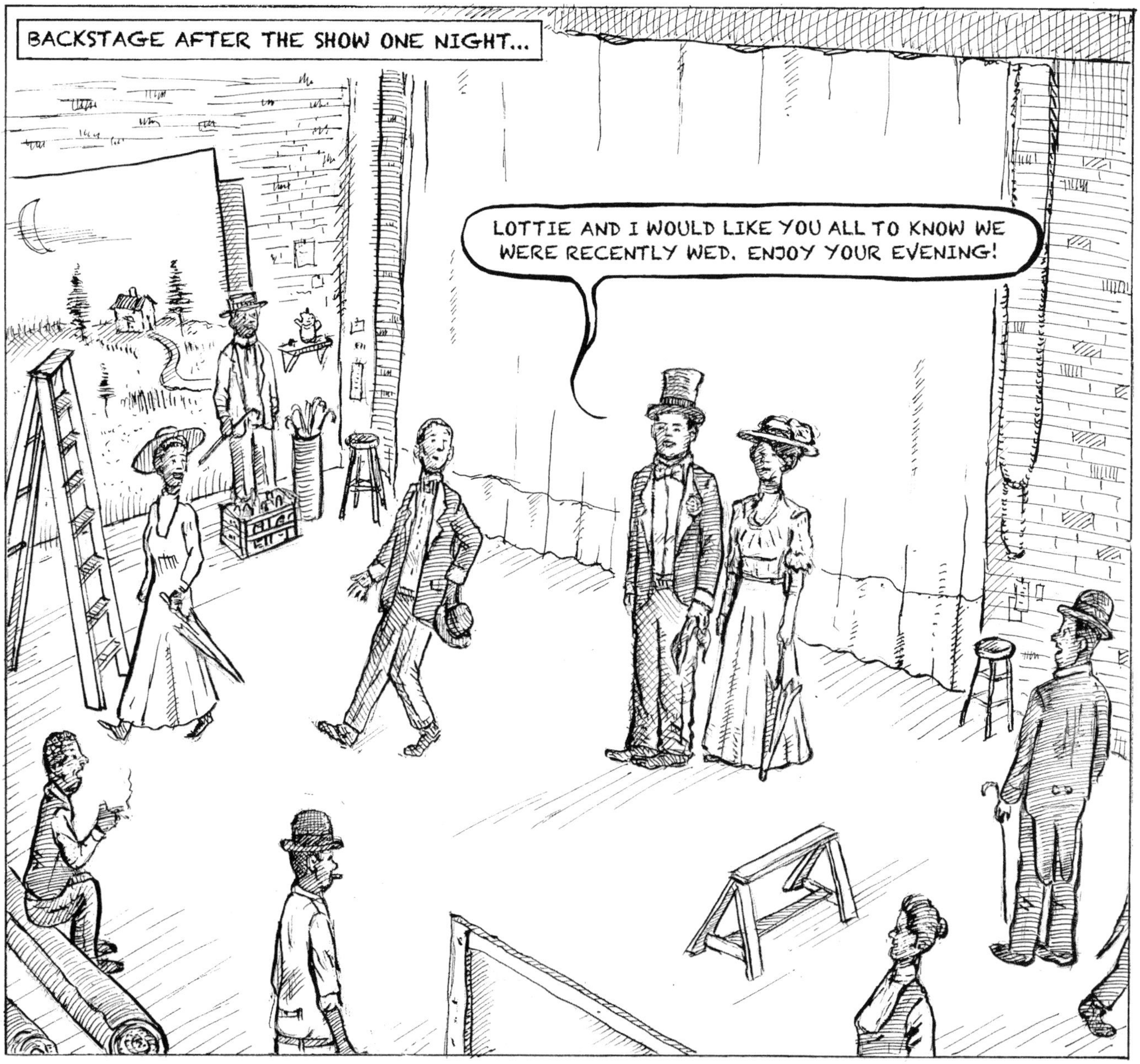
BACKSTAGE AFTER THE SHOW ONE NIGHT...
LOTTIE AND I WOULD LIKE YOU ALL TO KNOW WE WERE RECENTLY WED. ENJOY YOUR EVENING!

EIGHT YEARS OLDER THAN WILLIAMS, EITHER WIDOWED OR DIVORCED (THE FACTS ARE UNCLEAR), CHARLOTTE (LOTTIE) THOMPSON WAS A STATELY WOMAN WITH A STRONG, CLEAR SINGING VOICE. SHE JOINED WILLIAMS AND WALKER AS AN ENSEMBLE SINGER, AND SHE IMPRESSED WILLIAMS WITH HER SAVVY ONSTAGE AND OFF.

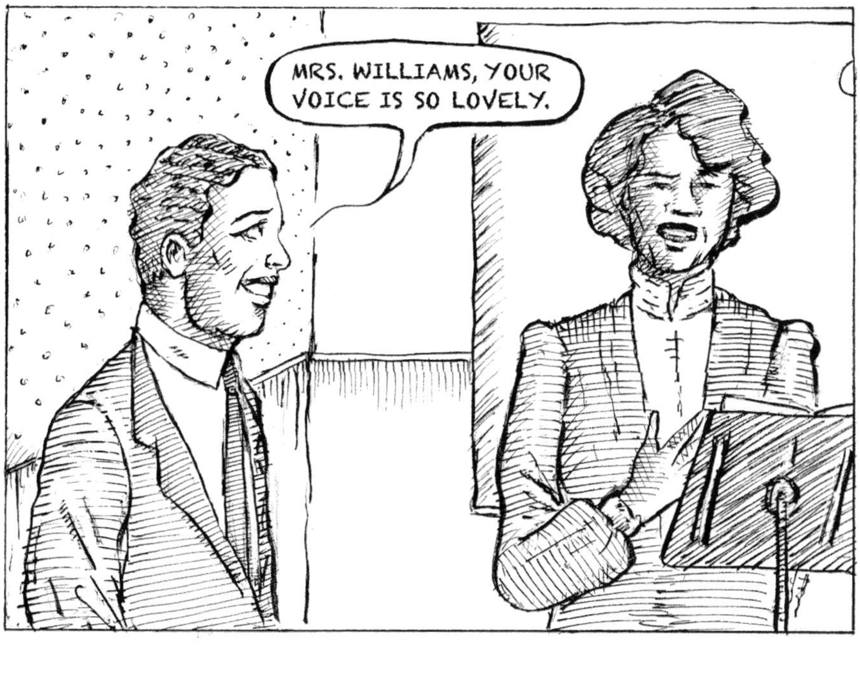
MRS. WILLIAMS, YOUR VOICE IS SO LOVELY.

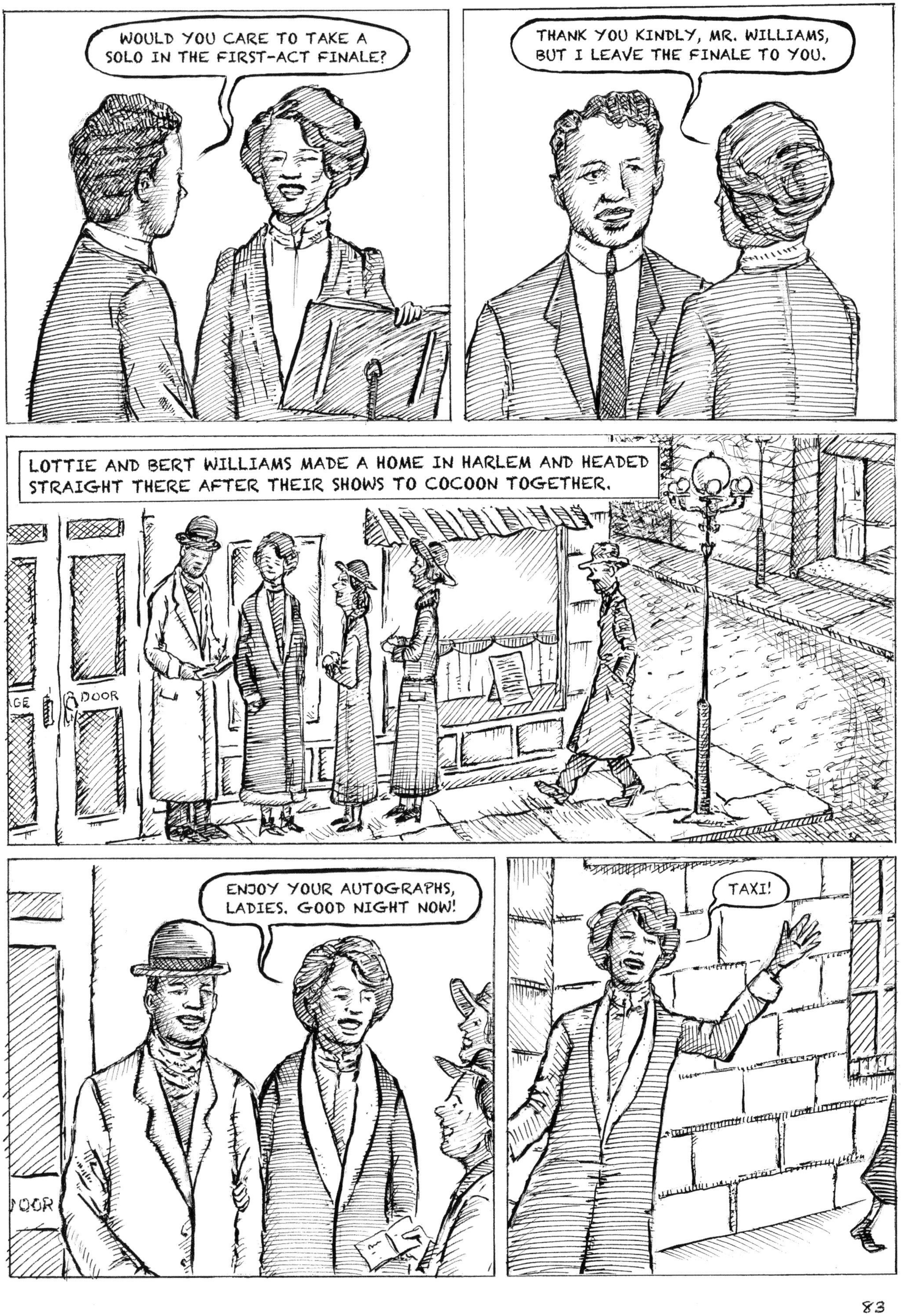
WOULD YOU CARE TO TAKE A SOLO IN THE FIRST-ACT FINALE?
THANK YOU KINDLY, MR. WILLIAMS, BUT I LEAVE THE FINALE TO YOU.
LOTTIE AND BERT WILLIAMS MADE A HOME IN HARLEM AND HEADED STRAIGHT THERE AFTER THEIR SHOWS TO COCOON TOGETHER.
DOOR
ENJOY YOUR AUTOGRAPHS, LADIES. GOOD NIGHT NOW!
TAXI!

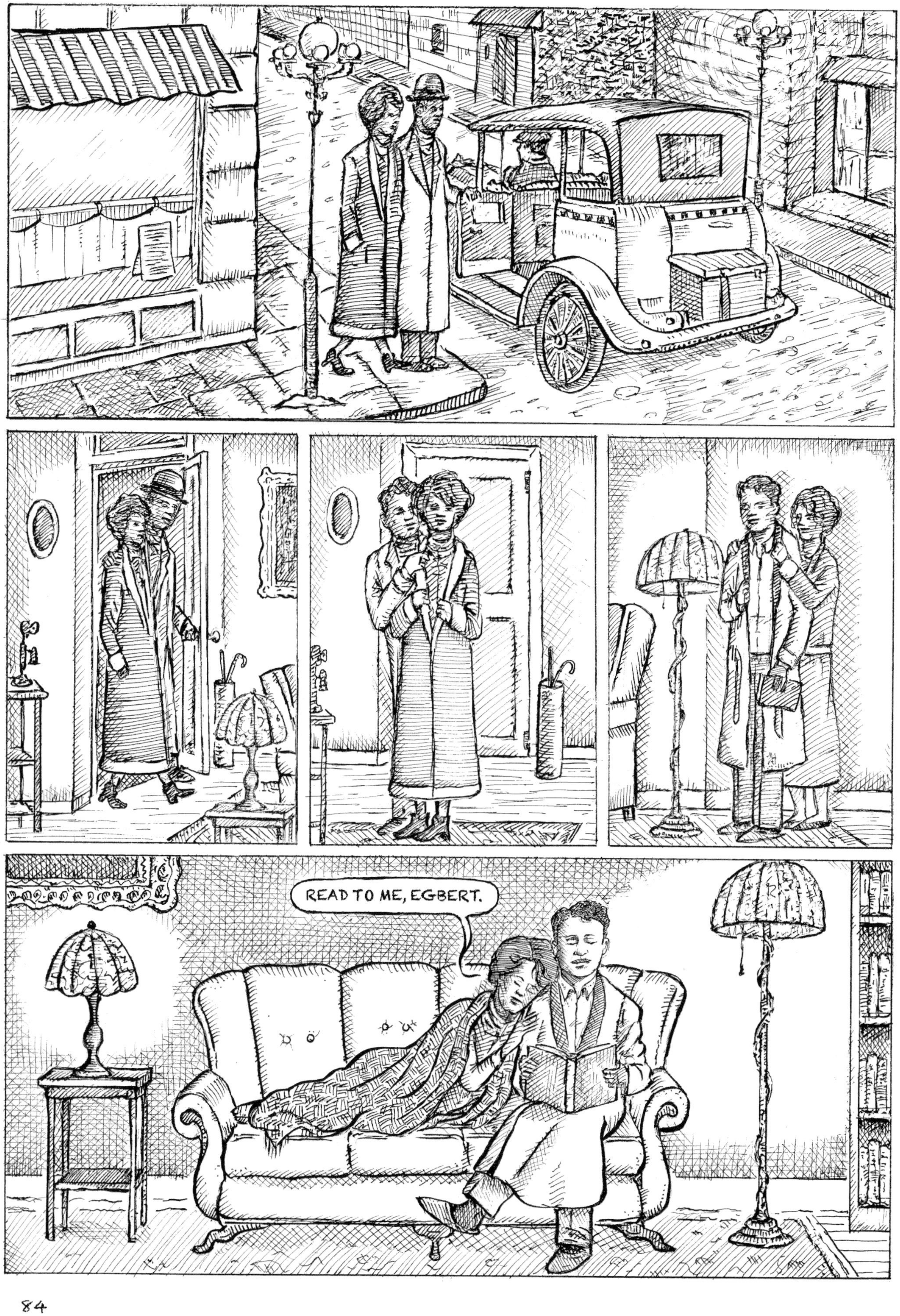
READ TO ME, EGBERT.

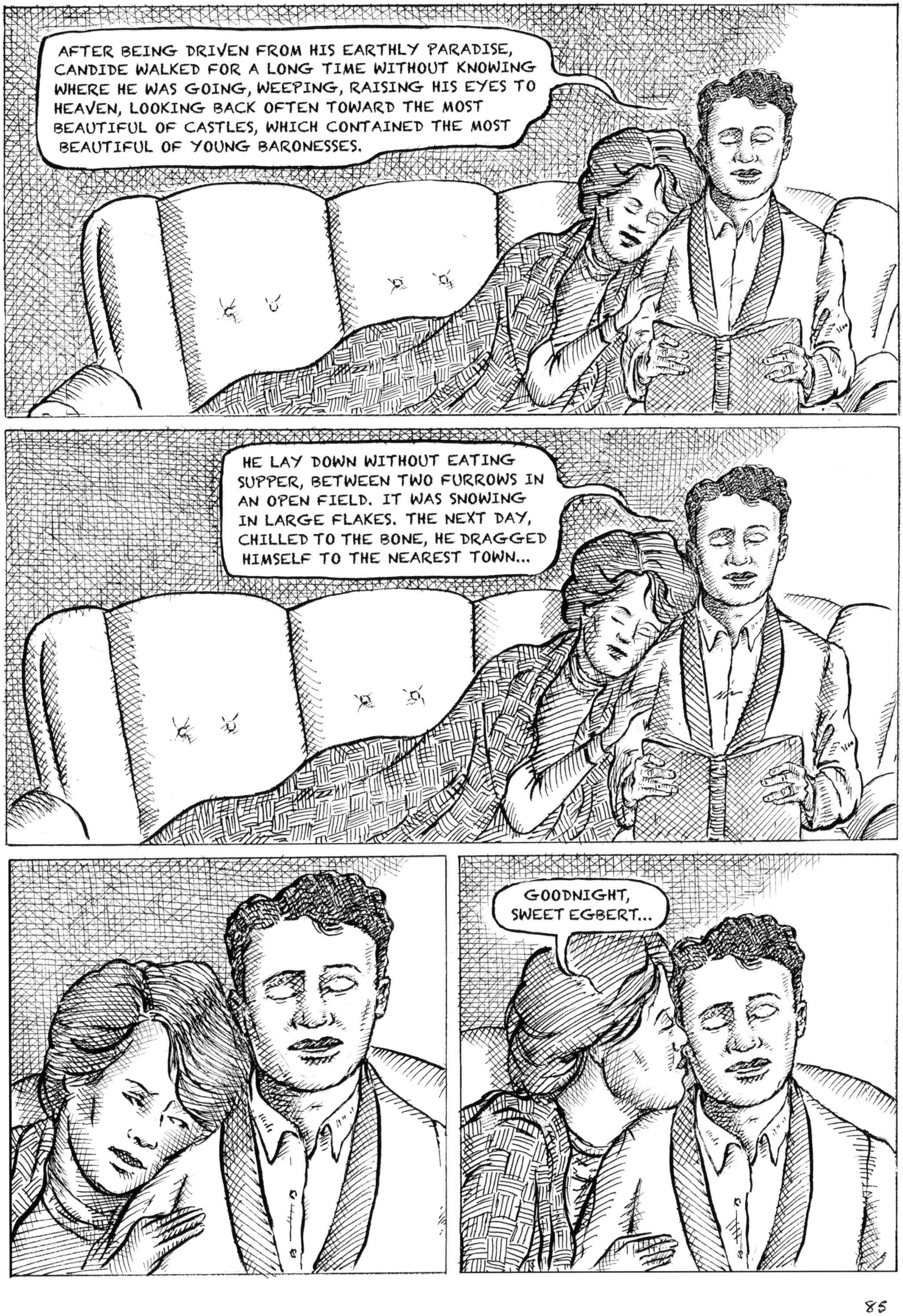
AFTER BEING DRIVEN FROM HIS EARTHLY PARADISE, CANDIDE WALKED FOR A LONG TIME WITHOUT KNOWING WHERE HE WAS GOING, WEEPING, RAISING HIS EYES TO HEAVEN, LOOKING BACK OFTEN TOWARD THE MOST BEAUTIFUL OF CASTLES, WHICH CONTAINED THE MOST BEAUTIFUL OF YOUNG BARONESSES.
HE LAY DOWN WITHOUT EATING SUPPER, BETWEEN TWO FURROWS IN AN OPEN FIELD. IT WAS SNOWING IN LARGE FLAKES. THE NEXT DAY, CHILLED TO THE BONE, HE DRAGGED HIMSELF TO THE NEAREST TOWN...
GOODNIGHT, SWEET EGBERT...

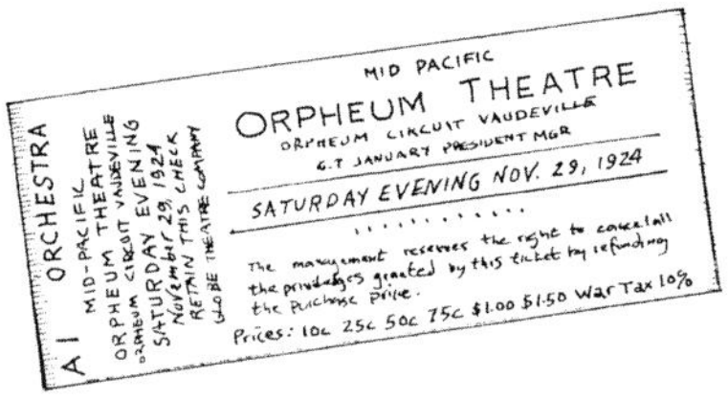
A1 ORCHESTRA
MID-PACIFIC
ORPHEUM THEATRE
ORPHEUM CIRCUIT VAUDEVILLE
SATURDAY EVENING
November 29, 1924
RETAIN THIS CHECK
GLOBE THEATRE COMPANY
MID PACIFIC
ORPHEUM THEATRE
ORPHEUM CIRCUIT VAUDEVILLE
G.T JANUARY PRESIDENT MGR
SATURDAY EVENING NOV. 29, 1924
The management reserves the right to cancel all the privileges granted by this ticket by refunding the purchase price.
Prices: 10c 25c 50c 75c $1.00 $1.50 War Tax 10%

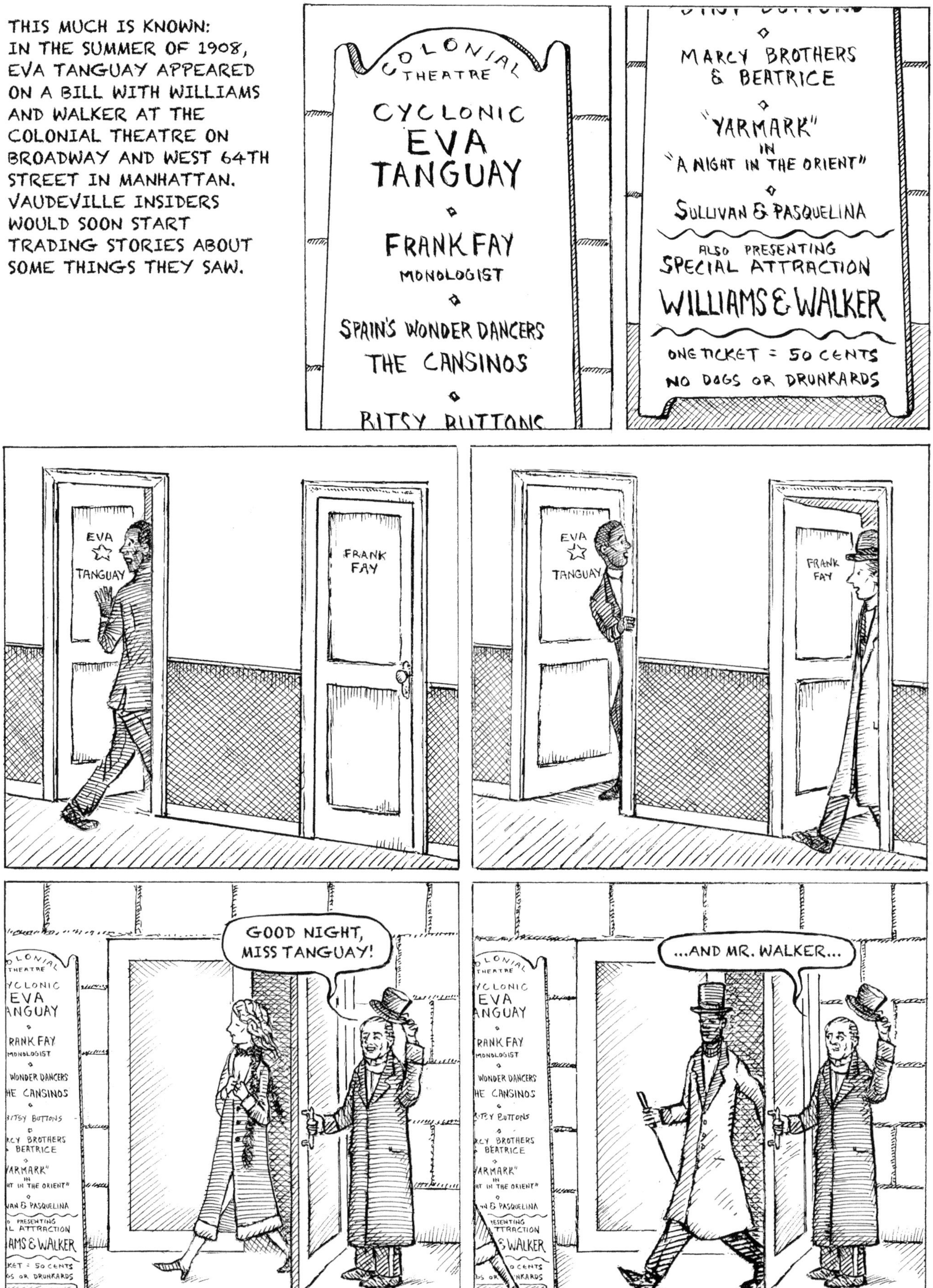
THIS MUCH IS KNOWN: IN THE SUMMER OF 1908, EVA TANGUAY APPEARED ON A BILL WITH WILLIAMS AND WALKER AT THE COLONIAL THEATRE ON BROADWAY AND WEST 64TH STREET IN MANHATTAN. VAUDEVILLE INSIDERS WOULD SOON START TRADING STORIES ABOUT SOME THINGS THEY SAW.
COLONIAL THEATRE
CYCLONIC EVA TANGUAY
FRANK FAY MONOLOGIST
SPAIN'S WONDER DANCERS THE CANSINOS
MARCY BROTHERS & BEATRICE
"YARMARK" IN "A NIGHT IN THE ORIENT"
SULLIVAN & PASQUELINA
ALSO PRESENTING SPECIAL ATTRACTION
WILLIAMS & WALKER
ONE TICKET = 50 CENTS
NO DOGS OR DRUNKARDS
EVA ☆ TANGUAY
FRANK FAY
GOOD NIGHT, MISS TANGUAY!
...AND MR. WALKER...

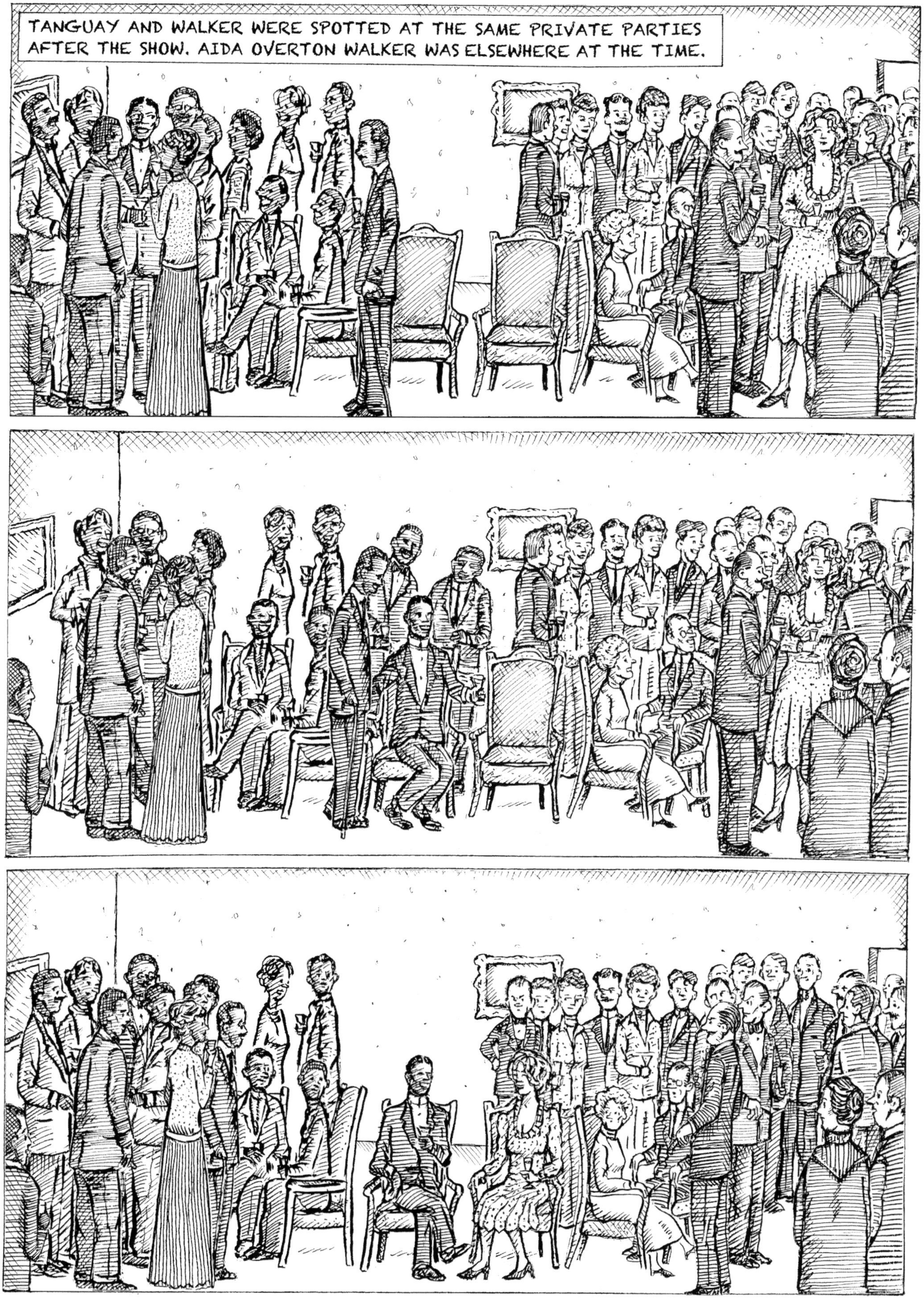
TANGUAY AND WALKER WERE SPOTTED AT THE SAME PRIVATE PARTIES AFTER THE SHOW. AIDA OVERTON WALKER WAS ELSEWHERE AT THE TIME.

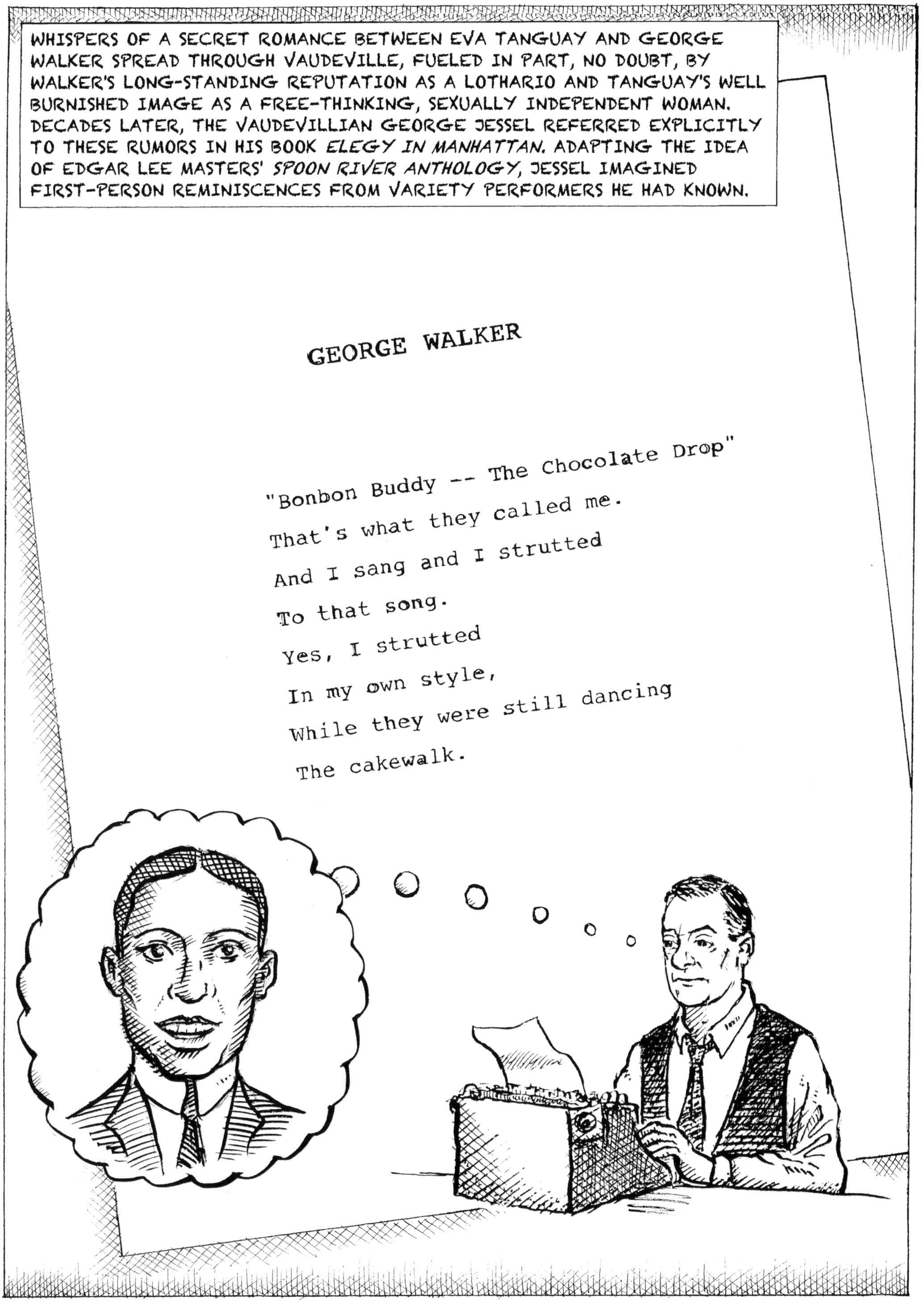
WHISPERS OF A SECRET ROMANCE BETWEEN EVA TANGUAY AND GEORGE WALKER SPREAD THROUGH VAUDEVILLE, FUELED IN PART, NO DOUBT, BY WALKER'S LONG-STANDING REPUTATION AS A LOTHARIO AND TANGUAY'S WELL BURNISHED IMAGE AS A FREE-THINKING, SEXUALLY INDEPENDENT WOMAN. DECADES LATER, THE VAUDEVILLIAN GEORGE JESSEL REFERRED EXPLICITLY TO THESE RUMORS IN HIS BOOK *ELEGY IN MANHATTAN*. ADAPTING THE IDEA OF EDGAR LEE MASTERS' *SPOON RIVER ANTHOLOGY*, JESSEL IMAGINED FIRST-PERSON REMINISCENCES FROM VARIETY PERFORMERS HE HAD KNOWN.
GEORGE WALKER
"Bonbon Buddy -- The Chocolate Drop"
That's what they called me.
And I sang and I strutted
To that song.
Yes, I strutted
In my own style,
While they were still dancing
The cakewalk.

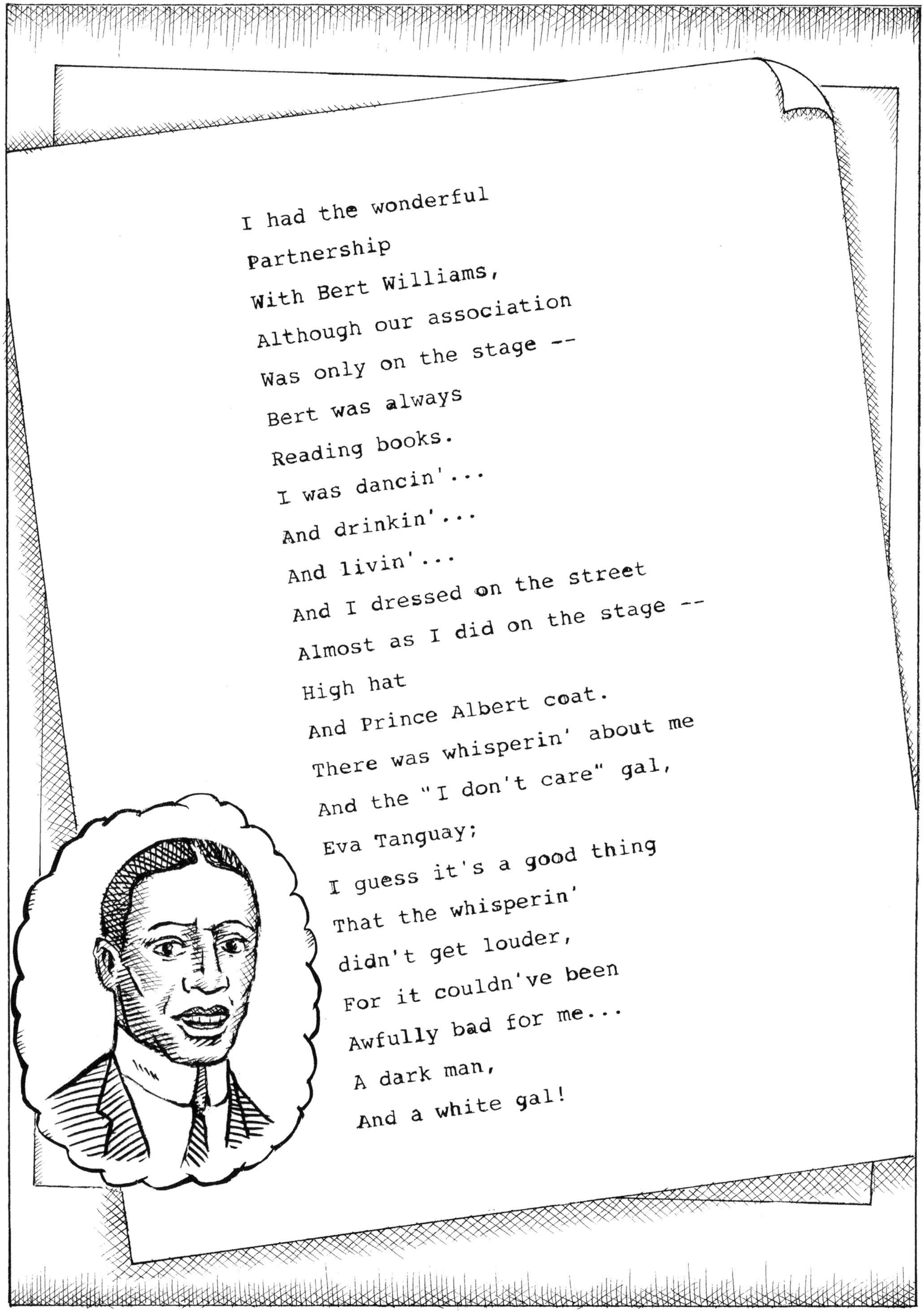
I had the wonderful
Partnership
With Bert Williams,
Although our association
Was only on the stage --
Bert was always
Reading books.
I was dancin'...
And drinkin'...
And livin'...
And I dressed on the street
Almost as I did on the stage --
High hat
And Prince Albert coat.
There was whisperin' about me
And the "I don't care" gal,
Eva Tanguay;
I guess it's a good thing
That the whisperin'
didn't get louder,
For it couldn've been
Awfully bad for me...
A dark man,
And a white gal!

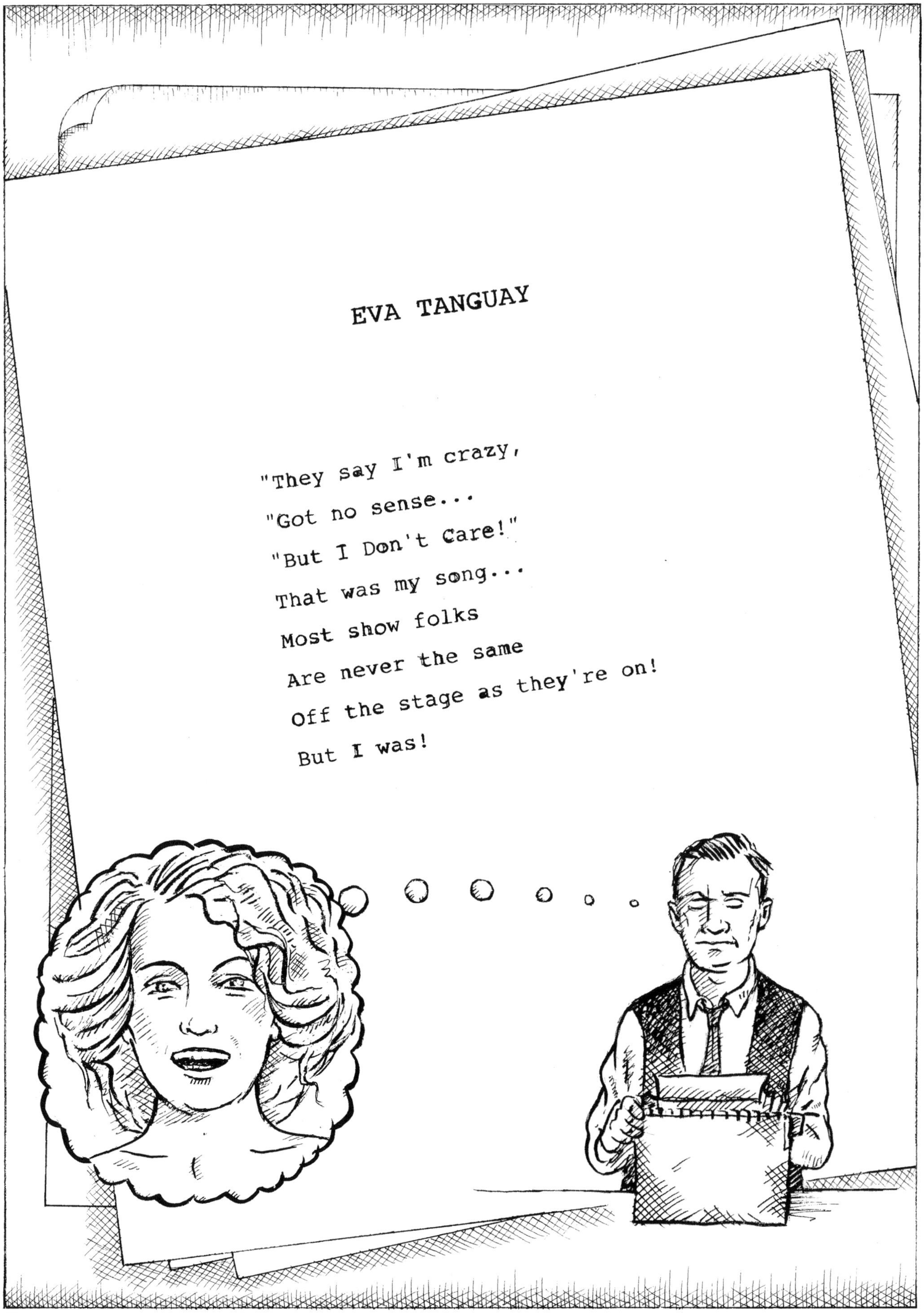
EVA TANGUAY
"They say I'm crazy,
"Got no sense...
"But I Don't Care!"
That was my song...
Most show folks
Are never the same
Off the stage as they're on!
But I was!

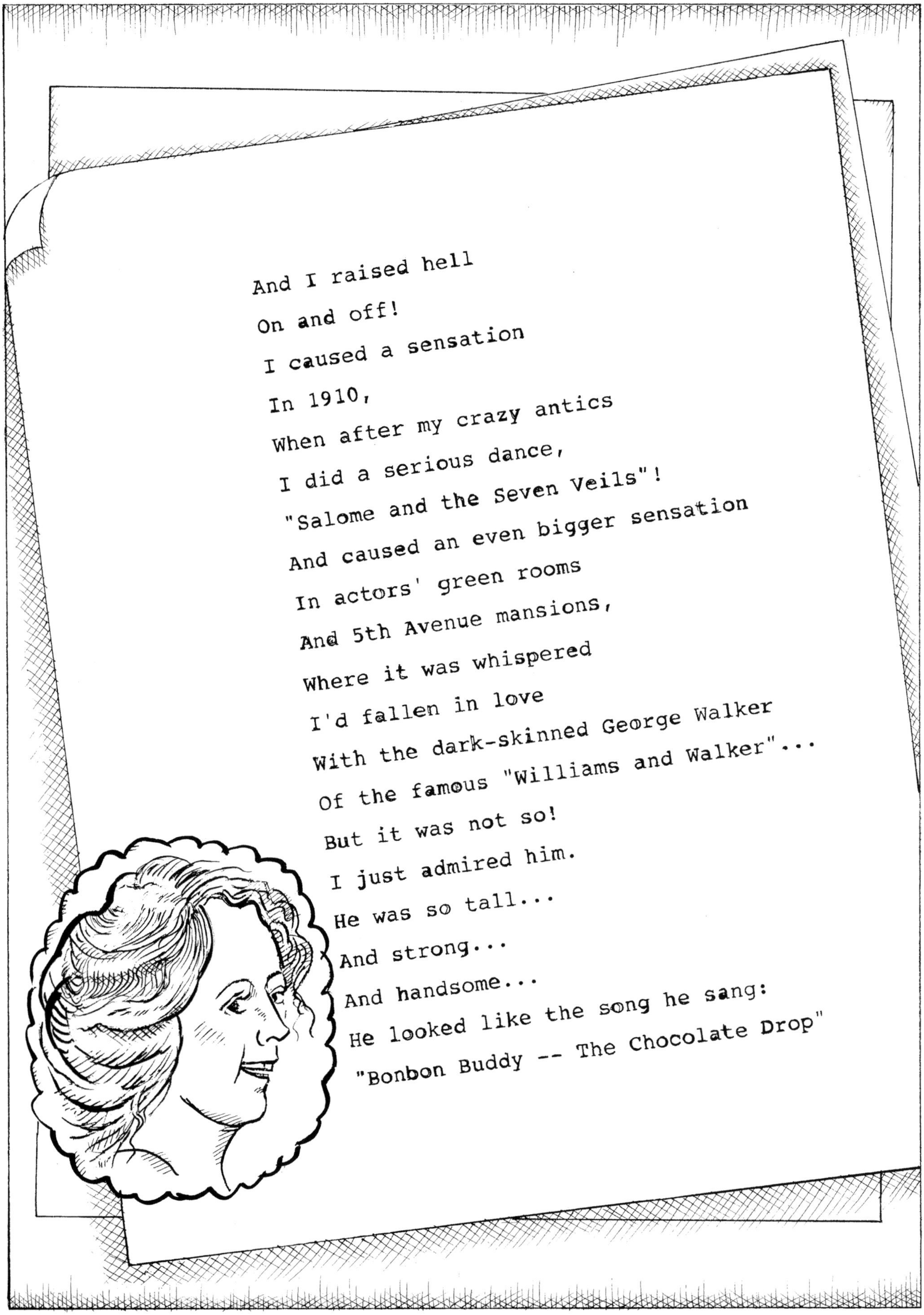
And I raised hell
On and off!
I caused a sensation
In 1910,
When after my crazy antics
I did a serious dance,
"Salome and the Seven Veils"!
And caused an even bigger sensation
In actors' green rooms
And 5th Avenue mansions,
Where it was whispered
I'd fallen in love
With the dark-skinned George Walker
Of the famous "Williams and Walker"...
But it was not so!
I just admired him.
He was so tall...
And strong...
And handsome...
He looked like the song he sang:
"Bonbon Buddy -- The Chocolate Drop"

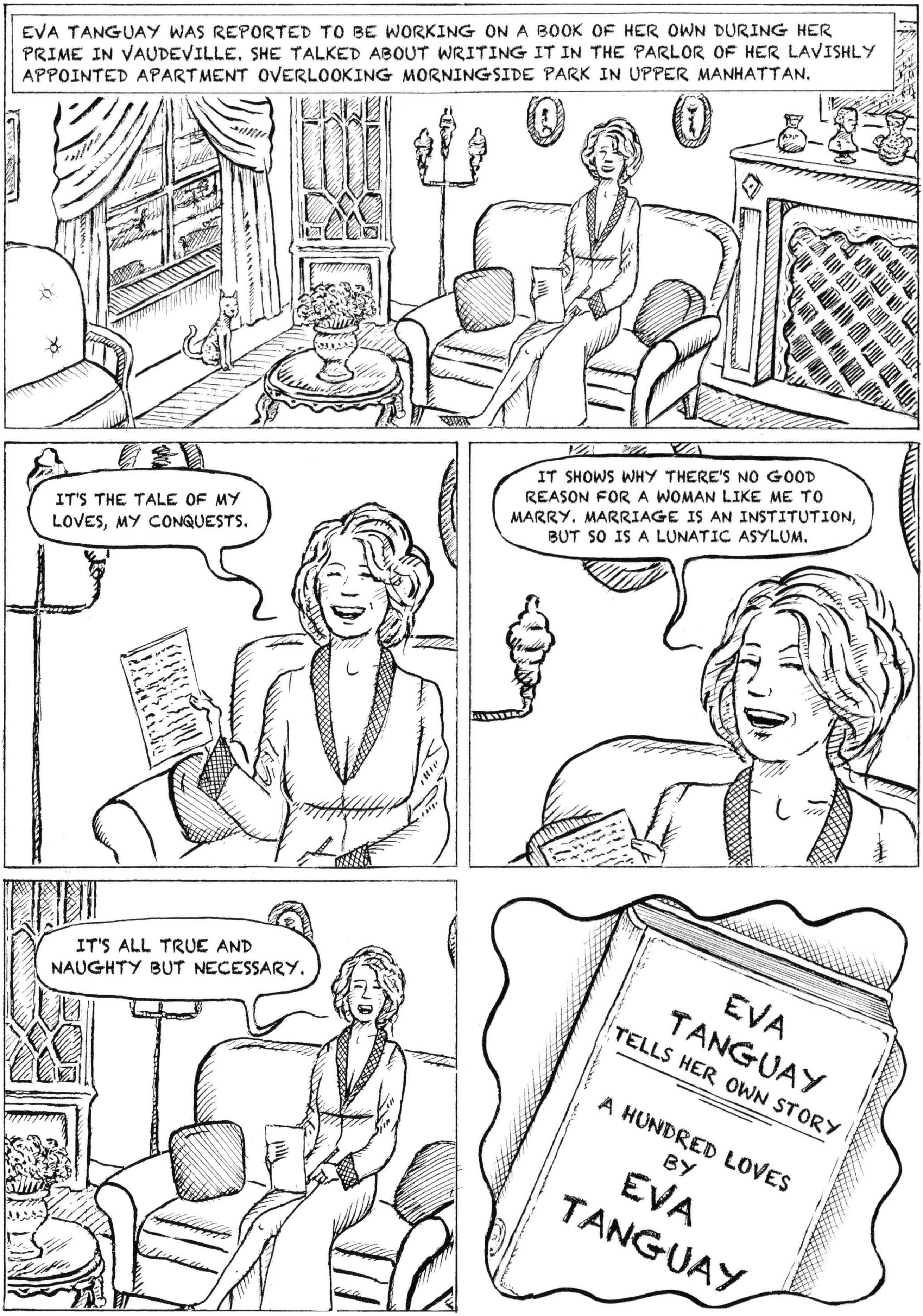
EVA TANGUAY WAS REPORTED TO BE WORKING ON A BOOK OF HER OWN DURING HER PRIME IN VAUDEVILLE. SHE TALKED ABOUT WRITING IT IN THE PARLOR OF HER LAVISHLY APPOINTED APARTMENT OVERLOOKING MORNINGSIDE PARK IN UPPER MANHATTAN.
IT'S THE TALE OF MY LOVES, MY CONQUESTS.
IT SHOWS WHY THERE'S NO GOOD REASON FOR A WOMAN LIKE ME TO MARRY. MARRIAGE IS AN INSTITUTION, BUT SO IS A LUNATIC ASYLUM.
IT'S ALL TRUE AND NAUGHTY BUT NECESSARY.
EVA TANGUAY TELLS HER OWN STORY
A HUNDRED LOVES BY EVA TANGUAY

ALTHOUGH TANGUAY'S BOOK WAS NEVER PUBLISHED (AND PROBABLY NEVER COMPLETED), TO BOAST PUBLICLY OF HAVING A HUNDRED LOVERS WAS ITSELF A RADICAL ACT, AND THE CLAIM WAS CREDIBLE. PAPERS AROUND THE COUNTRY WERE FILLED WITH STORIES OF TANGUAY'S AMOROUS AND CARNAL ADVENTURES.

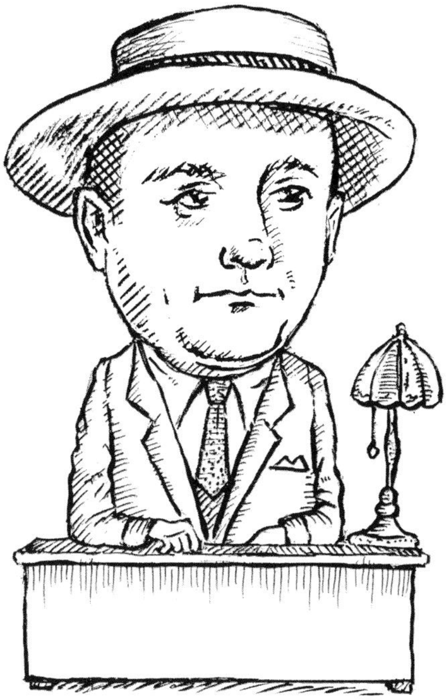

MELVILLE COLLINS

MUSICIAN, SONGWRITER, AND ACTOR IN *THE SAMBO GIRL* WHO WROTE WORDS AND MUSIC FOR SEVERAL TANGUAY SONGS AND CONNECTED WITH HER IN WAYS LOST TO HISTORY. DECADES LATER, AN AUTHOR WHO INTERVIEWED TANGUAY'S NIECES CALLED COLLINS THE "LOVE OF EVA'S LIFE."

ALEXANDER POLLOCK MOORE

PUBLISHER AND OWNER OF THE *PITTSBURGH LEADER* NEWSPAPER, MOORE (LEFT) PURSUED TANGUAY BRIEFLY AND PROPOSED MARRIAGE. WEEKS AFTER TANGUAY DECLINED, HE TRIED TANGUAY'S RIVAL LILLIAN RUSSELL, AND MOORE BECAME RUSSELL'S FOURTH HUSBAND. MOORE WOULD GO ON TO PARLAY HIS INFLUENCE AS A PUBLISHER TO BE NAMED AMBASSADOR TO SPAIN, PERU, AND POLAND.

MEN IN THE LIFE OF EVA TANGUAY

YOUNG LOCAL MILLIONAIRE

IN MARCH OF 1910, TANGUAY FAILED TO APPEAR FOR A PERFORMANCE IN PITTSBURGH. NEWSPAPERS REPORTED THAT SHE HAD LAST BEEN SEEN AROUND MIDNIGHT THE PREVIOUS EVENING, IN THE CAR OF A "YOUNG LOCAL MILLIONAIRE" WITH THE SURNAME MORGAN. WHILE SUCH EVENTS WOULD HAVE BEEN DEVASTATING TO THE CAREER OF MOST OTHER ENTERTAINERS, THEY ONLY ENHANCED TANGUAY'S REPUTATION AS A RADICALLY FREE-SPIRITED WOMAN.

"THE WANDERER"

IN A SYNDICATED EXCERPT OF A MEMOIR-IN-PROGRESS PUBLISHED LATE IN HER LIFE, TANGUAY TOLD A MELODRAMATIC TALE OF BEING LURED INTO A ROMANCE WITH A MYSTERIOUS CON MAN SHE IDENTIFIED ONLY AS "THE WANDERER." HE PILFERED JEWELRY FROM HER MORNINGSIDE HEIGHTS APARTMENT AND TRICKED HER INTO PAYING EXPENSES FOR HIS SECRET GIRLFRIEND, TANGUAY WROTE. THE TALE OF EVA TANGUAY AS A WOEFUL VICTIM STANDS APART FROM HER KNOWN HISTORY WITH MEN.

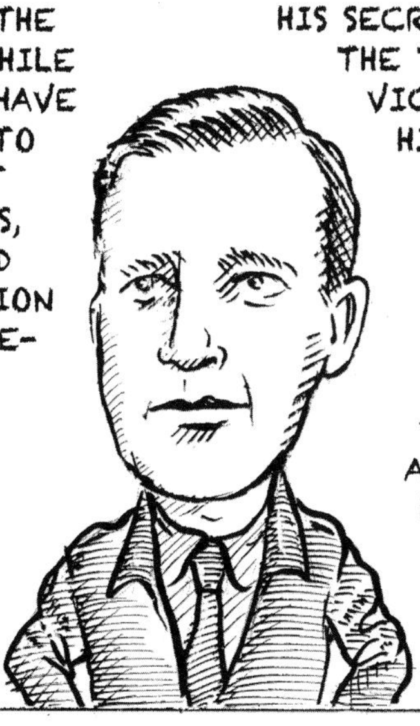

SYLVESTER L. "TONY" VON PHUL

A RECORD-HOLDING BALLOONIST IN THE HEYDAY OF HOT-AIR AVIATION, VON PHUL (LEFT) TOOK TANGUAY ON A BALLOON EXCURSION OUTSIDE ST. LOUIS AND, WHILE IN THE CLOUDS, PROPOSED MARRIAGE. SHE DECLINED BUT CONTINUED BALLOONING WITH OTHERS.

HAVEMEYER, "THE SUGAR KING"

REPORTS FROM HER EARLY CAREER TELL STORIES OF TANGUAY BEING FOLLOWED AROUND THE COUNTRY BY ONE FREDERICK C. HAVEMEYER, HEIR TO THE DOMINO SUGAR FORTUNE. THIS HAVEMEYER, SAID TO BE OVER 70 AND A WIDOWER, GAVE TANGUAY FUR COATS, A $7,000 TIARA, AND $1,000 CASH FOR A SMILE FROM THE STAGE. THE TALE HAS HOLES: FREDERICK C. HAVEMEYER DIED IN 1898, AND HIS SON FREDERICK C. HAVEMEYER JR. WOULD HAVE BEEN IN HIS MID-TWENTIES AT THE TIME OF THE NEWSPAPER ACCOUNTS. ANOTHER HAVEMEYER, HENRY OSBORNE (RIGHT), WOULD HAVE BEEN AROUND 60, BUT MARRIED, AND COULD HAVE BEEN TANGUAY'S SUGAR DADDY.

MR. LEACH

TRAVELING ON TOUR, TANGUAY HAD A TUSSLE WITH THE BRAKEMAN ON A RAIL LINE WHEN A MAN PULLED A HANDGUN ON THE BRAKEMAN IN TANGUAY'S DEFENSE, REFERRING TO TANGUAY AS HIS WIFE. LATER, TANGUAY STAYED IN A HOTEL ROOM BOOKED IN THE NAMES OF "MR. AND MRS. LEACH." THEY WERE NOT MARRIED.

A SAMPLING FROM HER EARLY YEARS

CARL F. ZITTEL

EDITOR OF *ZIT'S THEATRICAL WEEKLY*, WHO INVENTED A SYSTEM OF RANKING VAUDEVILLE POPULARITY, A PRECURSOR TO BOX-OFFICE CHARTS. DETECTIVES HIRED BY HIS WIFE FOUND ZITTEL AND TANGUAY IN A HOTEL SUITE, REGISTERED AS "TANGUAY AND WIFE," AND MRS. ZITTEL NAMED EVA TANGUAY AS CO-RESPONDENT IN HER SUIT FOR DIVORCE.

EDWARD DARLING

RIGHT-HAND MAN TO VAUDEVILLE MOGUL E.F. ALBEE, DARLING HAD AN ON-AND-OFF ROMANCE WITH TANGUAY AND PROPOSED MARRIAGE AT LEAST ONCE. IN ONE NEWSPAPER STORY IN 1909, TANGUAY CLAIMED SHE AND DARLING WERE MARRIED BUT WERE RARELY TOGETHER. "MARRIED PEOPLE MUSTN'T SEE TOO MUCH OF EACH OTHER," SHE SAID. "IT'S A MISTAKE." SOON AFTER, SHE RECANTED THE CLAIM OF THEIR MARRIAGE.

JOHNNY FORD

NOT TO BE CONFUSED WITH THE GREAT FILM DIRECTOR, JOHNNY FORD (LEFT) WAS A CLOG DANCER IN A FAMILY ACT WHO WORKED HIS WAY UP AND INTO TANGUAY'S TOURING COMPANY. THOUGH THEY WERE NOT LINKED ROMANTICALLY FOR LONG, FORD PERSUADED TANGUAY TO MARRY HIM IN A HURRIED CIVIL CEREMONY IN ANN ARBOR IN 1913. THE COUPLE WOULD DIVORCE FOUR YEARS LATER.

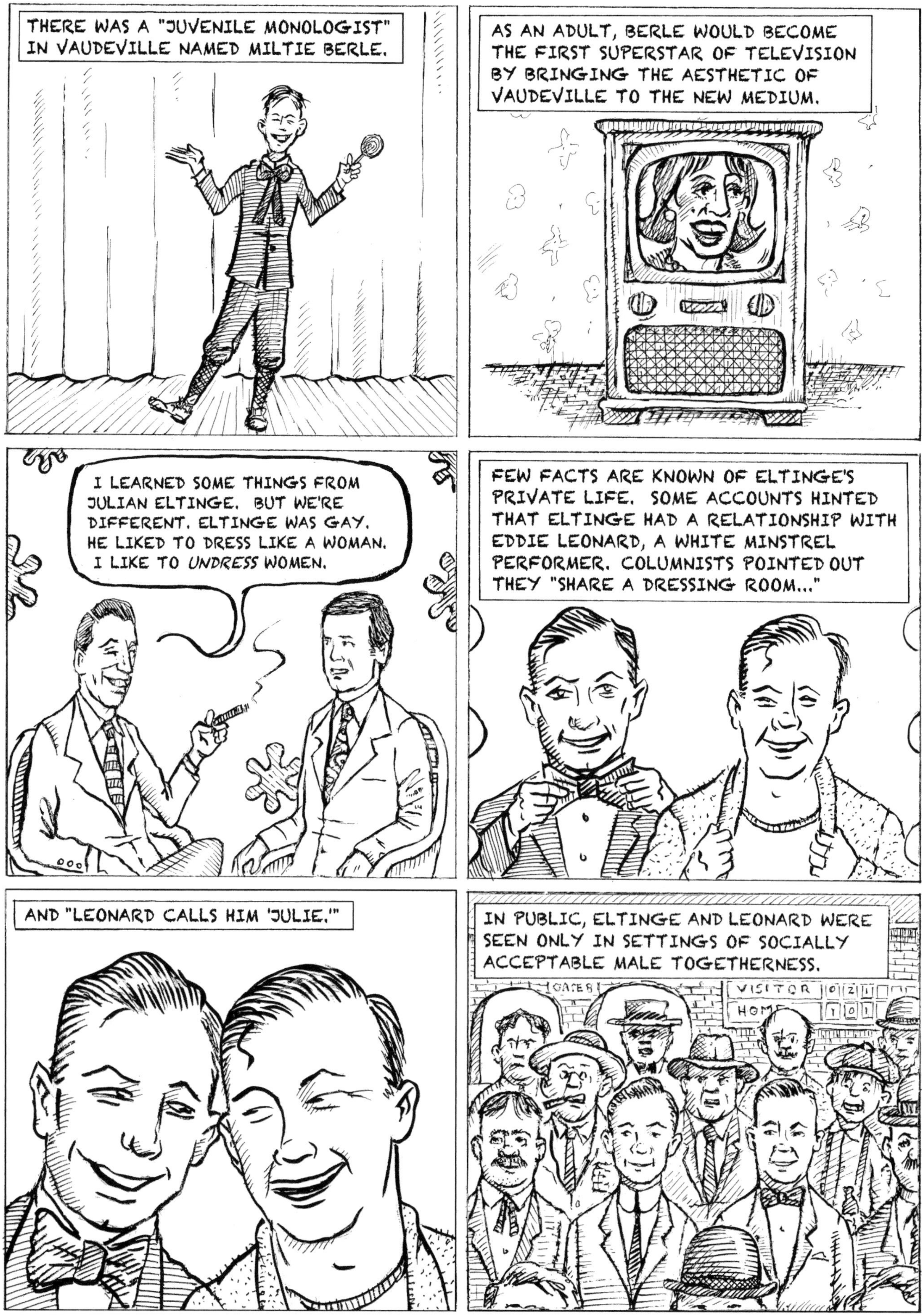
THERE WAS A "JUVENILE MONOLOGIST" IN VAUDEVILLE NAMED MILTIE BERLE.
AS AN ADULT, BERLE WOULD BECOME THE FIRST SUPERSTAR OF TELEVISION BY BRINGING THE AESTHETIC OF VAUDEVILLE TO THE NEW MEDIUM.
I LEARNED SOME THINGS FROM JULIAN ELTINGE. BUT WE'RE DIFFERENT. ELTINGE WAS GAY. HE LIKED TO DRESS LIKE A WOMAN. I LIKE TO *UNDRESS* WOMEN.
FEW FACTS ARE KNOWN OF ELTINGE'S PRIVATE LIFE. SOME ACCOUNTS HINTED THAT ELTINGE HAD A RELATIONSHIP WITH EDDIE LEONARD, A WHITE MINSTREL PERFORMER. COLUMNISTS POINTED OUT THEY "SHARE A DRESSING ROOM..."
AND "LEONARD CALLS HIM 'JULIE.'"
IN PUBLIC, ELTINGE AND LEONARD WERE SEEN ONLY IN SETTINGS OF SOCIALLY ACCEPTABLE MALE TOGETHERNESS.
VISITOR
HOME

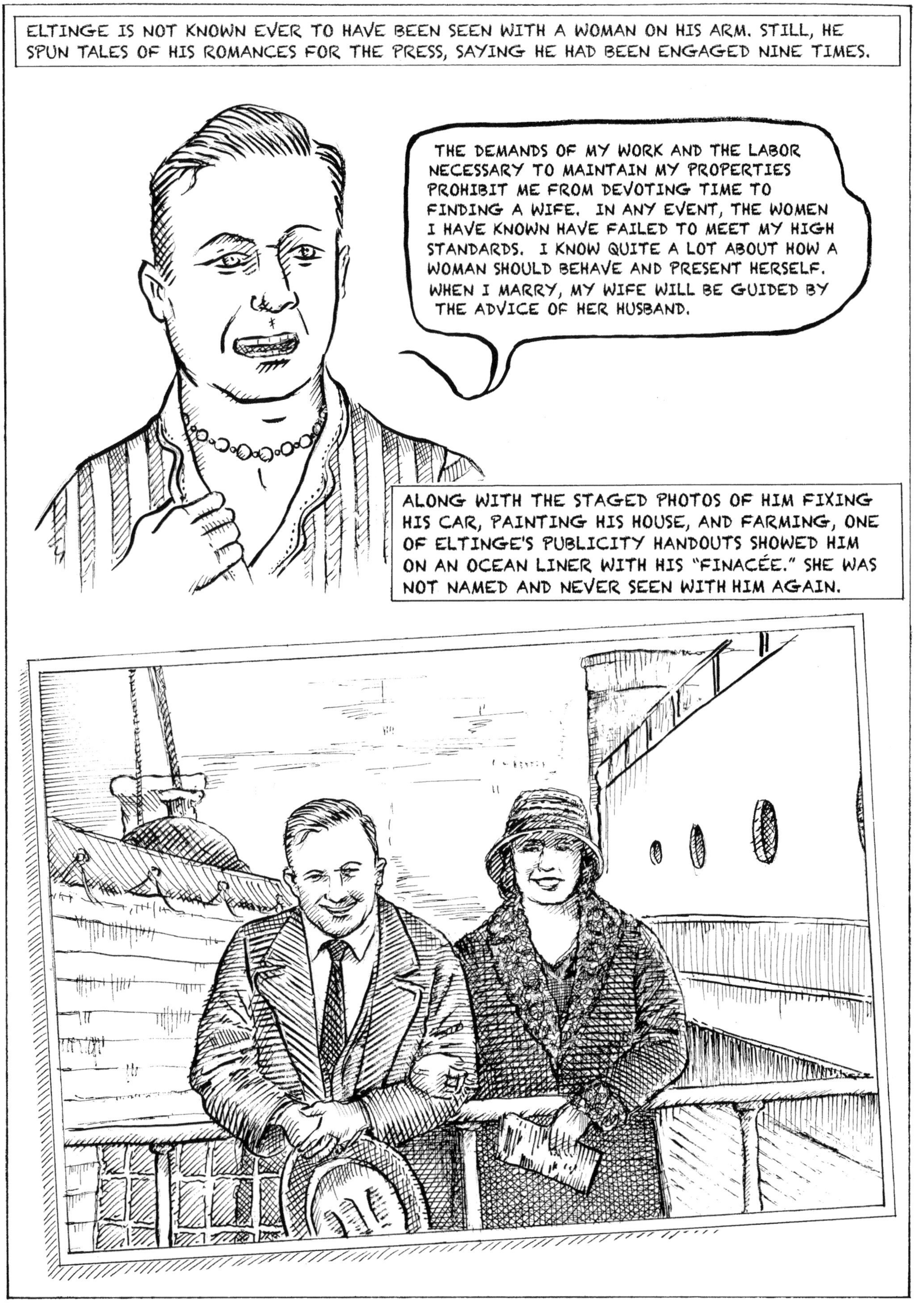
ELTINGE IS NOT KNOWN EVER TO HAVE BEEN SEEN WITH A WOMAN ON HIS ARM. STILL, HE SPUN TALES OF HIS ROMANCES FOR THE PRESS, SAYING HE HAD BEEN ENGAGED NINE TIMES.
THE DEMANDS OF MY WORK AND THE LABOR NECESSARY TO MAINTAIN MY PROPERTIES PROHIBIT ME FROM DEVOTING TIME TO FINDING A WIFE. IN ANY EVENT, THE WOMEN I HAVE KNOWN HAVE FAILED TO MEET MY HIGH STANDARDS. I KNOW QUITE A LOT ABOUT HOW A WOMAN SHOULD BEHAVE AND PRESENT HERSELF. WHEN I MARRY, MY WIFE WILL BE GUIDED BY THE ADVICE OF HER HUSBAND.
ALONG WITH THE STAGED PHOTOS OF HIM FIXING HIS CAR, PAINTING HIS HOUSE, AND FARMING, ONE OF ELTINGE'S PUBLICITY HANDOUTS SHOWED HIM ON AN OCEAN LINER WITH HIS "FINACÉE." SHE WAS NOT NAMED AND NEVER SEEN WITH HIM AGAIN.

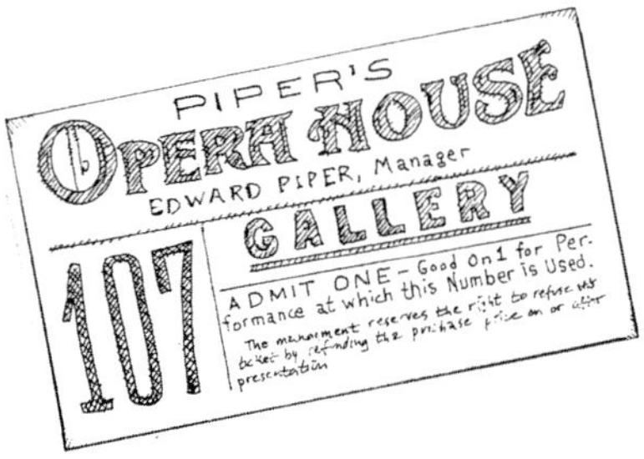
PIPER'S
OPERA HOUSE
EDWARD PIPER, Manager
GALLERY
107
ADMIT ONE – Good On 1 for Per-
formance at which this Number is Used.

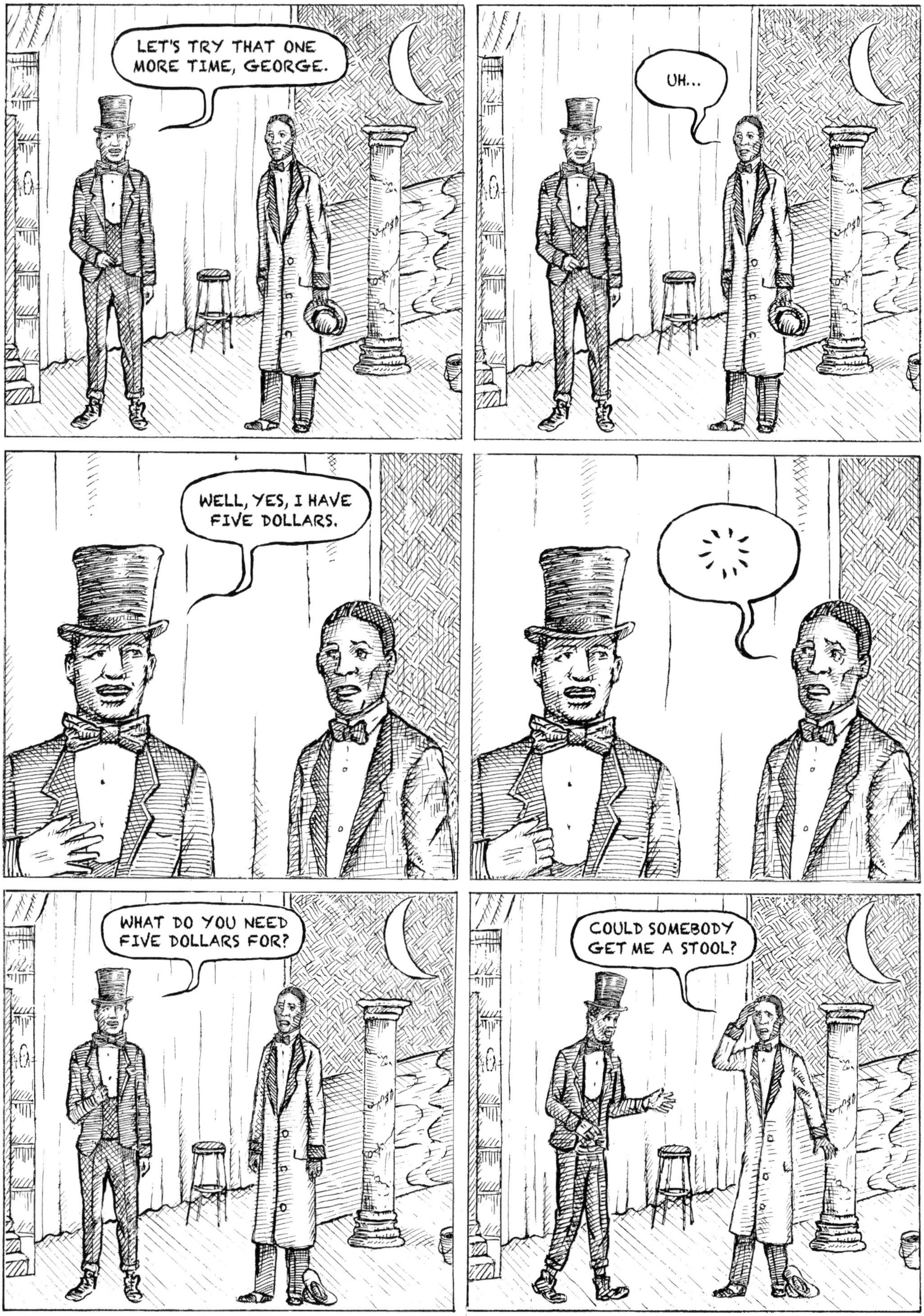
LET'S TRY THAT ONE MORE TIME, GEORGE.
UH...
WELL, YES, I HAVE FIVE DOLLARS.
WHAT DO YOU NEED FIVE DOLLARS FOR?
COULD SOMEBODY GET ME A STOOL?

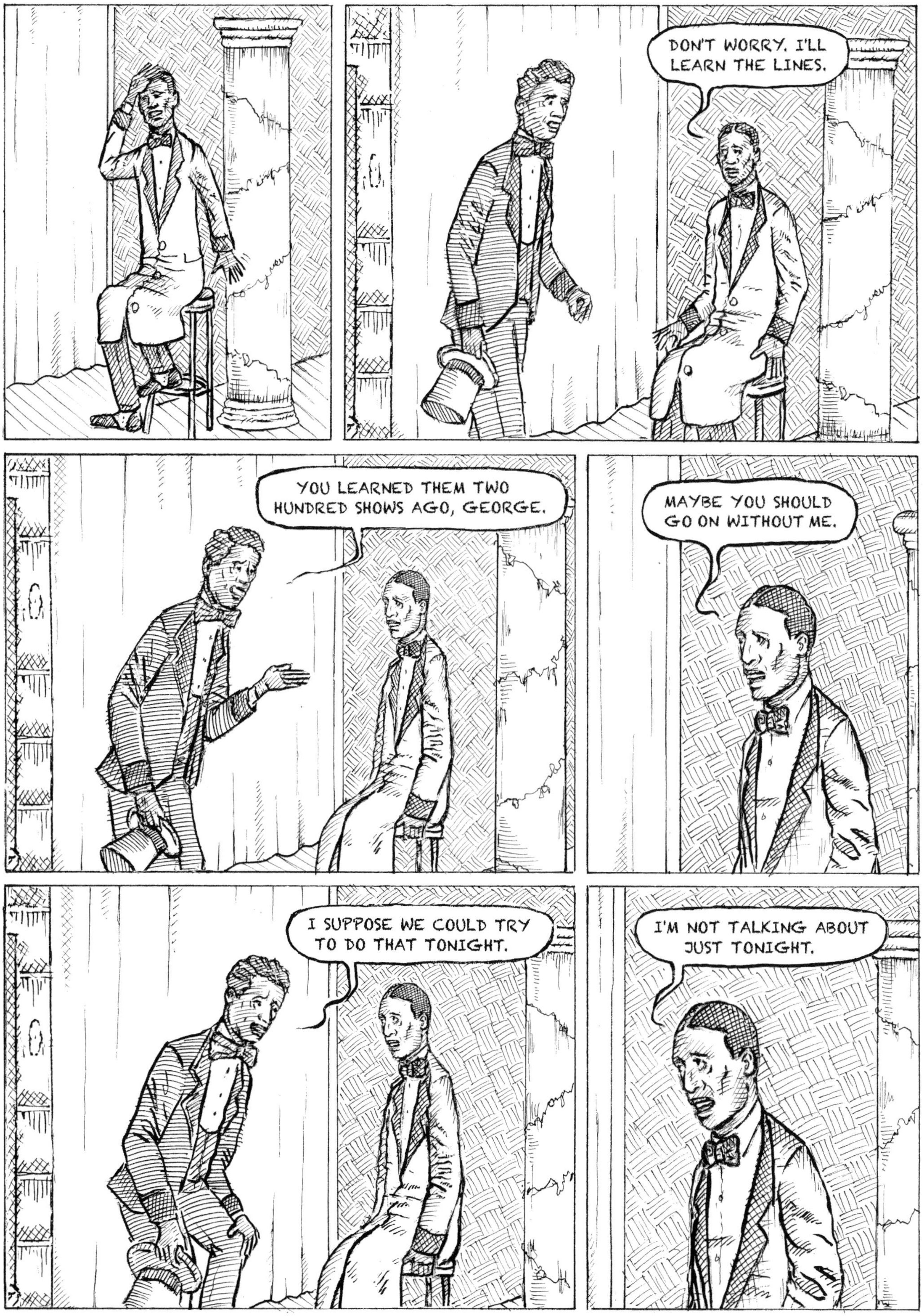
DON'T WORRY. I'LL LEARN THE LINES.
YOU LEARNED THEM TWO HUNDRED SHOWS AGO, GEORGE.
MAYBE YOU SHOULD GO ON WITHOUT ME.
I SUPPOSE WE COULD TRY TO DO THAT TONIGHT.
I'M NOT TALKING ABOUT JUST TONIGHT.

GEORGE WALKER, SUFFERING FROM PROGRESSIVE WEAKNESS AND MEMORY LOSS, WAS DIAGNOSED WITH SYPHILIS AND FORCED TO GIVE UP SHOW BUSINESS. THE WILLIAMS AND WALKER TROUPE CARRIED ON WITHOUT HIM FOR A WHILE, WITH AIDA OVERTON WALKER TAKING ON HER HUSBAND'S PART IN ROUTINES WITH WILLIAMS, DRESSED IN MALE DRAG. GEORGE WALKER DEGENERATED IN THE "STATE ASYLUM" IN ISLIP, LONG ISLAND, WHERE HE DIED ON JANUARY 8, 1911.

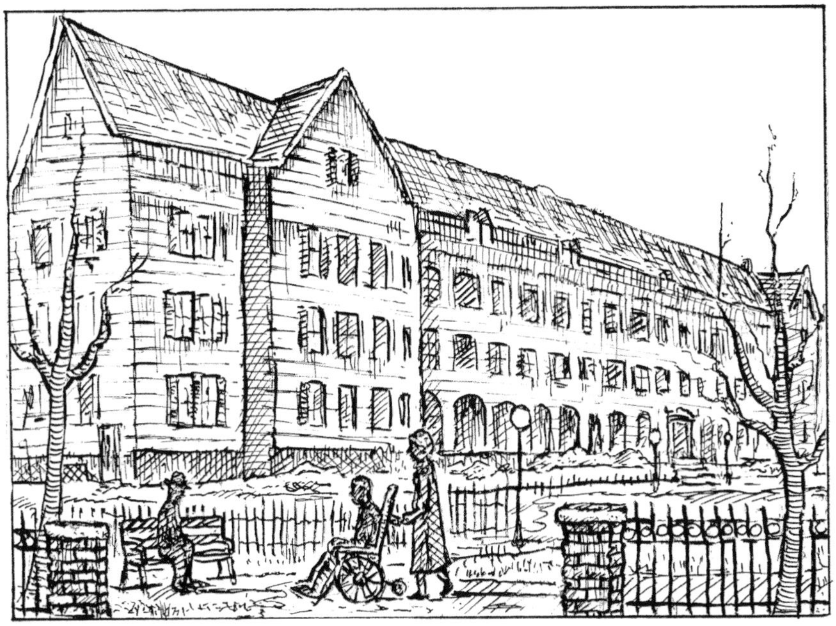

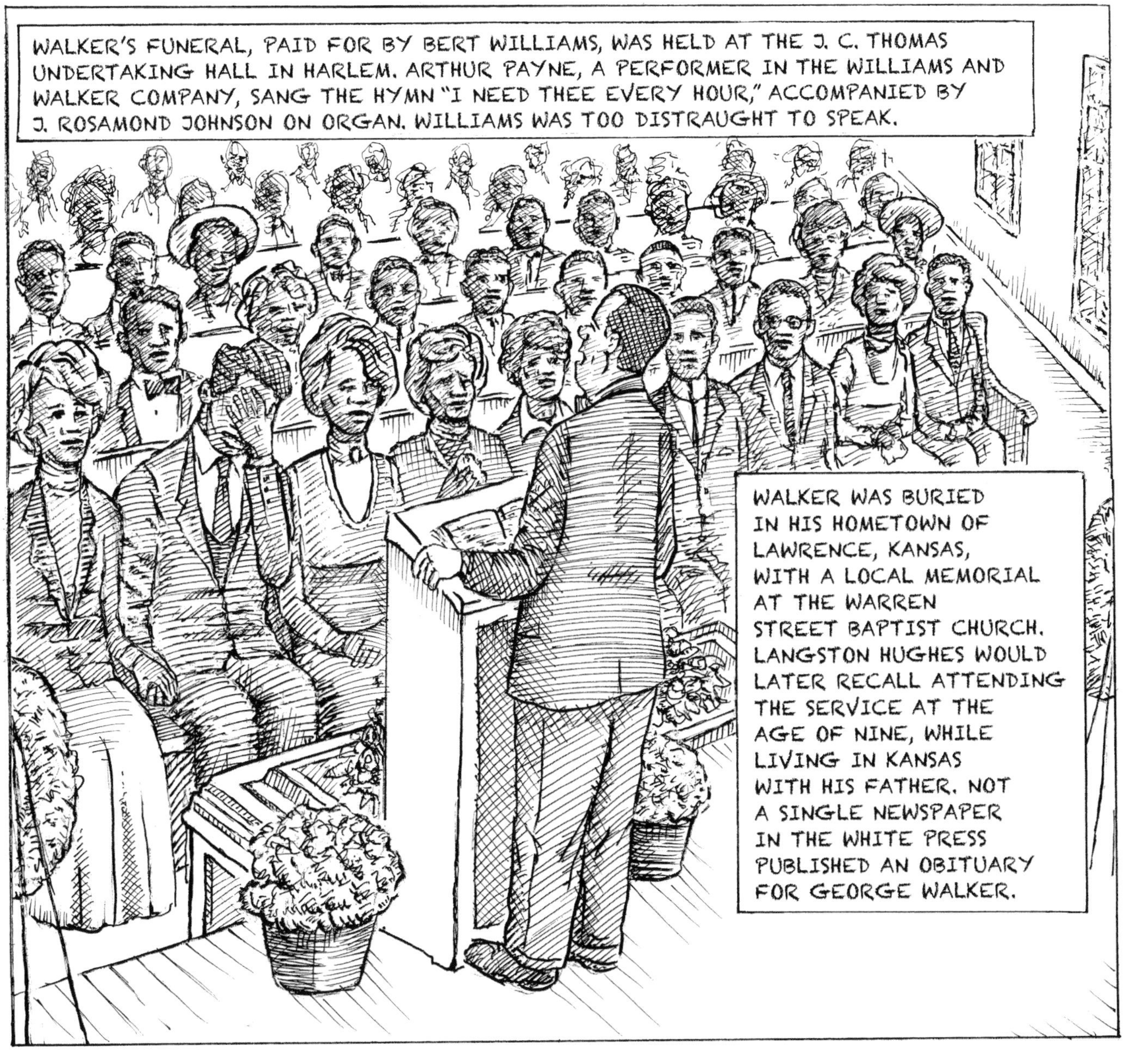
WALKER'S FUNERAL, PAID FOR BY BERT WILLIAMS, WAS HELD AT THE J. C. THOMAS UNDERTAKING HALL IN HARLEM. ARTHUR PAYNE, A PERFORMER IN THE WILLIAMS AND WALKER COMPANY, SANG THE HYMN "I NEED THEE EVERY HOUR," ACCOMPANIED BY J. ROSAMOND JOHNSON ON ORGAN. WILLIAMS WAS TOO DISTRAUGHT TO SPEAK.
WALKER WAS BURIED IN HIS HOMETOWN OF LAWRENCE, KANSAS, WITH A LOCAL MEMORIAL AT THE WARREN STREET BAPTIST CHURCH. LANGSTON HUGHES WOULD LATER RECALL ATTENDING THE SERVICE AT THE AGE OF NINE, WHILE LIVING IN KANSAS WITH HIS FATHER. NOT A SINGLE NEWSPAPER IN THE WHITE PRESS PUBLISHED AN OBITUARY FOR GEORGE WALKER.

BERT WILLIAMS WORKED UP A SOLO ACT, ABANDONING THE BROAD "COON" HUMOR OF THE WILLIAMS AND WALKER SHOWS IN FAVOR OF NUANCED PANTOMIME AND GENTLE STORYTELLING. OFFSTAGE, HE GREW EVER MORE RECLUSIVE, RARELY SEEN OUTSIDE HIS HOME.

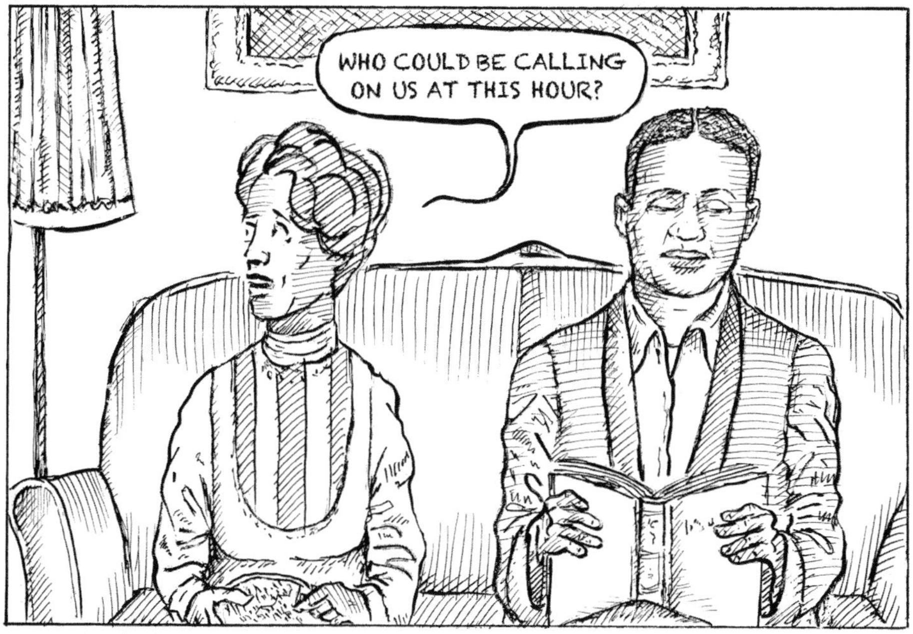
WHO COULD BE CALLING ON US AT THIS HOUR?

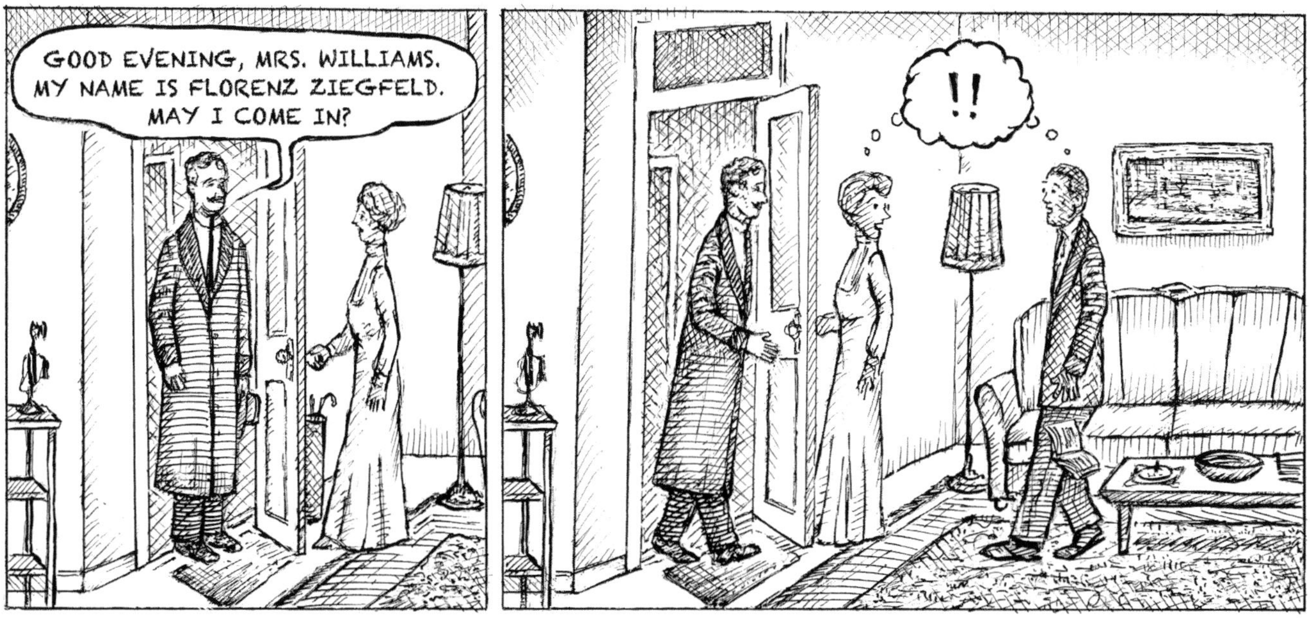
GOOD EVENING, MRS. WILLIAMS. MY NAME IS FLORENZ ZIEGFELD. MAY I COME IN?
!!

NOT LONG AFTER HE WENT SOLO, BERT WILLIAMS BECAME THE FIRST BLACK ARTIST SIGNED TO STAR IN THE PREMIERE ATTRACTION IN VARIETY ENTERTAINMENT, THE ZIEGFELD FOLLIES. WILLIAMS INSISTED THAT HIS CONTRACT PROHIBIT HIM FROM APPEARING ONSTAGE WITH THE NEARLY NUDE WHITE "FOLLIES GIRLS." HE WAS ATTUNED TO THE BENEFITS, AS WELL AS THE DANGERS, THE FOLLIES OFFERED HIM.

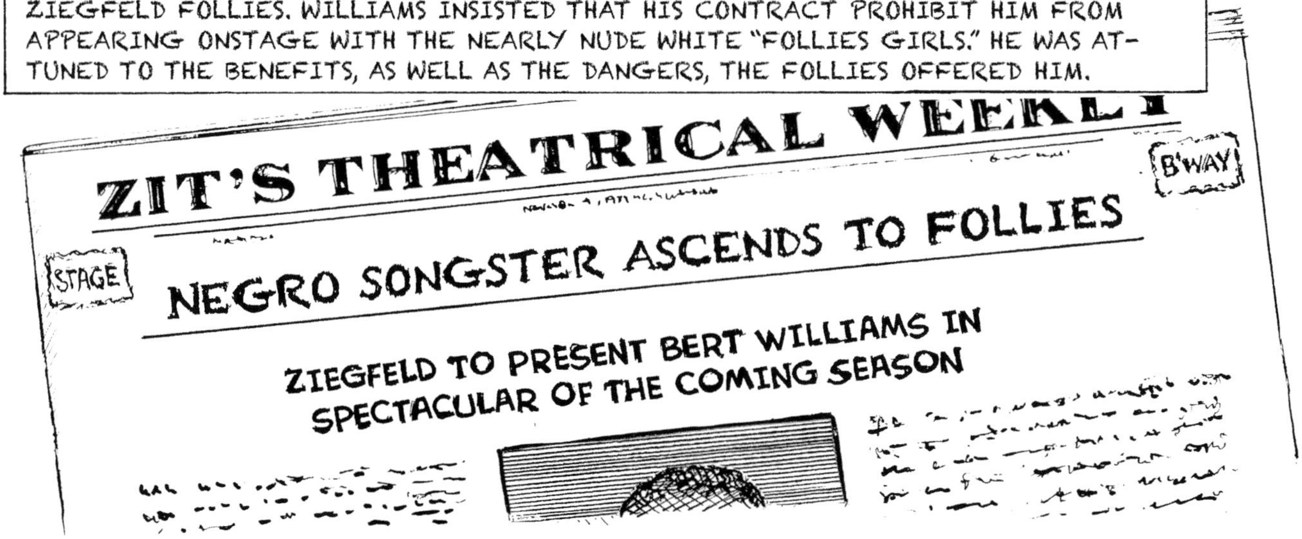
ZIT'S THEATRICAL WEEKLY
B'WAY
STAGE
NEGRO SONGSTER ASCENDS TO FOLLIES
ZIEGFELD TO PRESENT BERT WILLIAMS IN SPECTACULAR OF THE COMING SEASON

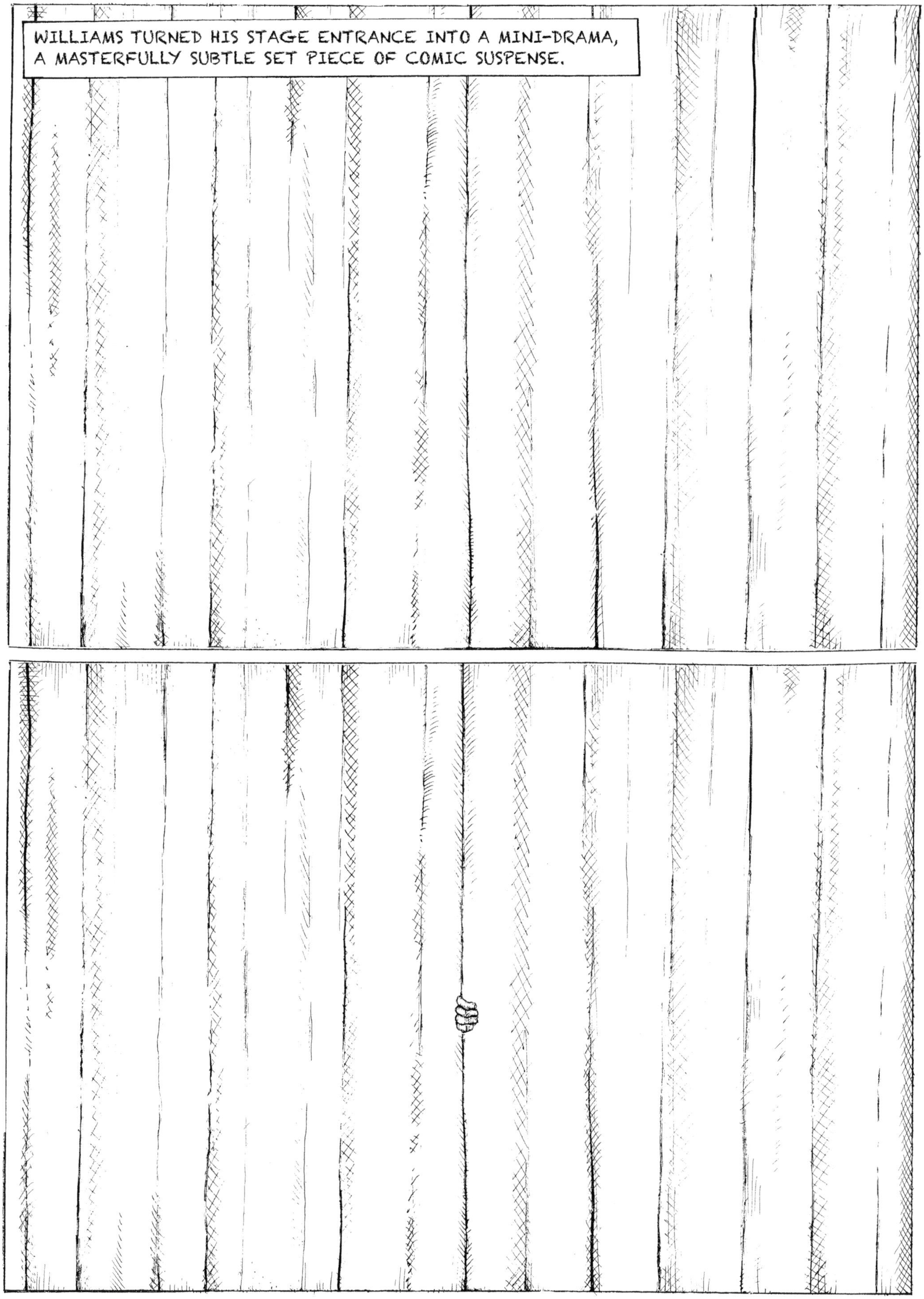
WILLIAMS TURNED HIS STAGE ENTRANCE INTO A MINI-DRAMA, A MASTERFULLY SUBTLE SET PIECE OF COMIC SUSPENSE.

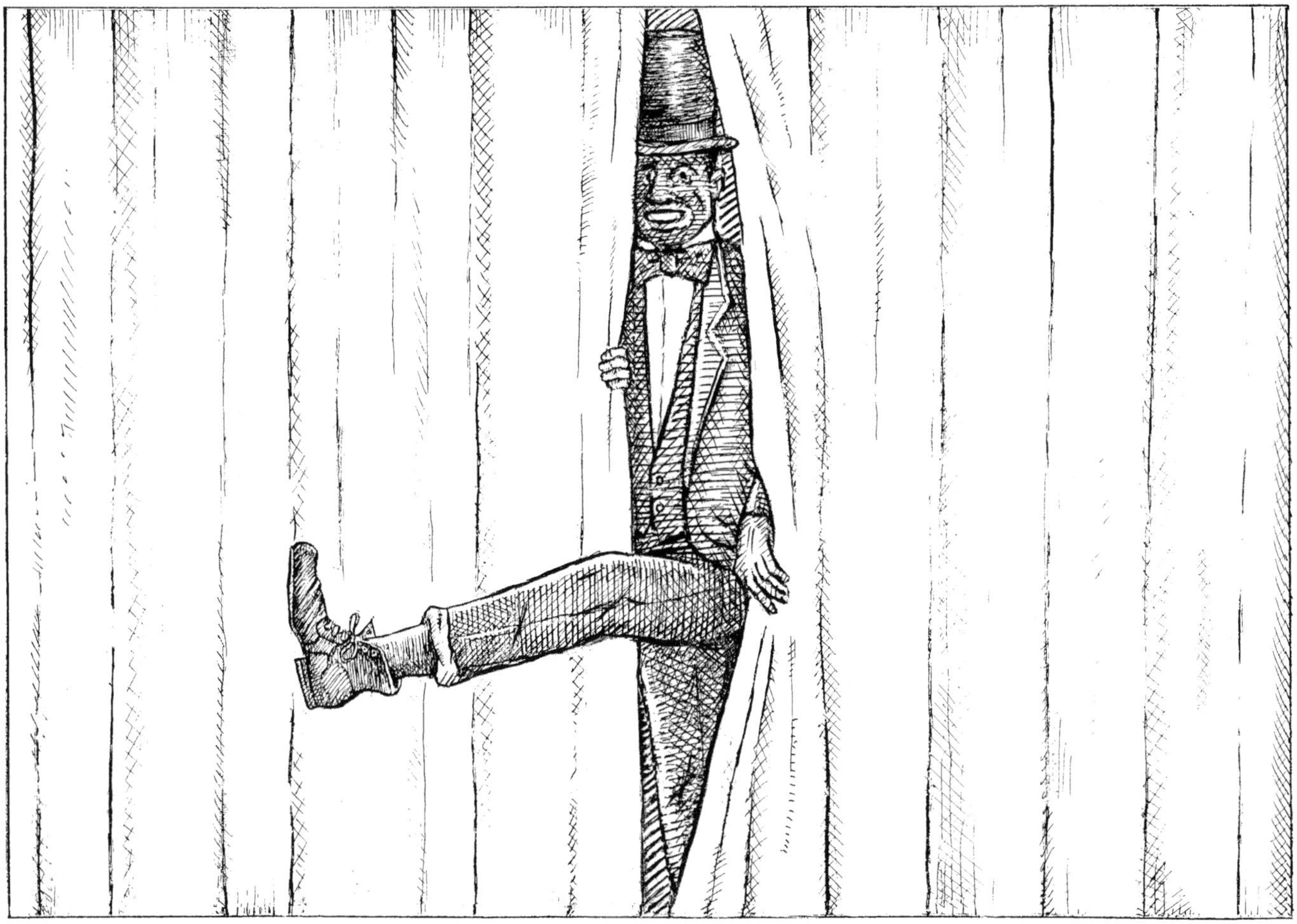

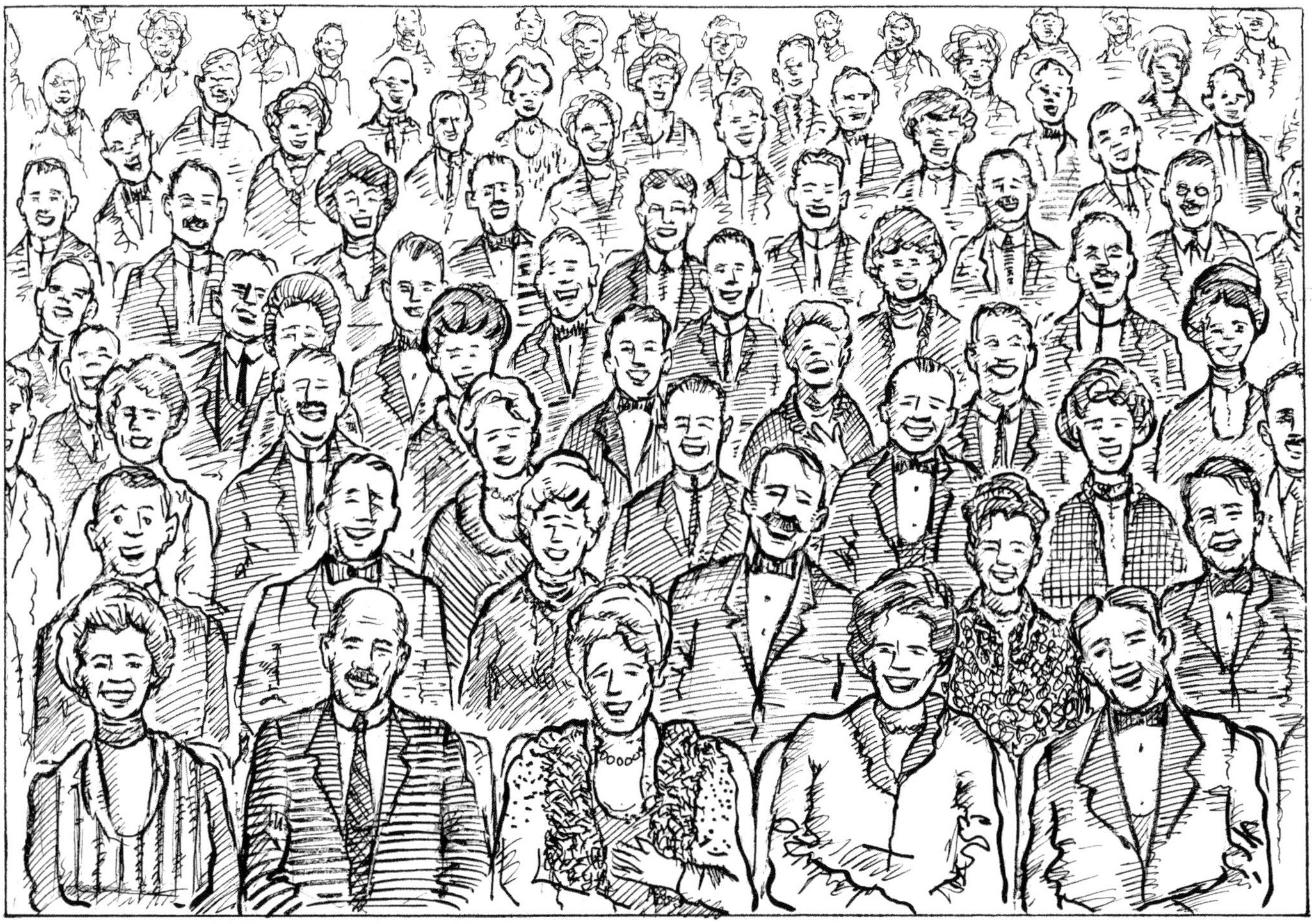

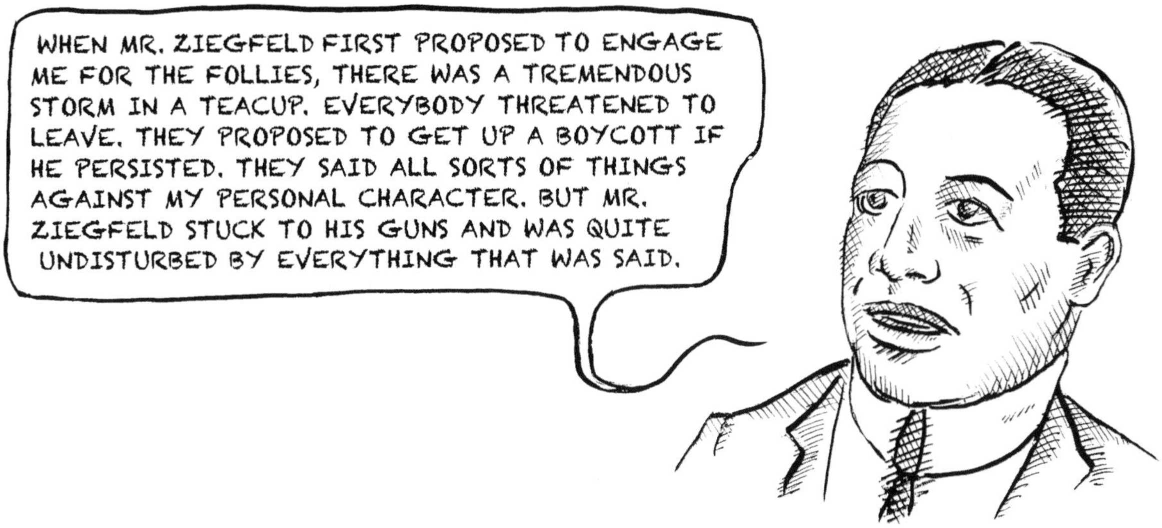
WHEN MR. ZIEGFELD FIRST PROPOSED TO ENGAGE ME FOR THE FOLLIES, THERE WAS A TREMENDOUS STORM IN A TEACUP. EVERYBODY THREATENED TO LEAVE. THEY PROPOSED TO GET UP A BOYCOTT IF HE PERSISTED. THEY SAID ALL SORTS OF THINGS AGAINST MY PERSONAL CHARACTER. BUT MR. ZIEGFELD STUCK TO HIS GUNS AND WAS QUITE UNDISTURBED BY EVERYTHING THAT WAS SAID.

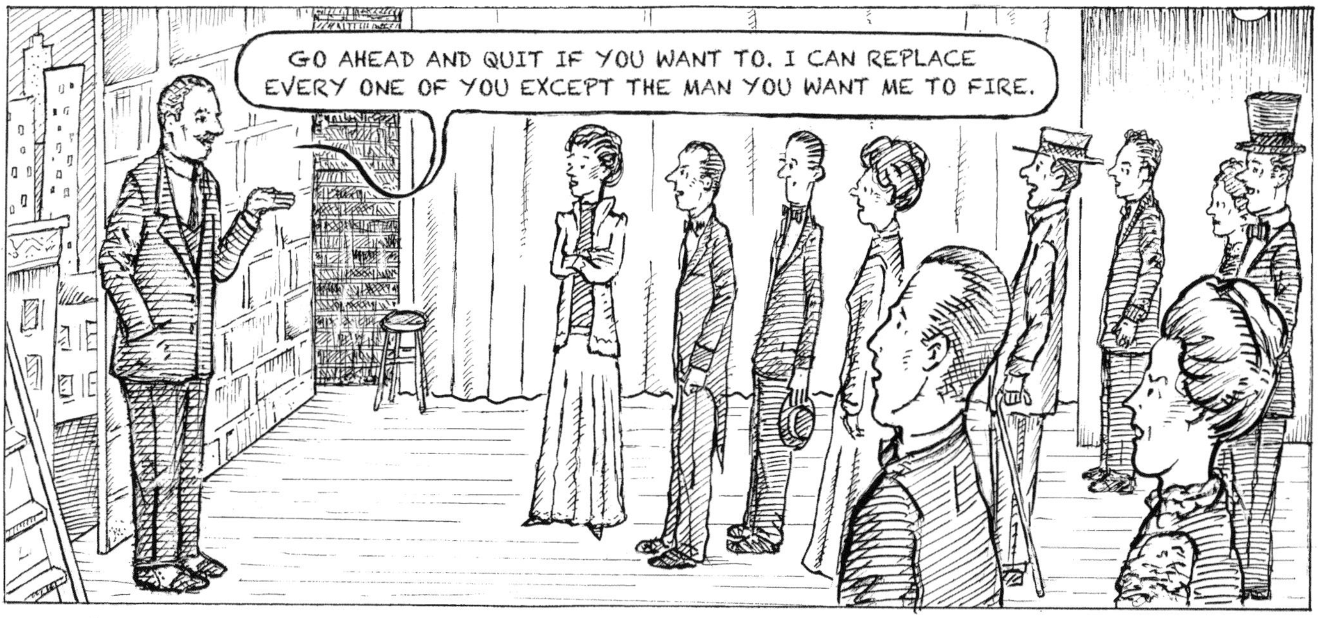
GO AHEAD AND QUIT IF YOU WANT TO. I CAN REPLACE EVERY ONE OF YOU EXCEPT THE MAN YOU WANT ME TO FIRE.

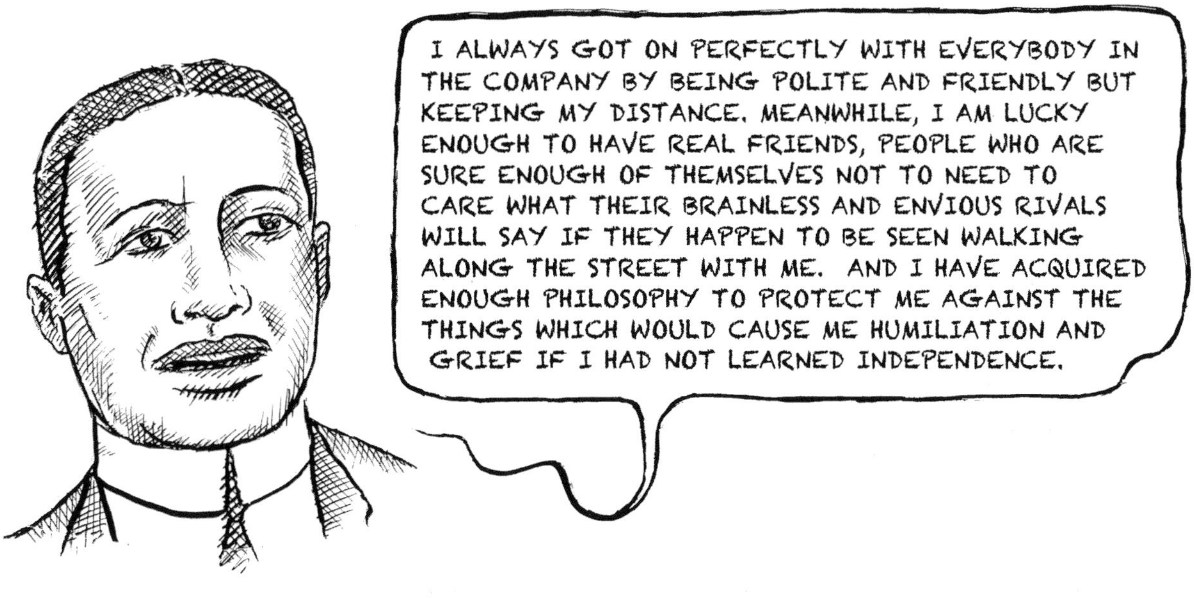
I ALWAYS GOT ON PERFECTLY WITH EVERYBODY IN THE COMPANY BY BEING POLITE AND FRIENDLY BUT KEEPING MY DISTANCE. MEANWHILE, I AM LUCKY ENOUGH TO HAVE REAL FRIENDS, PEOPLE WHO ARE SURE ENOUGH OF THEMSELVES NOT TO NEED TO CARE WHAT THEIR BRAINLESS AND ENVIOUS RIVALS WILL SAY IF THEY HAPPEN TO BE SEEN WALKING ALONG THE STREET WITH ME. AND I HAVE ACQUIRED ENOUGH PHILOSOPHY TO PROTECT ME AGAINST THE THINGS WHICH WOULD CAUSE ME HUMILIATION AND GRIEF IF I HAD NOT LEARNED INDEPENDENCE.

WILLIAMS PERFORMED ALONE ONSTAGE, BANNED FROM ENSEMBLE NUMBERS WITH THE OTHERWISE ALL-WHITE CAST OF THE FOLLIES. IN ONE EXCEPTION, A YOUNG COMEDIAN, EDDIE CANTOR, JOINED WILLIAMS FOR A FATHER-AND-SON ROUTINE. BOTH WORE BLACKFACE. OFFSTAGE, CANTOR AND WILLIAMS SOMETIMES SOCIALIZED, WITH COMPLICATIONS CANTOR AND OTHERS WOULD LATER RECALL.

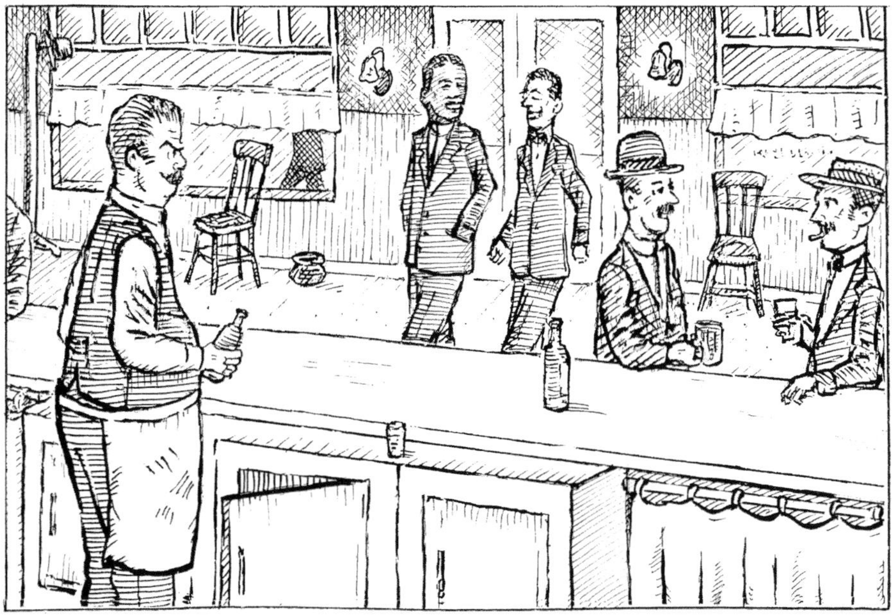

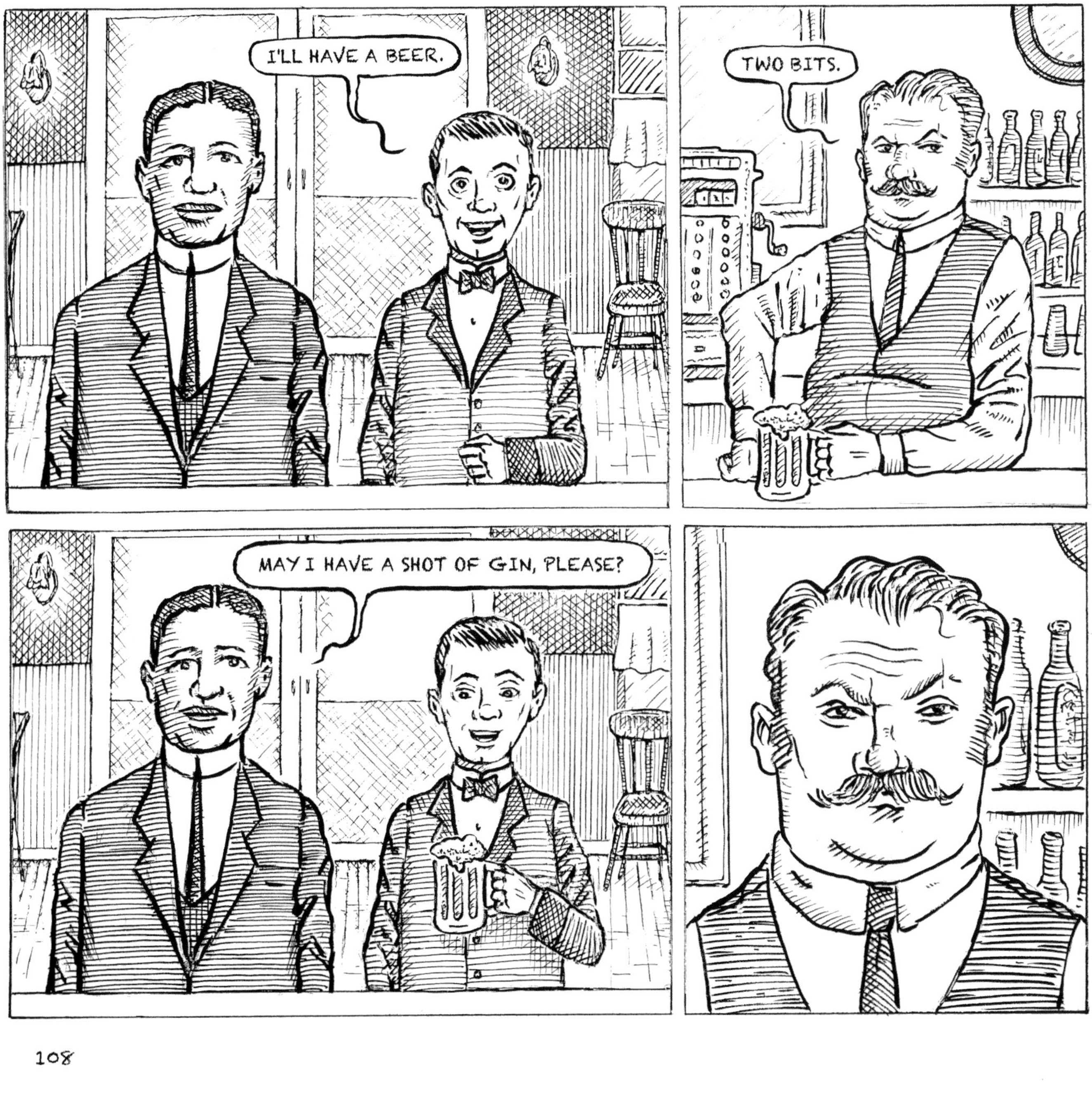
I'LL HAVE A BEER.
TWO BITS.
MAY I HAVE A SHOT OF GIN, PLEASE?

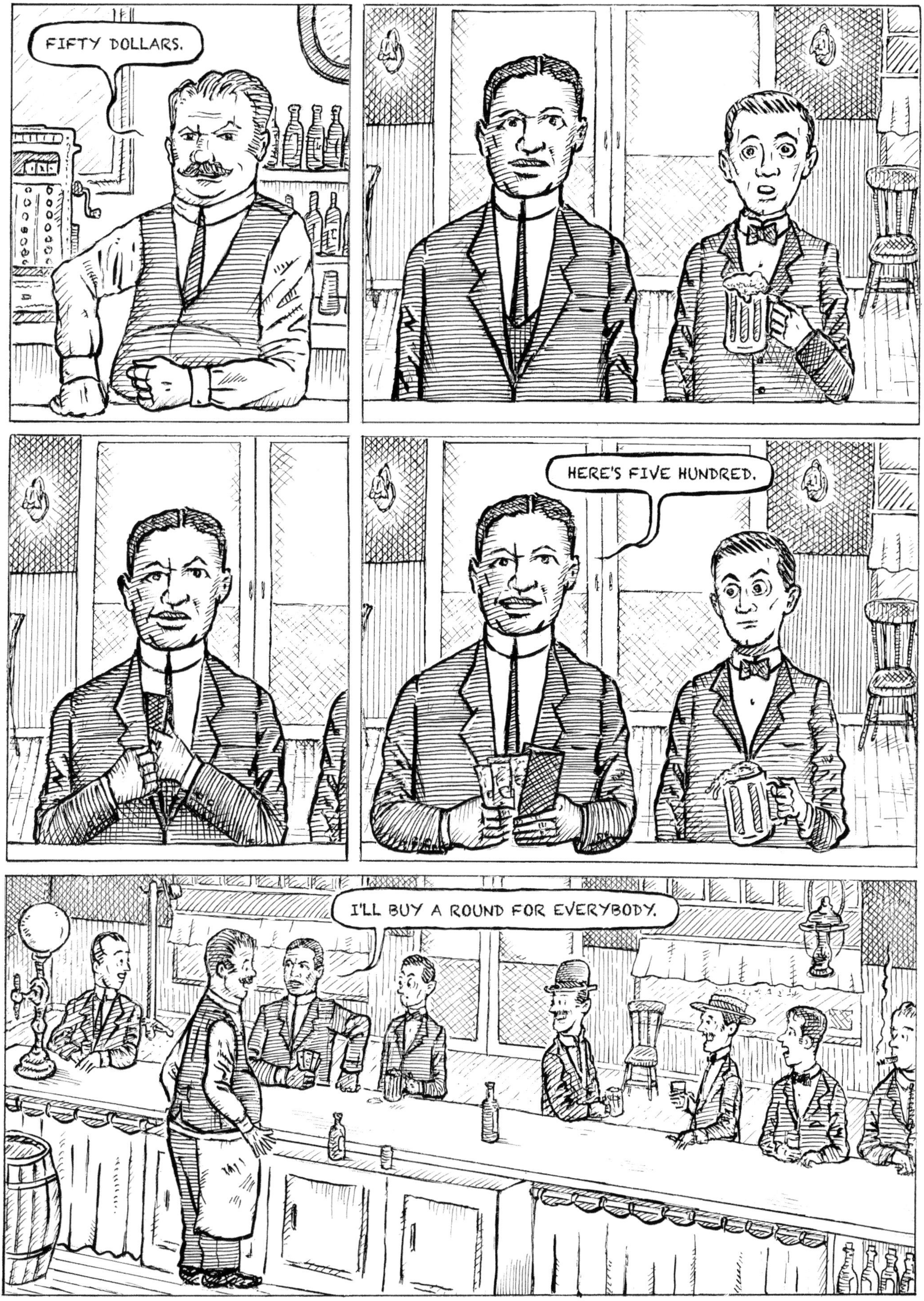
FIFTY DOLLARS.
HERE'S FIVE HUNDRED.
I'LL BUY A ROUND FOR EVERYBODY.

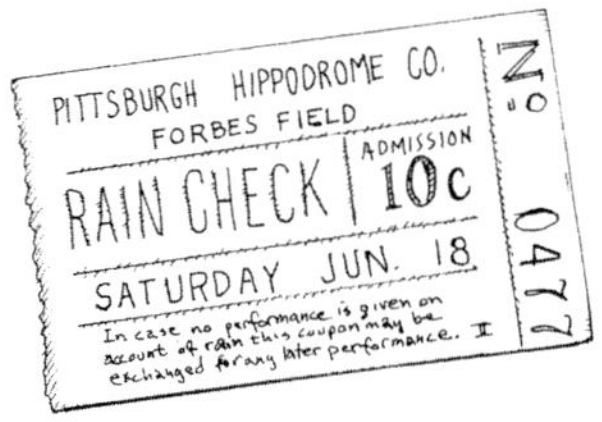
PITTSBURGH HIPPODROME CO.
FORBES FIELD
RAIN CHECK
ADMISSION
10c
SATURDAY JUN. 18
In case no performance is given on account of rain this coupon may be exchanged for any later performance.
No 0477

JULIAN ELTINGE WAS GROUNDBREAKING NOT ONLY AS A CROSS-DRESSER BUT ALSO AS A CROSS-MERCHANDISER. ONCE ESTABLISHED AS AN AUTHORITY ON WOMANHOOD, HE ADVANCED AND EXPLOITED THAT REPUTATION BY PUBLISHING A MAGAZINE HE NAMED FOR HIMSELF. IT WAS A PRECURSOR TO TWO SUPERFICIALLY DISTINCT BUT ELEMENTALLY PARALLEL GENRES OF GLOSSIES TO COME: "WOMEN'S MAGAZINES" OF HEALTH AND BEAUTY TIPS AND "MEN'S MAGAZINES" OF TIPS FOR GROOMING AND HOME CONSTRUCTION PROJECTS.

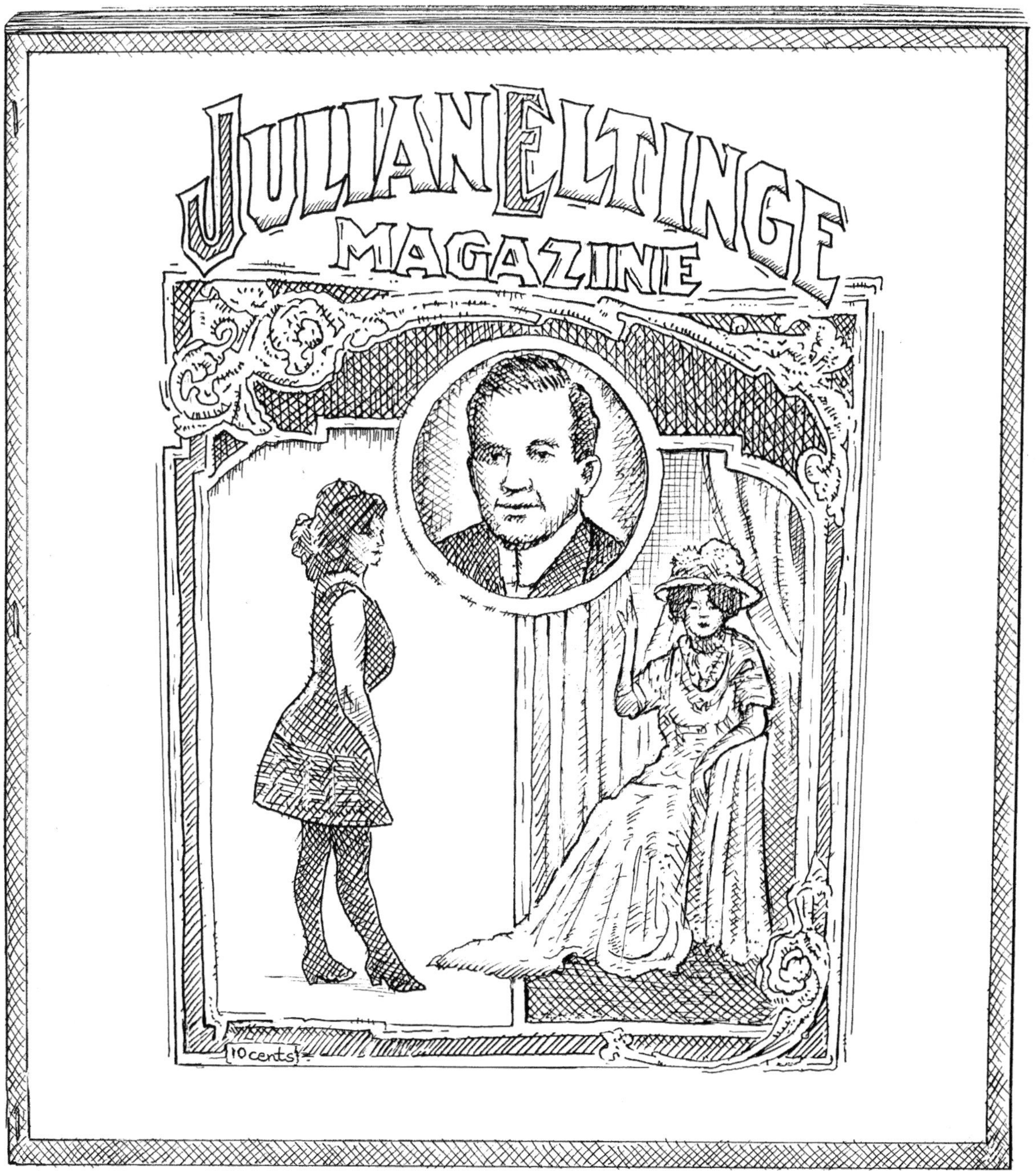
JULIAN ELTINGE
MAGAZINE
10 cents

PRESENTED FROM THE POINT OF VIEW OF A MAN WHO FAMOUSLY REBUILT HIMSELF AS A WOMAN, *JULIAN ELTINGE MAGAZINE* SENT JUMBLED MESSAGES ABOUT THE MALLEABILITY OF GENDER AND THE GLORY OF A FEMININE IDEAL DESIGNED BY MEN. ALL THE ADS IN THE MAGAZINE WERE FOR ELTINGE'S OWN GOODS: HIS SHOWS, THE SHEET MUSIC FOR THE SONGS IN THOSE SHOWS, AND THE JULIAN ELTINGE-BRAND PRODUCTS WRITTEN ABOUT IN THE ARTICLES OF BEAUTY TIPS. THE EDITORIAL CONTENT WAS ADVERTISING FOR THE ADVERTISING.

IN MAGAZINES OTHER THAN HIS OWN, JULIAN ELTINGE APPEARED IN ADVERTISEMENTS FOR PRODUCTS FOR WOMEN AND ALSO PRODUCTS FOR MEN. HE LEVERAGED BOTH HIS IMAGES FOR PROMOTIONAL FEES AND PUBLICITY FOR HIS STAGE ACT.

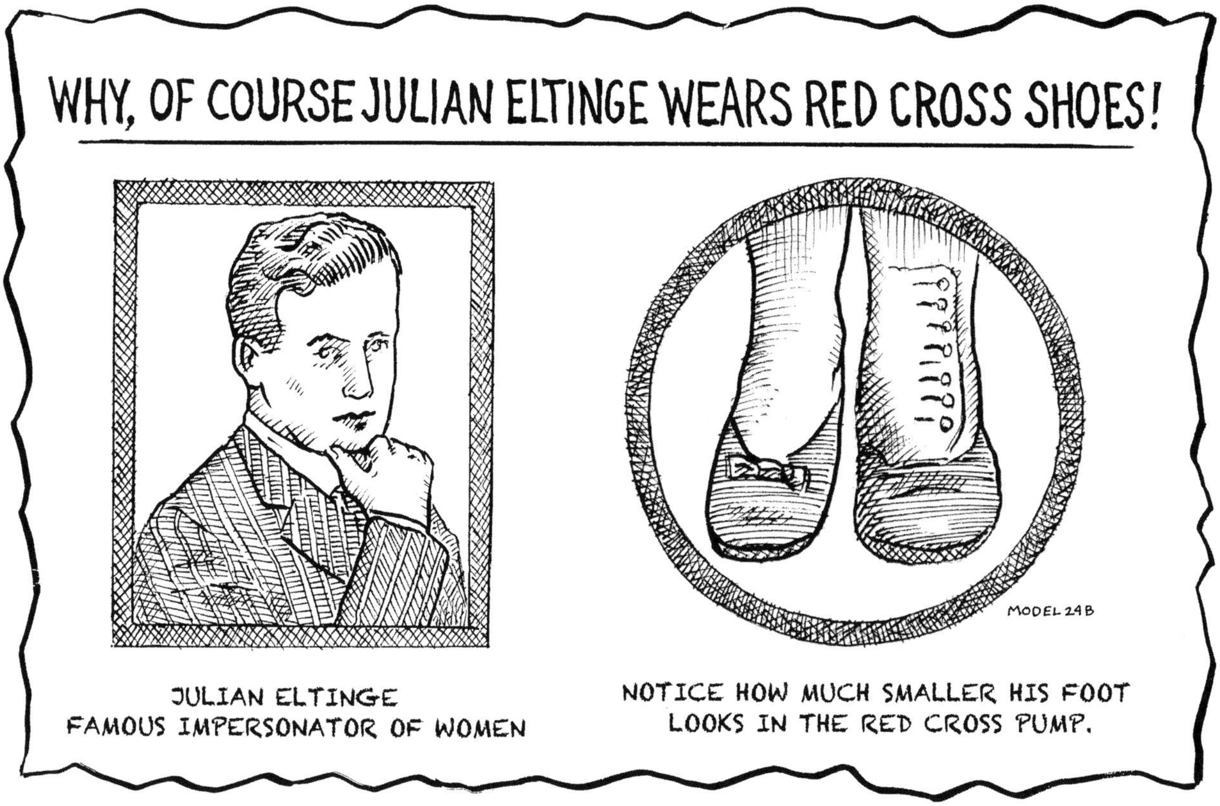

WHY, OF COURSE JULIAN ELTINGE WEARS RED CROSS SHOES!
MODEL 24B
JULIAN ELTINGE
FAMOUS IMPERSONATOR OF WOMEN
NOTICE HOW MUCH SMALLER HIS FOOT LOOKS IN THE RED CROSS PUMP.

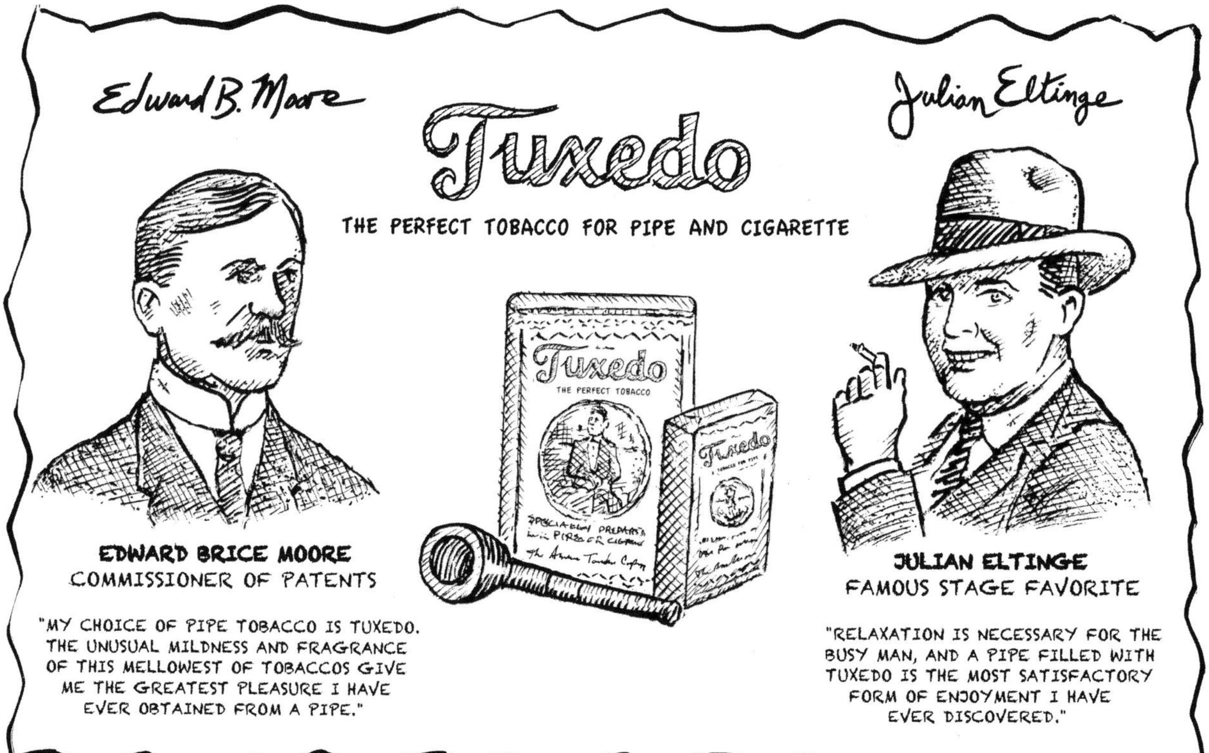

Edward B. Moore
Tuxedo
Julian Eltinge
THE PERFECT TOBACCO FOR PIPE AND CIGARETTE
Tuxedo
THE PERFECT TOBACCO
Tuxedo
EDWARD BRICE MOORE
COMMISSIONER OF PATENTS
"MY CHOICE OF PIPE TOBACCO IS TUXEDO. THE UNUSUAL MILDNESS AND FRAGRANCE OF THIS MELLOWEST OF TOBACCOS GIVE ME THE GREATEST PLEASURE I HAVE EVER OBTAINED FROM A PIPE."
JULIAN ELTINGE
FAMOUS STAGE FAVORITE
"RELAXATION IS NECESSARY FOR THE BUSY MAN, AND A PIPE FILLED WITH TUXEDO IS THE MOST SATISFACTORY FORM OF ENJOYMENT I HAVE EVER DISCOVERED."

JULIAN ELTINGE'S MANAGER WAS A BARNUMESQUE SHOWMAN AND THEATER PRODUCER NAMED A. H. WOODS. HE CAME UP IN THE ROUSTABOUT WORLD OF CHEAP-TICKET BOWERY THEATERS, MANAGING THE "GAIETY BURLESQUERERS." A PIONEER OF BELITTLING SHOW-BIZ GLAD-HANDING, HE CALLED EVERYONE OF ANY AGE OR SEX "SWEETHEART" OR "KID."

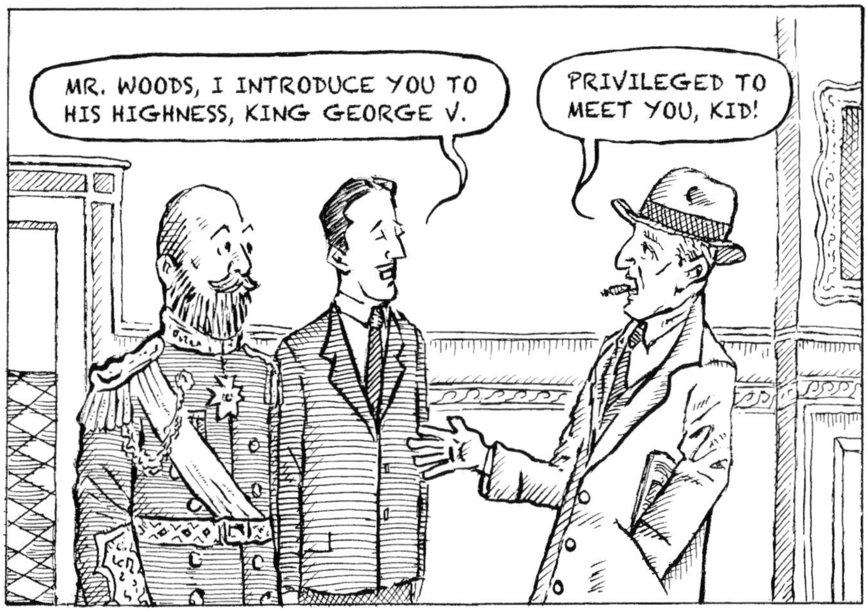
MR. WOODS, I INTRODUCE YOU TO HIS HIGHNESS, KING GEORGE V.
PRIVILEGED TO MEET YOU, KID!

WOODS BECAME FAMOUS AS "THE KING OF THE MELODRAMA" FOR STAGING PLAYS THOUGHT TO HAVE "FEMININE APPEAL," SUCH AS *THE EVIL THAT MEN DO*, *BERTHA THE SEWING MACHING GIRL*, AND *NELLIE THE BEAUTIFUL CLOAK MODEL*.

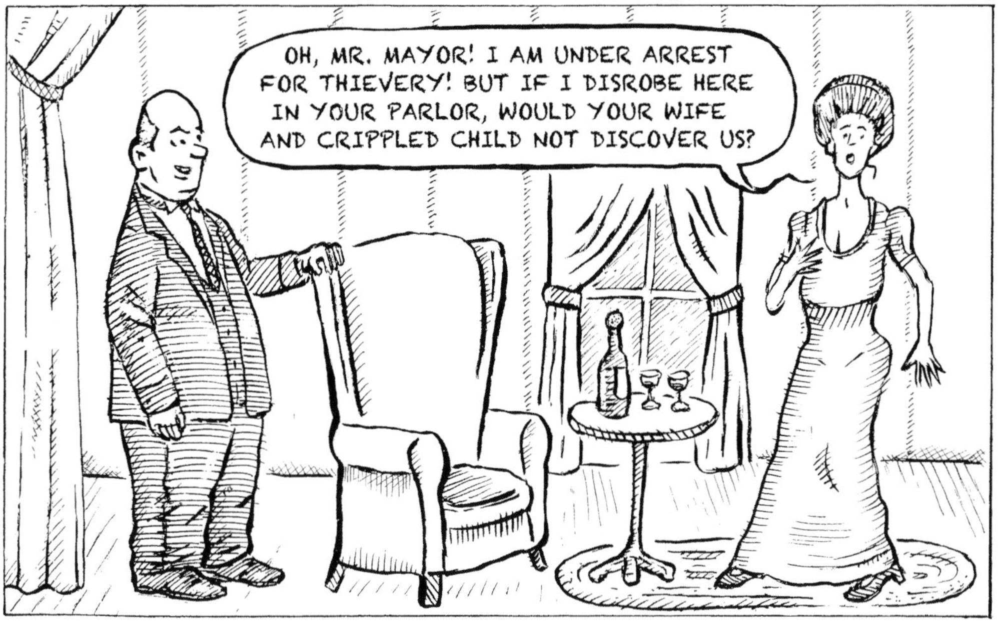
OH, MR. MAYOR! I AM UNDER ARREST FOR THIEVERY! BUT IF I DISROBE HERE IN YOUR PARLOR, WOULD YOUR WIFE AND CRIPPLED CHILD NOT DISCOVER US?

WOODS SET OUT TO ESTABLISH HIMSELF ON BROADWAY BY BUILDING A THEATER OF HIS OWN ON 42ND STREET, WHERE HE COULD PRESENT HIS STAR CLIENT, ELTINGE, IN BEDROOM FARCES DESIGNED FOR ELTINGE TO PLAY BOTH MALE AND FEMALE ROLES. ELTINGE ASSISTED IN THE PLANNING FOR THE THEATER.

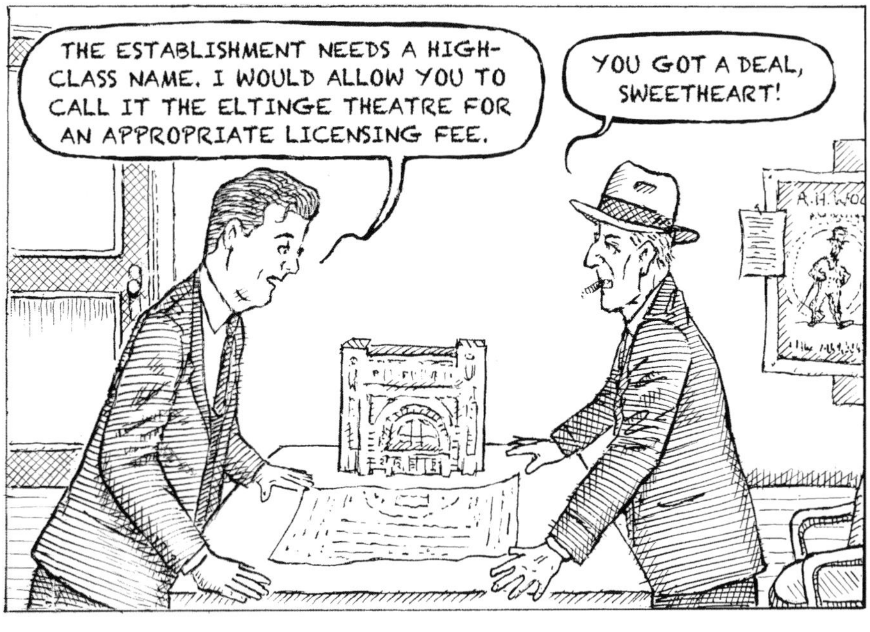
THE ESTABLISHMENT NEEDS A HIGH-CLASS NAME. I WOULD ALLOW YOU TO CALL IT THE ELTINGE THEATRE FOR AN APPROPRIATE LICENSING FEE.
YOU GOT A DEAL, SWEETHEART!

THE ELTINGE THEATRE, OPENED IN 1912, WAS THE FIRST AND ONLY BROADWAY HOUSE EVER NAMED FOR A VAUDEVILLE STAR. DESIGNED BY THE THEATER ARCHITECT THOMAS W. LAMB, IT WAS AN ORNATE SHOWPLACE WITH FEATURES DRAWN FREELY FROM CLASSICAL CULTURE. ABOVE A PROSCENIUM TOPPED WITH RELIEF SCULPTURES OF TWO SPHINXES, THERE WAS A MURAL BY ARTIST ARTHUR BROUNET DEPICTING THREE FLESHY GREEK WOMEN IN ROBES. ELTINGE WAS SAID TO HAVE BEEN THE MODEL FOR THE WOMEN.

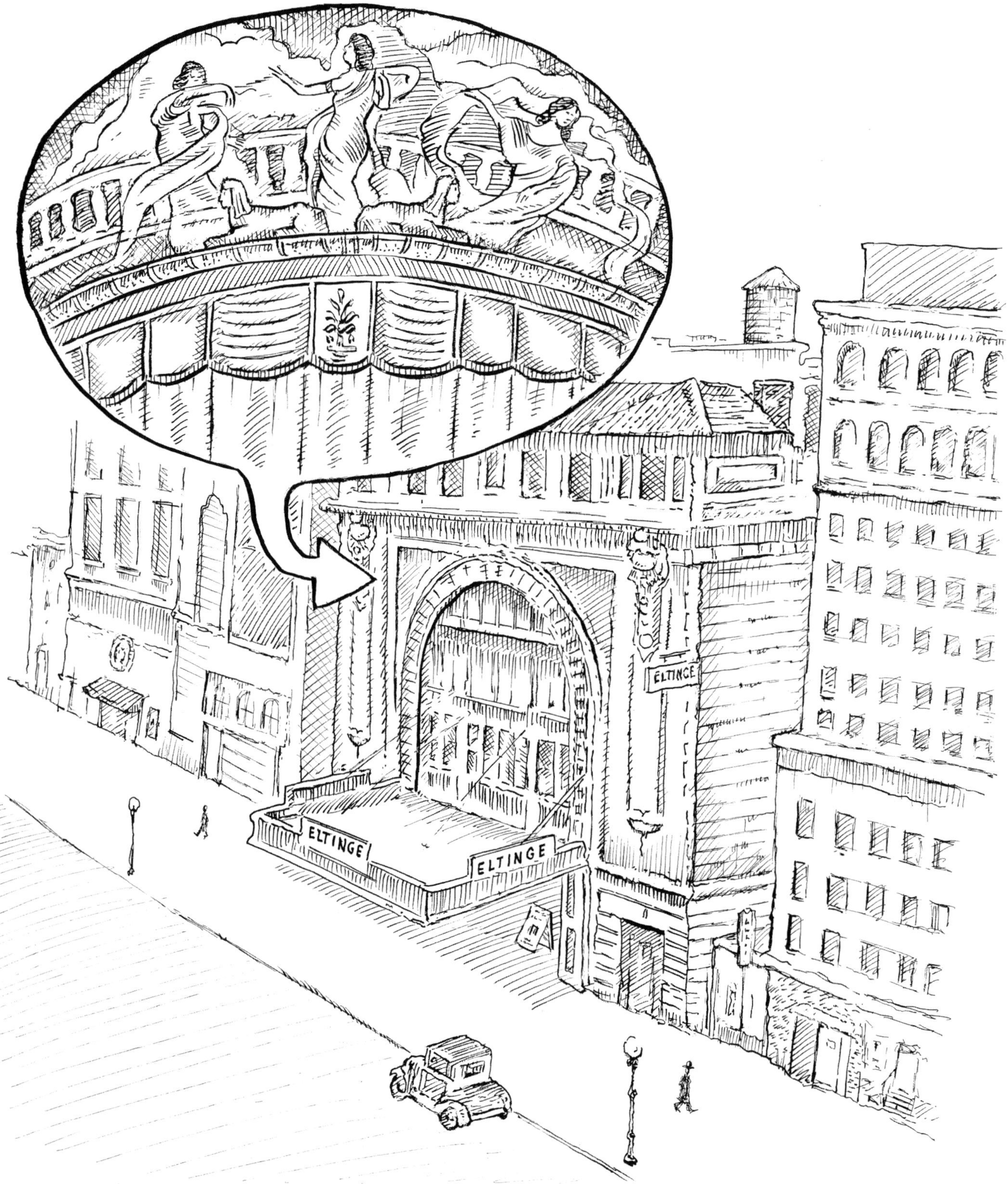
ELTINGE
ELTINGE
ELTINGE

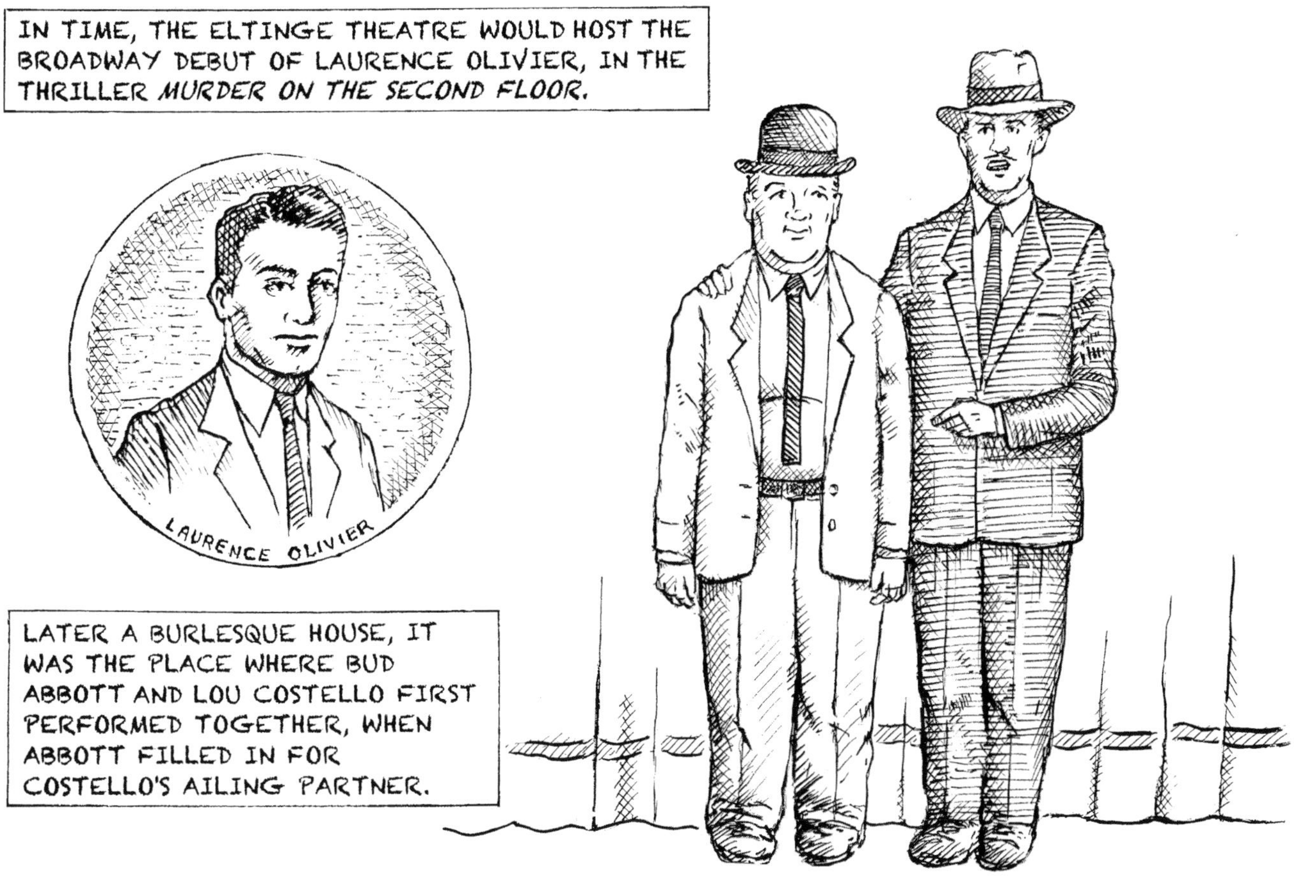
IN TIME, THE ELTINGE THEATRE WOULD HOST THE BROADWAY DEBUT OF LAURENCE OLIVIER, IN THE THRILLER *MURDER ON THE SECOND FLOOR.*
LAURENCE OLIVIER
LATER A BURLESQUE HOUSE, IT WAS THE PLACE WHERE BUD ABBOTT AND LOU COSTELLO FIRST PERFORMED TOGETHER, WHEN ABBOTT FILLED IN FOR COSTELLO'S AILING PARTNER.

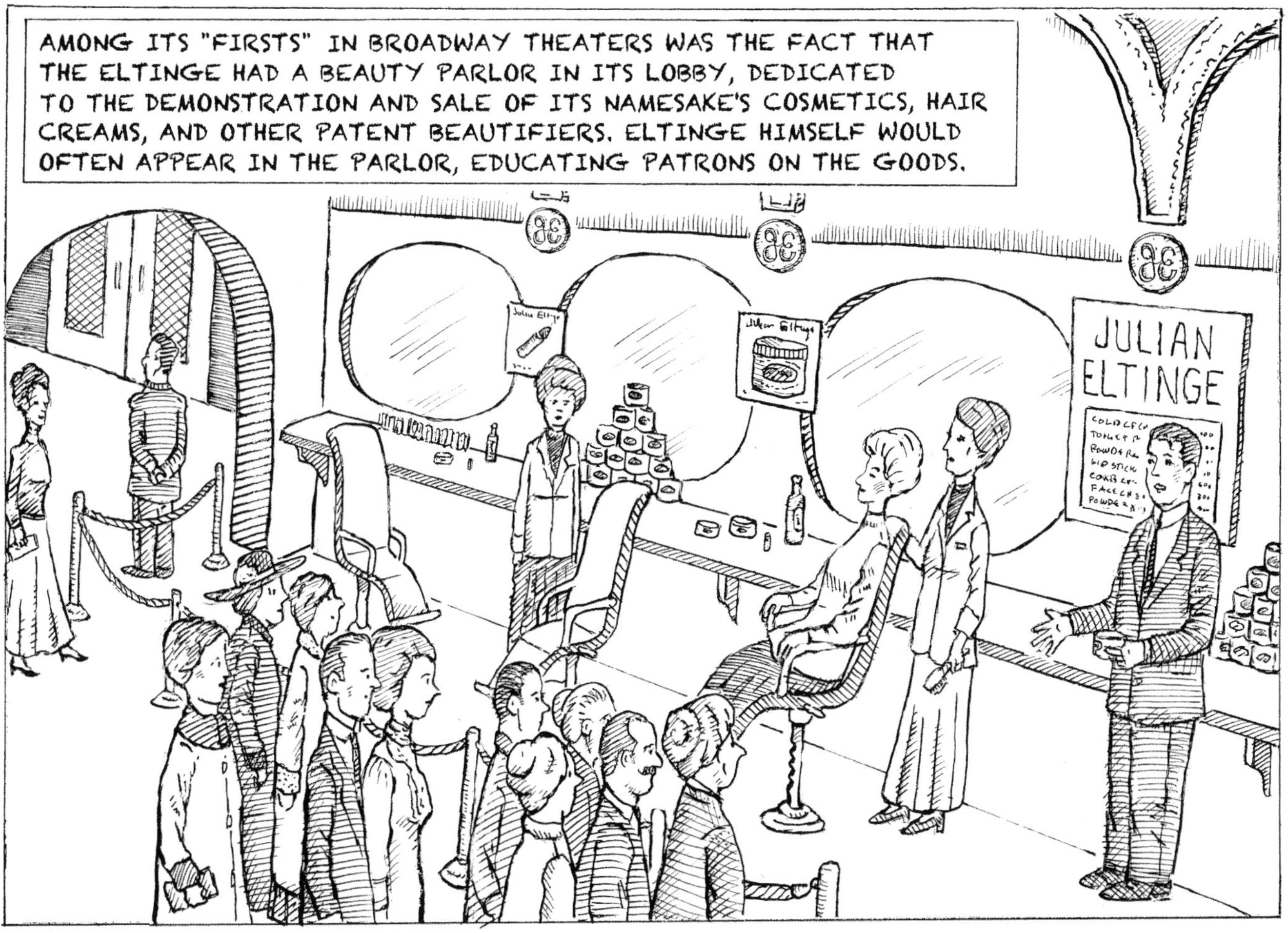
AMONG ITS "FIRSTS" IN BROADWAY THEATERS WAS THE FACT THAT THE ELTINGE HAD A BEAUTY PARLOR IN ITS LOBBY, DEDICATED TO THE DEMONSTRATION AND SALE OF ITS NAMESAKE'S COSMETICS, HAIR CREAMS, AND OTHER PATENT BEAUTIFIERS. ELTINGE HIMSELF WOULD OFTEN APPEAR IN THE PARLOR, EDUCATING PATRONS ON THE GOODS.
JULIAN ELTINGE

IF JULIAN ELTINGE WAS THE MOST BEAUTIFUL WOMAN IN VAUDEVILLE, EVA TANGUAY WAS THE MOST POPULAR. BEAUTY, FOR TANGUAY, WAS JUST ANOTHER THING NOT TO CARE ABOUT. AT THE PEAK OF THEIR CAREERS, THE TWO STARS HATCHED A PLOT TO MAKE NEWS TOGETHER. THE OCCASION WAS TANGUAY'S OPENING AT THE ALHAMBRA THEATRE IN HARLEM.

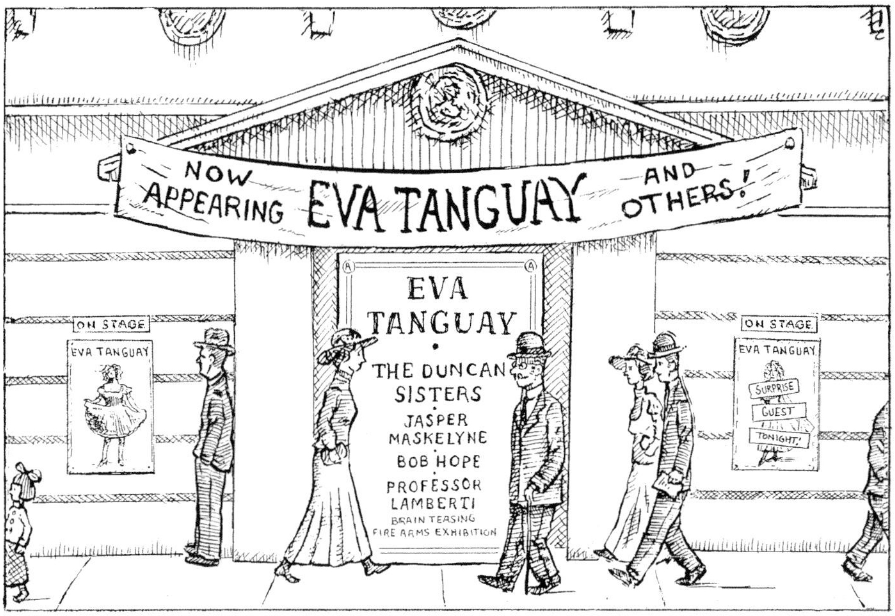
NOW APPEARING EVA TANGUAY AND OTHERS!
ON STAGE
EVA TANGUAY
EVA TANGUAY • THE DUNCAN SISTERS • JASPER MASKELYNE • BOB HOPE • PROFESSOR LAMBERTI BRAIN TEASING FIRE ARMS EXHIBITION
ON STAGE
EVA TANGUAY
SURPRISE GUEST TONIGHT!

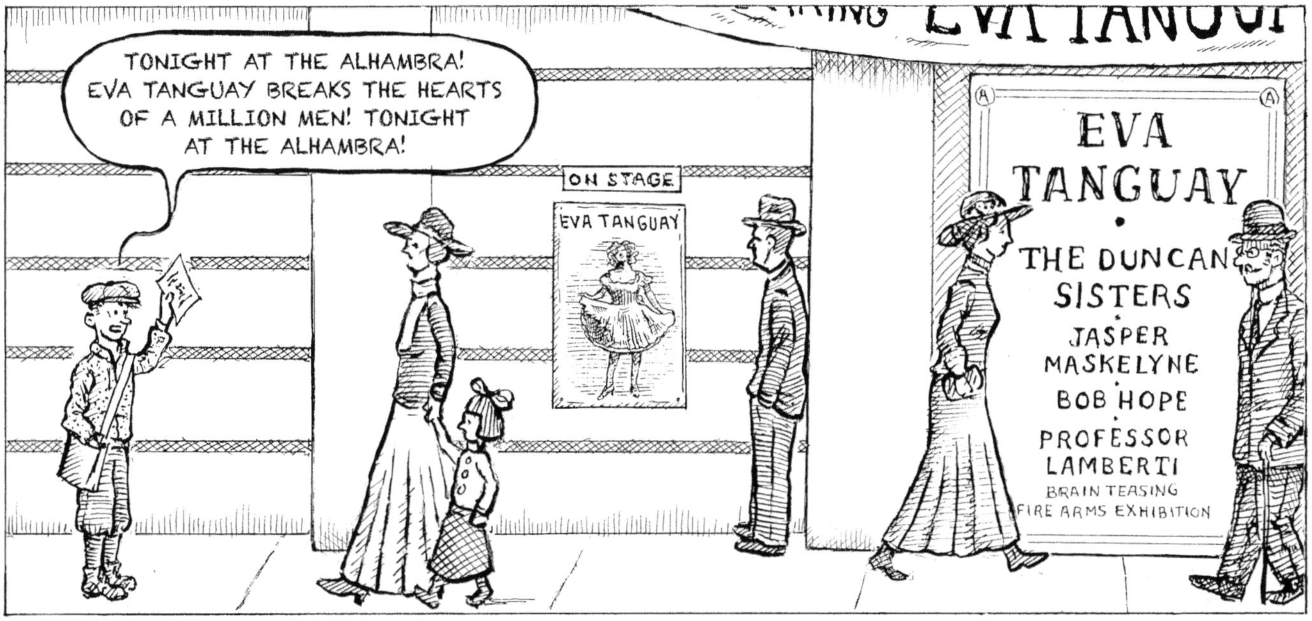
TONIGHT AT THE ALHAMBRA! EVA TANGUAY BREAKS THE HEARTS OF A MILLION MEN! TONIGHT AT THE ALHAMBRA!
ON STAGE
EVA TANGUAY
EVA TANGUAY • THE DUNCAN SISTERS • JASPER MASKELYNE • BOB HOPE • PROFESSOR LAMBERTI BRAIN TEASING FIRE ARMS EXHIBITION

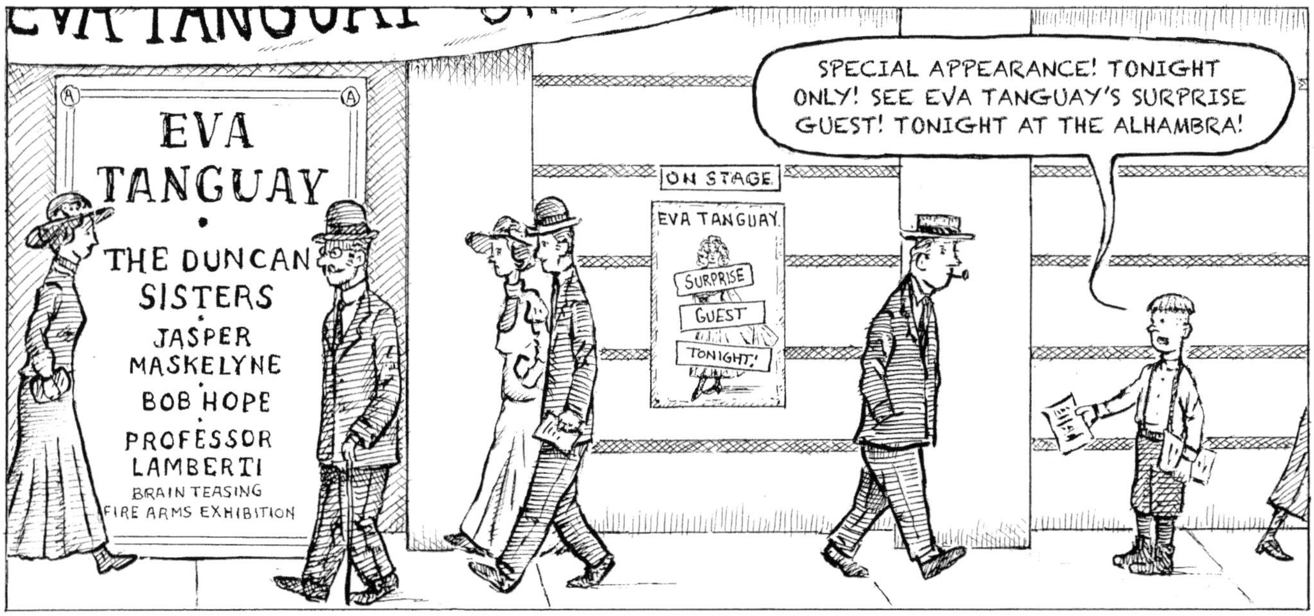
EVA TANGUAY • THE DUNCAN SISTERS • JASPER MASKELYNE • BOB HOPE • PROFESSOR LAMBERTI BRAIN TEASING FIRE ARMS EXHIBITION
SPECIAL APPEARANCE! TONIGHT ONLY! SEE EVA TANGUAY'S SURPRISE GUEST! TONIGHT AT THE ALHAMBRA!
ON STAGE
EVA TANGUAY
SURPRISE
GUEST
TONIGHT!

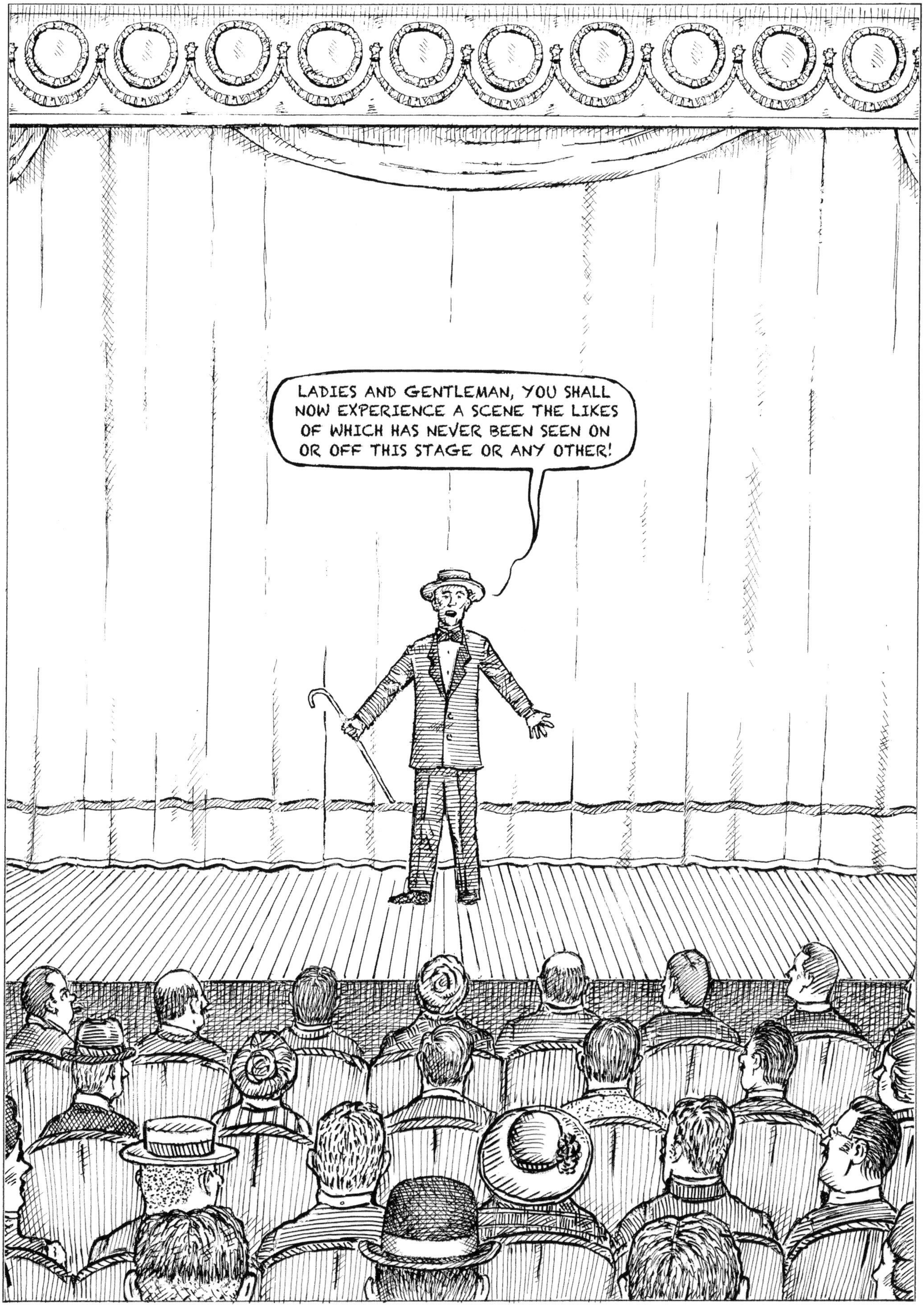
LADIES AND GENTLEMAN, YOU SHALL NOW EXPERIENCE A SCENE THE LIKES OF WHICH HAS NEVER BEEN SEEN ON OR OFF THIS STAGE OR ANY OTHER!

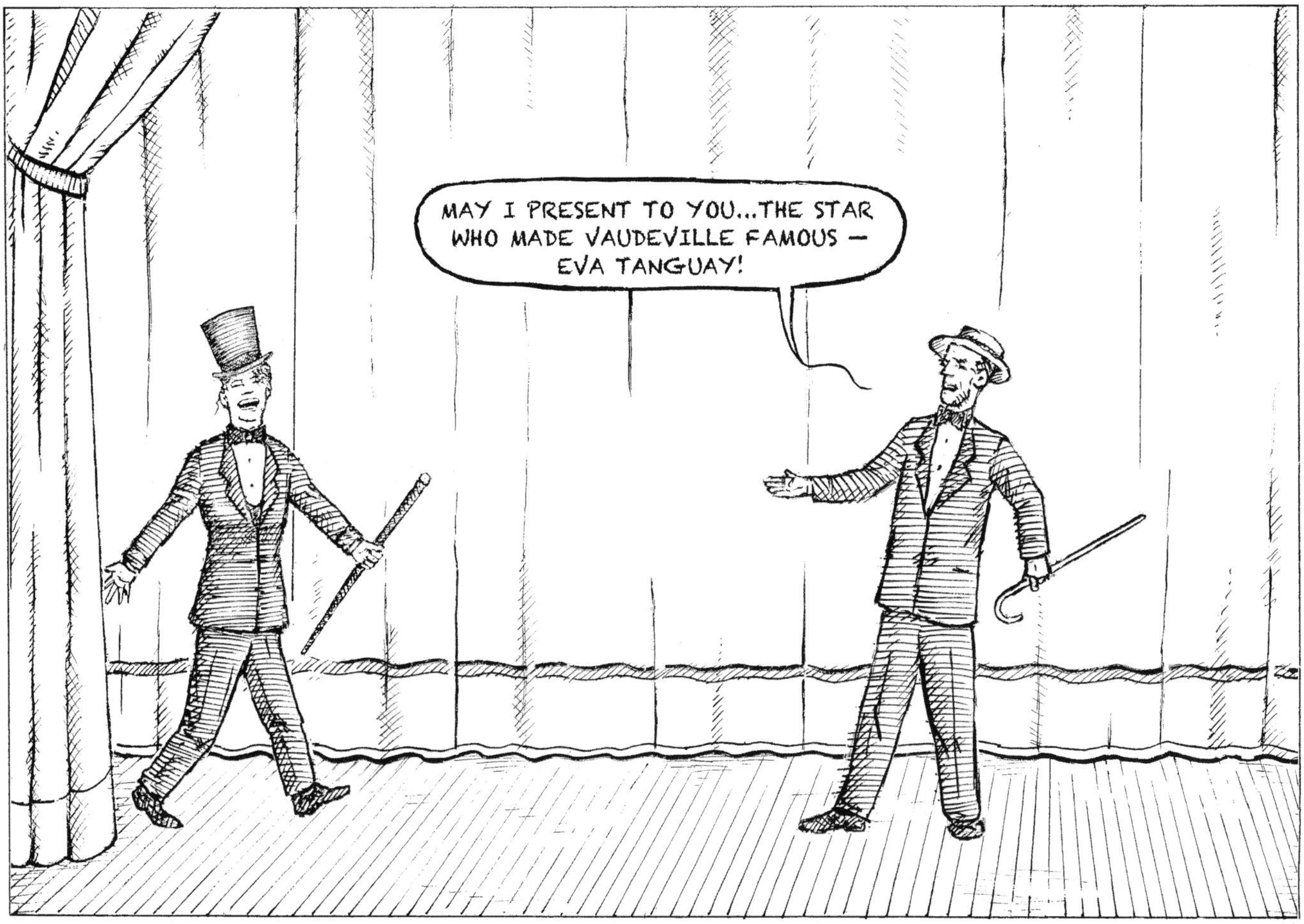
MAY I PRESENT TO YOU...THE STAR WHO MADE VAUDEVILLE FAMOUS — EVA TANGUAY!

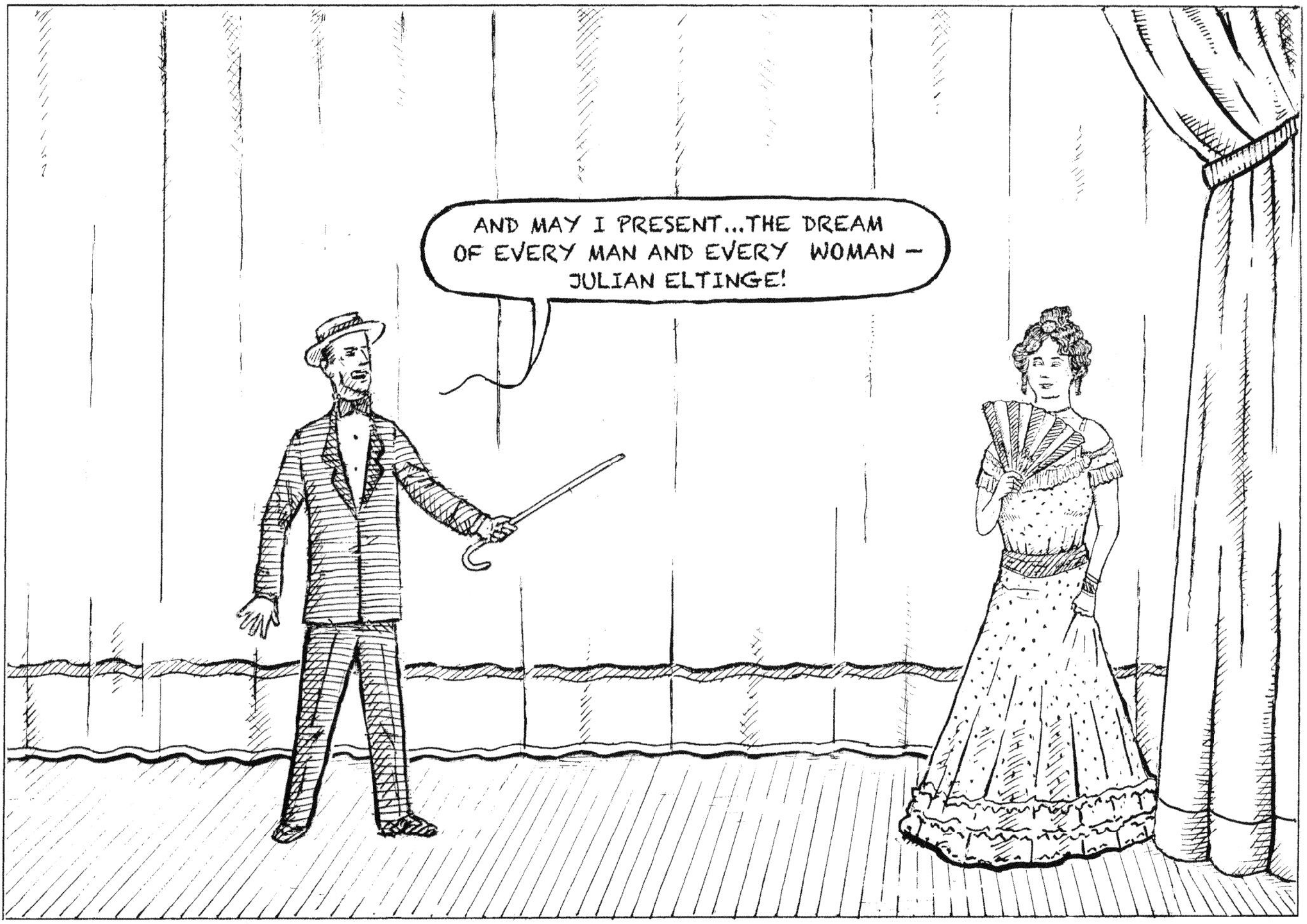
AND MAY I PRESENT...THE DREAM OF EVERY MAN AND EVERY WOMAN — JULIAN ELTINGE!

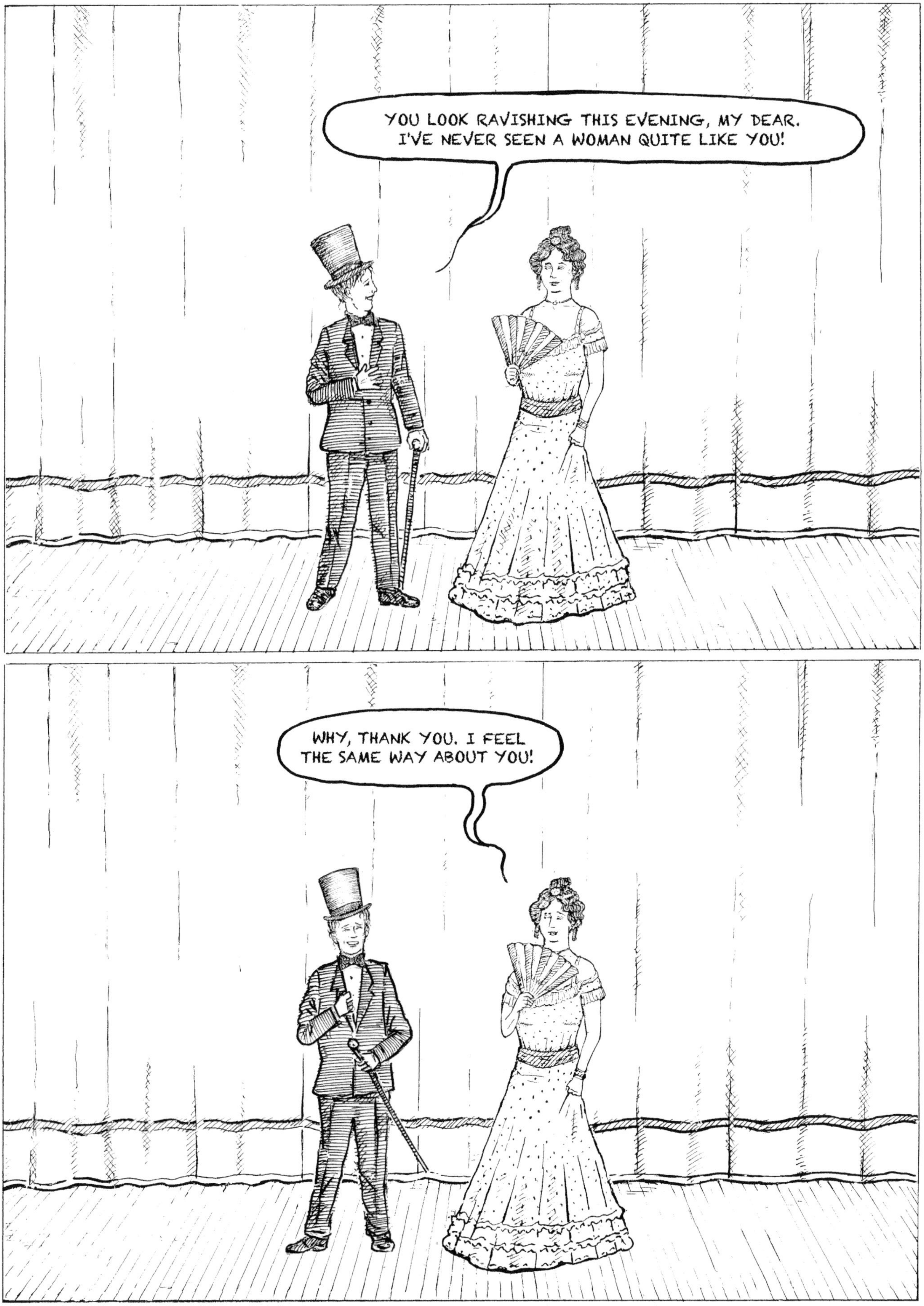
YOU LOOK RAVISHING THIS EVENING, MY DEAR. I'VE NEVER SEEN A WOMAN QUITE LIKE YOU!
WHY, THANK YOU. I FEEL THE SAME WAY ABOUT YOU!

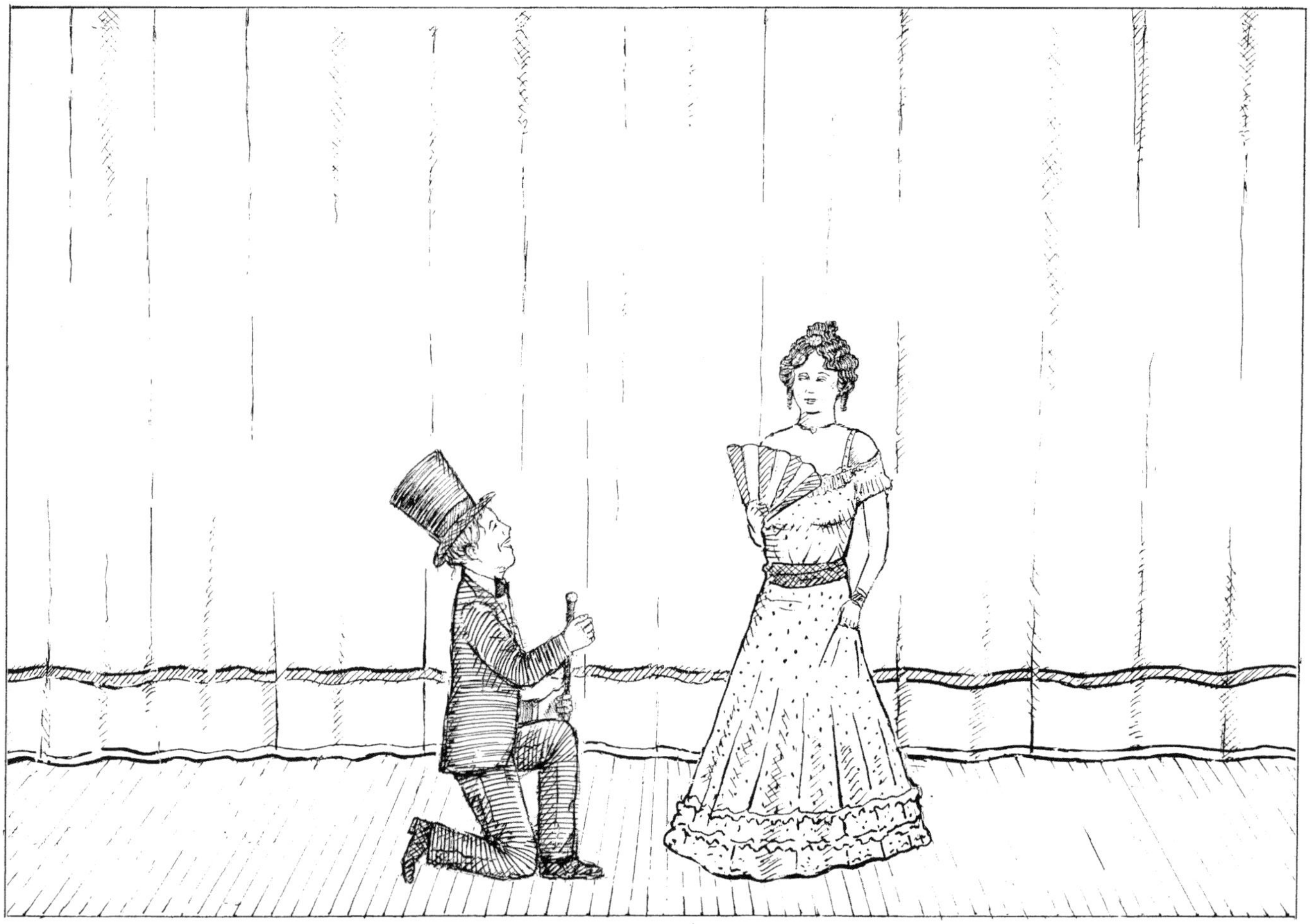

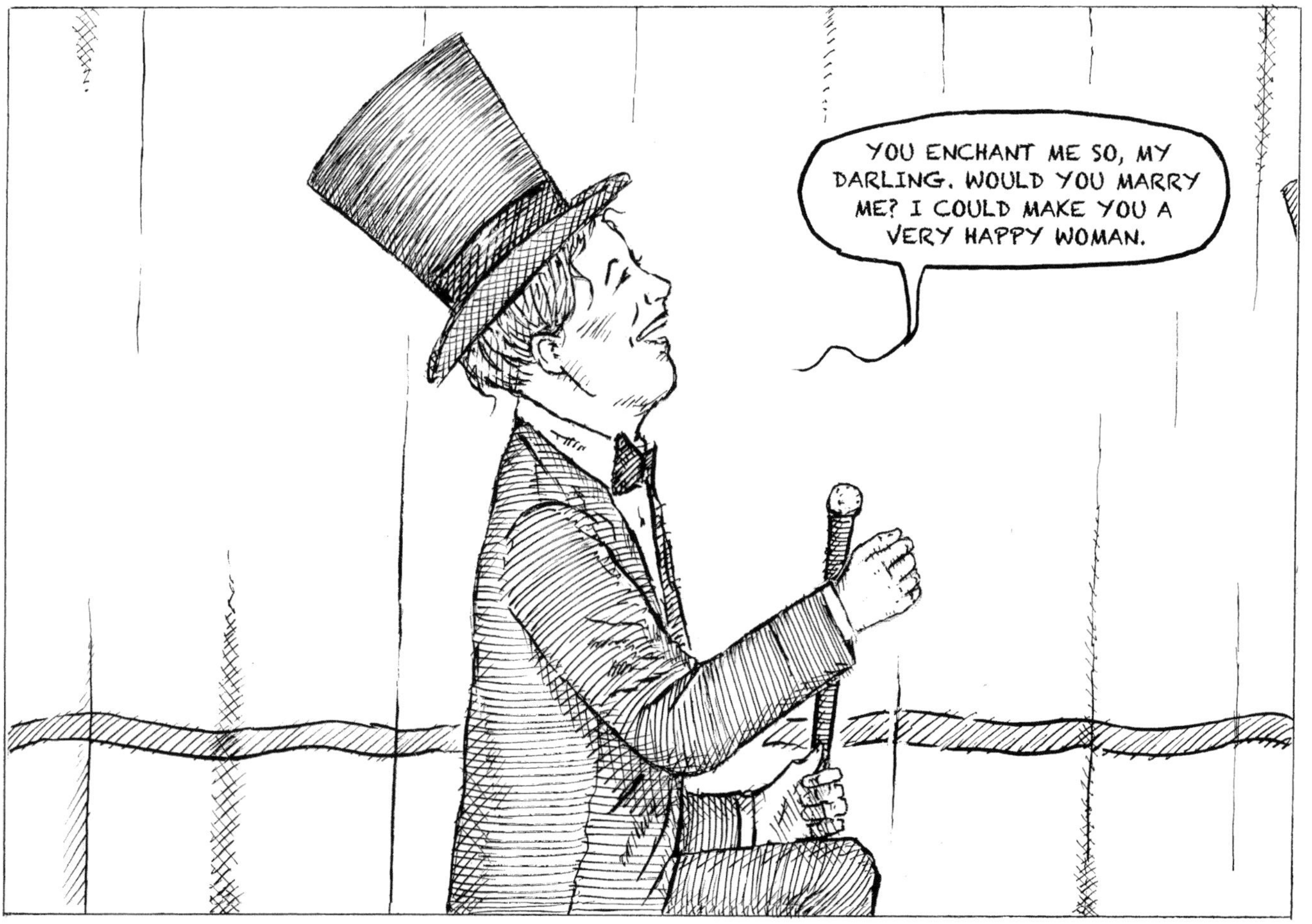
YOU ENCHANT ME SO, MY DARLING. WOULD YOU MARRY ME? I COULD MAKE YOU A VERY HAPPY WOMAN.

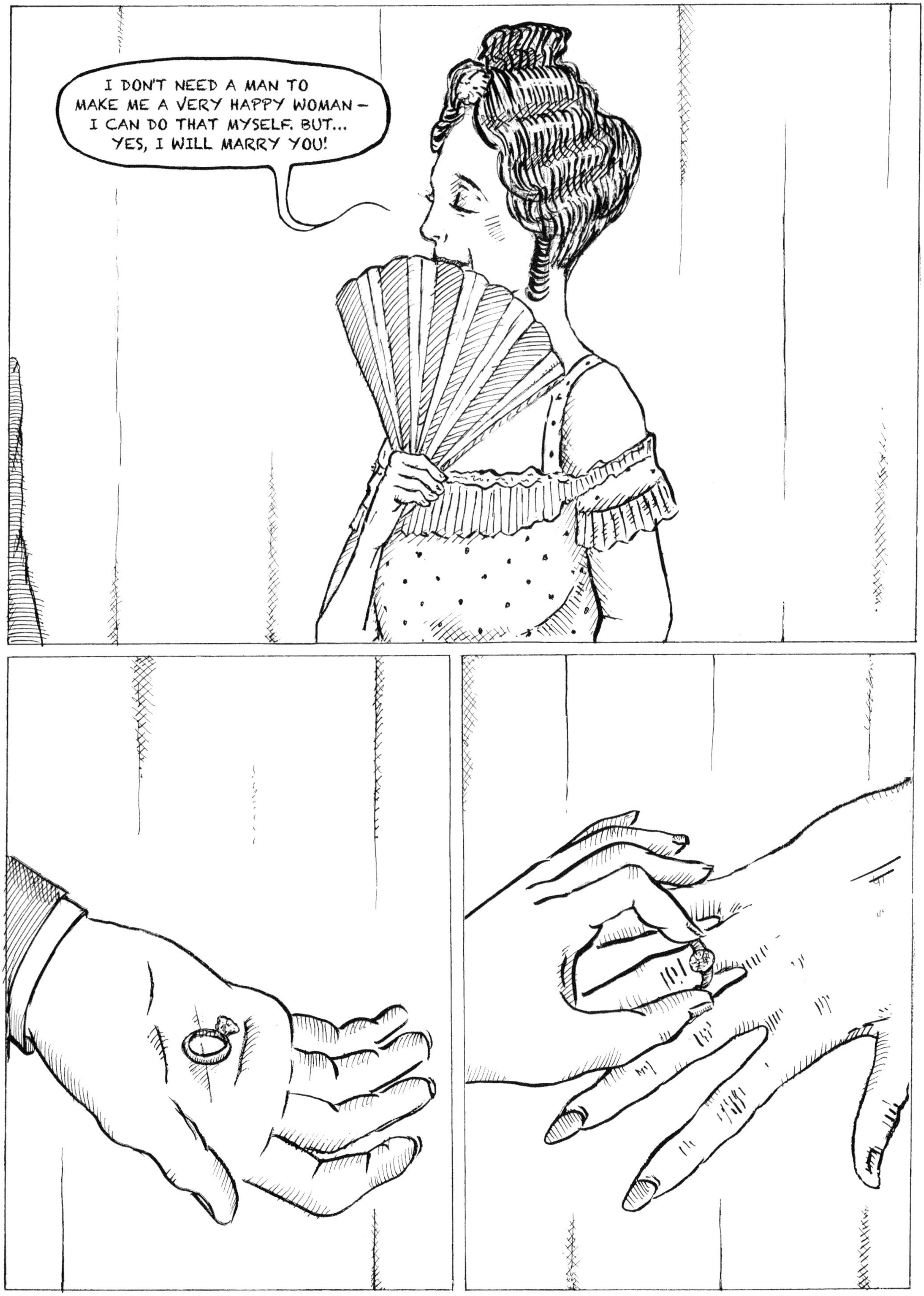
I DON'T NEED A MAN TO MAKE ME A VERY HAPPY WOMAN— I CAN DO THAT MYSELF. BUT... YES, I WILL MARRY YOU!

NEWS OF THE TANGUAY-ELTINGE BETROTHAL MADE HEADLINES ACROSS THE COUNTRY, FROM WASHINGTON TO NORTH DAKOTA.

EVA TANGUAY, THE FAMOUS SALOME, IS TO MARRY JULIAN ELTINGE, THE NOTED FEMALE IMPERSONATOR, AND TONGUES WAG THEATRICAL

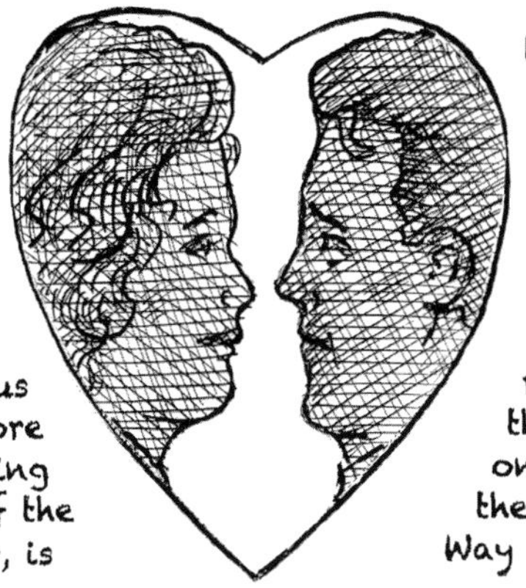

New York, Aug. 19 - The latest phase of the Salome craze has set all New York to wriggling it out. Eva Tanguay is to marry Julian Eltinge.

Eva, the "Queen of the Vaudevilles," who has discarded her famous "I Don't Care" for the more exciting pastime of showing her gyroscopic version of the original wicked wriggler, is to give her hand — if she can keep it still long enough — to the good-looking Harvard graduate, who is now Saloming a few himself.

While the first announcement of the engagement startled Broadway sufficiently, it has recovered its breath, and the wedding promises to be one that will go down in the annals of the Gay White Way folklore.

BISMARCK TRIBUNE

WHEN GIRL-BOY WEDS BOY-GIRL, WHO'LL BE BOSS?

TANGUAY LOOKS BETTER THAN ELTINGE IN BOY'S CLOTHES, AND VICE VERSA

NEW YORK, Aug. 18 — There's an exciting promise of an astonishing matrimonial team in vaudeville after Oct. 14 next.

On or about that date, according to present announcements, "Salome Dancer" Julian Eltinge is to become the husband of Boy-Impersonator Eva Tanguay.

The prospective bridegroom, a graduate of Harvard, is famous for his skirted portrayals of female roles, his Salome dance being as much like the real thing, it is said, as the best efforts of Gertrude Hoffman or Maud Allan.

NEW YORK EVENING WORLD

EVA TANGUAY'S COMING WEDDING TALK OF THE STAGE

JULIAN ELTINGE, THE BRIDEGROOM, A FAMOUS IMPERSONATOR OF WOMEN.

When Eva Tanguay marries Julian Eltinge there will be a wedding the like of which has not excited stageland for a long time. The announcement of the engagement sounds simple enough, even commonplace; but the wonder comes when one realizes that the bridegroom-elect is one of the best-known impersonators of women, while Miss Tanguay has won no small amount of notice impersonating men.

ST. LOUIS POST-DISPATCH

ELTINGE MAY WED TANGUAY

LATEST FROM NEW YORK SAYS THE TWO SALOMES ARE TO MARRY

A union of the Salomes is the latest announcement on the dancing boards.

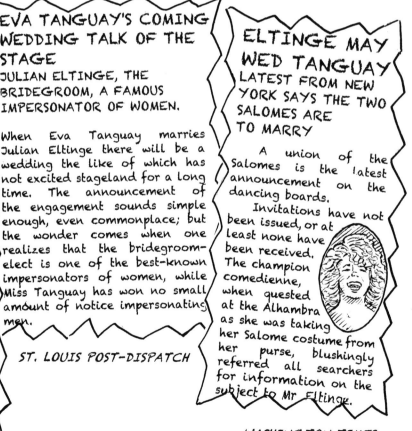

Invitations have not been issued, or at least none have been received. The champion comedienne, when quested at the Alhambra as she was taking her Salome costume from her purse, blushingly referred all searchers for information on the subject to Mr Eltinge.

WASHINGTON TIMES

TANGUAY SAYS SHE WILL WED IMPERSONATOR ELTINGE; BOTH "SALOMES"

NEW YORK, Aug. 17 — Eva Tanguay, comedienne, says she is going to marry Julian Eltinge, whose chief glory is the fact that he can impersonate a sweet young girl with greater accuracy than any other man. Eva says the ceremony will be performed on or before Oct. 1, and Julian, when investigated, blushes coyly and admits the soft impeachment.

DETROIT TIMES

WHO WILL WEAR THE BREECHES?

It's a question that has agitated the world ever since mankind began to wear breeches, and many an otherwise happy household has been disrupted over the issue. Now, however, it's a singularly vital question, and there's simply no telling what may happen if it becomes a point of contention between Mr. and Mrs. Eltinge.

Because - well, everybody knows what an audacious and swaggering tom-boy EvaTanguay can be, and there's a lurking suspicion that she'd rather wear trousers than skirts any old day. The one ray of hope lies in the fact that Julian Eltinge has been so successful in skirts that he may not in the least mind surrendering the breeches to Eva Tanguay when she shall have become Mrs. Julian Eltinge.

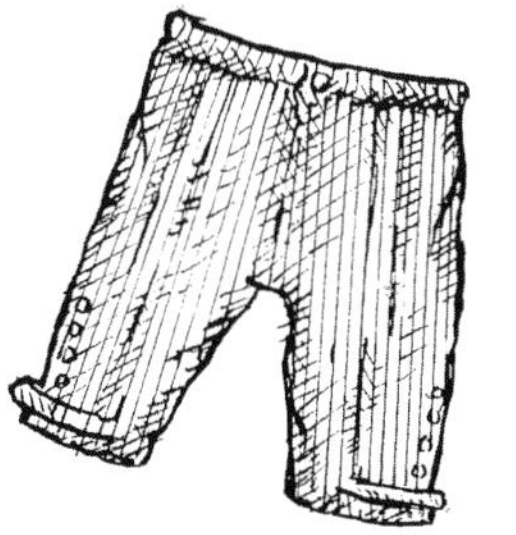

ASSOCIATED PRESS

FOUR WEEKS AFTER THE BETROTHAL WAS MADE PUBLIC, TANGUAY ANNOUNCED THAT SHE WAS BREAKING IT OFF. THE NEWS HAPPENED TO CORRESPOND WITH THE END OF TANGUAY'S OTHER ENGAGEMENT, THE ONE AT THE ALHAMBRA THEATRE.

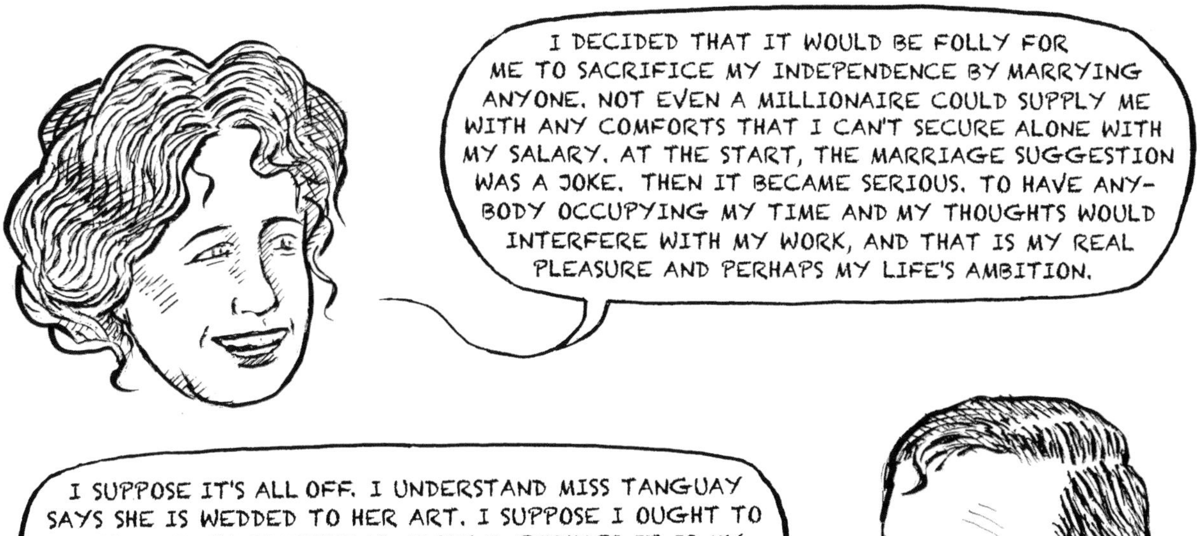
I DECIDED THAT IT WOULD BE FOLLY FOR ME TO SACRIFICE MY INDEPENDENCE BY MARRYING ANYONE. NOT EVEN A MILLIONAIRE COULD SUPPLY ME WITH ANY COMFORTS THAT I CAN'T SECURE ALONE WITH MY SALARY. AT THE START, THE MARRIAGE SUGGESTION WAS A JOKE. THEN IT BECAME SERIOUS. TO HAVE ANYBODY OCCUPYING MY TIME AND MY THOUGHTS WOULD INTERFERE WITH MY WORK, AND THAT IS MY REAL PLEASURE AND PERHAPS MY LIFE'S AMBITION.

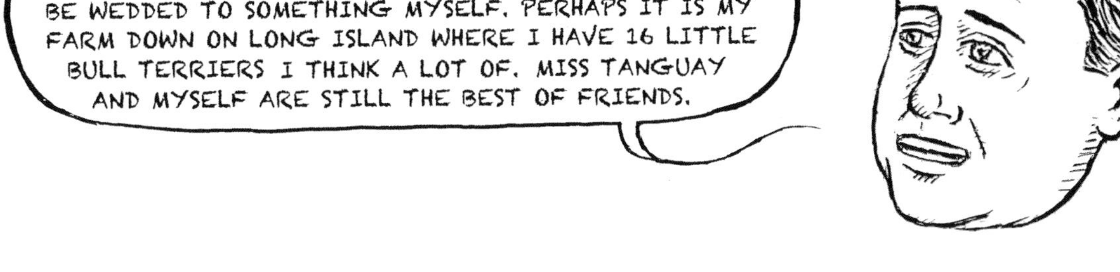
I SUPPOSE IT'S ALL OFF. I UNDERSTAND MISS TANGUAY SAYS SHE IS WEDDED TO HER ART. I SUPPOSE I OUGHT TO BE WEDDED TO SOMETHING MYSELF. PERHAPS IT IS MY FARM DOWN ON LONG ISLAND WHERE I HAVE 16 LITTLE BULL TERRIERS I THINK A LOT OF. MISS TANGUAY AND MYSELF ARE STILL THE BEST OF FRIENDS.

W.C. FIELDS PAID A CALL ON BERT WILLIAMS TO INVITE HIM PERSONALLY TO JOIN ACTORS EQUITY. AS FIELDS WOULD LATER RECALL, HE FOUND WILLIAMS PLEASED TO SEE HIM BUT OTHERWISE "SAD AND WISTFUL."

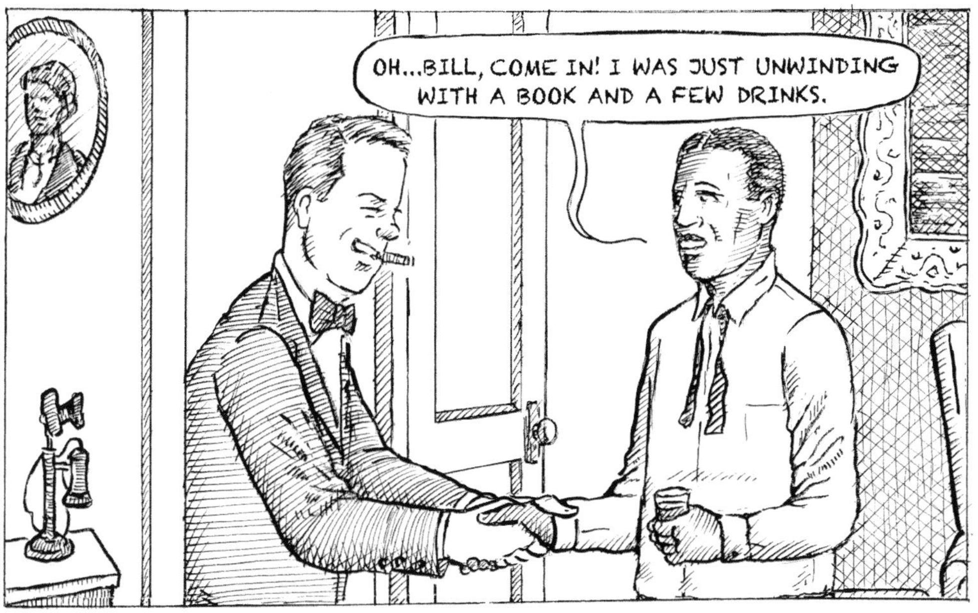
OH...BILL, COME IN! I WAS JUST UNWINDING WITH A BOOK AND A FEW DRINKS.

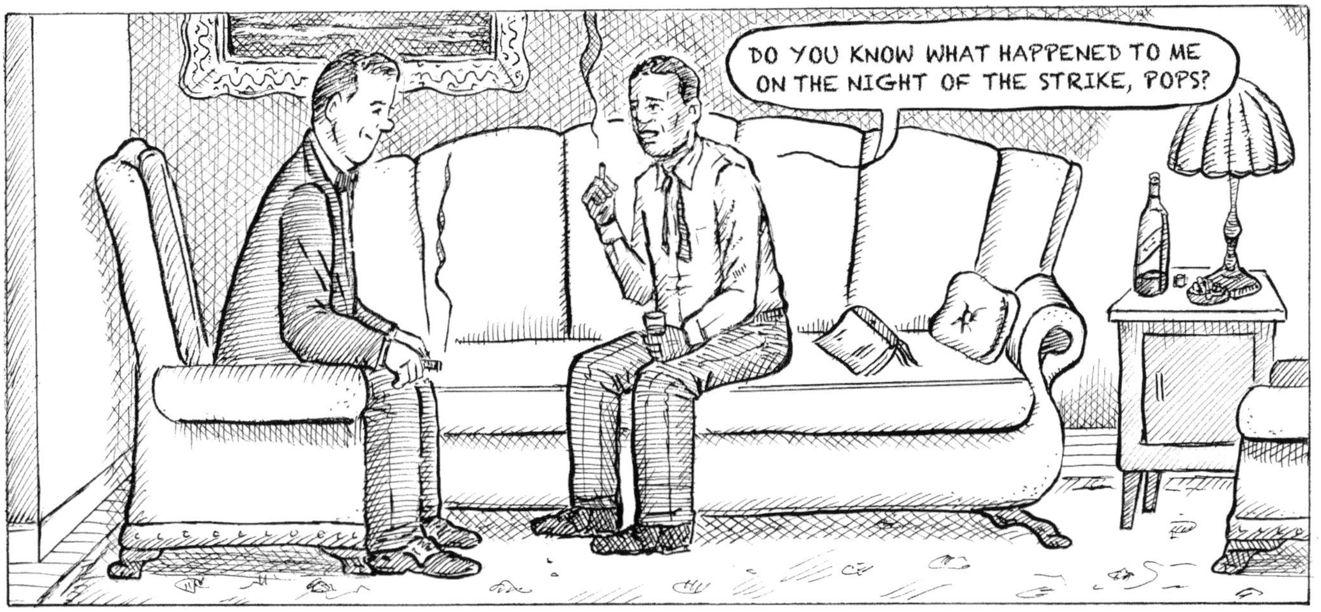
DO YOU KNOW WHAT HAPPENED TO ME ON THE NIGHT OF THE STRIKE, POPS?

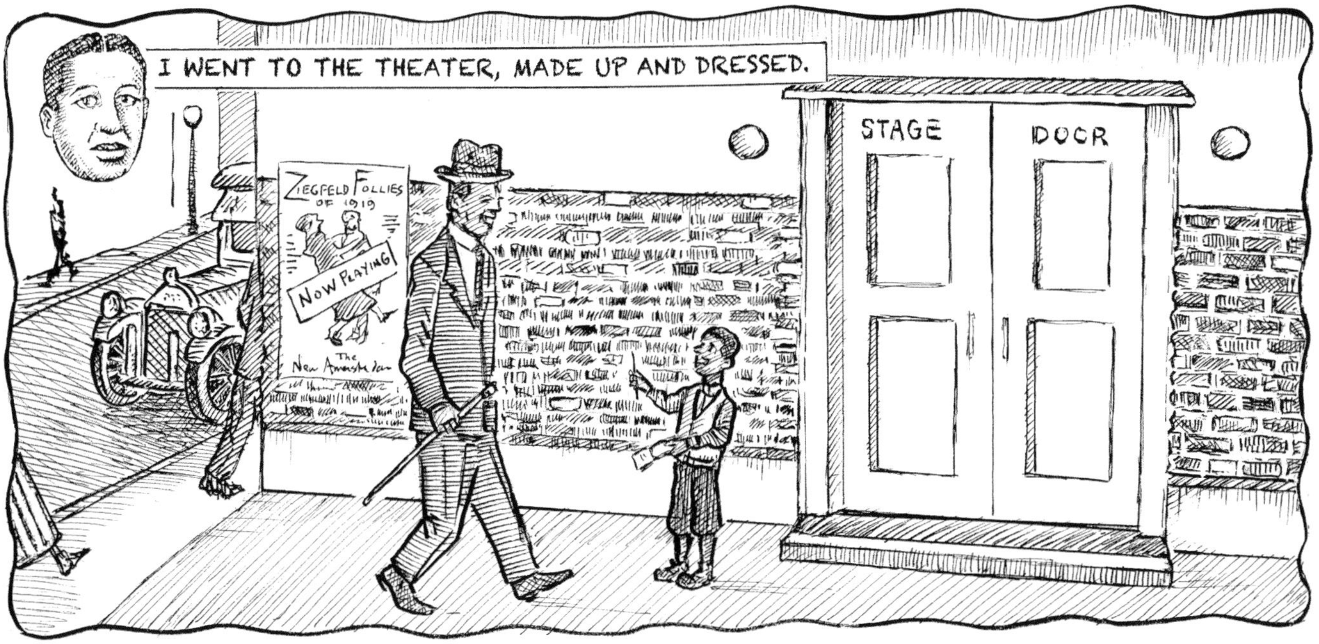
I WENT TO THE THEATER, MADE UP AND DRESSED.
ZIEGFELD FOLLIES OF 1919
NOW PLAYING
STAGE DOOR

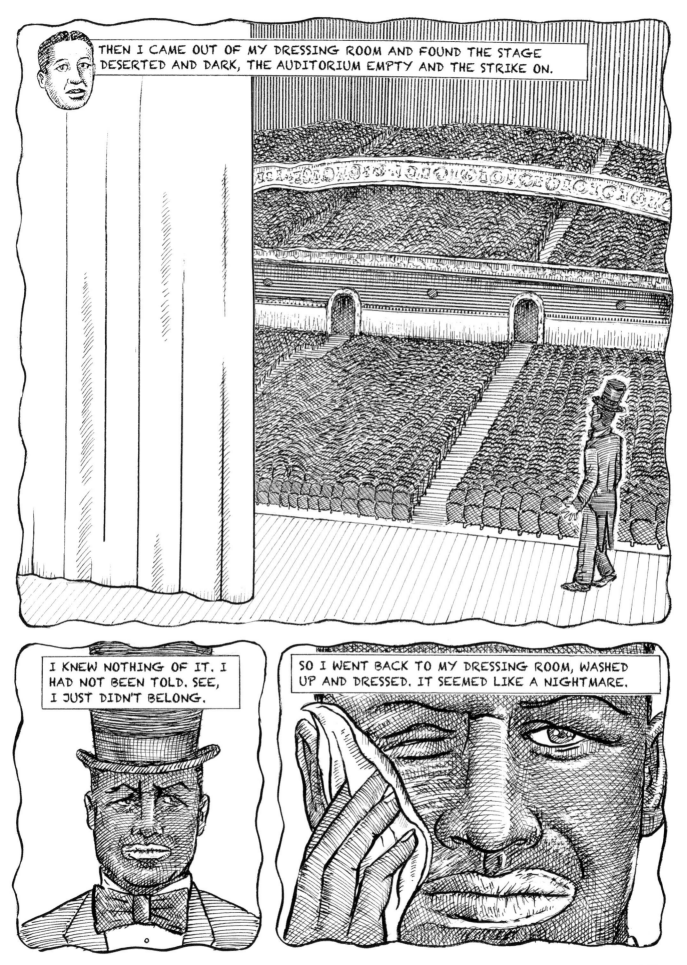

THEN I CAME OUT OF MY DRESSING ROOM AND FOUND THE STAGE DESERTED AND DARK, THE AUDITORIUM EMPTY AND THE STRIKE ON.

I KNEW NOTHING OF IT. I HAD NOT BEEN TOLD. SEE, I JUST DIDN'T BELONG.

SO I WENT BACK TO MY DRESSING ROOM, WASHED UP AND DRESSED. IT SEEMED LIKE A NIGHTMARE.

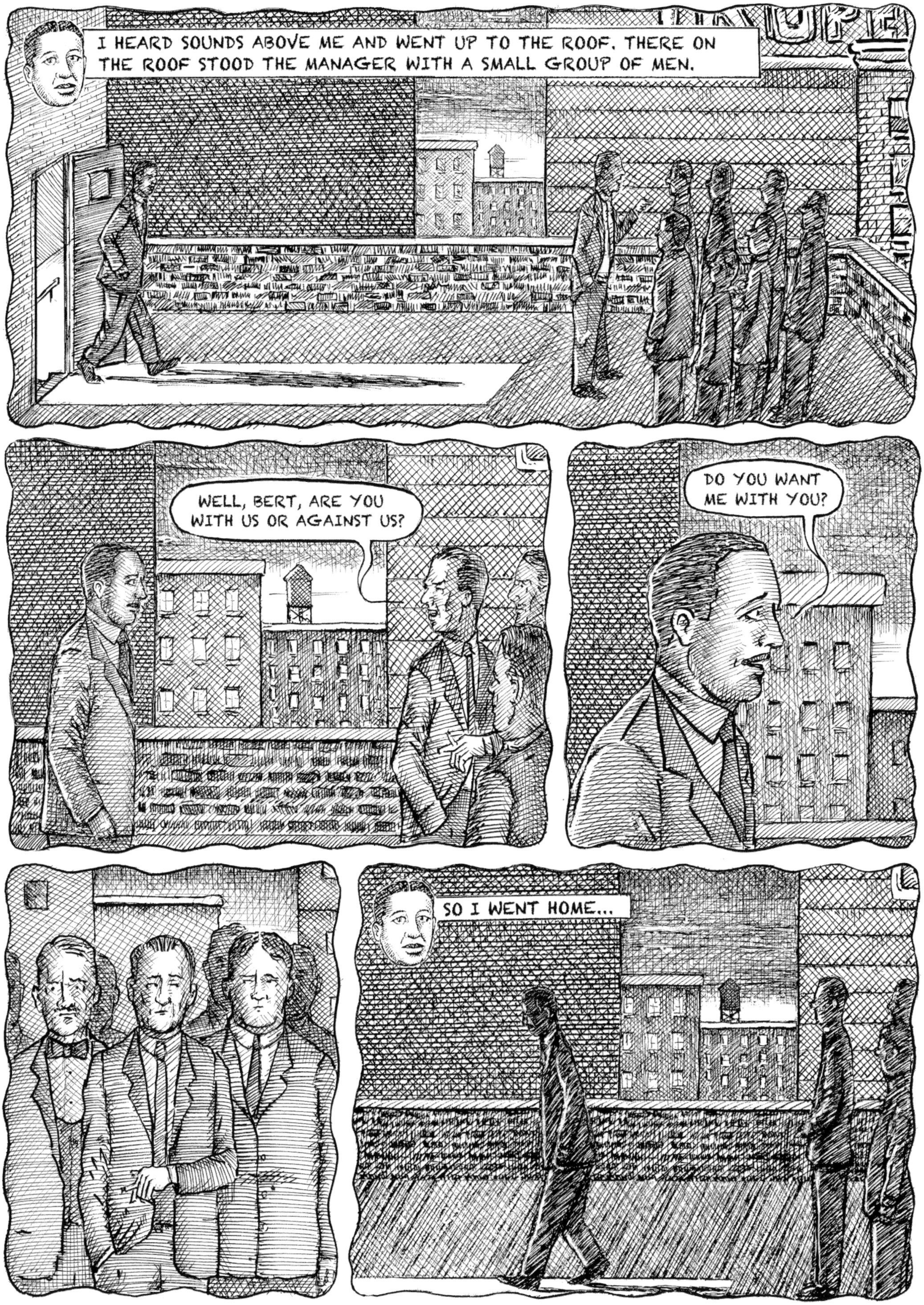
I HEARD SOUNDS ABOVE ME AND WENT UP TO THE ROOF. THERE ON THE ROOF STOOD THE MANAGER WITH A SMALL GROUP OF MEN.
WELL, BERT, ARE YOU WITH US OR AGAINST US?
DO YOU WANT ME WITH YOU?
SO I WENT HOME...

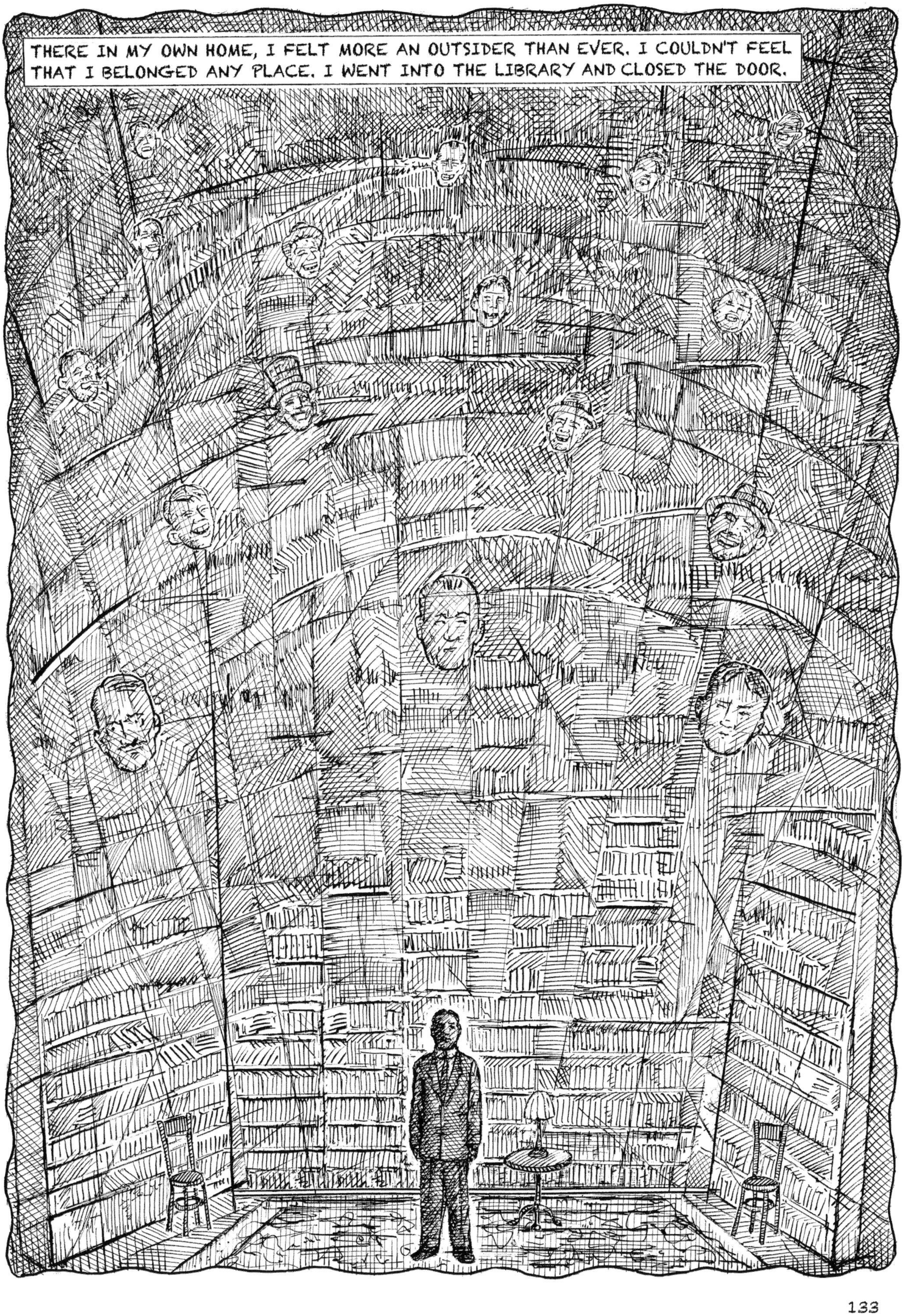
THERE IN MY OWN HOME, I FELT MORE AN OUTSIDER THAN EVER. I COULDN'T FEEL THAT I BELONGED ANY PLACE. I WENT INTO THE LIBRARY AND CLOSED THE DOOR.

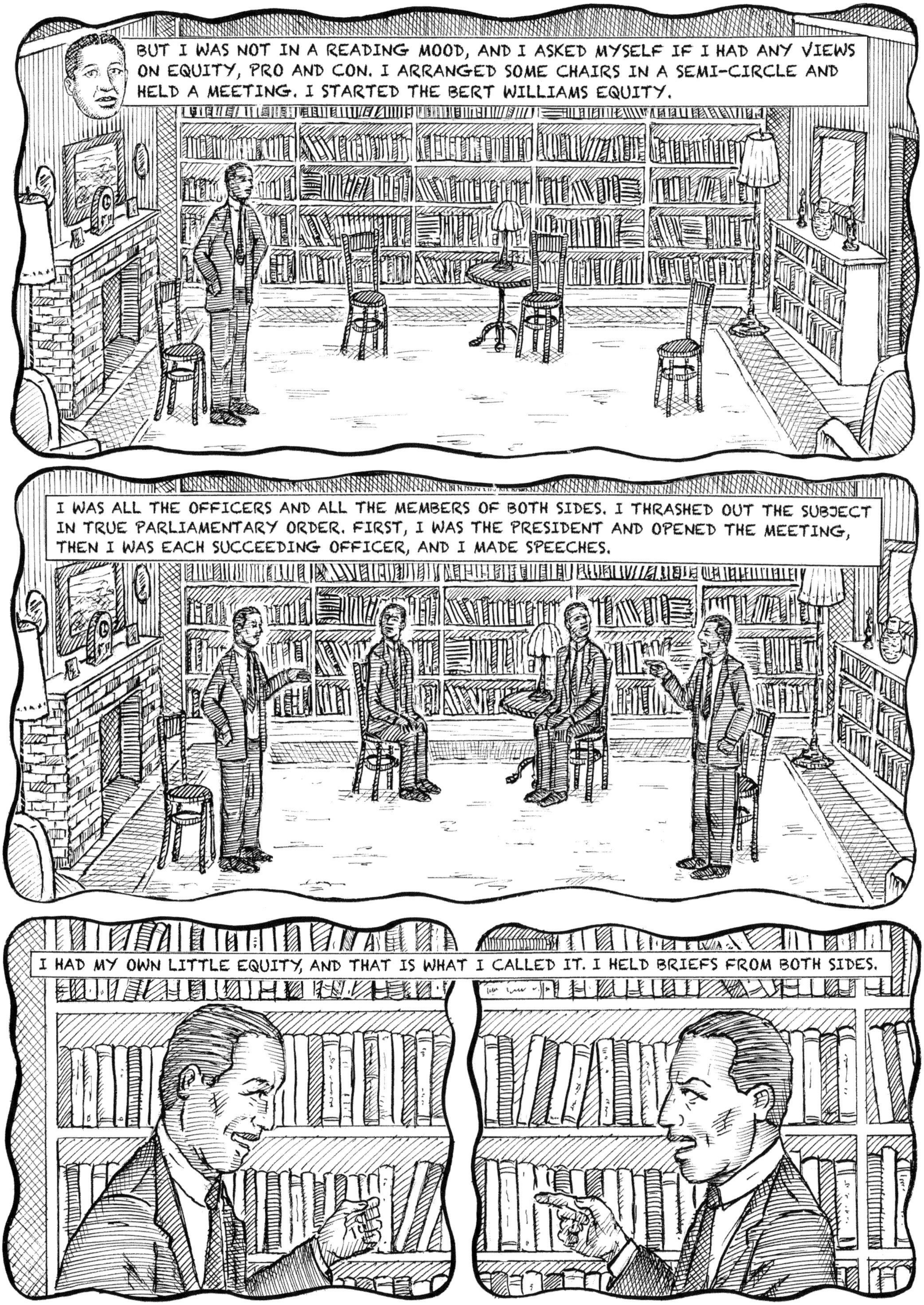
BUT I WAS NOT IN A READING MOOD, AND I ASKED MYSELF IF I HAD ANY VIEWS ON EQUITY, PRO AND CON. I ARRANGED SOME CHAIRS IN A SEMI-CIRCLE AND HELD A MEETING. I STARTED THE BERT WILLIAMS EQUITY.
I WAS ALL THE OFFICERS AND ALL THE MEMBERS OF BOTH SIDES. I THRASHED OUT THE SUBJECT IN TRUE PARLIAMENTARY ORDER. FIRST, I WAS THE PRESIDENT AND OPENED THE MEETING, THEN I WAS EACH SUCCEEDING OFFICER, AND I MADE SPEECHES.
I HAD MY OWN LITTLE EQUITY, AND THAT IS WHAT I CALLED IT. I HELD BRIEFS FROM BOTH SIDES.

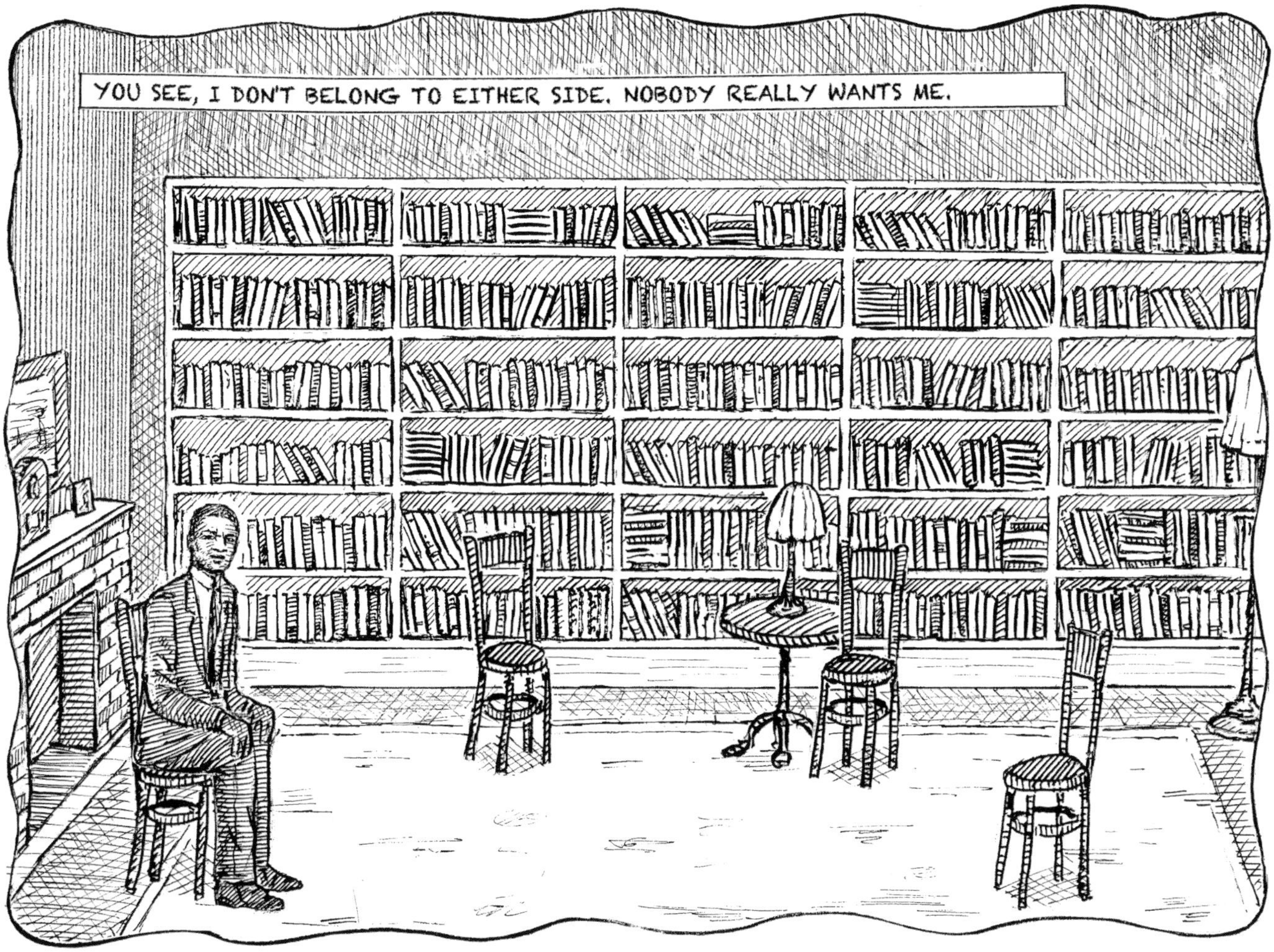
YOU SEE, I DON'T BELONG TO EITHER SIDE. NOBODY REALLY WANTS ME.

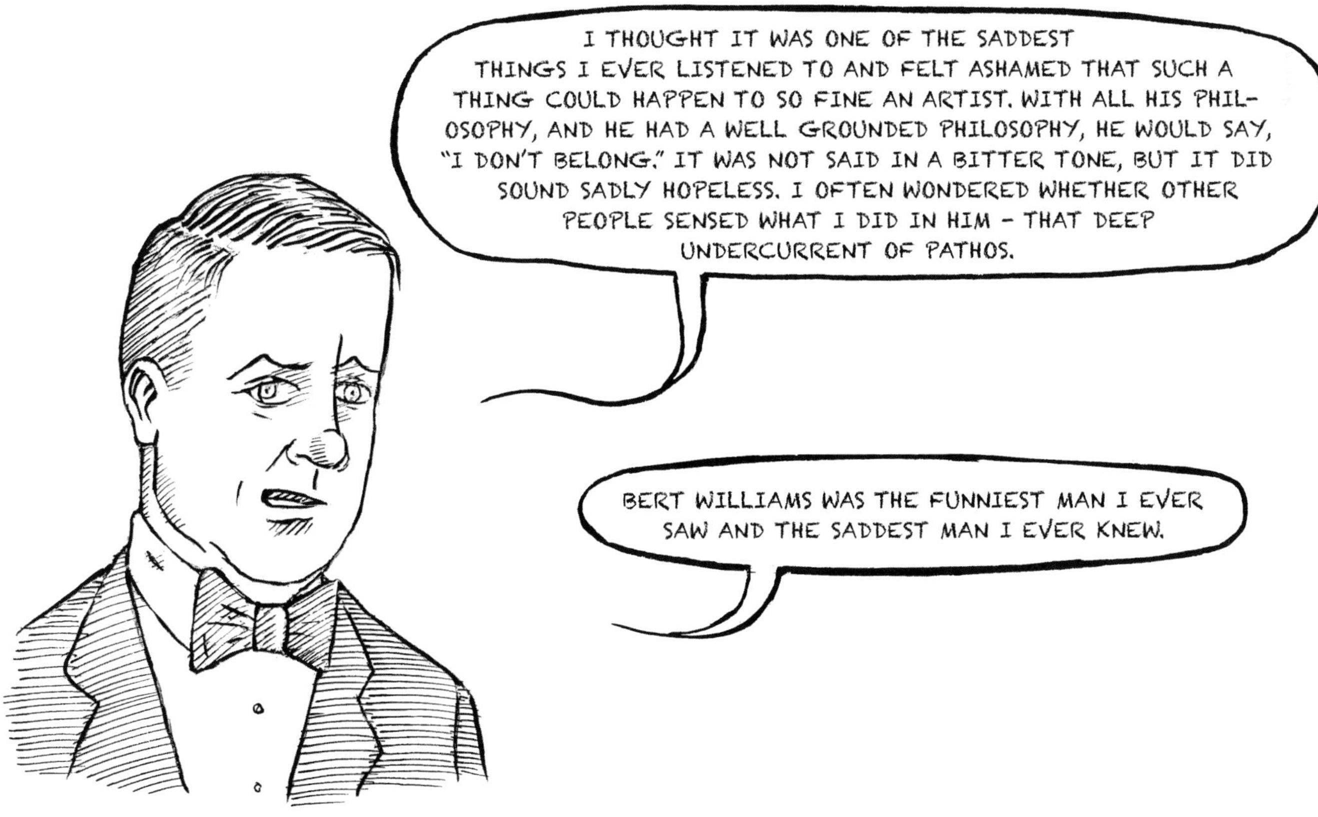
I THOUGHT IT WAS ONE OF THE SADDEST THINGS I EVER LISTENED TO AND FELT ASHAMED THAT SUCH A THING COULD HAPPEN TO SO FINE AN ARTIST. WITH ALL HIS PHIL-OSOPHY, AND HE HAD A WELL GROUNDED PHILOSOPHY, HE WOULD SAY, "I DON'T BELONG." IT WAS NOT SAID IN A BITTER TONE, BUT IT DID SOUND SADLY HOPELESS. I OFTEN WONDERED WHETHER OTHER PEOPLE SENSED WHAT I DID IN HIM - THAT DEEP UNDERCURRENT OF PATHOS.
BERT WILLIAMS WAS THE FUNNIEST MAN I EVER SAW AND THE SADDEST MAN I EVER KNEW.

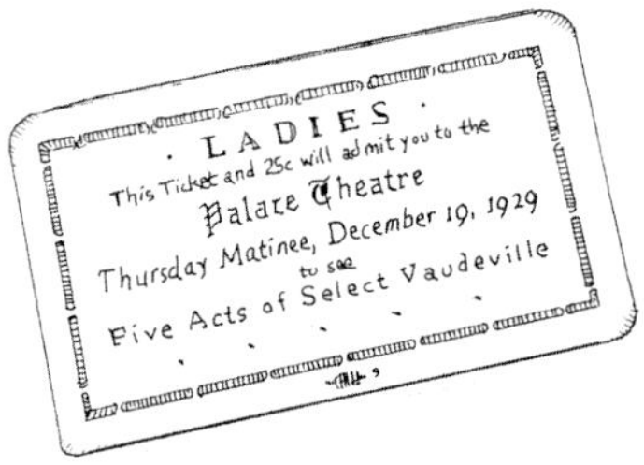
LADIES
This Ticket and 25c will admit you to the
Palace Theatre
Thursday Matinee, December 19, 1929
to see
Five Acts of Select Vaudeville

IN THE SOUTHERN MEDITERRANEAN REGION OF EUROPE, THERE IS A GENUS OF SPIDERS, STEGODYPHUS LINEATUS. THE MOTHERS NURTURE THEIR OFFSPRING BY DIGESTING FOOD AND REGURGITATING IT INTO THEIR MOUTHS. WHEN THE MOTHERS' SUPPLY OF NOURISHMENT IS DEPLETED, THE YOUNG SPIDERS EAT THEIR MOTHERS ALIVE.

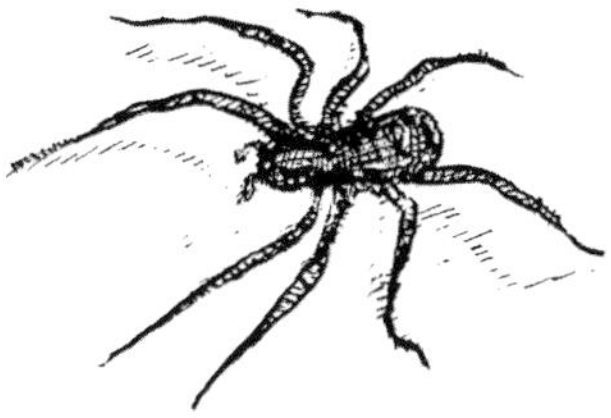

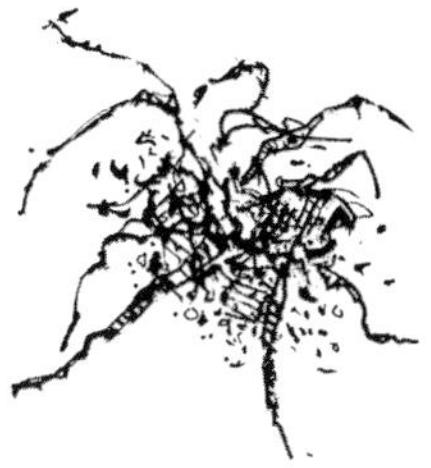

IN BIOSCIENCE, THE PHENOMENON IS CALLED MATRIPHAGY. IN SHOW BUSINESS HISTORY, IT IS KNOWN AS CINEMA IN THE VAUDEVILLE AGE.

IN THE EARLIEST YEARS OF MOTION PICTURES, VAUDEVILLE THEATERS NURTURED THE NEW FORM OF POPULAR ENTERTAINMENT. KOSTER AND BIAL'S MUSIC HALL AND KEITH'S UNION SQUARE THEATRE PRESENTED SOME OF THE FIRST FILMS IN 1896. BY THE SECOND DECADE OF THE TWENTIETH CENTURY, THE MAJORITY OF VARIETY HOUSES INCLUDED SILENT "SHORT SUBJECTS" IN THEIR PROGRAMS, THOUGH TYPICALLY IN THE "CHASER" SLOT AT THE END OF THE BILL RESERVED FOR THE WEAKEST PART OF THE SHOW.

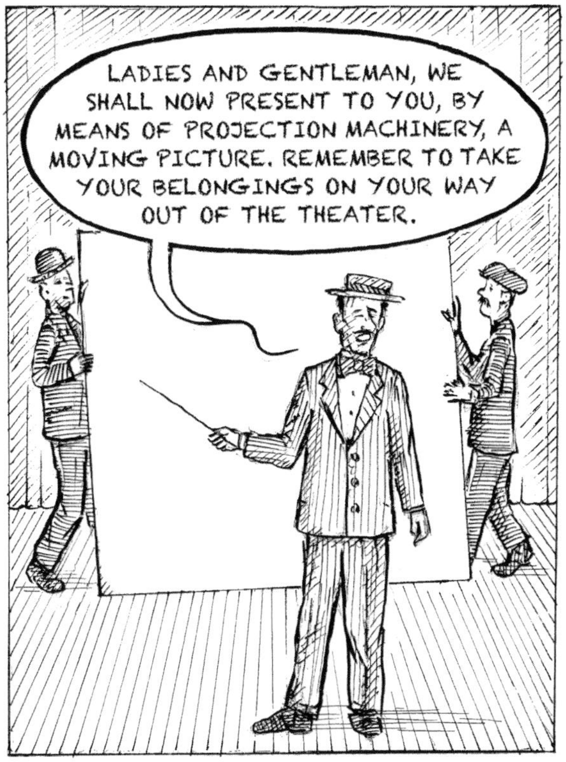
LADIES AND GENTLEMAN, WE SHALL NOW PRESENT TO YOU, BY MEANS OF PROJECTION MACHINERY, A MOVING PICTURE. REMEMBER TO TAKE YOUR BELONGINGS ON YOUR WAY OUT OF THE THEATER.

SINGERS, MUSICIANS, AND MONOLOGISTS WERE ILL-SUITED TO SILENT ENTERTAINMENT, OF COURSE, AND MANY DANCERS AND PANTOMIME ARTISTS SUCCESSFUL IN VAUDEVILLE WERE RELUCTANT TO HAVE THEIR ACTS FILMED, OUT OF FEAR THAT ONCE AUDIENCES SAW THEM ONSCREEN, THEY WOULD NO LONGER WANT TO PAY TO SEE THEM IN PERSON.

FEW STARS OF SILENT PICTURES CAME FROM THE TOP RANKS OF VAUDEVILLE. CHARLIE CHAPLIN WAS A TRANSPLANT FROM THE ENGLISH MUSIC HALL. SO WAS STAN LAUREL. HIS PARTNER, OLIVER HARDY, DID SOME SINGING AS A BOY, THEN WORKED AS A FILM PROJECTIONIST. BUSTER KEATON GREW UP IN VAUDEVILLE AS A CHILD STAR IN A FAMILY ACT, BUT WAS NEVER A SOLO STAGE PERFORMER. FILM, LIKE TELEVISION LATER, MADE ITS OWN STARS.

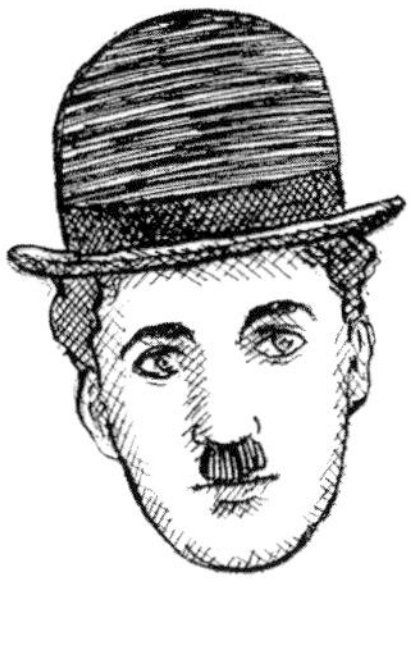

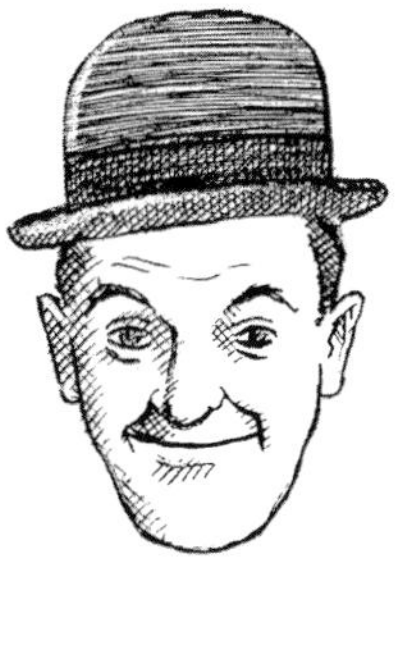

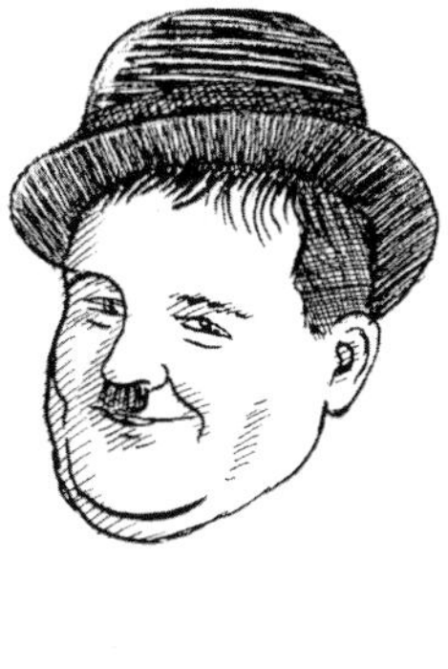

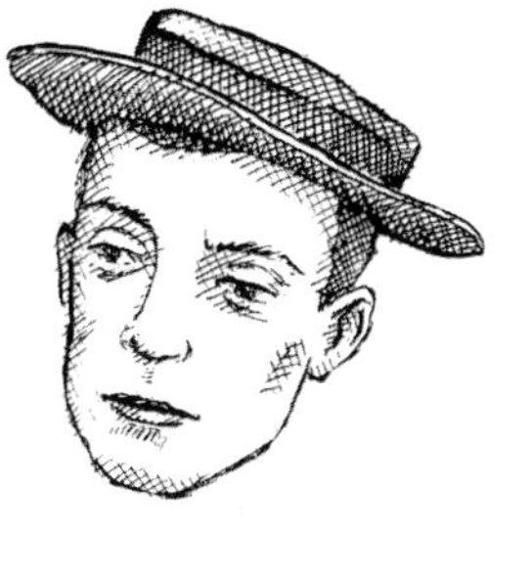

By 1915, silent movies had grown in scale and ambition into full-length features, presented in dedicated movie houses competing with vaudeville theaters for ticket buyers. Show-biz reporters would ask variety stars when, not if, they planned to venture into film.

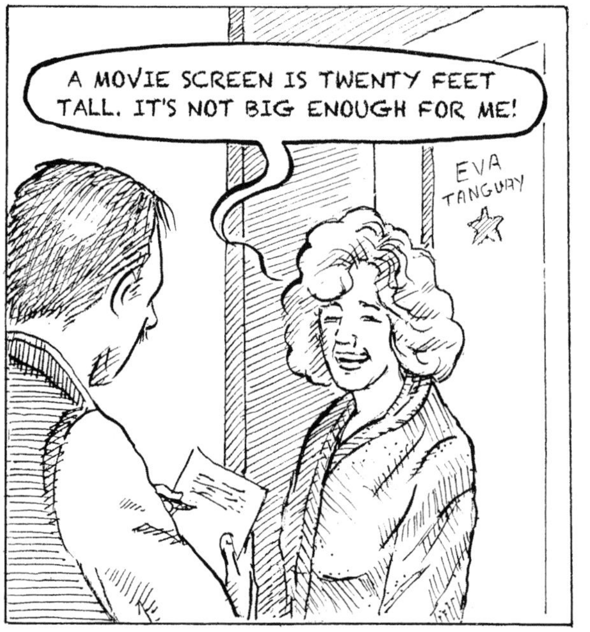
A MOVIE SCREEN IS TWENTY FEET TALL. IT'S NOT BIG ENOUGH FOR ME!
EVA TANGUAY

Eva Tanguay's first appearance onscreen, in a short subject shot in 1915 called *Energetic Eva*, has not survived. The following year, Tanguay made her feature debut in *The Wild Girl*, a film written and named for her.

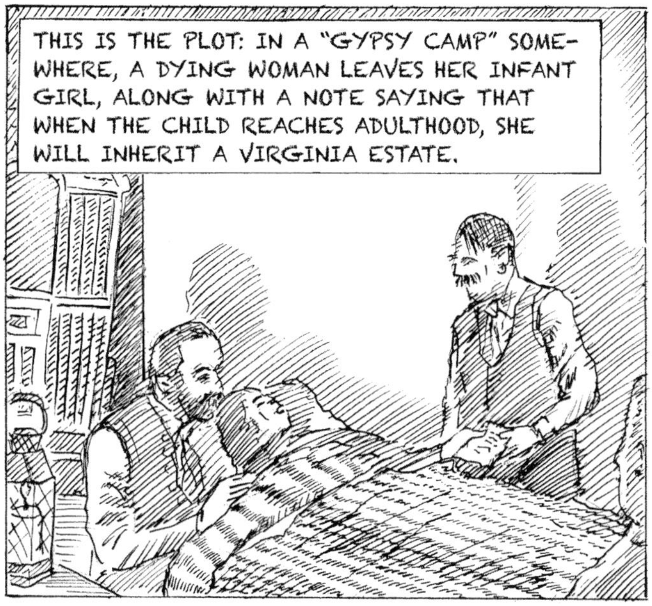
THIS IS THE PLOT: IN A "GYPSY CAMP" SOMEWHERE, A DYING WOMAN LEAVES HER INFANT GIRL, ALONG WITH A NOTE SAYING THAT WHEN THE CHILD REACHES ADULTHOOD, SHE WILL INHERIT A VIRGINIA ESTATE.

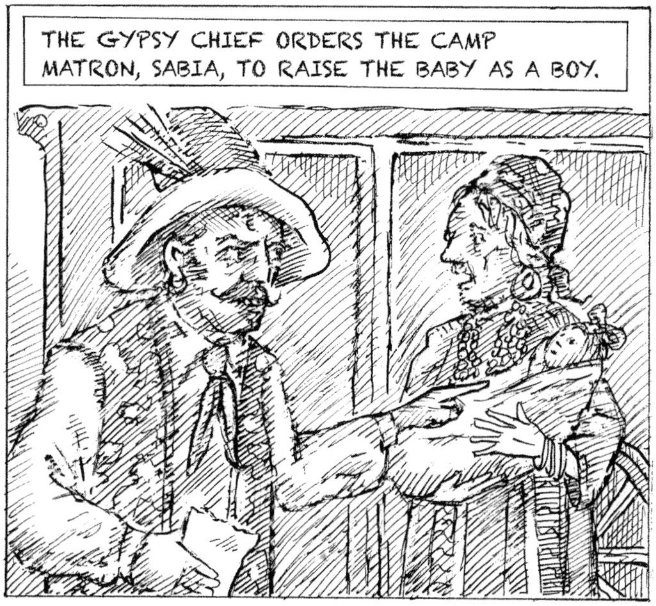
THE GYPSY CHIEF ORDERS THE CAMP MATRON, SABIA, TO RAISE THE BABY AS A BOY.

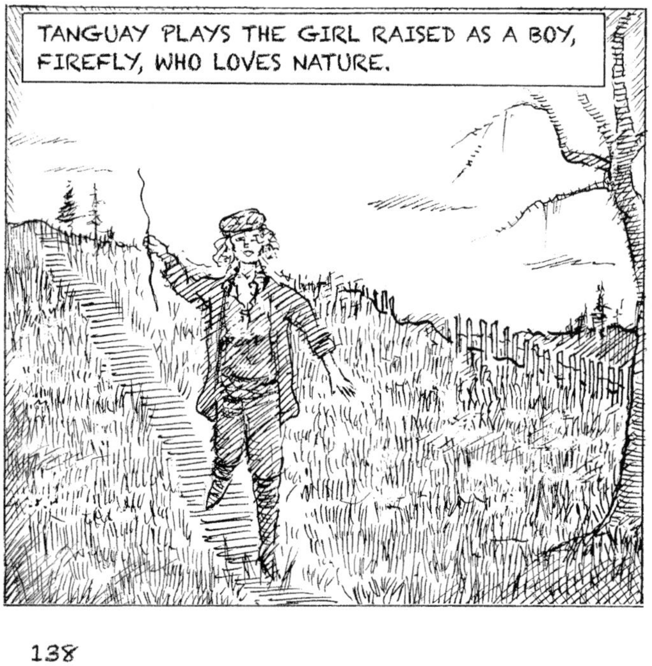
TANGUAY PLAYS THE GIRL RAISED AS A BOY, FIREFLY, WHO LOVES NATURE.

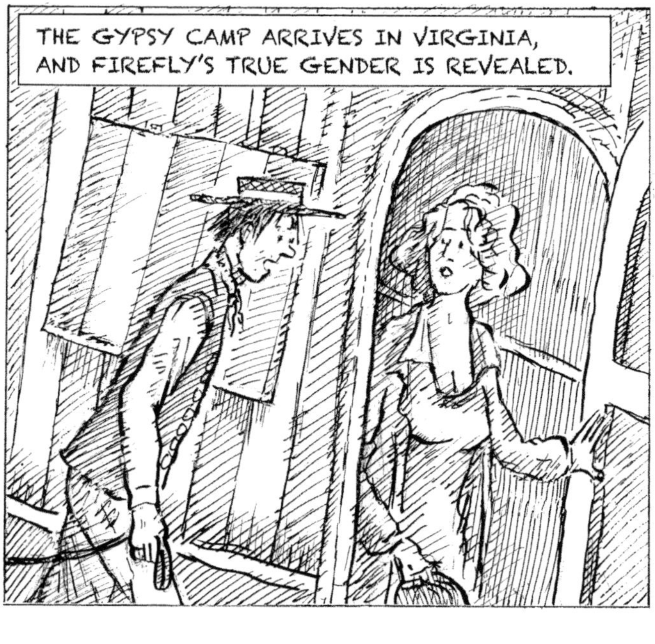
THE GYPSY CAMP ARRIVES IN VIRGINIA, AND FIREFLY'S TRUE GENDER IS REVEALED.

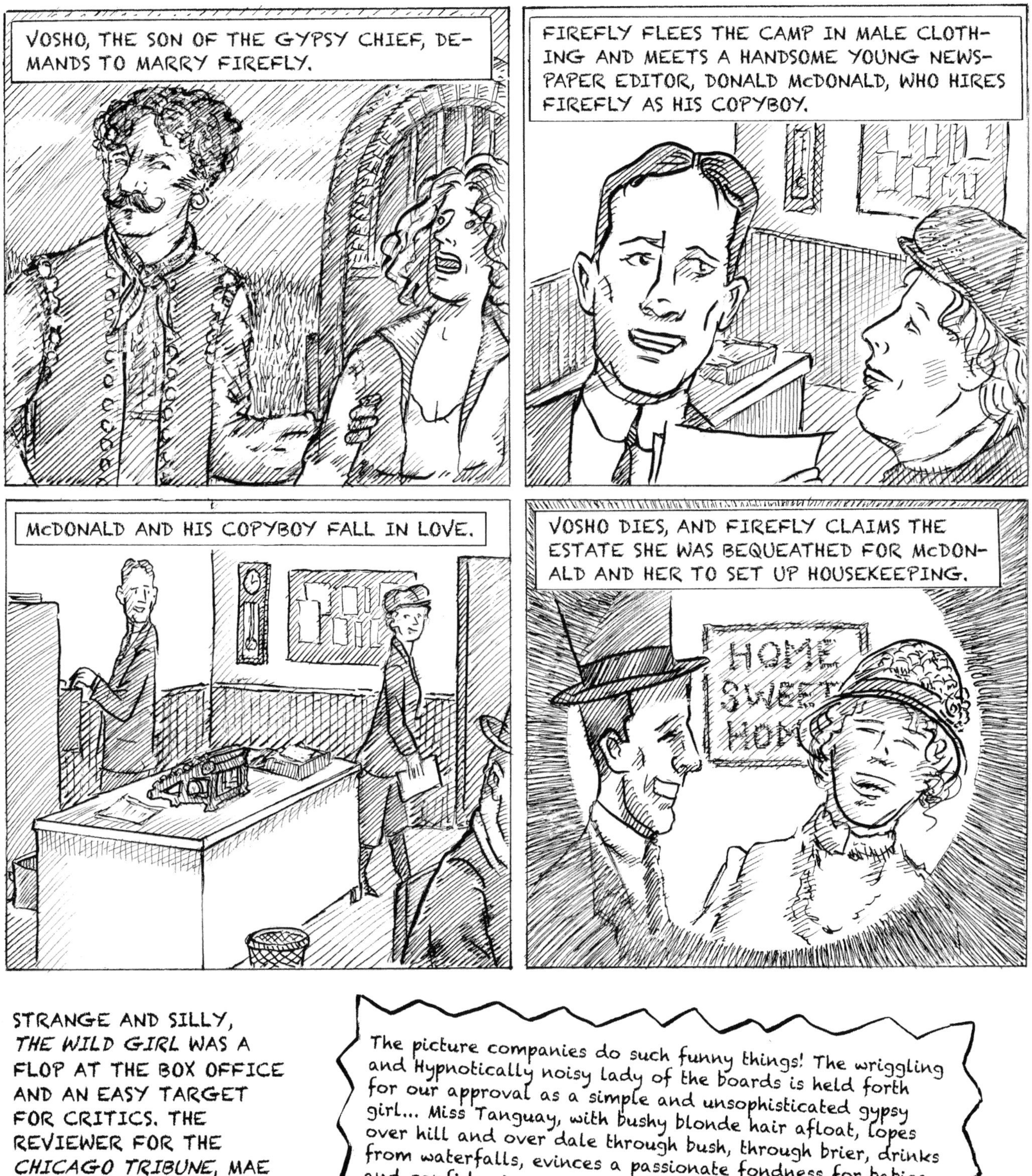
VOSHO, THE SON OF THE GYPSY CHIEF, DEMANDS TO MARRY FIREFLY.
FIREFLY FLEES THE CAMP IN MALE CLOTHING AND MEETS A HANDSOME YOUNG NEWSPAPER EDITOR, DONALD McDONALD, WHO HIRES FIREFLY AS HIS COPYBOY.
McDONALD AND HIS COPYBOY FALL IN LOVE.
VOSHO DIES, AND FIREFLY CLAIMS THE ESTATE SHE WAS BEQUEATHED FOR McDONALD AND HER TO SET UP HOUSEKEEPING.
HOME SWEET HOM

STRANGE AND SILLY, *THE WILD GIRL* WAS A FLOP AT THE BOX OFFICE AND AN EASY TARGET FOR CRITICS. THE REVIEWER FOR THE *CHICAGO TRIBUNE*, MAE TINEE, CAPTURED THE FAILURE OF THE FILM TO TAP THE WILDNESS IN THE GIRL.

The picture companies do such funny things! The wriggling and Hypnotically noisy lady of the boards is held forth for our approval as a simple and unsophisticated gypsy girl... Miss Tanguay, with bushy blonde hair afloat, lopes over hill and over dale through bush, through brier, drinks from waterfalls, evinces a passionate fondness for babies and confides in a queer blackbird with an enormous beak. Wild she is, all right — but it is neither the wildness of the present day nor the primitive. The story lands her in the company of Tom Moore, and we know that, though the fact is almost beyond our imagination, here is the man whose love will tame her and whose coffee she will pour. I second the wail of someone behind me as I quote it, "Why couldn't they of left her stay tough!"

EVA TANGUAY WOULD NEVER MAKE ANOTHER MOVIE.

IN THE YEAR AFTER *THE WILD GIRL* WAS RELEASED, THE *NASHVILLE TENNESSEAN* PUBLISHED AN ITEM UNDER THE HEADING "NEWS OF INTEREST TO COLORED PEOPLE." IT ANNOUNCED THE RELEASE OF A FILM STARRING BERT WILLIAMS, "THE FAMOUS COLORED COMEDIAN," WHO WAS "ONE OF THE FEW NEGRO PERFORMERS REGULARLY EMPLOYED BY THE BIG MOVIE PRODUCERS, BEING WITH THE BIOGRAPH COMPANY."

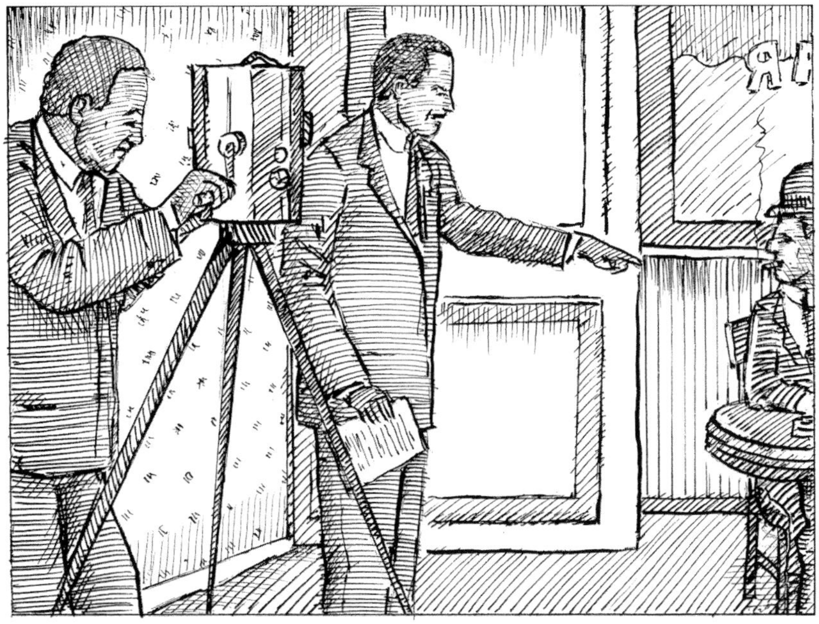

TWO COMEDY SHORTS BY WILLIAMS WERE RELEASED BY BIOGRAPH: *NATURAL BORN GAMBLER* AND *FISH*. IN THE FIRST, A TWO-REELER, WILLIAMS PLAYS A MEMBER OF A SOCIAL GROUP, THE INDEPENDENT ORDER OF CALCIMINE ARTISTS OF AMERICA.

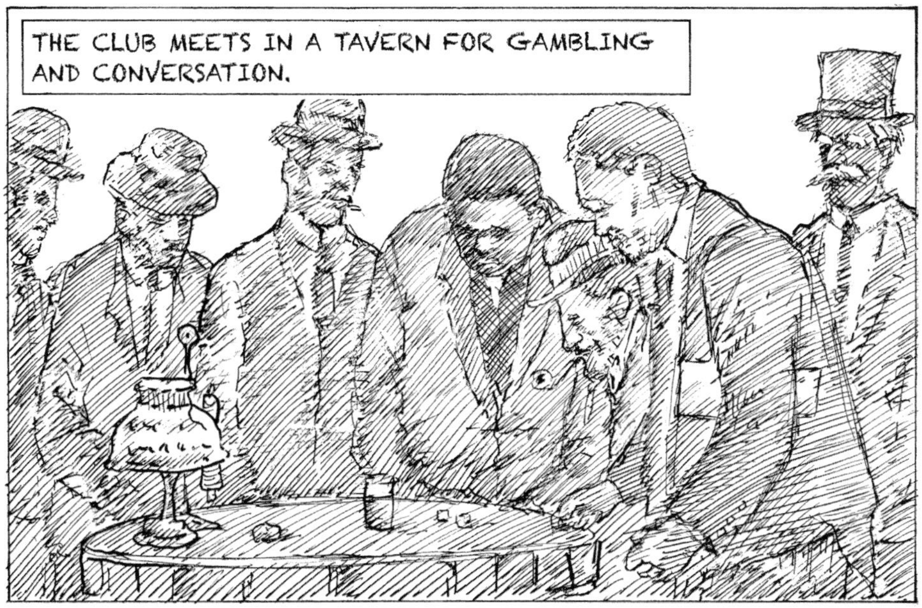
THE CLUB MEETS IN A TAVERN FOR GAMBLING AND CONVERSATION.

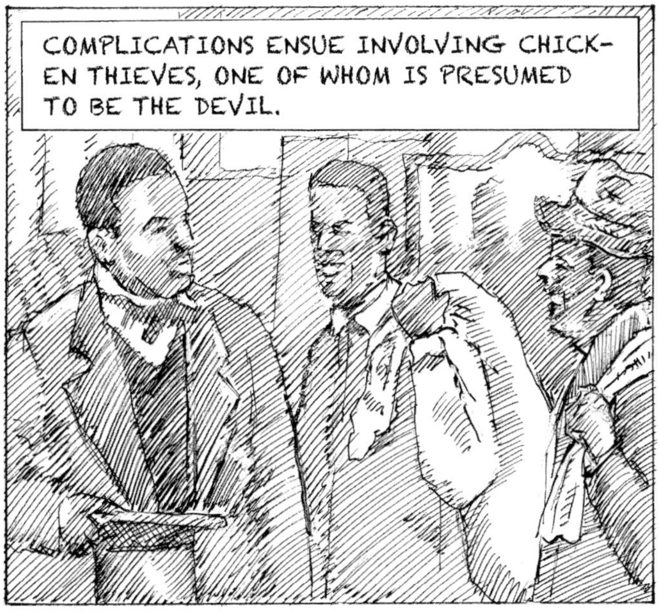
COMPLICATIONS ENSUE INVOLVING CHICKEN THIEVES, ONE OF WHOM IS PRESUMED TO BE THE DEVIL.

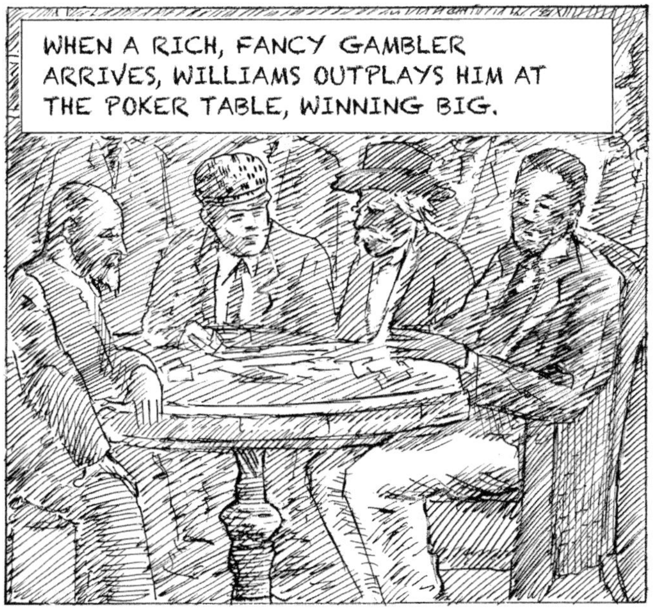
WHEN A RICH, FANCY GAMBLER ARRIVES, WILLIAMS OUTPLAYS HIM AT THE POKER TABLE, WINNING BIG.

CAUGHT BY THE COPS, THE WILLIAMS CHARACTER IS JAILED. BEHIND BARS, HE DREAMS OF PLAYING POKER AGAIN. IN THE CLOSING SCENE OF THE FILM, WILLIAMS RE-CREATES THE ONE-MAN IMAGINARY CARD GAME THAT WAS A SIGNATURE OF HIS PERFORMANCES IN VAUDEVILLE.

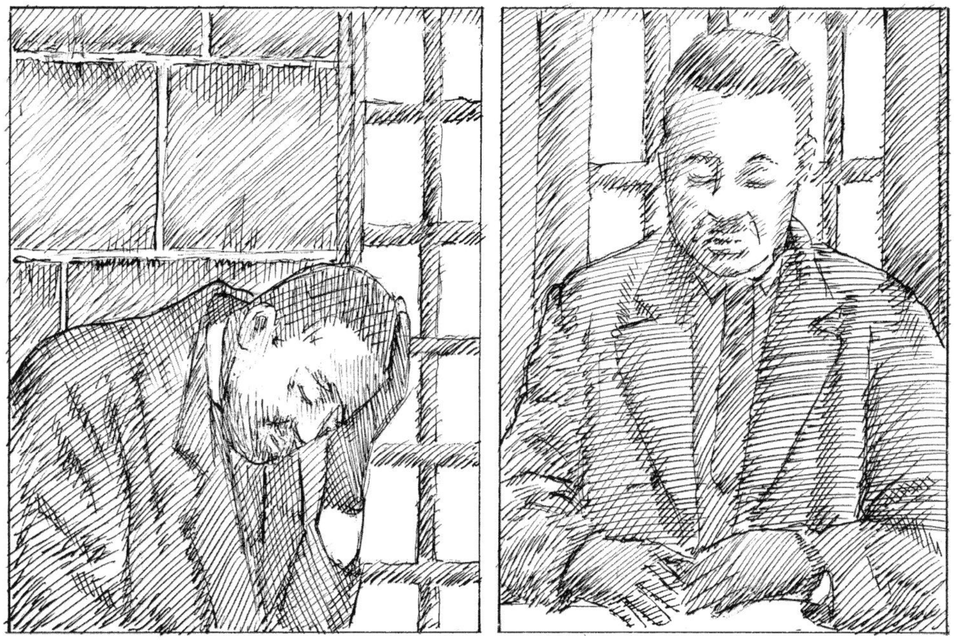

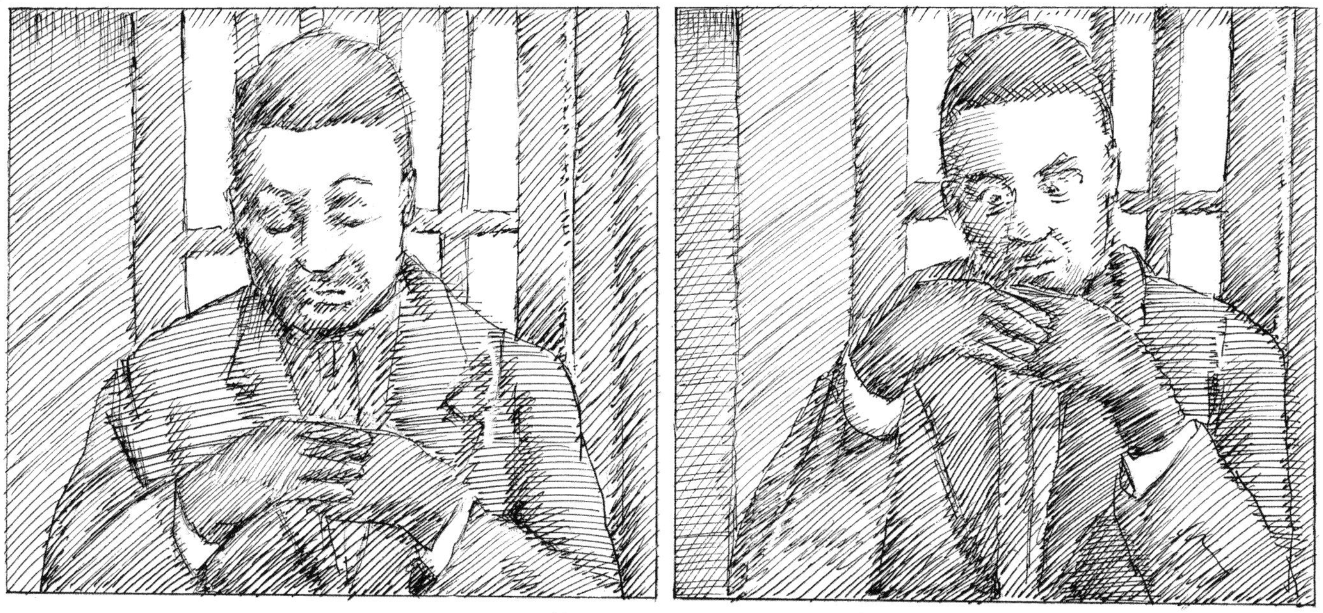

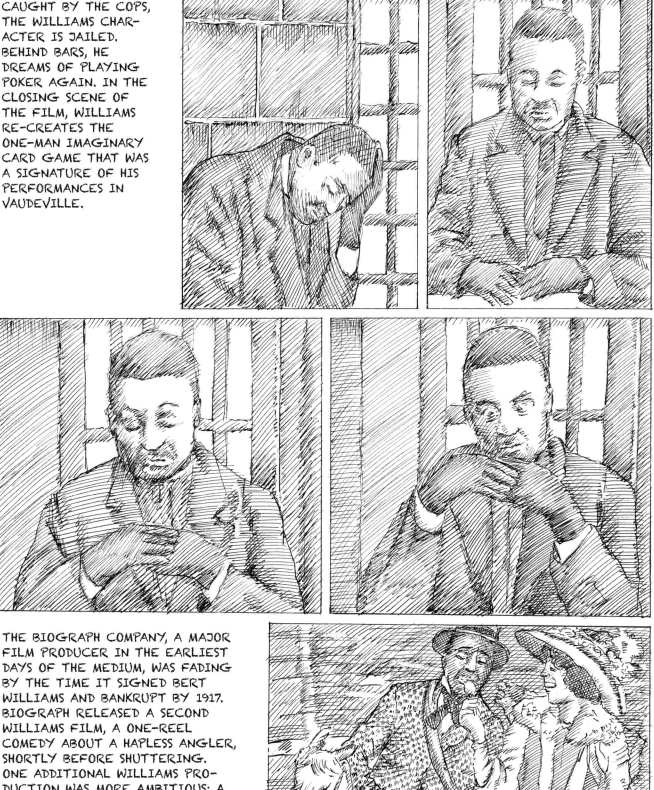

THE BIOGRAPH COMPANY, A MAJOR FILM PRODUCER IN THE EARLIEST DAYS OF THE MEDIUM, WAS FADING BY THE TIME IT SIGNED BERT WILLIAMS AND BANKRUPT BY 1917. BIOGRAPH RELEASED A SECOND WILLIAMS FILM, A ONE-REEL COMEDY ABOUT A HAPLESS ANGLER, SHORTLY BEFORE SHUTTERING. ONE ADDITIONAL WILLIAMS PRODUCTION WAS MORE AMBITIOUS: A MULTIREEL SOCIAL COMEDY WITH AN ALL-BLACK CAST, STARRING WILLIAMS AND ODESSA WARREN GREY AS SUITORS.

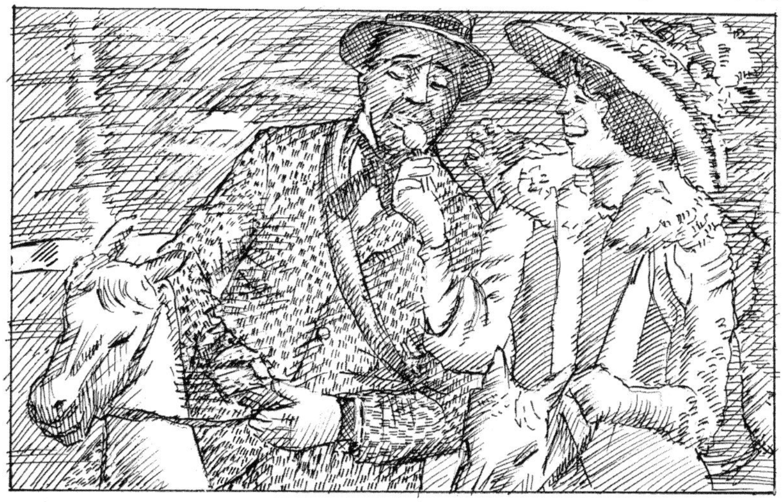

THE MOVIE WAS UNFINISHED AND UNKNOWN UNTIL IT WAS FOUND, IN 2013, IN CANISTERS OF UNEDITED FILM.

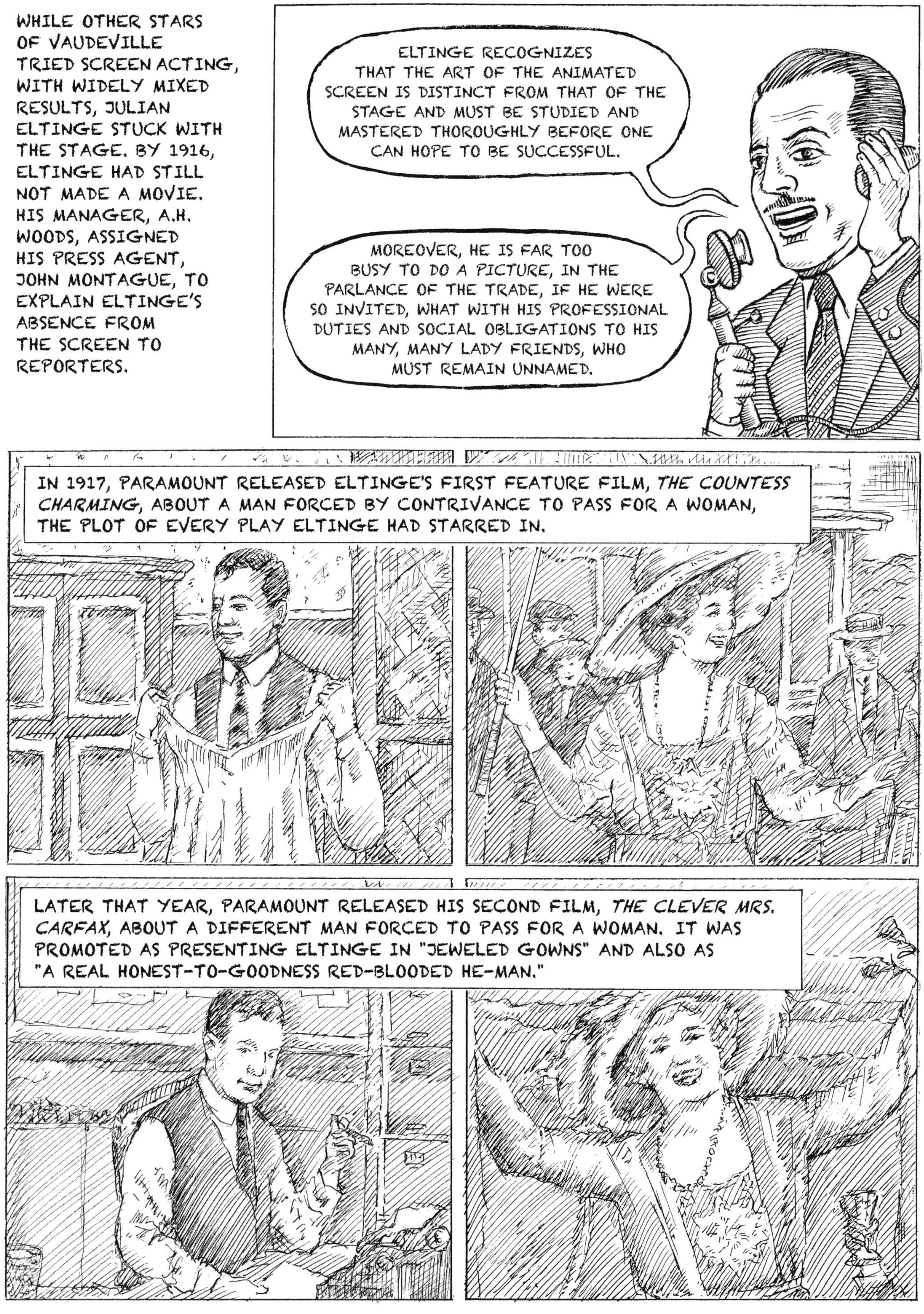
WHILE OTHER STARS OF VAUDEVILLE TRIED SCREEN ACTING, WITH WIDELY MIXED RESULTS, JULIAN ELTINGE STUCK WITH THE STAGE. BY 1916, ELTINGE HAD STILL NOT MADE A MOVIE. HIS MANAGER, A.H. WOODS, ASSIGNED HIS PRESS AGENT, JOHN MONTAGUE, TO EXPLAIN ELTINGE'S ABSENCE FROM THE SCREEN TO REPORTERS.
ELTINGE RECOGNIZES THAT THE ART OF THE ANIMATED SCREEN IS DISTINCT FROM THAT OF THE STAGE AND MUST BE STUDIED AND MASTERED THOROUGHLY BEFORE ONE CAN HOPE TO BE SUCCESSFUL.
MOREOVER, HE IS FAR TOO BUSY TO *DO A PICTURE*, IN THE PARLANCE OF THE TRADE, IF HE WERE SO INVITED, WHAT WITH HIS PROFESSIONAL DUTIES AND SOCIAL OBLIGATIONS TO HIS MANY, MANY LADY FRIENDS, WHO MUST REMAIN UNNAMED.
IN 1917, PARAMOUNT RELEASED ELTINGE'S FIRST FEATURE FILM, *THE COUNTESS CHARMING*, ABOUT A MAN FORCED BY CONTRIVANCE TO PASS FOR A WOMAN, THE PLOT OF EVERY PLAY ELTINGE HAD STARRED IN.
LATER THAT YEAR, PARAMOUNT RELEASED HIS SECOND FILM, *THE CLEVER MRS. CARFAX*, ABOUT A DIFFERENT MAN FORCED TO PASS FOR A WOMAN. IT WAS PROMOTED AS PRESENTING ELTINGE IN "JEWELED GOWNS" AND ALSO AS "A REAL HONEST-TO-GOODNESS RED-BLOODED HE-MAN."

BY 1918, ELTINGE HAD MOVED TO SOUTHERN CALIFORNIA TO PURSUE A FILM CAREER. WITH WEALTH FROM HIS STAGE WORK, HE BUILT A MANSION IN THE SILVER LAKE AREA AND CALLED IT VILLA CAPISTRANO. NEWSPAPERS FAWNED OVER THE "CASTLE-LIKE RESIDENCE," WITH ITS ITALIANATE FLOURISHES, SUNKEN GARDEN, "RARE OLD FURNITURE AND TAPESTRIES BROUGHT FROM ABROAD," AND "NAUGHTY LITTLE STATUES IN THE NICHES OF ITS CHAPEL-LIKE CORRIDORS." POSTCARDS OF THE PROPERTY WERE SOLD IN TOURIST SHOPS.

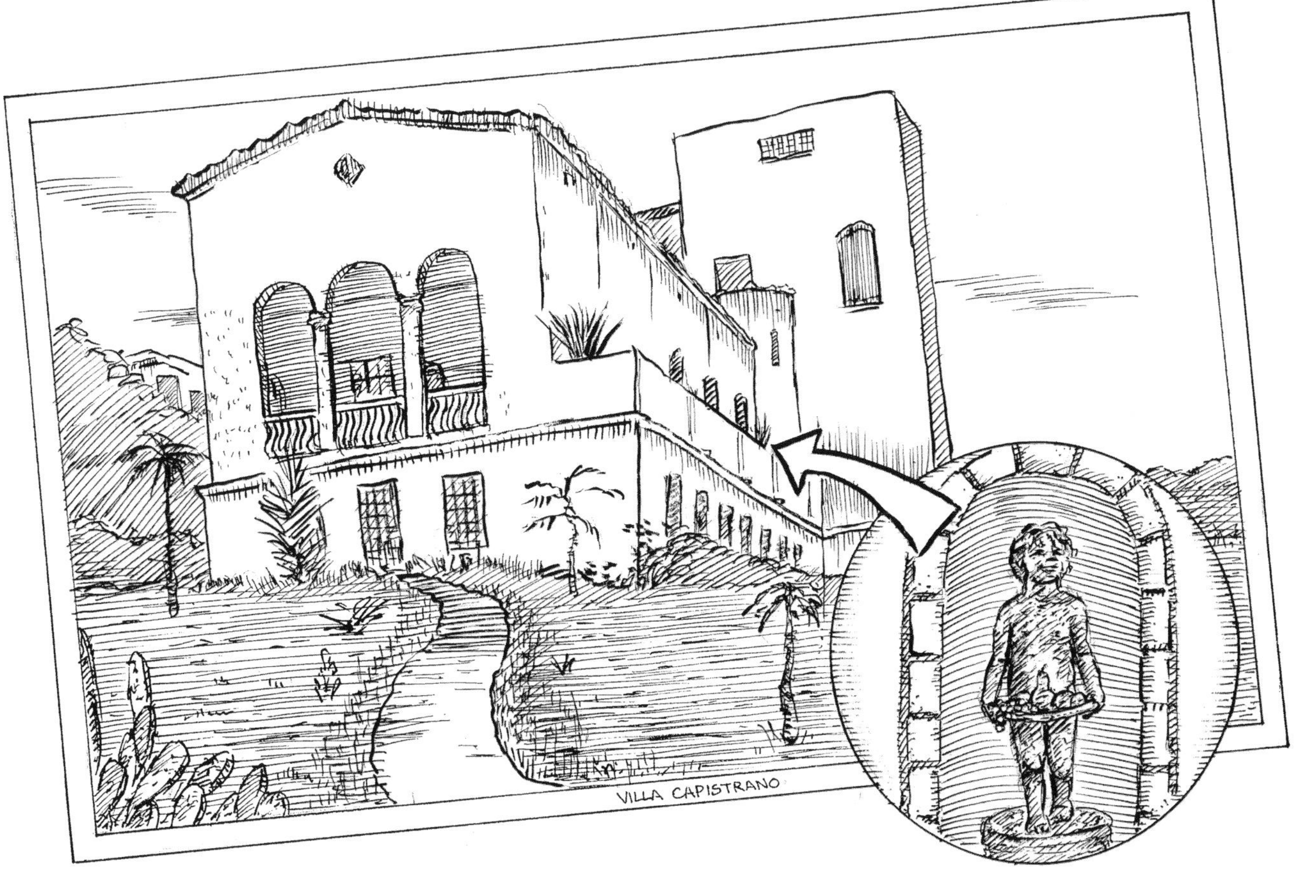
VILLA CAPISTRANO

IN HIS THIRD FILM FOR PARAMOUNT, *THE WIDOW'S MIGHT*, ELTINGE PLAYED A NEW YORK GENTLEMAN WHO BUYS A RANCH IN CALIFORNIA AND, TO TRICK SOME CROOKS, PASSES FOR A WOMAN. ADS FOR THE MOVIE IMPLORED, "GET A NEW VIEWPOINT ON EUGENICS! SEE A MAN MOTHER A BABY AND GIVE NEW IMPETUS TO THE SUFFRAGE CAUSE!"

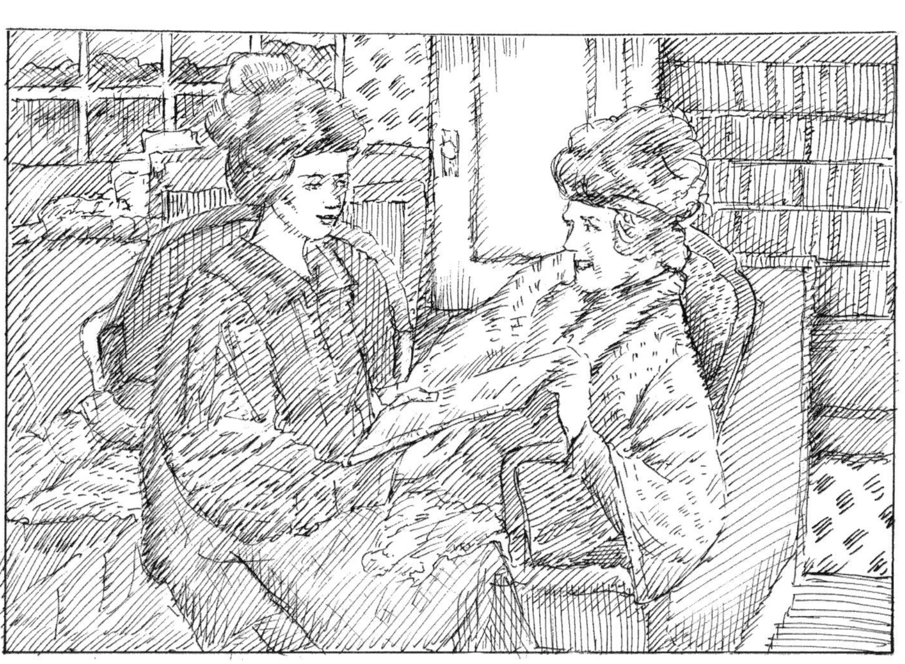

ELTINGE HIMSELF STARTED BUYING ACREAGE IN THE DESERT OF THE IMPERIAL VALLEY, A VAST SWATH OF HARD-TO-REACH AND HARDER-TO-TAME LAND NORTHEAST OF SAN DIEGO. HE CHARMED SHOW-BIZ REPORTERS FOR *THE LOS ANGELES TIMES* WITH DETAILS OF HIS PLANS TO BUILD A LUXURIOUS RETREAT FOR ARTISTS AND PATRONS OF THE ARTS AT LEISURE: A COMBINATION HEALTH SPA/MUSEUM/ARTISTS' COLONY.

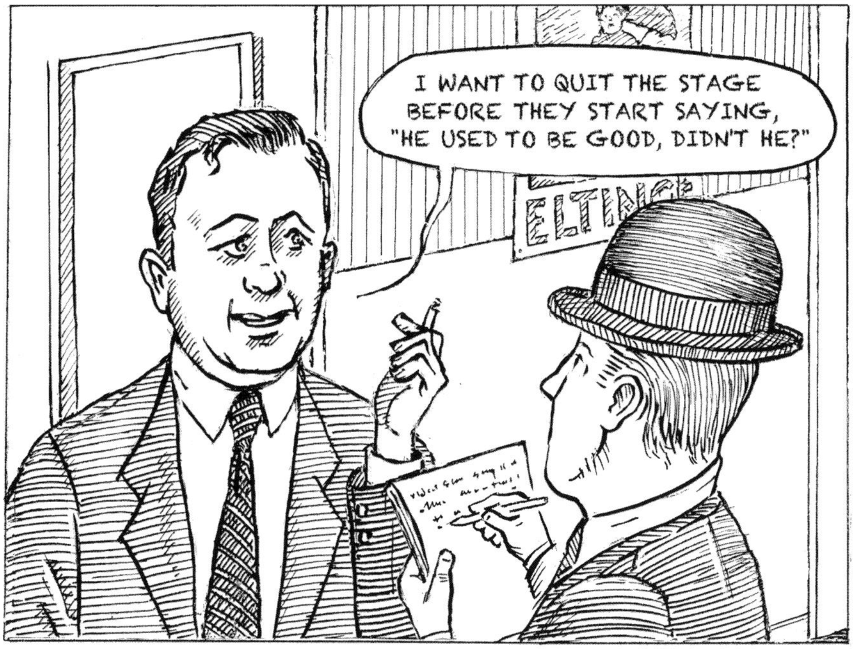
I WANT TO QUIT THE STAGE BEFORE THEY START SAYING, "HE USED TO BE GOOD, DIDN'T HE?"

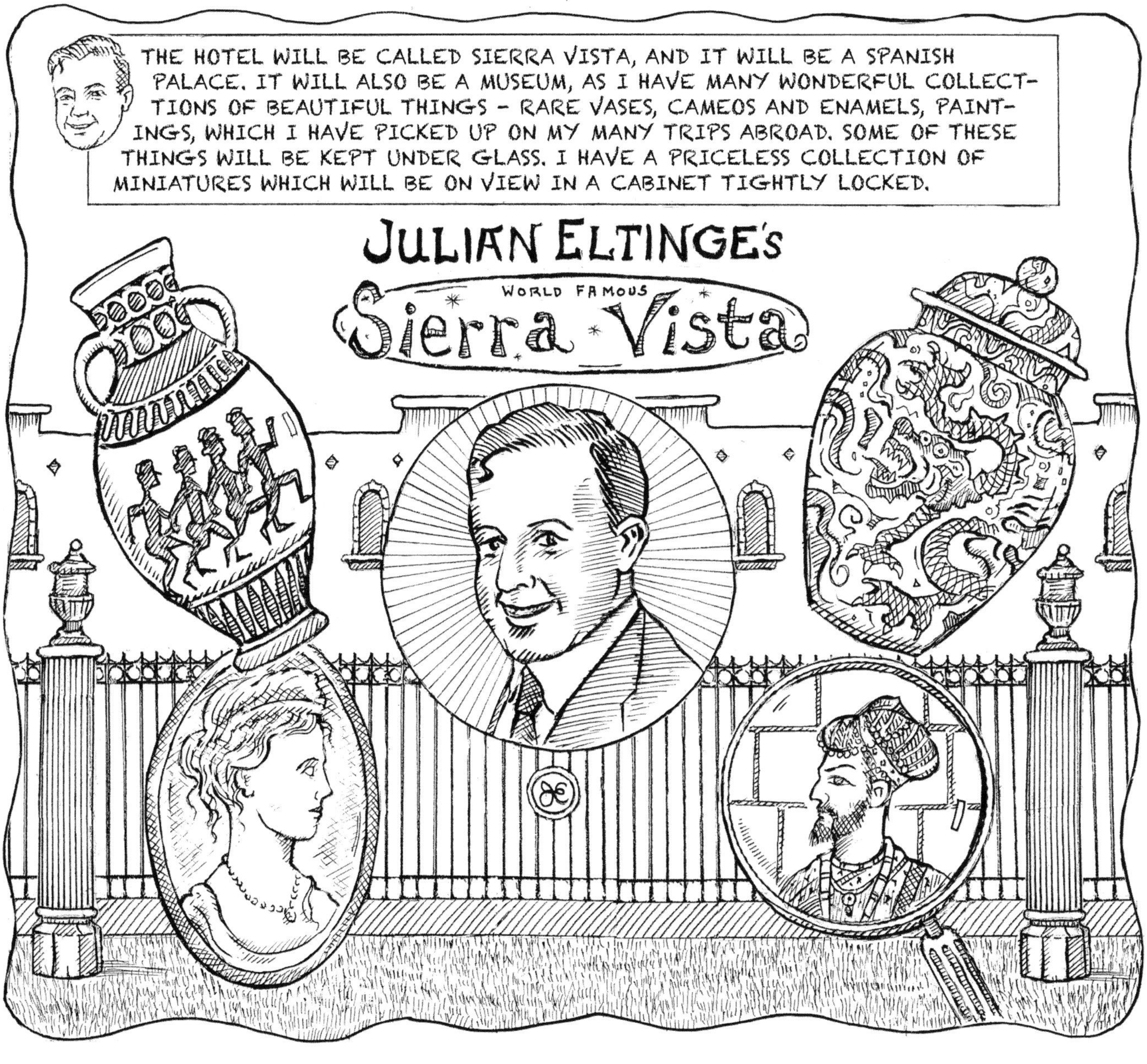
THE HOTEL WILL BE CALLED SIERRA VISTA, AND IT WILL BE A SPANISH PALACE. IT WILL ALSO BE A MUSEUM, AS I HAVE MANY WONDERFUL COLLECTIONS OF BEAUTIFUL THINGS - RARE VASES, CAMEOS AND ENAMELS, PAINTINGS, WHICH I HAVE PICKED UP ON MY MANY TRIPS ABROAD. SOME OF THESE THINGS WILL BE KEPT UNDER GLASS. I HAVE A PRICELESS COLLECTION OF MINIATURES WHICH WILL BE ON VIEW IN A CABINET TIGHTLY LOCKED.
JULIAN ELTINGE'S
WORLD FAMOUS
Sierra Vista

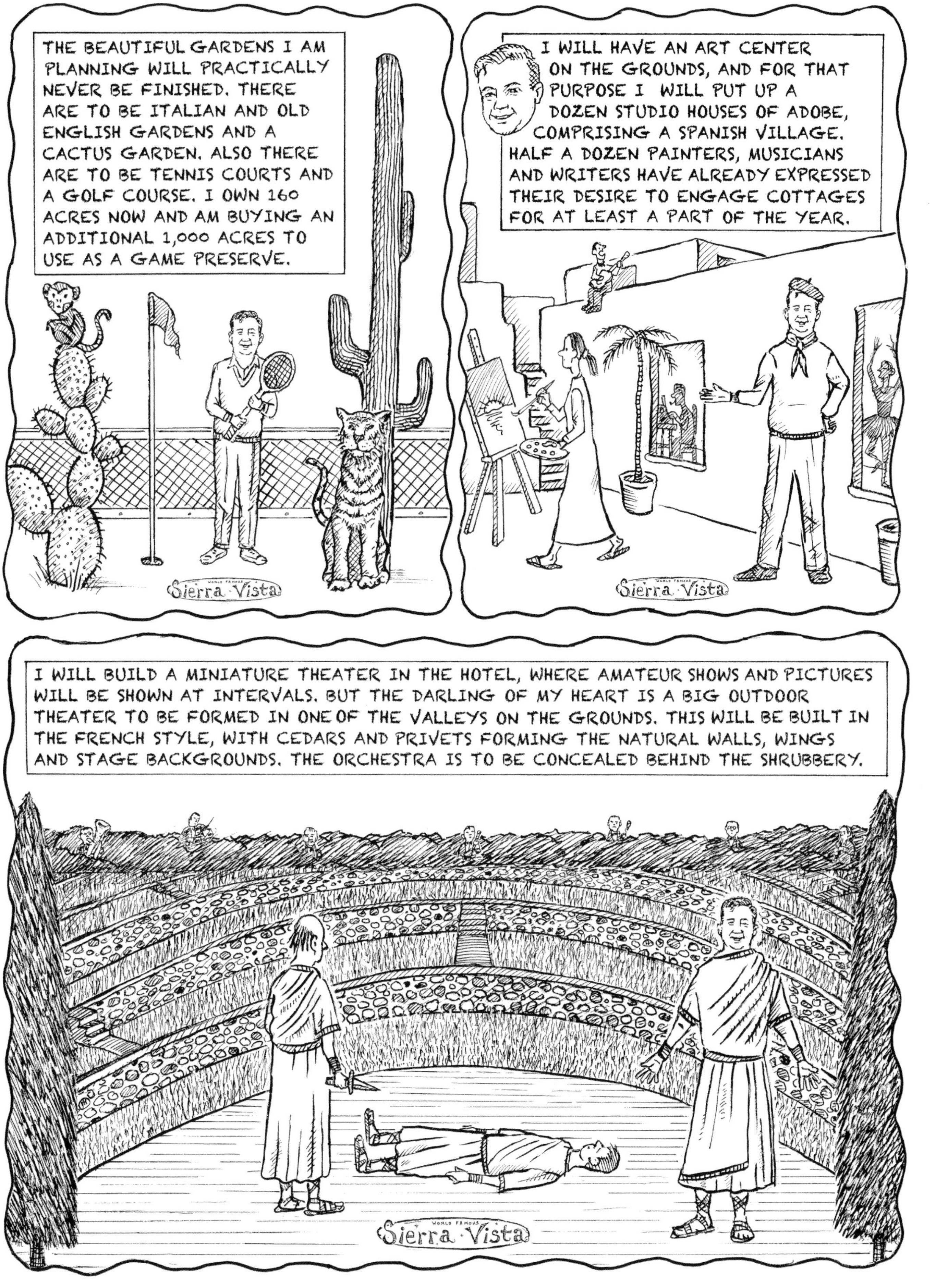
THE BEAUTIFUL GARDENS I AM PLANNING WILL PRACTICALLY NEVER BE FINISHED. THERE ARE TO BE ITALIAN AND OLD ENGLISH GARDENS AND A CACTUS GARDEN. ALSO THERE ARE TO BE TENNIS COURTS AND A GOLF COURSE. I OWN 160 ACRES NOW AND AM BUYING AN ADDITIONAL 1,000 ACRES TO USE AS A GAME PRESERVE.
WORLD FAMOUS Sierra Vista
I WILL HAVE AN ART CENTER ON THE GROUNDS, AND FOR THAT PURPOSE I WILL PUT UP A DOZEN STUDIO HOUSES OF ADOBE, COMPRISING A SPANISH VILLAGE. HALF A DOZEN PAINTERS, MUSICIANS AND WRITERS HAVE ALREADY EXPRESSED THEIR DESIRE TO ENGAGE COTTAGES FOR AT LEAST A PART OF THE YEAR.
WORLD FAMOUS Sierra Vista
I WILL BUILD A MINIATURE THEATER IN THE HOTEL, WHERE AMATEUR SHOWS AND PICTURES WILL BE SHOWN AT INTERVALS. BUT THE DARLING OF MY HEART IS A BIG OUTDOOR THEATER TO BE FORMED IN ONE OF THE VALLEYS ON THE GROUNDS. THIS WILL BE BUILT IN THE FRENCH STYLE, WITH CEDARS AND PRIVETS FORMING THE NATURAL WALLS, WINGS AND STAGE BACKGROUNDS. THE ORCHESTRA IS TO BE CONCEALED BEHIND THE SHRUBBERY.
WORLD FAMOUS Sierra Vista

IN HIS FOURTH FILM, *OVER THE RHINE*, ELTINGE PLAYED AN AMERICAN SPY CALLED IN PATRIOTIC DUTY TO PASS FOR A WOMAN. HIS FOURTH FIZZLE AT THE BOX OFFICE, THE FILM WAS REPACKAGED TWO YEARS LATER AS *THE ADVENTURESS*, AFTER ONE OF THE SECONDARY PLAYERS, R. DE VALENTINA, BECAME FAMOUS AS RUDOLPH VALENTINO. BUT IT WAS WITHDRAWN AFTER ANOTHER OF THE SECONDARY PLAYERS, VIRGINIA RAPPE, DIED IN A SCANDAL THAT ENDED FATTY ARBUCKLE'S CAREER. IT WAS LATER RE-RELEASED AS *ISLE OF LOVE*, WITH RAPPE NO LONGER BILLED.

CAPTURED IN CLOSE-UP AND BLOWN UP ON SCREEN, ELTINGE WAS LESS THAN IMPRESSIVE AS A WOMAN ON FILM. HE NEVER BECAME A MOVIE STAR. OVEREXTENDED FINANCIALLY, HE LOST EVERYTHING HE INVESTED IN HIS HEALTH FARM/ARTISTS' COLONY, ALONG WITH THE PROPERTY, AND ENDED UP HAVING TO SELL VILLA CAPISTRANO, AS WELL.

FORECLOSED

By Order of
The Office of the Comptroller
San Diego County

MEANWHILE, YOUNG PERFORMERS INSPIRED BY ELTINGE WERE TAKING THE THEATRICAL PERFORMANCE OF GENDER INTO A NEW REALM OF THEATRICALITY. FEMALE IMPERSONATORS – AND SOME FEMALES IMPERSONATING MALES – WERE MOVING PAST THE IDEALIZATION OF VICTORIAN PROPRIETY THAT ELTINGE PERSONIFIED TO DISRUPT ESTABLISHED GENDER VALUES THROUGH PARODY, BAWDY HUMOR, AND A WILDLY EXTRAVAGANT KIND OF IRONY THAT WAS STILL YEARS FROM BEING IDENTIFIED AS "CAMP." THE EMERGING PHENOMENON OF DRAG PERFORMANCE WOULD COME TO BE KNOWN AS...

THE "PANSY CRAZE"

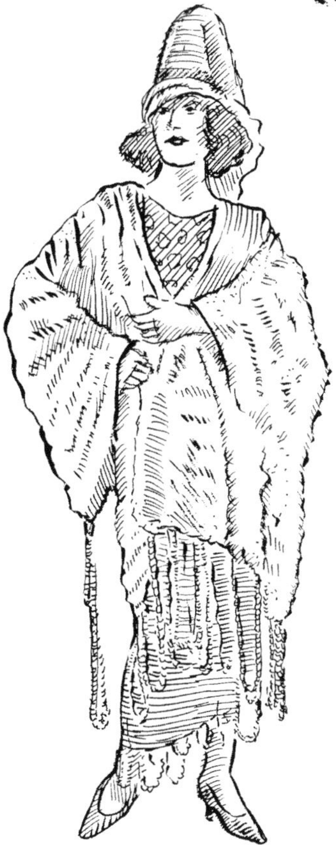

KARYL NORMAN

AN ITALIAN AMERICAN WHO STARTED OUT IN MINSTREL SHOWS, NORMAN MADE HIS NAME IN FEMALE IMPERSONATION AS "THE CREOLE FASHION PLATE." BY THE 1920s, *THE WASHINGTON POST* WAS CALLING HIM "JULIAN ELTINGE'S SUCCESSOR." IN LATER YEARS, HE WOULD BECOME A STAPLE AT FINNOCHIO'S, AN UNDERGROUND GAY CLUB IN SAN FRANCISCO.

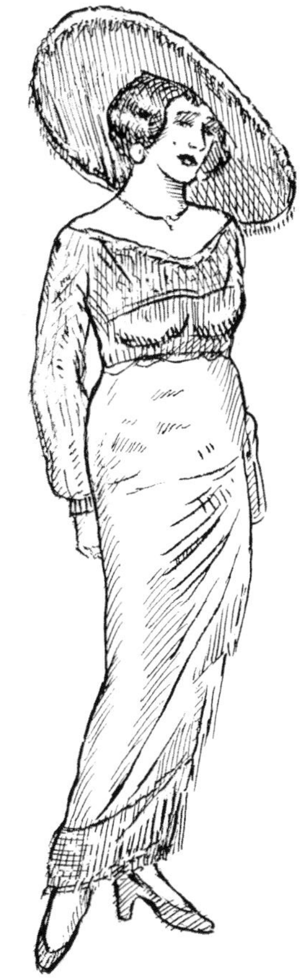

BERT SAVOY

SINGING AND DANCING AS AN OVERSEXED COQUETTE, SAVOY WAS AN EARLY INNOVATOR OF THE DRAG AESTHETIC. MAE WEST IS SAID TO HAVE BEEN INFLUENCED BY BOTH SAVOY AND EVA TANGUAY. HE WOULD DIE IN 1923 WHEN HE MADE A SASSY JOKE ABOUT "MISS GOD" TO SOME FRIENDS AND WAS STRUCK BY LIGHTNING.

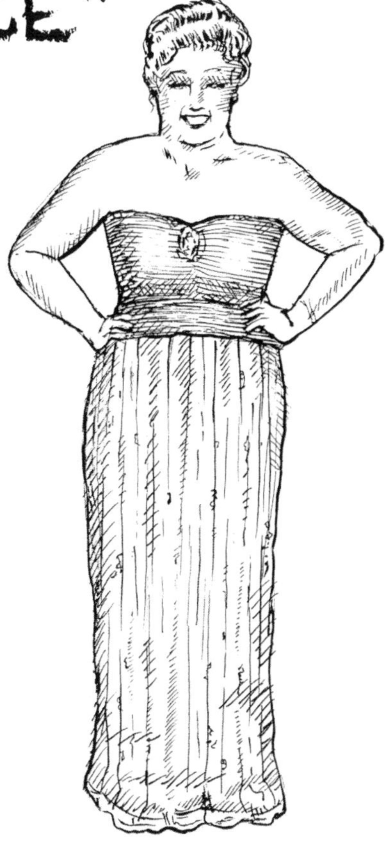

RAY BOURBON

A PROFESSIONAL FABULIST WHO MAY OR MAY NOT HAVE HAD FAILED (OR SUCCESSFUL) SEX-CHANGE SURGERY IN MEXICO, BOURBON CAME UP IN VAUDEVILLE AS THE NON-STRAIGHT PARTNER OF STRAIGHT MAN BERT SHERRY. AS A FEMALE IMPERSONATOR, HE SPECIALIZED IN OUTRAGEOUS VULGARITY IN AN ACT CALLED "BOYS WILL BE GIRLS" AND WOULD DIE IN PRISON WHILE SERVING TIME ON A CONVICTION AS ACCOMPLICE TO MURDER IN AN INCIDENT INVOLVING A TRAILER FULL OF PET DOGS.

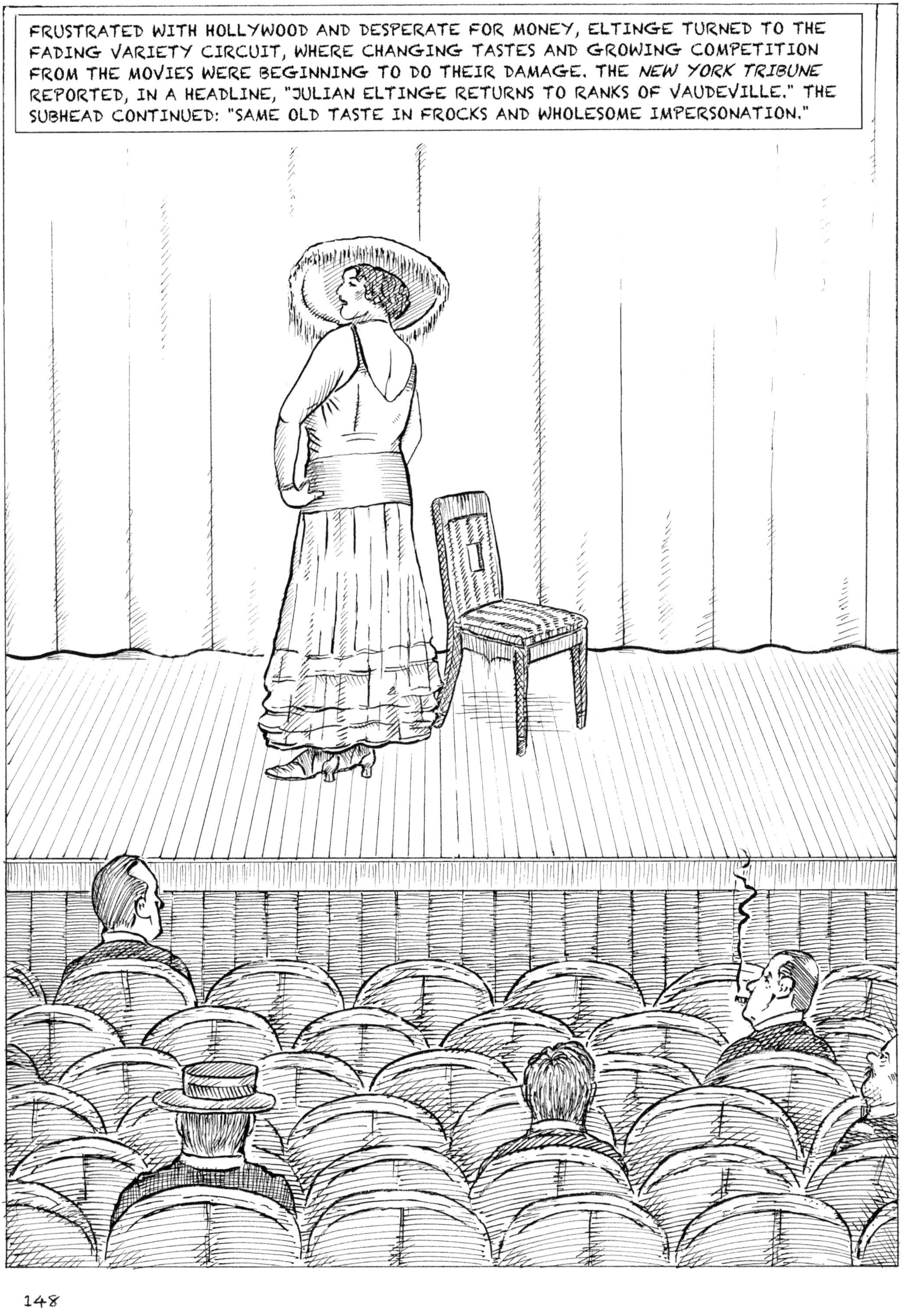
FRUSTRATED WITH HOLLYWOOD AND DESPERATE FOR MONEY, ELTINGE TURNED TO THE FADING VARIETY CIRCUIT, WHERE CHANGING TASTES AND GROWING COMPETITION FROM THE MOVIES WERE BEGINNING TO DO THEIR DAMAGE. THE *NEW YORK TRIBUNE* REPORTED, IN A HEADLINE, "JULIAN ELTINGE RETURNS TO RANKS OF VAUDEVILLE." THE SUBHEAD CONTINUED: "SAME OLD TASTE IN FROCKS AND WHOLESOME IMPERSONATION."

THE TOURING SYSTEM OF THE VAUDEVILLE CIRCUITS LULLED PERFORMERS INTO COMPLACENCY. AN ARTIST COULD HOP FROM TOWN TO TOWN ACROSS THE COUNTRY AND DO THE SAME ACT FOR A DIFFERENT AUDIENCE EVERY NIGHT, AND IT WOULD COME ACROSS AS SOMETHING NEW. THIS WORKED WELL OVER LONG STRETCHES OF DISTANCE, BUT NOT SO WELL OVER LONG STRETCHES OF TIME.

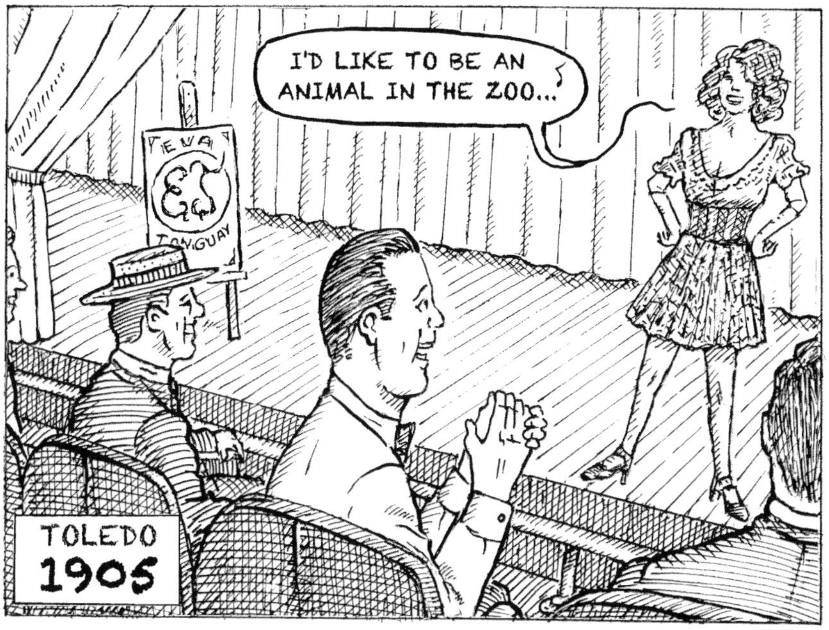
I'D LIKE TO BE AN ANIMAL IN THE ZOO...
EVA TANGUAY
TOLEDO 1905

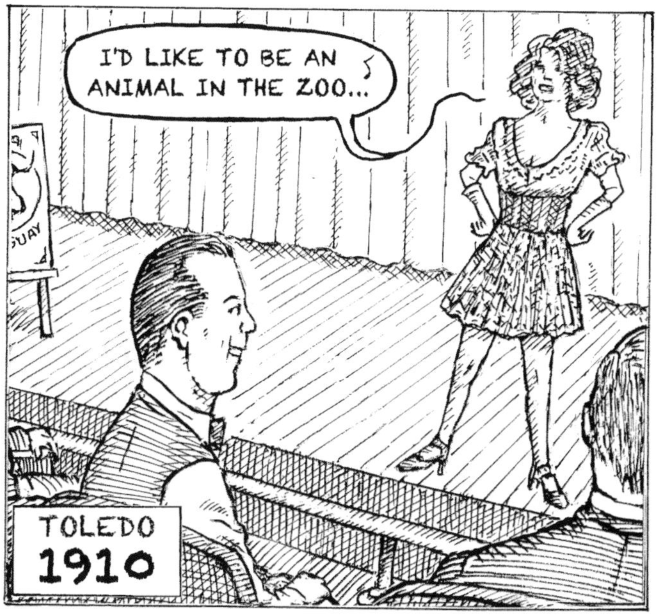
I'D LIKE TO BE AN ANIMAL IN THE ZOO...
TOLEDO 1910

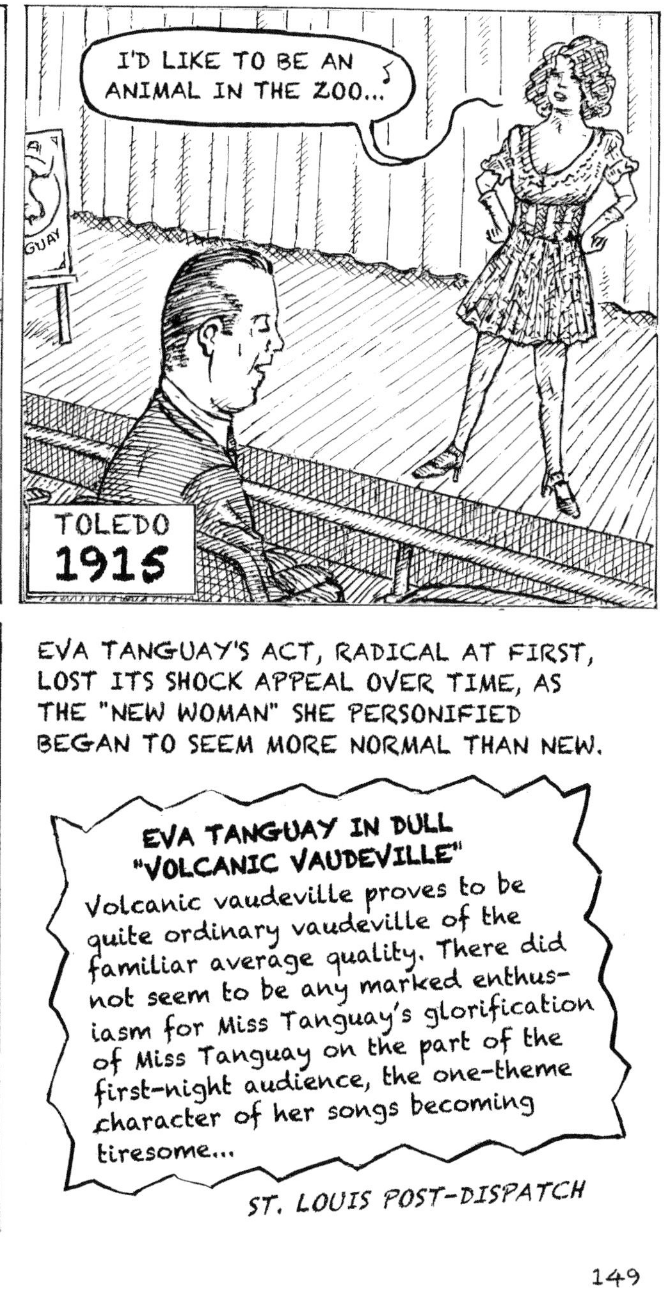
I'D LIKE TO BE AN ANIMAL IN THE ZOO...
TOLEDO 1915

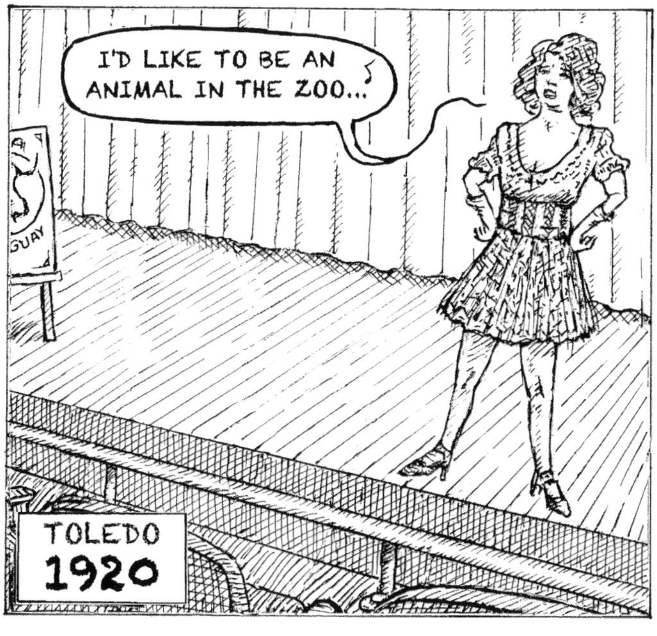
I'D LIKE TO BE AN ANIMAL IN THE ZOO...
TOLEDO 1920

EVA TANGUAY'S ACT, RADICAL AT FIRST, LOST ITS SHOCK APPEAL OVER TIME, AS THE "NEW WOMAN" SHE PERSONIFIED BEGAN TO SEEM MORE NORMAL THAN NEW.

EVA TANGUAY IN DULL "VOLCANIC VAUDEVILLE"

Volcanic vaudeville proves to be quite ordinary vaudeville of the familiar average quality. There did not seem to be any marked enthusiasm for Miss Tanguay's glorification of Miss Tanguay on the part of the first-night audience, the one-theme character of her songs becoming tiresome...

ST. LOUIS POST-DISPATCH

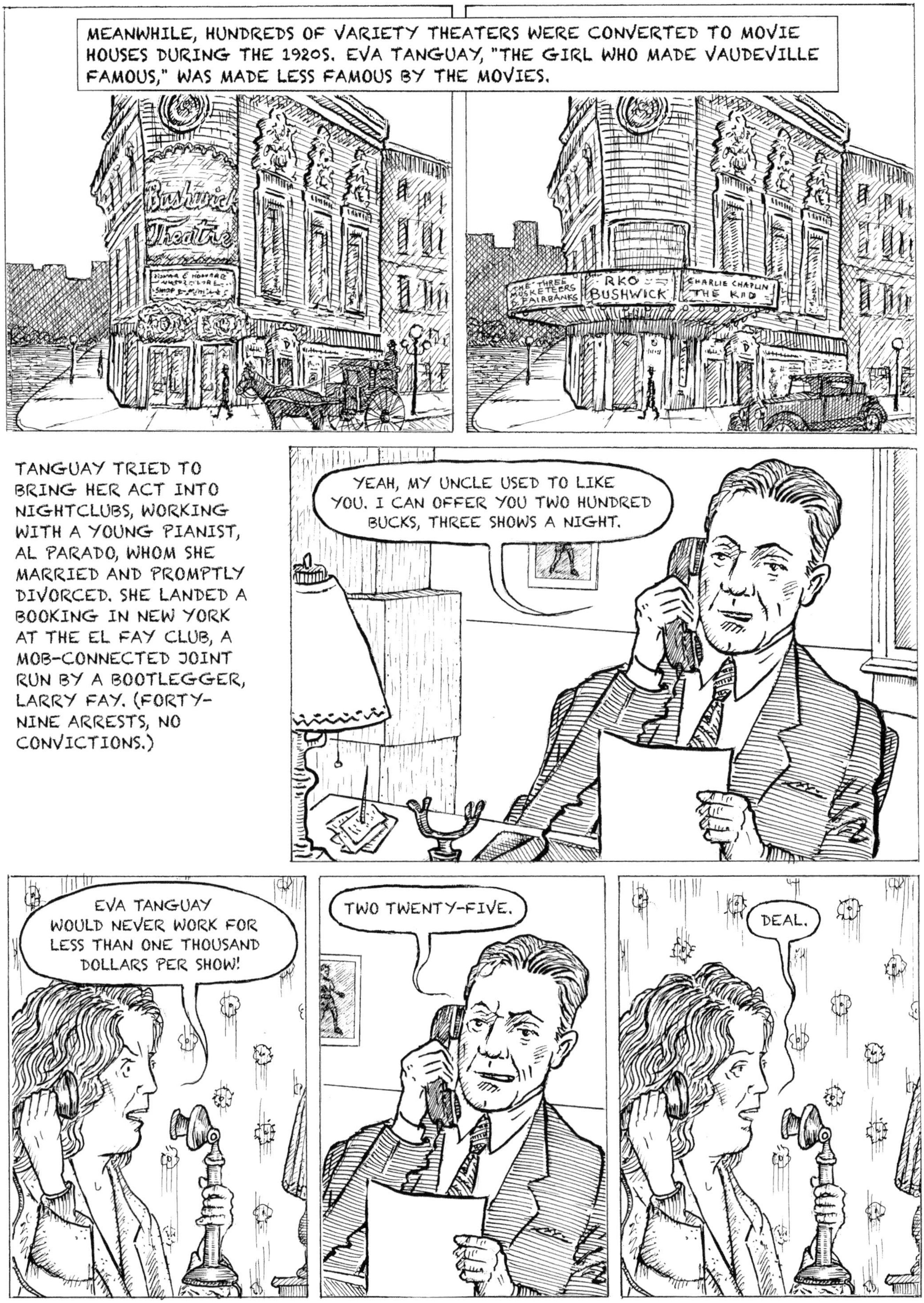
MEANWHILE, HUNDREDS OF VARIETY THEATERS WERE CONVERTED TO MOVIE HOUSES DURING THE 1920S. EVA TANGUAY, "THE GIRL WHO MADE VAUDEVILLE FAMOUS," WAS MADE LESS FAMOUS BY THE MOVIES.
Bushwick Theatre
THE THREE MUSKETEERS D. FAIRBANKS
RKO BUSHWICK
CHARLIE CHAPLIN THE KID
TANGUAY TRIED TO BRING HER ACT INTO NIGHTCLUBS, WORKING WITH A YOUNG PIANIST, AL PARADO, WHOM SHE MARRIED AND PROMPTLY DIVORCED. SHE LANDED A BOOKING IN NEW YORK AT THE EL FAY CLUB, A MOB-CONNECTED JOINT RUN BY A BOOTLEGGER, LARRY FAY. (FORTY-NINE ARRESTS, NO CONVICTIONS.)
YEAH, MY UNCLE USED TO LIKE YOU. I CAN OFFER YOU TWO HUNDRED BUCKS, THREE SHOWS A NIGHT.
EVA TANGUAY WOULD NEVER WORK FOR LESS THAN ONE THOUSAND DOLLARS PER SHOW!
TWO TWENTY-FIVE.
DEAL.

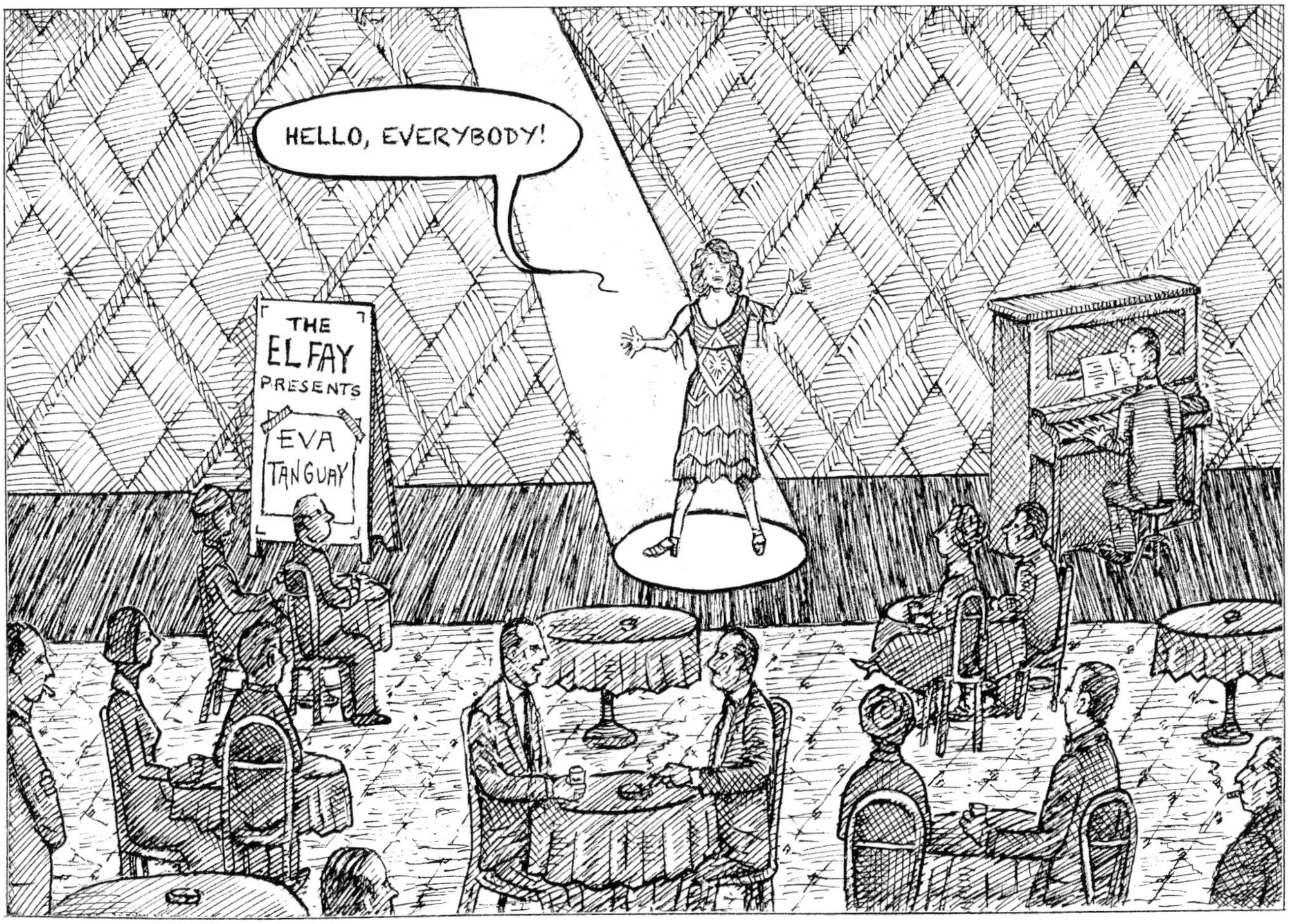
HELLO, EVERYBODY!
THE EL FAY PRESENTS
EVA TANGUAY

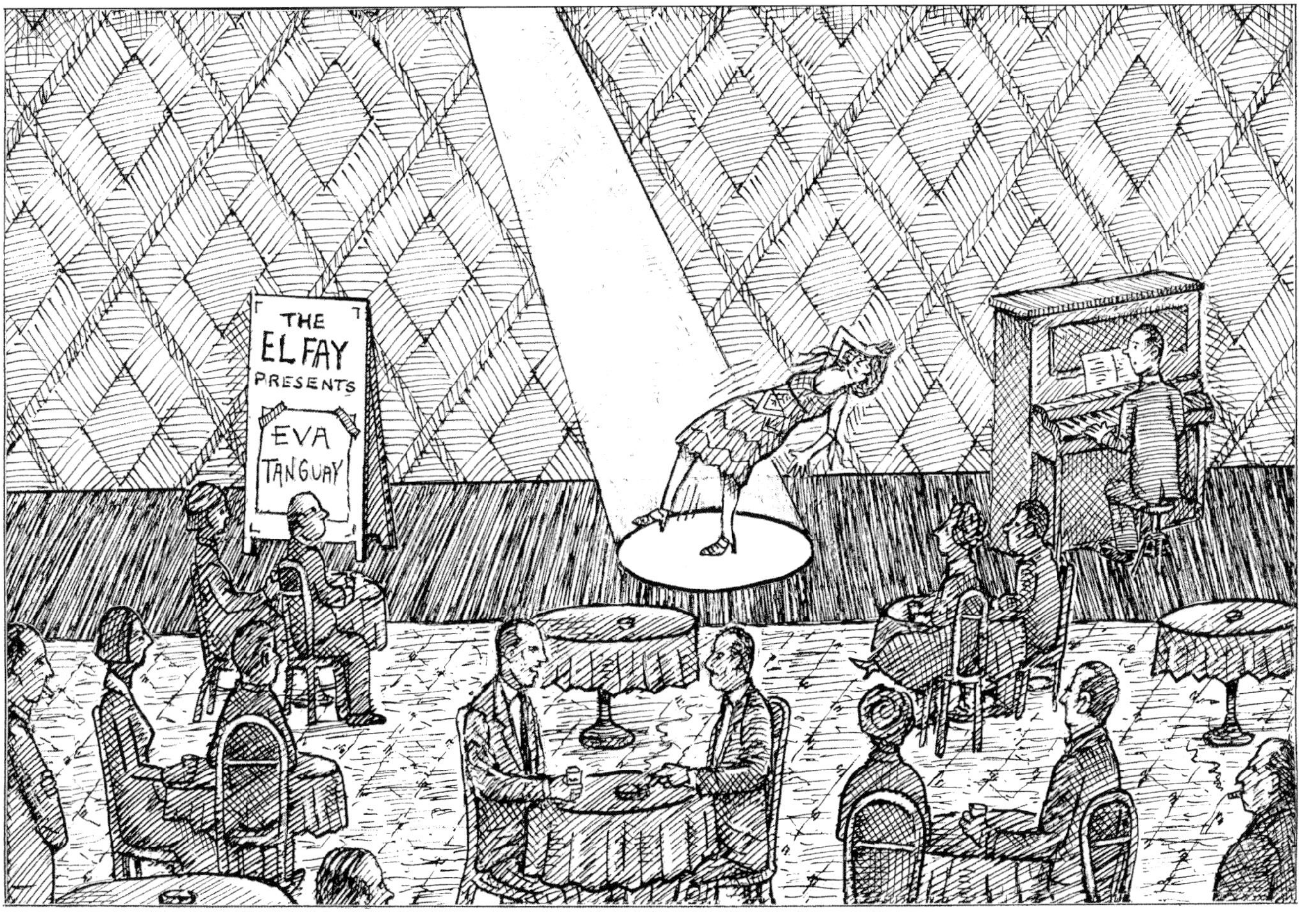
THE EL FAY PRESENTS
EVA TANGUAY

IN THE YEARS IMMEDIATELY FOLLOWING HIS FILM WORK FOR THE BIOGRAPH COMPANY, BERT WILLIAMS HAD GROWING HEALTH PROBLEMS. DESPONDENT, HE WAS DRINKING HEAVILY AND SUFFERED FROM SEVERE PAIN IN HIS JOINTS. HE WENT FOR A REST CURE, CHECKING INTO A BLACK-OWNED HEALTH RESORT IN WEST BADEN SPRINGS, INDIANA.

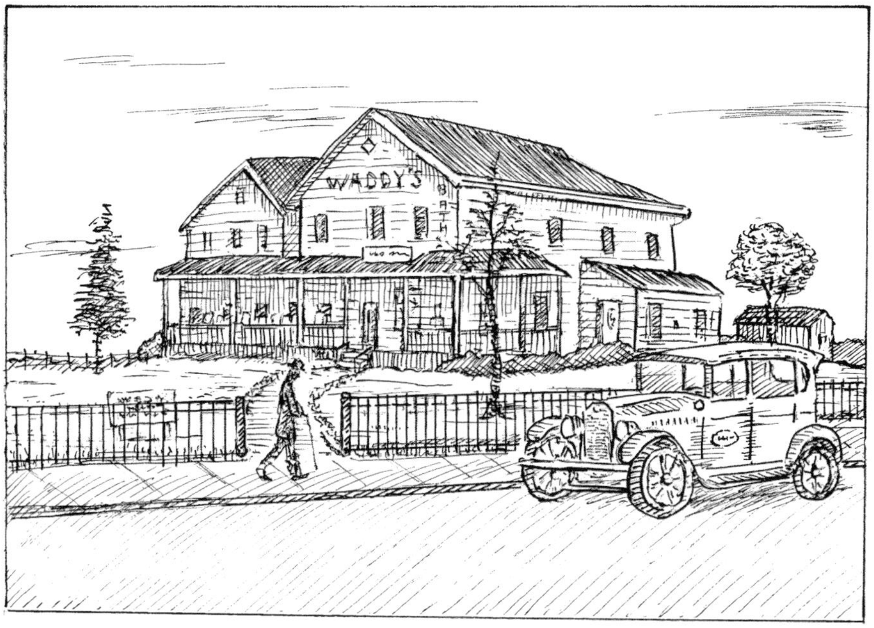
WADDY'S

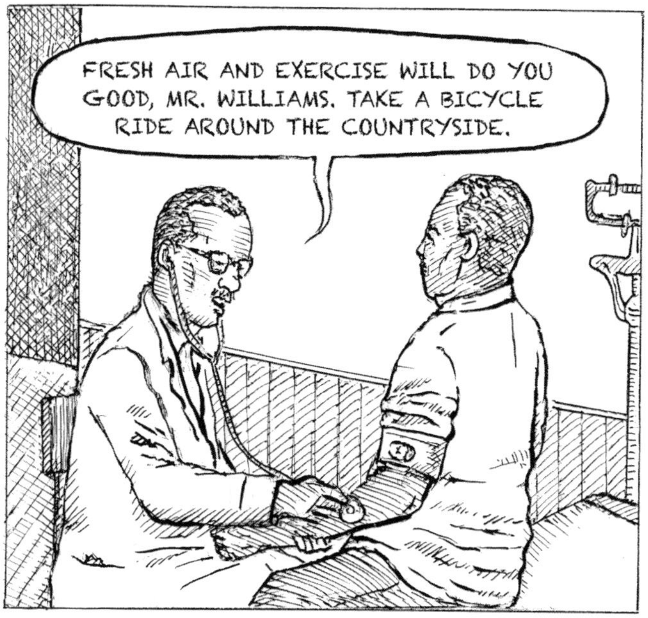
FRESH AIR AND EXERCISE WILL DO YOU GOOD, MR. WILLIAMS. TAKE A BICYCLE RIDE AROUND THE COUNTRYSIDE.

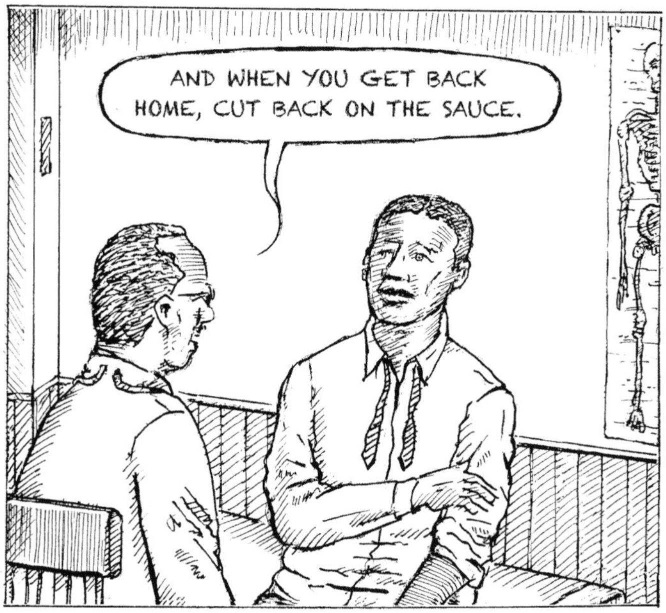
AND WHEN YOU GET BACK HOME, CUT BACK ON THE SAUCE.

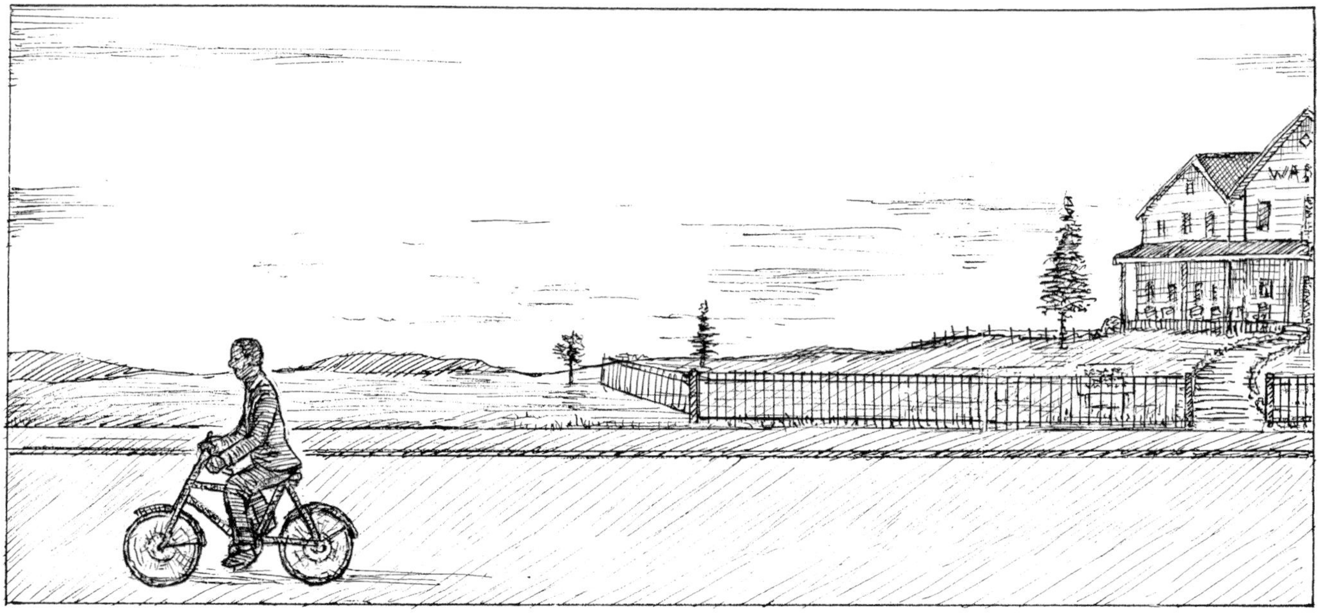

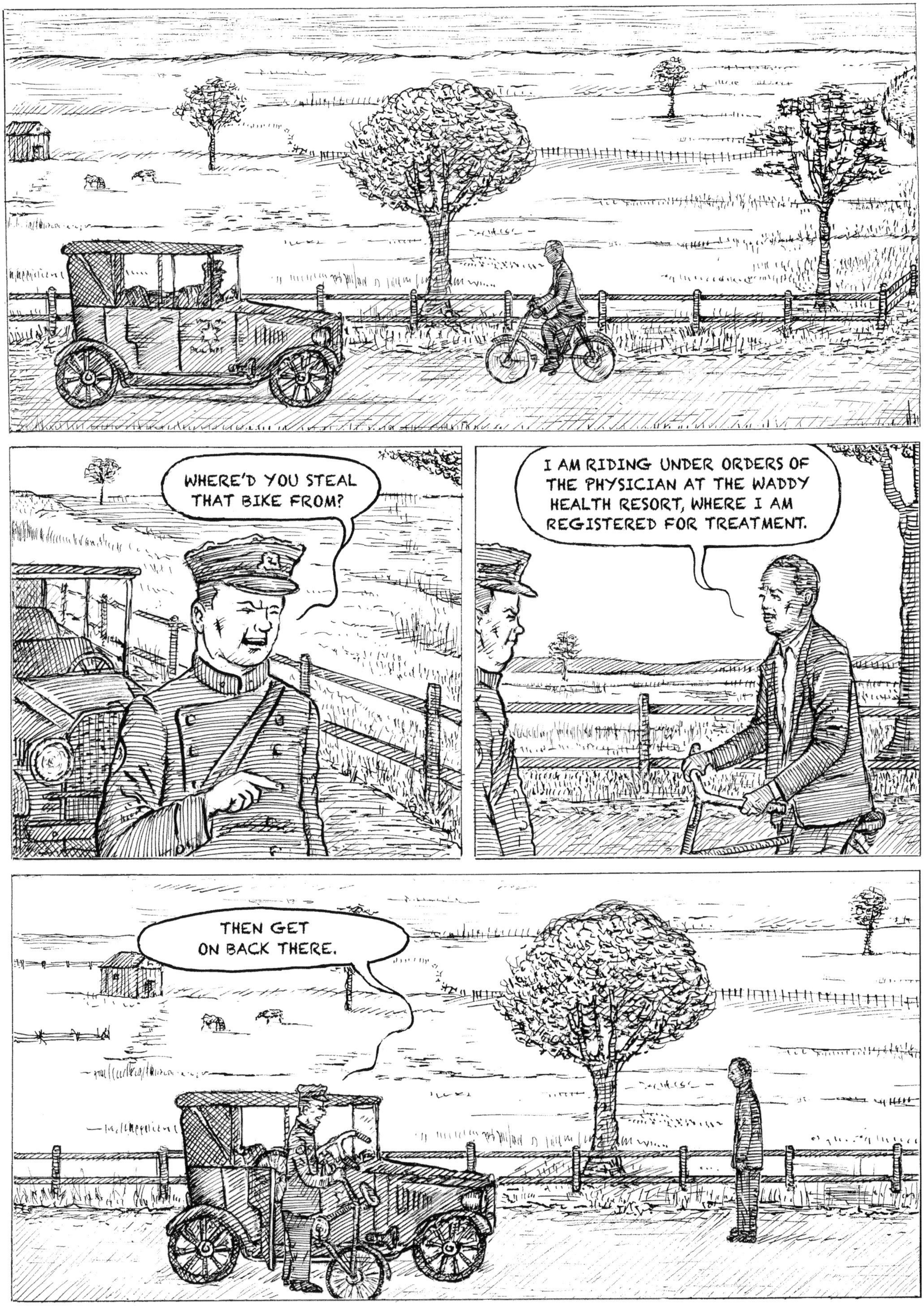
WHERE'D YOU STEAL THAT BIKE FROM?
I AM RIDING UNDER ORDERS OF THE PHYSICIAN AT THE WADDY HEALTH RESORT, WHERE I AM REGISTERED FOR TREATMENT.
THEN GET ON BACK THERE.

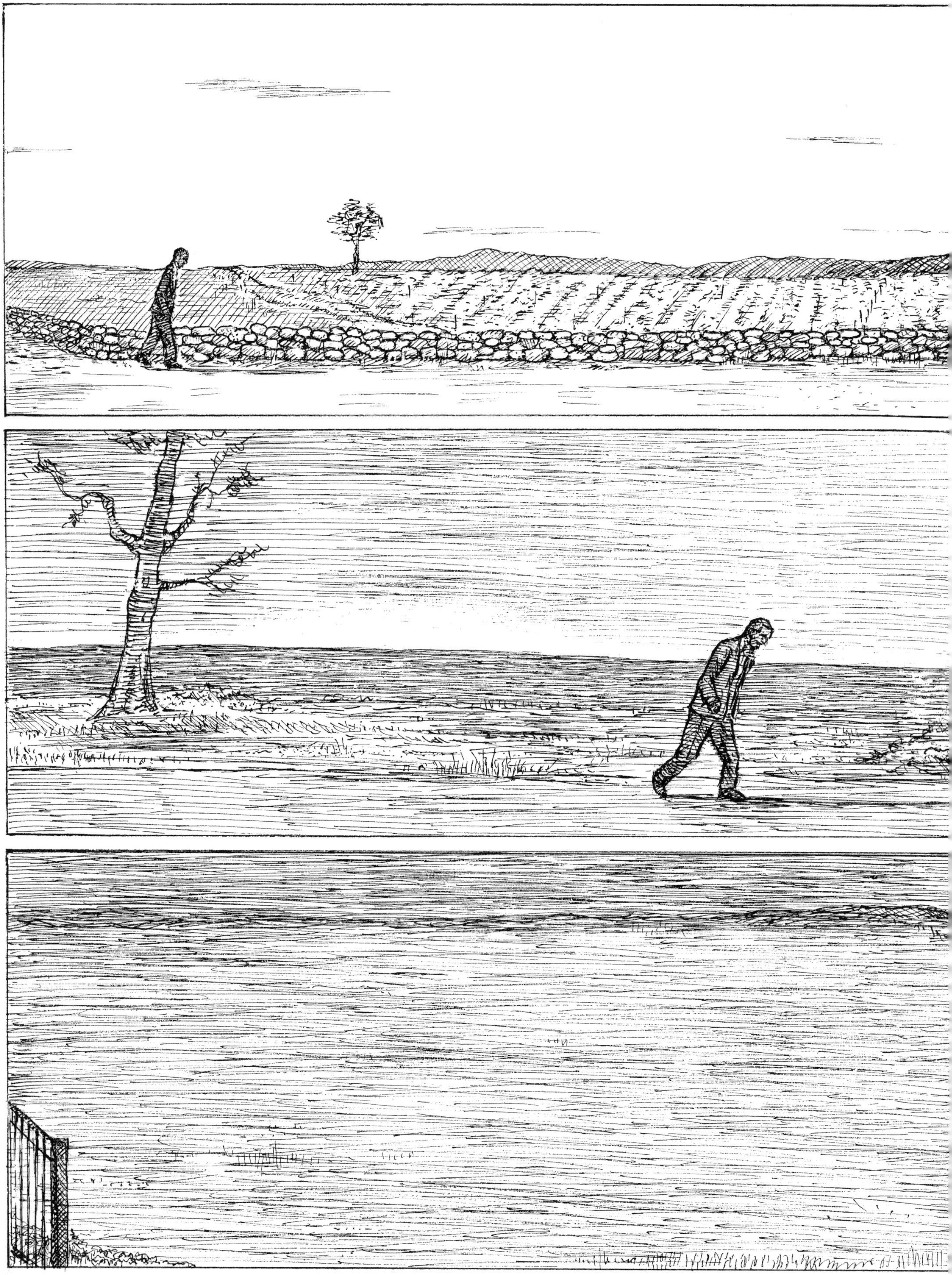

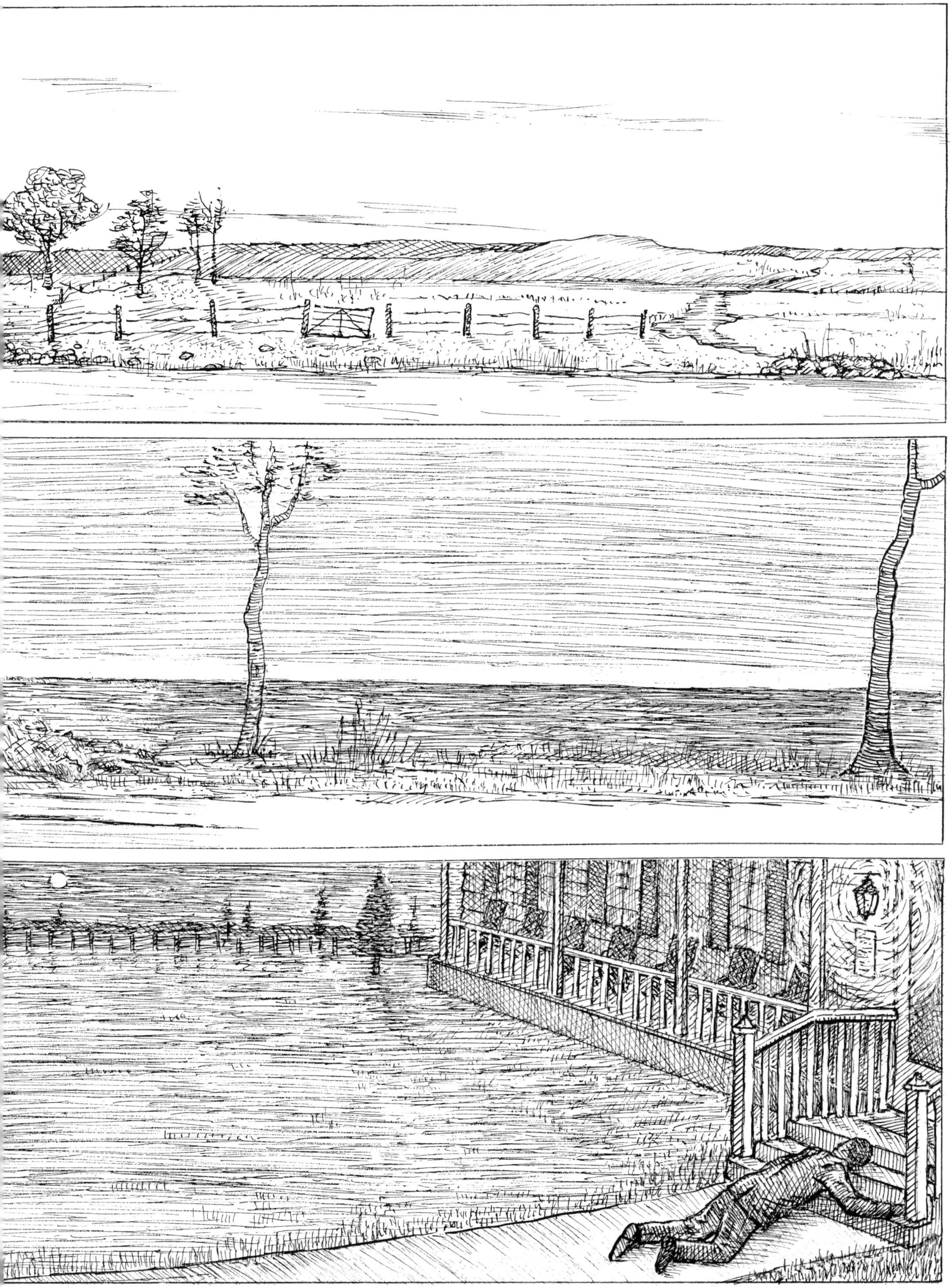

BERT WILLIAMS DECLINED MORE RAPIDLY THAN VAUDEVILLE. TOO WEAK TO CONTINUE IN THE FOLLIES, HE RESTED AT HOME UNTIL PRODUCER A. H. WOODS LURED HIM BACK TO THE STAGE. WOODS COMMISSIONED THE BLACK COMPOSER WILL VODERY TO WRITE SONGS FOR A NEW MUSICAL TAILORED TO WILLIAMS, *THE PINK SLIP*. WILLIAMS SIGNED ON, AND WOODS ANNOUNCED THAT THE SHOW WOULD OPEN IN SEPTEMBER 1922 AT THE ELTINGE THEATRE.

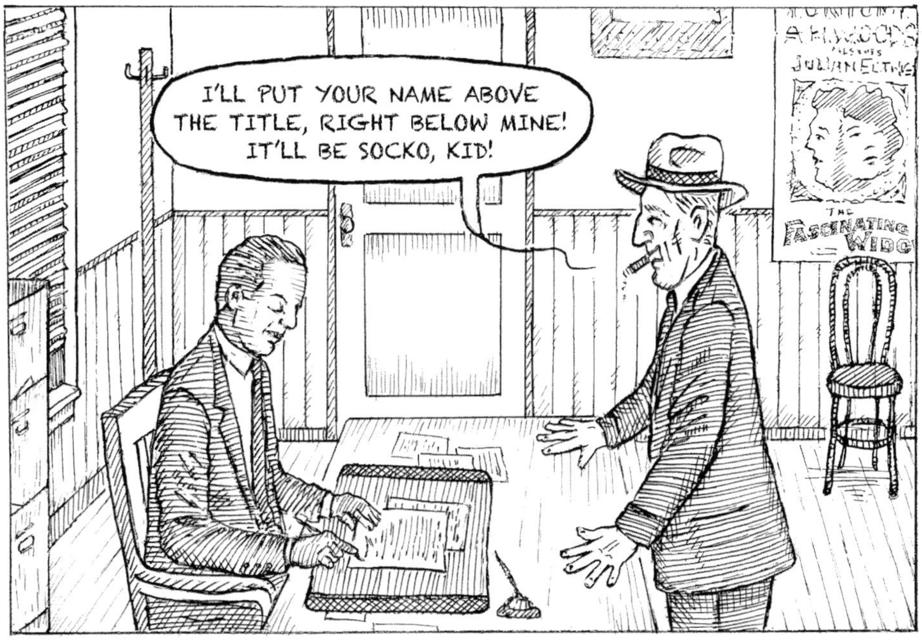
I'LL PUT YOUR NAME ABOVE THE TITLE, RIGHT BELOW MINE! IT'LL BE SOCKO, KID!

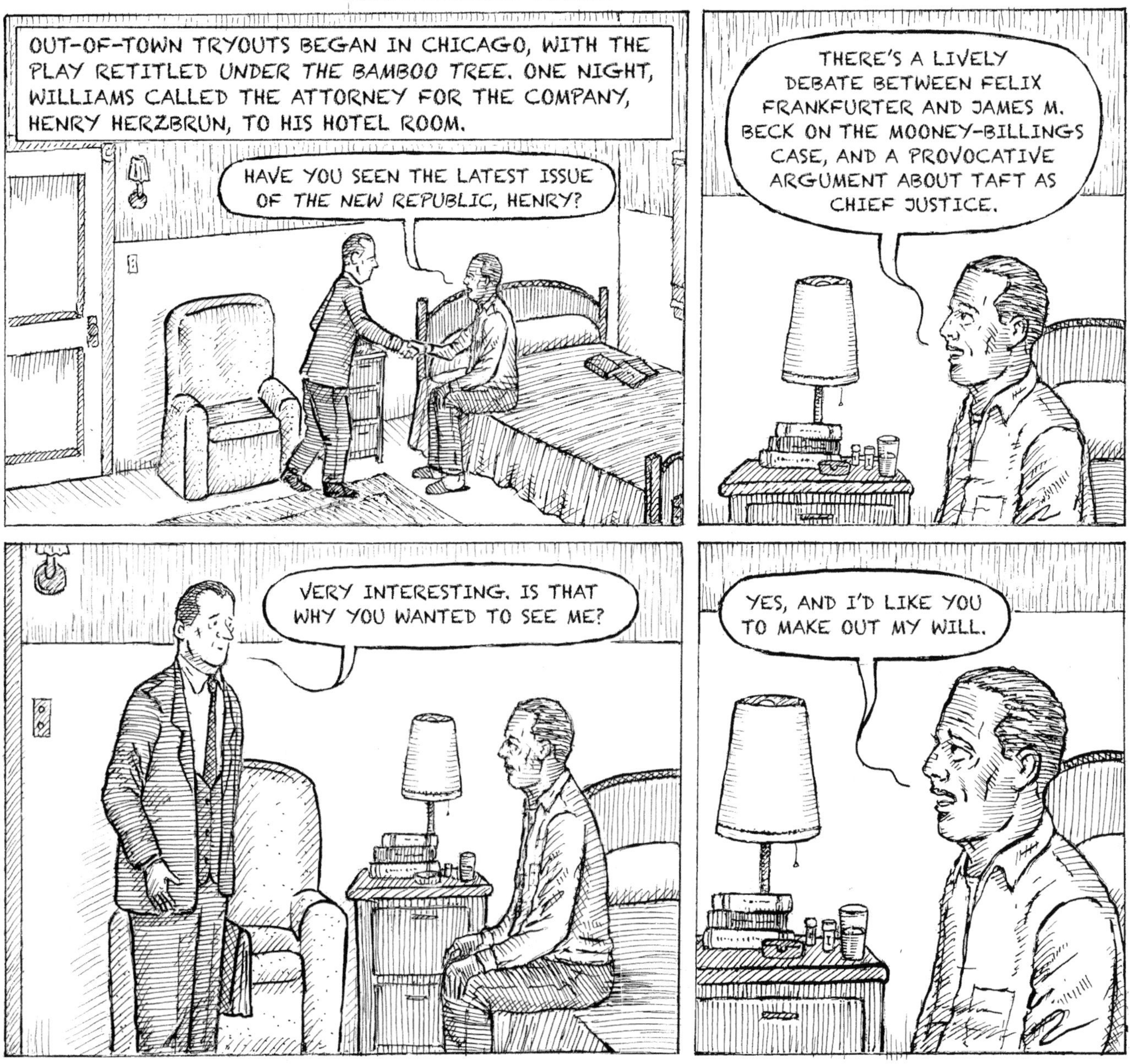
OUT-OF-TOWN TRYOUTS BEGAN IN CHICAGO, WITH THE PLAY RETITLED *UNDER THE BAMBOO TREE*. ONE NIGHT, WILLIAMS CALLED THE ATTORNEY FOR THE COMPANY, HENRY HERZBRUN, TO HIS HOTEL ROOM.
HAVE YOU SEEN THE LATEST ISSUE OF *THE NEW REPUBLIC*, HENRY?
THERE'S A LIVELY DEBATE BETWEEN FELIX FRANKFURTER AND JAMES M. BECK ON THE MOONEY-BILLINGS CASE, AND A PROVOCATIVE ARGUMENT ABOUT TAFT AS CHIEF JUSTICE.
VERY INTERESTING. IS THAT WHY YOU WANTED TO SEE ME?
YES, AND I'D LIKE YOU TO MAKE OUT MY WILL.

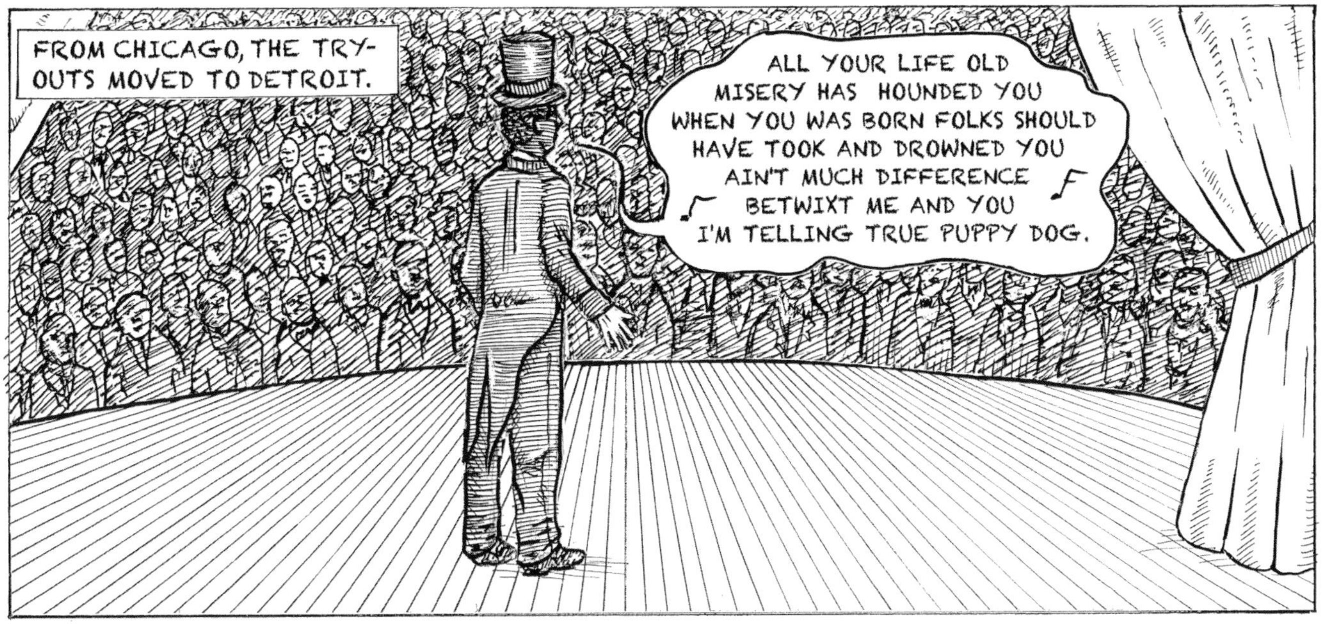
FROM CHICAGO, THE TRY-OUTS MOVED TO DETROIT.
ALL YOUR LIFE OLD MISERY HAS HOUNDED YOU WHEN YOU WAS BORN FOLKS SHOULD HAVE TOOK AND DROWNED YOU AIN'T MUCH DIFFERENCE BETWIXT ME AND YOU I'M TELLING TRUE PUPPY DOG.

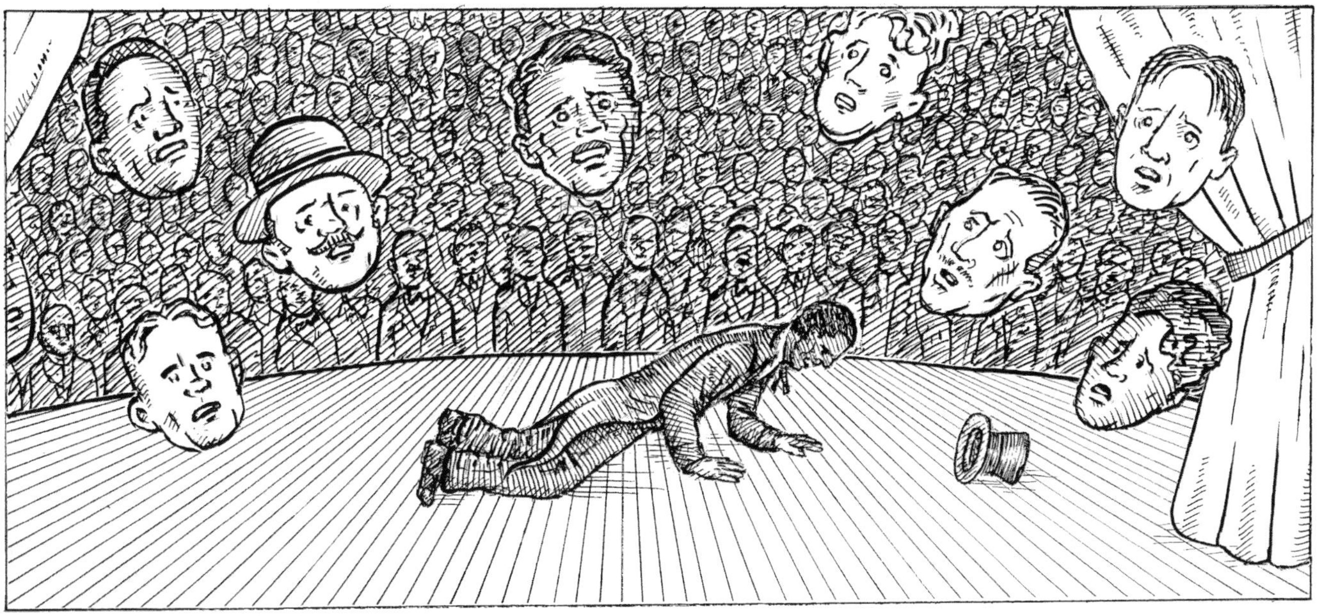

GRAVELY ILL WITH PNEUMONIA AND HEART DISEASE, BERT WILLIAMS WAS TRANSPORTED BACK TO NEW YORK BY TRAIN. HIS WIFE LOTTIE NURSED HIM AT HOME AS HE SLIPPED IN AND OUT OF CONSCIOUSNESS.
WILLIAMS DIED, AT AGE 47, ON MARCH 4, 1922. SOME 5,000 MOURNERS, BLACK AND WHITE, PASSED THROUGH ST. PHILIP'S EPISCOPAL CHURCH IN HARLEM TO VIEW HIS BODY. AN ESTIMATED 10,000 MORE LINED UP OUTSIDE IN THE RAIN, UNABLE TO GET IN.

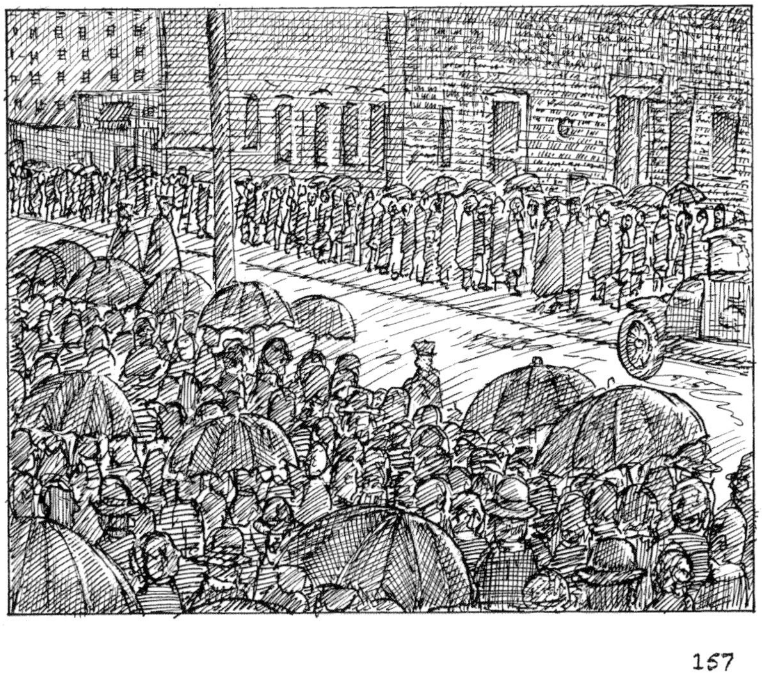

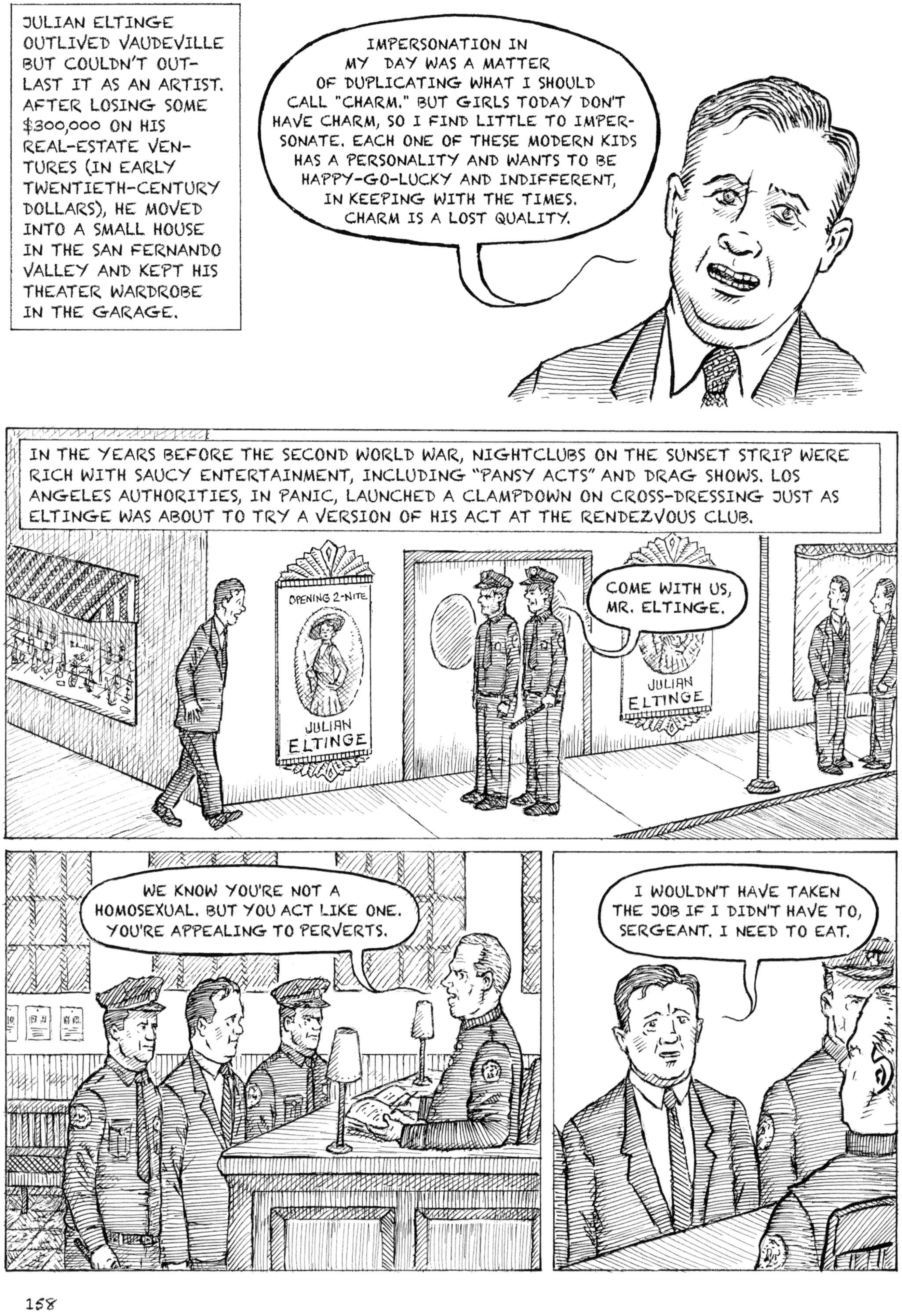
JULIAN ELTINGE OUTLIVED VAUDEVILLE BUT COULDN'T OUTLAST IT AS AN ARTIST. AFTER LOSING SOME $300,000 ON HIS REAL-ESTATE VENTURES (IN EARLY TWENTIETH-CENTURY DOLLARS), HE MOVED INTO A SMALL HOUSE IN THE SAN FERNANDO VALLEY AND KEPT HIS THEATER WARDROBE IN THE GARAGE.
IMPERSONATION IN MY DAY WAS A MATTER OF DUPLICATING WHAT I SHOULD CALL "CHARM." BUT GIRLS TODAY DON'T HAVE CHARM, SO I FIND LITTLE TO IMPERSONATE. EACH ONE OF THESE MODERN KIDS HAS A PERSONALITY AND WANTS TO BE HAPPY-GO-LUCKY AND INDIFFERENT, IN KEEPING WITH THE TIMES. CHARM IS A LOST QUALITY.
IN THE YEARS BEFORE THE SECOND WORLD WAR, NIGHTCLUBS ON THE SUNSET STRIP WERE RICH WITH SAUCY ENTERTAINMENT, INCLUDING "PANSY ACTS" AND DRAG SHOWS. LOS ANGELES AUTHORITIES, IN PANIC, LAUNCHED A CLAMPDOWN ON CROSS-DRESSING JUST AS ELTINGE WAS ABOUT TO TRY A VERSION OF HIS ACT AT THE RENDEZVOUS CLUB.
OPENING 2-NITE
JULIAN ELTINGE
COME WITH US, MR. ELTINGE.
JULIAN ELTINGE
WE KNOW YOU'RE NOT A HOMOSEXUAL. BUT YOU ACT LIKE ONE. YOU'RE APPEALING TO PERVERTS.
I WOULDN'T HAVE TAKEN THE JOB IF I DIDN'T HAVE TO, SERGEANT. I NEED TO EAT.

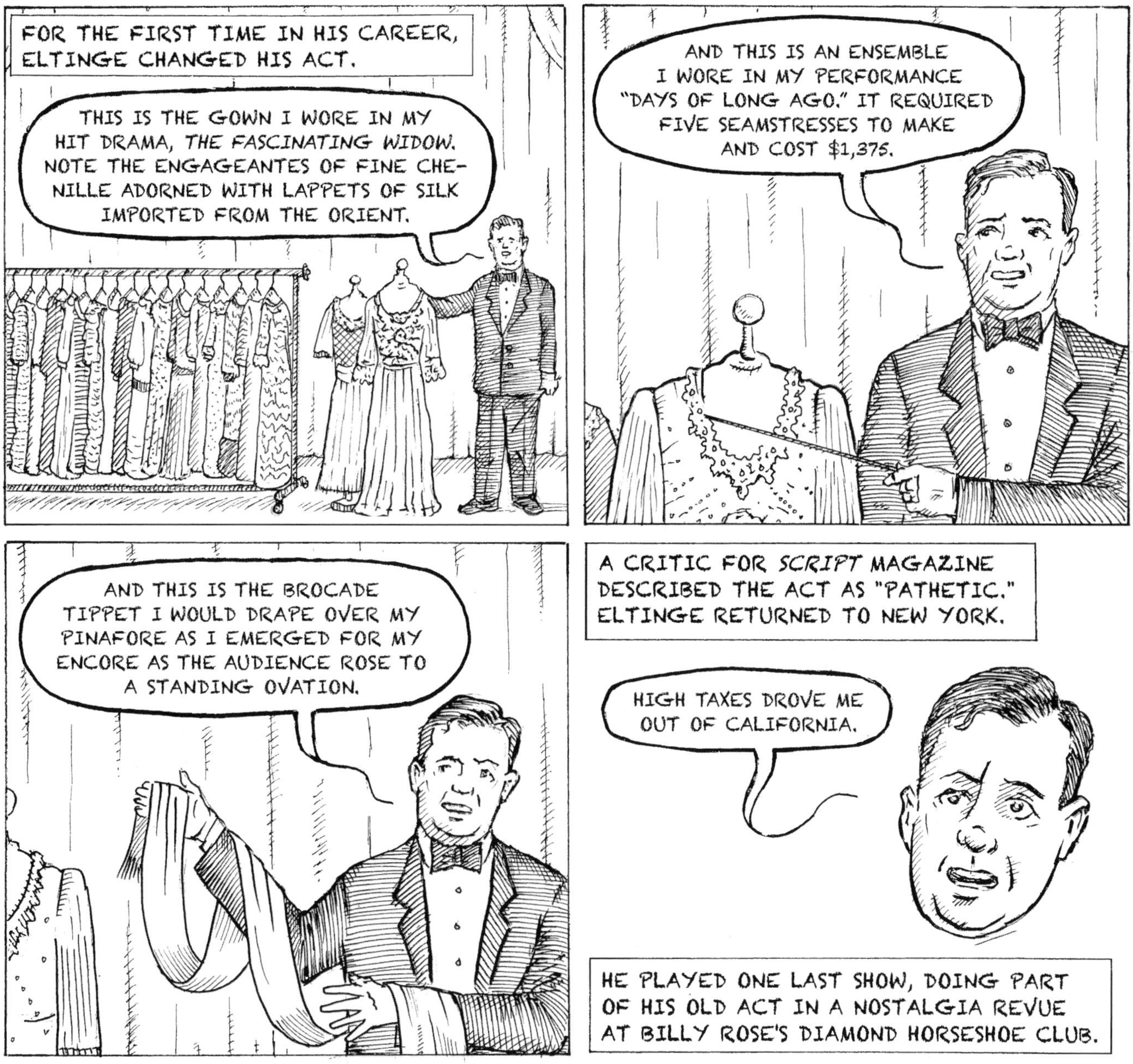
FOR THE FIRST TIME IN HIS CAREER, ELTINGE CHANGED HIS ACT.
THIS IS THE GOWN I WORE IN MY HIT DRAMA, *THE FASCINATING WIDOW*. NOTE THE ENGAGEANTES OF FINE CHENILLE ADORNED WITH LAPPETS OF SILK IMPORTED FROM THE ORIENT.
AND THIS IS AN ENSEMBLE I WORE IN MY PERFORMANCE "DAYS OF LONG AGO." IT REQUIRED FIVE SEAMSTRESSES TO MAKE AND COST $1,375.
AND THIS IS THE BROCADE TIPPET I WOULD DRAPE OVER MY PINAFORE AS I EMERGED FOR MY ENCORE AS THE AUDIENCE ROSE TO A STANDING OVATION.
A CRITIC FOR *SCRIPT* MAGAZINE DESCRIBED THE ACT AS "PATHETIC." ELTINGE RETURNED TO NEW YORK.
HIGH TAXES DROVE ME OUT OF CALIFORNIA.
HE PLAYED ONE LAST SHOW, DOING PART OF HIS OLD ACT IN A NOSTALGIA REVUE AT BILLY ROSE'S DIAMOND HORSESHOE CLUB.

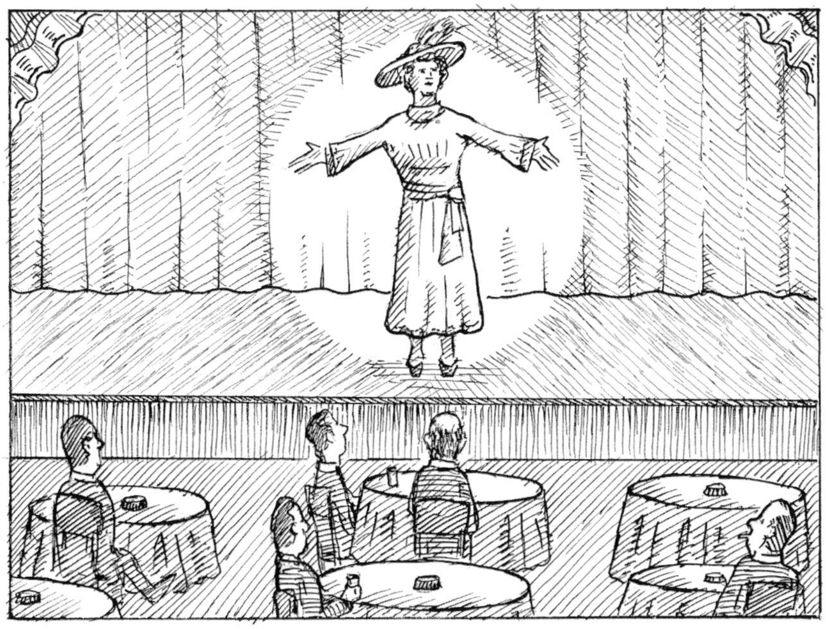

ELTINGE COLLAPSED BACKSTAGE AT BILLY ROSE'S CLUB AND DIED TEN DAYS LATER, ON MARCH 7, 1941, AT 59. HIS DEATH CERTIFICATE CITED CEREBRAL HEMORRHAGE AS THE CAUSE, THOUGH HE WAS KNOWN TO HAVE HEART TROUBLE AND KIDNEY PROBLEMS LIKELY RELATED TO HIS HAVING SQUEEZED HIS ORGANS IN TIGHT CORSETS FOR YEARS. RUMORS THAT ELTINGE HAD COMMITTED SUICIDE WITH AN OVERDOSE OF SLEEPING PILLS MADE THEIR WAY INTO KENNETH ANGER'S *HOLLYWOOD BABYLON*.

EVA TANGUAY RECOVERED FROM HER FALL AT THE EL FAY CLUB ONLY TO FIND HER EYESIGHT DETERIORATING AND OVERALL HEALTH WANING. WIDELY REPORTED TO BE BLIND OR GOING BLIND, SHE UNDERWENT A SERIES OF RISKY EYE SURGERIES PAID FOR BY SOPHIE TUCKER, WHOSE PERSONA OF SEXUALLY COMPLICATED BRIO WAS INSPIRED BY TANGUAY. IN TIME, SHE WAS WELL ENOUGH TO DO ONE FINAL TOUR, SINGING "I DON'T CARE" IN A "STARS OF YESTERYEAR" SHOW.

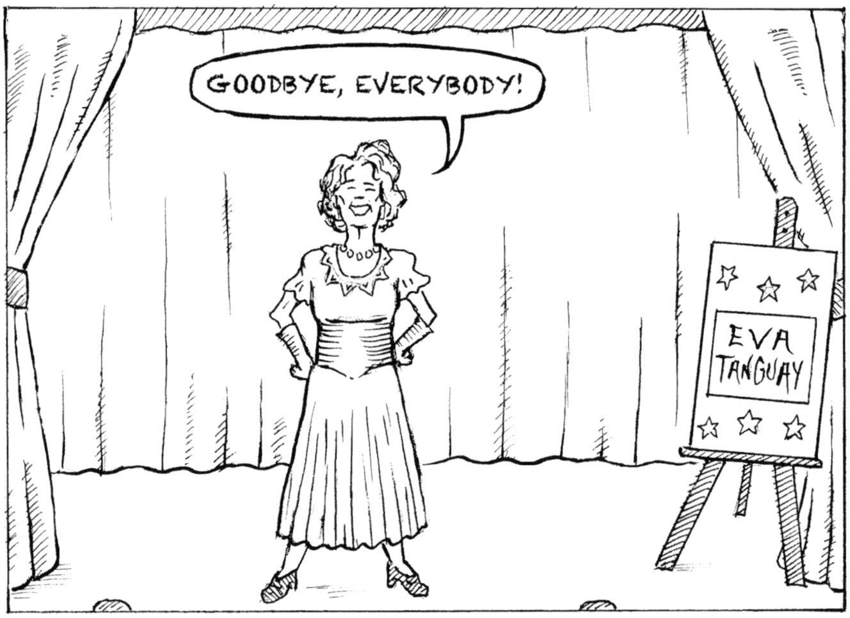
GOODBYE, EVERYBODY!
EVA TANGUAY

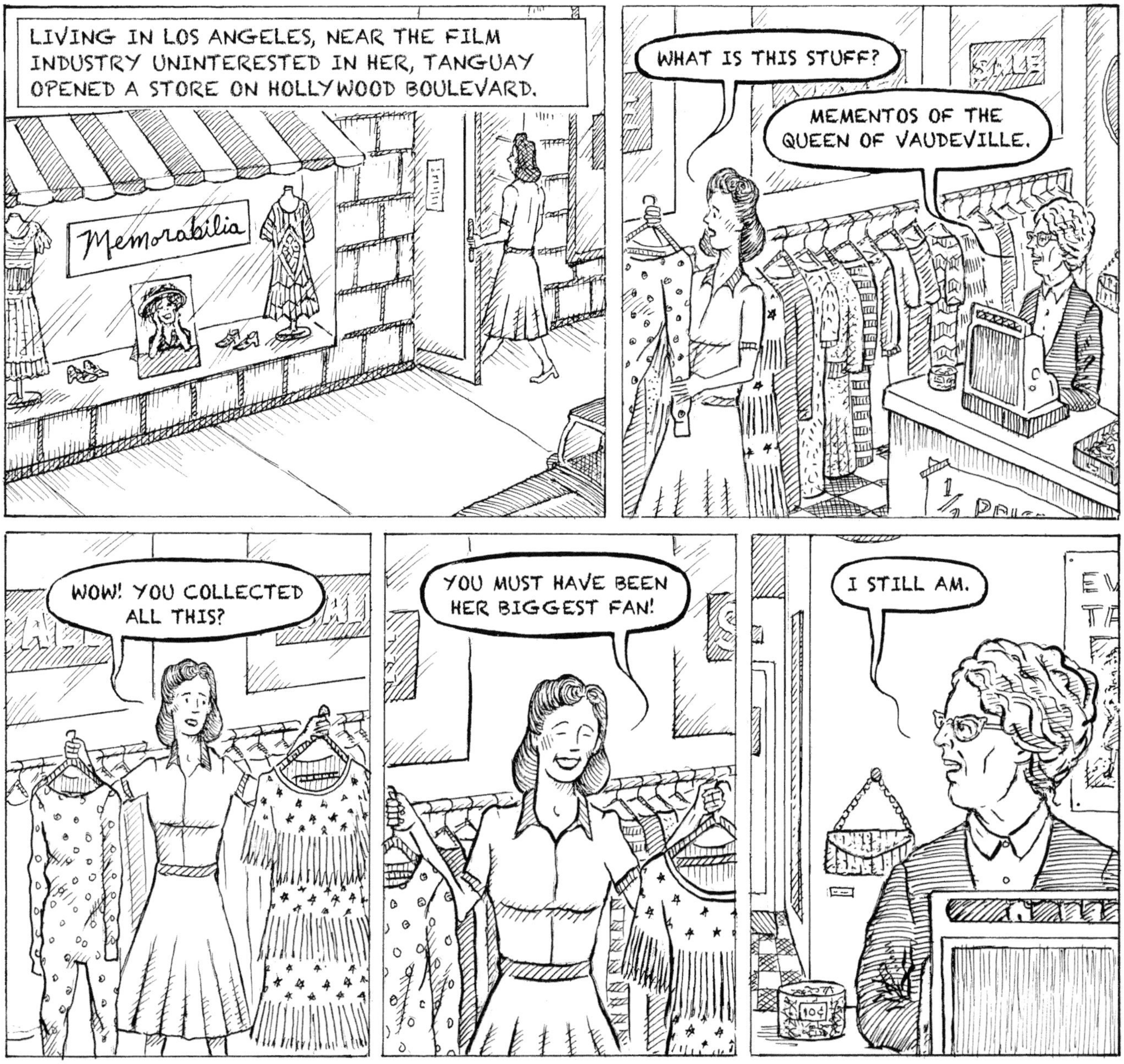
LIVING IN LOS ANGELES, NEAR THE FILM INDUSTRY UNINTERESTED IN HER, TANGUAY OPENED A STORE ON HOLLYWOOD BOULEVARD.
Memorabilia
WHAT IS THIS STUFF?
MEMENTOS OF THE QUEEN OF VAUDEVILLE.
WOW! YOU COLLECTED ALL THIS?
YOU MUST HAVE BEEN HER BIGGEST FAN!
I STILL AM.
10¢

TANGUAY'S HEALTH WORSENED AS SHE BATTLED RHEUMATISM, ARTHRITIS, HEART TROUBLE, AND KIDNEY DISEASE, ALONG WITH ONGOING VISION PROBLEMS. THERE WAS TALK THAT TANGUAY, LIKE HER RUMORED LOVER GEORGE WALKER, HAD SYPHILIS.

EVA TANGUAY ILL – DOCTOR SAYS "HOPELESS"

WASHINGTON POST (DEC. 1, 1938)

EX-VAUDEVILLE STAR IS REPORTED BETTER

AUSTIN STATESMAN (DEC. 12, 1938)

EVA TANGUAY FIGHTS FOR LIFE; DOCTOR HOLDS LITTLE HOPE FOR RECOVERY OF STAR

LOS ANGELES TIMES (DEC. 12, 1938)

"I'M FEELING SWELL," SAYS TANGUAY

ATLANTA CONSTITUTION (DEC. 13, 1938)

EVA TANGUAY'S CONDITION GRAVE

NEW YORK TIMES (DEC. 14, 1938)

EVA TANGUAY MUCH IMPROVED

HARTFORD COURANT (DEC. 16, 1938)

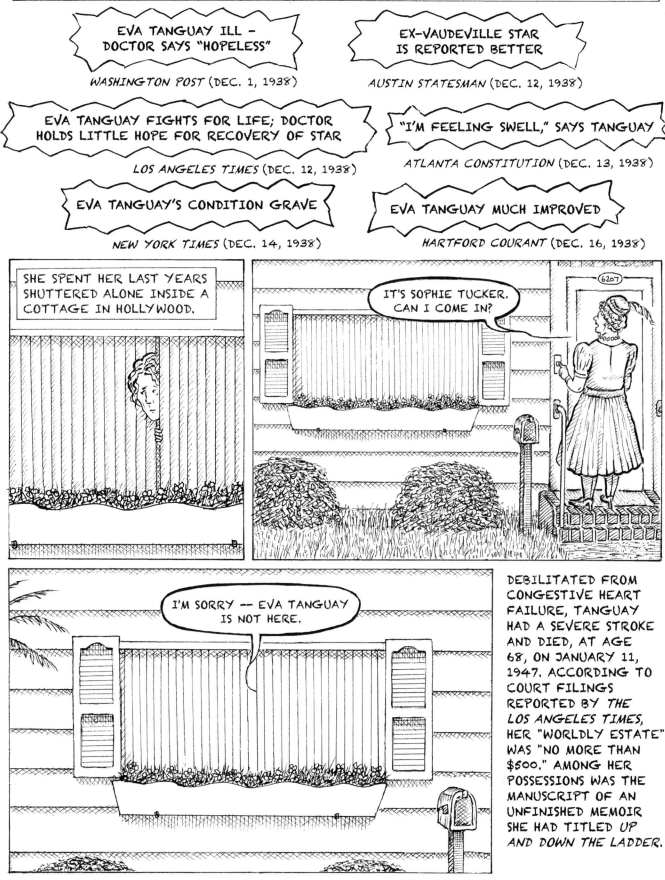

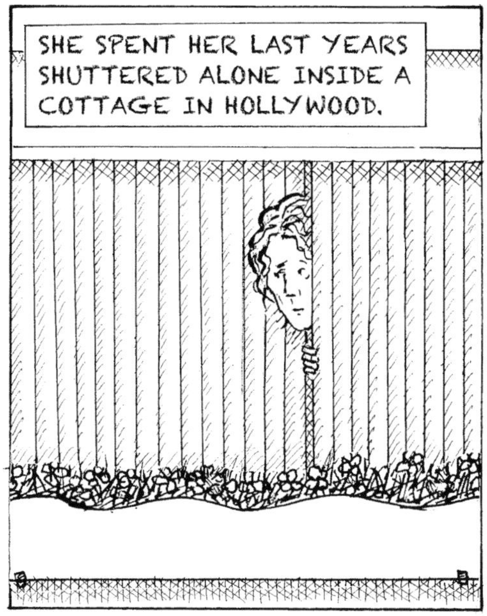
SHE SPENT HER LAST YEARS SHUTTERED ALONE INSIDE A COTTAGE IN HOLLYWOOD.

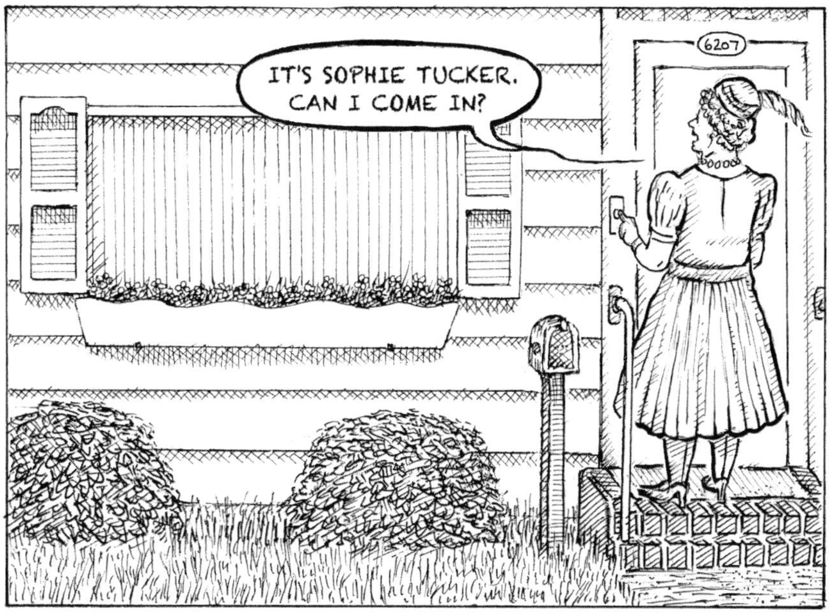
6207
IT'S SOPHIE TUCKER. CAN I COME IN?

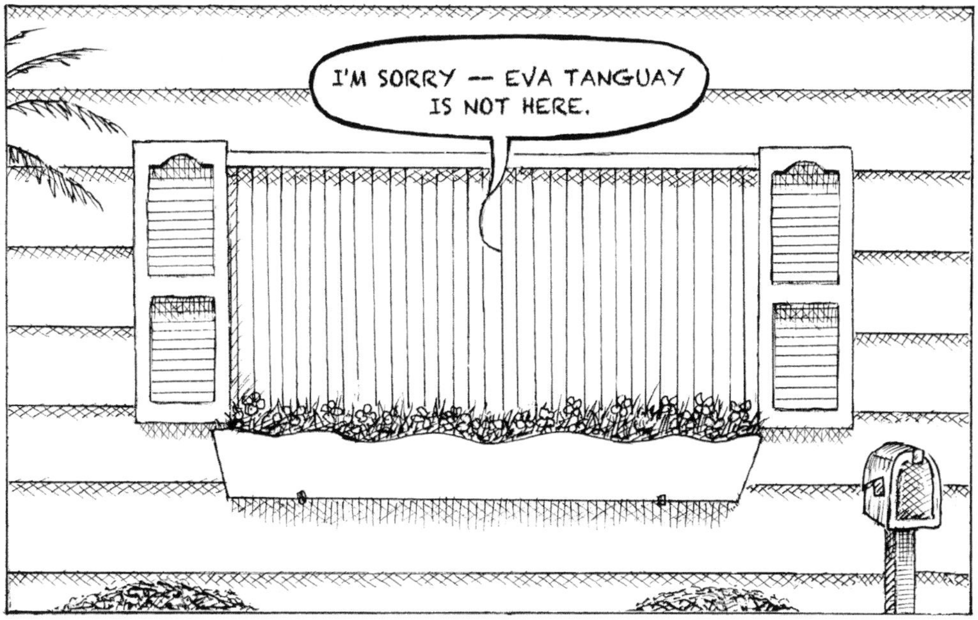
I'M SORRY -- EVA TANGUAY IS NOT HERE.

DEBILITATED FROM CONGESTIVE HEART FAILURE, TANGUAY HAD A SEVERE STROKE AND DIED, AT AGE 68, ON JANUARY 11, 1947. ACCORDING TO COURT FILINGS REPORTED BY *THE LOS ANGELES TIMES*, HER "WORLDLY ESTATE" WAS "NO MORE THAN $500." AMONG HER POSSESSIONS WAS THE MANUSCRIPT OF AN UNFINISHED MEMOIR SHE HAD TITLED *UP AND DOWN THE LADDER*.

IN THE 50 YEARS FROM 1881, WHEN TONY PASTOR OPENED THE 14TH STREET THEATRE, TO 1931, WHEN FLO ZIEGFELD SHUT DOWN THE FOLLIES, TICKET TAKERS TOOK TICKETS FOR MORE THAN 10 MILLION SHOWS IN VAUDEVILLE THEATERS AROUND THE UNITED STATES. AN ESTIMATED 60 MILLION PEOPLE SAW NEARLY A MILLION DIFFERENT ACTS, WHOSE VARIETY GAVE THE ENTERTAINMENT FORM ITS NAME. THERE WERE PERFORMANCES OF EVERY CONCEIVABLE KIND, INCLUDING SOME THAT DEFIED THE CONCEPTIONS OF THE DAY, DISRUPTING AND EXPANDING WHAT WAS CONCEIVABLE.

THE FIRST AUDIENCES FOR VAUDEVILLE WERE VICTORIANS, AND THE LAST WERE MODERNS. IN THE TIME IN BETWEEN, A BLACK MAN SUFFERED FROM HORRIFIC RACISM WHILE LEVERAGING IT TO CHALLENGE THE STEREOTYPES OF MINSTRELSY. A WHITE WOMAN REJECTED EVERY STANDARD OF FEMININE PROPRIETY TO REDEFINE WOMANHOOD FOR A NEW DAY. AND AN ENTERTAINER OF MALLEABLE IDENTITY FORESHADOWED A LATER ERA OF GENDER FLUIDITY, PERFORMING AS BOTH AN IDEALIZED WOMAN AND AN IDEALIZED MAN. FOR 50 CENTS A SEAT (25 CENTS FOR THE BALCONY), THE PEOPLE WHO WENT TO SEE BERT WILLIAMS, EVA TANGUAY, AND JULIAN ELTINGE GOT TICKETS TO ANOTHER WORLD.

RESERVED
ADMIT ONE
SAT. MARCH 23
50¢
SPRINGFIELD
COUPON
072067
ORPHEUM
ADMIT
ADMIT ONE

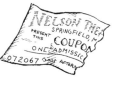

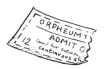

Baker Opera H
ADMIT
SATURDAY
The Davi
GRAND OPE
GALLERY TIC
HEUM THEATRE
CURCUIT VAUDEVILLE
EVENING JAN 31, 1923
ONE SHOW
ORCHESTRA
PIPER'S
GOOD FOR ONE PE
TONY PASTOR'S TH
Compliment
Memoria
ONE WEEK
Benne
SPECIAL
Colonia
Tuesday
Five Acts
VELTY
audeville
ADMIT ONE
No. 18
TON
CONTIN
Gallery T
ADMI

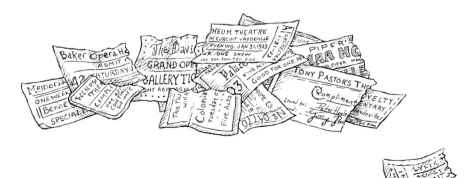

Sources and Further Reading

This is a work of dramatic nonfiction, grounded in history. We drew primarily from newspaper articles published during the period covered in the book, as well as from historical materials in the following archives: the American Variety Stage Collection at the Library of Congress; the Lincoln Center Library for the Performing Arts; the Keith/Albee Collection at the University of Iowa; the African American Culture Collection at the Smithsonian Institution; the American Vaudeville Museum Archive at the University of Arizona; the Vaudeville Collection at Princeton University; the Bonnie and Semoura Clark Black Vaudeville Collection at Yale University; the Oral History Archives at Columbia University; the American Vaudeville Collection at Harvard University; the Schomburg Center for Research in Black Culture; the Eva Tanguay Papers in the Benson Ford Research Center; the Chicago Theater Collection at the Chicago Public Library; the William F. Kilmer vaudeville collection at The Ohio State University; the Blondie Robinson Collection of African-American Minstrel and Vaudeville photographs at Brown University; the vaudeville archives of the New-York Historical Society Museum and Library; The Theater Collection of the Museum of the City of New York; vaudeville holdings of the Harry Ransom Center at the University of Texas; the American Museum of Vaudeville in Edgewood, New Mexico; and various digital archives and resources.

For additional reading on vaudeville and related subjects, we suggest the following books, all of which were useful in the making of this work:

Caffin, Caroline. *Vaudeville*. New York: M. Kennerley, 1914.

Cantor, Eddie. *As I Remember Them*. New York: Duell, Sloan and Pearce, 1963.

Cantor, Eddie, and Jane Kesner Ardmore. *Take My Life*. New York: Doubleday, 1957.

Charters, Ann. *Nobody: The Story of Bert Williams*. New York: Macmillan, 1970.

Chude-Sokei, Louis. *The Last "Darky": Bert Williams, Black-on-Black Minstrelsy, and the African Diaspora*. Durham NC: Duke University Press, 2006.

Cressy, Will M. *Continuous Vaudeville*. Boston: R. G. Badger, 1914.

Erdman, Andrew L. *Blue Vaudeville: Sex, Morals, and the Mass Marketing of Amusement, 1895–1915*. Jefferson, NC: McFarland, 2004.

——. *Queen of Vaudeville: The Story of Eva Tanguay*. Ithaca, NY: Cornell University Press, 2012.

Fields, Armond. *Tony Pastor, Father of Vaudeville*. Jefferson, NC: McFarland, 2007.

Fields, W. C., and Ronald J. Fields. *W. C. Fields by Himself: His Intended Autobiography*. Upper Saddle River, NJ: Prentice Hall, 1973.

Forbes, Camille F. *Introducing Bert Williams: Burnt Cork, Broadway, and the Story of America's First Black Star*. New York: Basic Books, 2008.

Garber, Marjorie. *Vested Interests: Cross-Dressing and Cultural Anxiety*. New York: Routledge, 1992.

Gilbert, Douglas. *American Vaudeville: Its Life and Times*. New York: McGraw-Hill, 1940.

Glenn, Susan A. *Female Spectacle: The Theatrical Roots of Modern Feminism*. Cambridge, MA: Harvard University Press, 2000.

Grau, Robert. *The Stage in the Twentieth Century: Third Volume*. Philadelphia: J. B. Lippincott, 1912.

Jessel, George. *Elegy in Manhattan*. New York: Holt, Rinehart and Winston, 1961.

Kibler, M. Alison. *Rank Ladies: Gender and Cultural Hierarchy in American Vaudeville*. Chapel Hill: University of North Carolina Press, 1999.

Krasner, David. *Resistance, Parody, and Double Consciousness in African American Theatre, 1895–1910*. New York: St. Martin's Press, 1997.

Laurie Jr., Joe. *Vaudeville: From the Honky Tonks to the Palace*. New York: Henry Holt, 1953.

Lewis, Robert M., ed. *From Traveling Show to Vaudeville: Theatrical Spectacle in America, 1830–1910*. Baltimore, MD: Johns Hopkins University Press, 2007.

McAllister, Marvin Edward. *Whiting Up: Whiteface Minstrels and Stage Europeans in African American Performance*. Chapel Hill: University of North Carolina Press, 2011.

McLean, Jr., Albert F. *American Vaudeville as Ritual*. Lexington: University Press of Kentucky, 1965.

Moore, F. Michael. *Julian Eltinge: Drag Diva of Broadway, Vaudeville, and Hollywood*. Self-published, 2020.

Mordden, Ethan. *Ziegfeld: The Man Who Invented Show Business*. New York: St. Martin's Press, 2008.

Nasaw, David. *Going Out: The Rise and Fall of Public Amusements*. New York: Basic Books, 1993.

Romeyn, Esther. *Street Scenes: Staging the Self in Immigrant New York, 1880–1924*. Minneapolis: University of Minnesota Press, 2008.

Rowland, Mabel, ed. *Bert Williams, Son of Laughter: A Symposium of Tribute to the Man and to His Work, by His Friends and Associates*. New York: English Crafters, 1923.

Slide, Anthony. *New York City Vaudeville*. Charleston, SC: Arcadia, 2006.

——. *The Encyclopedia of Vaudeville*. Westport, CT: Greenwood Press, 1994.

Smith, Bill. *The Vaudevillians*. New York: Macmillan, 1976.

Smith, Eric Ledell. *Bert Williams: A Biography of the Pioneer Black Comedian*. Jefferson, NC: McFarland, 1992.

Snyder, Robert W. *The Voice of the City: Vaudeville and Popular Culture in New York*. Oxford: Oxford University Press, 1989.

Strausbaugh, John. *Black Like You: Blackface, Whiteface, Insult and Imitation in American Popular Culture*. New York: Penguin, 2006.

Taylor, Yuval. *Darkest America: Black Minstrelsy from Slavery to Hip-Hop*. New York: Norton, 2012.

Trav, S. D. *No Applause—Just Throw Money*. London: Faber & Faber, 2005.

Wittke, Carl Frederick. *Tambo and Bones: A History of the American Minstrel Stage*. Durham, NC: Duke University Press, 1930.